An Introduction to Economic Theory:
MICROECONOMICS

In this textbook for intermediate microeconomics courses, the student is presented with the basic tools of neoclassical economic theory and some alternative approaches to explaining the behaviour of firms and markets. It differs from other textbooks in taking a critical approach to standard neoclassical economic theory, drawing attention repeatedly to the subtle implications of underlying assumptions and to the value judgements that permeate the neoclassical micro-theoretical structures. The results of empirical studies of cost curves and the pricing of manufactured goods are reflected in theoretical models that are offered as alternatives to standard neoclassical theory. The many discussions of economic events allow the student to understand the historical and institutional features of markets and put the theoretical structure into relief.

The use of mathematics is kept to a minimum in this book — the use of calculus is restricted to a few footnotes that illustrate alternative methods for the derivation of particular results. Questions and problems are attached to many of the chapters to help the student master the ideas and techniques discussed.

Clearly written and with each chapter containing an introduction, summary, bibliography, many diagrams, and problems oriented towards theory application, *An Introduction to Economic Theory: Microeconomics* offers a rich and illuminating study of its subject.

A. ASIMAKOPULOS has been Chairman, Department of Economics, McGill University, since 1974. He was Guest of the Institute, Massachusetts Institute of Technology, 1965-6; Visiting Professor, University of Washington, summer 1972; Visiting Fellow, Clare College, Cambridge University, 1972-3; and Visiting Professor, Monash University, 1973-4. He served as Managing Editor of the *Canadian Journal of Economics* from 1968 to 1972 and was elected a Fellow of the Royal Society of Canada in 1976.

An Introduction to Economic Theory:
MICROECONOMICS

A. Asimakopulos

McGill University

Toronto, Oxford, New York
OXFORD UNIVERSITY PRESS
1978

Canadian Cataloguing in Publication Data

Asimakopulos, A., 1930-
    An introduction to economic theory:
microeconomics

Includes bibliographies and index.
ISBN 0-19-540281-2

1. Microeconomics.   I. Title.

HB171.5.A85   330   C78-001149-X

© Oxford University Press (Canada) 1978
Diagrams by Fred Huffman and Fortunato Aglialoro
ISBN 0-19-540281-2
2 3 4 - 1 0
Printed in Canada by T.H. Best Printing Company Limited

To
MARIKA, ANNA, & JULIA

CONTENTS

PREFACE

This book covers the main topics taught in intermediate-level micro-economics courses, but it differs from competing textbooks in taking a more critical approach to standard neoclassical economic theory. I believe it is necessary to warn students that equilibrium positions may be irrelevant when the real world is subject to changing conditions over time, and when the expectations about the future that guide current actions are often mistaken. Microeconomics should not be restricted to examining situations in which the economy is necessarily at a full-employment equilibrium, and the microeconomic analysis of pricing should consider the effects on relative prices of fluctuations in economic activity. However, all the elements of neoclassical economic theory are presented in this book, along with careful statements of the assumptions on which this theory is based. The limitations of the neoclassical models in many applications are noted, and some alternative approaches are introduced. In teaching a micro-economics course for many years at McGill University (and at the University of Washington in the summer of 1972 and at Monash University in 1974), I have found that the interest of students is enhanced when they are encouraged to think critically about economic theory while they learn the techniques of analysis.

The results of empirical studies of cost curves and the pricing of manufactured goods are reflected in the theoretical models that are presented here as alternatives to standard neoclassical economic theory. References are made throughout the book to economic events to emphasize the need to understand the special historical and institutional features of the sector being studied if economic analysis is not to be misleading. The use of mathematics is kept to a minimum, since the mathematical approach tends to concentrate on the solution of sets of equations—on equilibrium positions—without paying enough attention to the economic, nonmathematical reasons why these solutions may be very special cases and not of much practical interest. The use of calculus is restricted to a few footnotes that illustrate alternative methods for the derivation of particular results. Questions and problems are appended to many of the chapters to help the student master the ideas and techniques discussed.

The distinction that I have made in this book between the forces determining the prices of primary goods and those determining the prices of manufactured goods is to be found in the writings of Joan Robinson. It was also clearly stated by Michal Kalecki, who wrote about 'demand-determined' and 'cost-determined' prices. In recent years Sir John Hicks has used the terms 'flexprice' and 'fixprice' markets to make the same distinction.

The publications of Joan Robinson have very much influenced my approach to economic theory over the last ten years, and in this book I have tried to observe the three methodological rules she drew attention to in the Preface to her *Exercises in Economic Analysis:* '(1) We must take time seriously. To make a comparison between two situations, each with its own future and its own past, is not the same thing as to trace a movement from one to the other. (2) A quantity has no meaning unless we can specify the units in which it is measured. (3) Technical and physical relations, between man and nature, must be distinguished from social relations, between man and man.'

While writing this book I have been greatly helped by the comments of students and colleagues on the various drafts of my typescript. I shall list alphabetically the names of those who were most active in this regard, but before doing so I must make special mention of John Burbidge of McMaster University. His enthusiasm for the approach taken was one of the reasons for writing the set of lecture notes that formed the basis for this book, and he read and provided extensive comments on all the drafts. I am also grateful to Louis Ascah, Helen Boss, Denis Cousineau, Takis Economopoulos, Chris Green, Sid Ingerman, Ruth Rose-Lizée, Lee Soderstrom, and Abe Tarasofsky for comments and advice. The final typescript greatly benefited from the editorial work of William Toye of the Oxford University Press. Many typists, on different continents, were involved with the drafts of the typescript, and I would like to acknowledge the patient work of Ruth Bennett, Lynn Boyle, Jenny Dobbie, Lynda Goralczyk, Ann Jackson, and Kim Reany.

Finally, I want to thank my wife Marika, who read and made editorial comments on the final drafts and shared all the proof-reading chores. Her encouragement and readiness to sacrifice many hours of leisure made it possible for me to write this book.

1

INTRODUCTION

1.1 Introduction

It is customary to begin an introductory book on economic theory with a definition of economics. Nothing, however, is settled by a definition, even if general agreement is reached on its appropriateness. Scholars are not going to be restricted by an arbitrary boundary for their discipline should their understanding be increased by letting it cross that boundary. There is much to be said for Jacob Viner's dictum, 'Economics is what economists do,'[1] which leads directly to an examination of the subjects covered by economists and the methods they use. It also suggests that the boundaries of the subject change as the range of subjects considered by economists changes.

This chapter will define economics in such a way as to emphasize its scope—without attaching undue significance to the definition. It will also consider the methods used by economists and will distinguish between microeconomics, the subject-matter of this book, and macroeconomics.

1.2 What is economics?

The definition of economics to be given here follows the tradition in English-speaking countries of relating it to 'material welfare'.[2] It states: *Economics is the subject concerned with the material welfare of individuals*

---

[1] Quoted in Kenneth E. Boulding, *Economic Analysis* (4th ed.; New York: Harper & Row, 1966), Vol. I, p. 3.

[2] Lionel Robbins (in *An Essay on the Nature and Significance of Economic Science* [2nd ed.; London: Macmillan & Co., 1935], p. 4) notes that the definition of economics that would probably command most adherents in Anglo-Saxon countries would relate it to material welfare. Robbins, however, favoured another definition (see Footnote 12).

and groups in societies.[3] This definition makes clear that economics is concerned with matters of public policy, a concern that was made explicit by the classical name for the discipline, 'political economy'. The _raison d'être_ of economics is its ability to provide some understanding of the factors that affect material welfare, and the ways in which these factors can be altered to improve welfare. Because of its intimate concern with welfare and policy, economics can never be value-free. Values do not suddenly appear when policy conclusions are being reached; they permeate the subject.[4] This statement may be somewhat controversial, for the term 'economic science' is not infrequently used in the literature, and the switch in designation from political economy to economics was in part inspired by the belief that the subject was sufficiently scientific to merit the termination -ics, as in physics.[5]

Economics tries, quite properly, to be scientific in its method. It proceeds, just as the natural sciences do, from observation of events to some hypothesis about the factors causing these events. On the basis of this hypothesis, it then makes predictions about what will happen in situations where these factors have particular values. If these predictions are not disproved by subsequent events, then the hypothesis can be said to have passed this test. The greater the number of such tests a hypothesis passes, the greater the confidence in its usefulness for understanding the operation of economies of the real world. Although this general approach is scientific, economics is a discipline where values impinge on conclusions because there are problems both in making observations and in testing hypotheses. In the natural sciences it is usually possible to test the predictions made by hypotheses with controlled experiments devised in a laboratory. These experiments can be repeated by different individuals at different times and places, and the findings can be confirmed. This is not the case with the

---

[3] This definition is derived from Edwin Cannan's definition of economics, as the subject 'having to do with material welfare' (_Wealth_ [3rd ed.; London: P.S. King & Son, 1928], p. 4), but it makes clear that the concern is with individuals (and groups) in societies. Alfred Marshall's definition of economics also makes this clear. 'Economics is a study of mankind in the ordinary business of life; it examines that part of individual and social action which is most closely connected with the attainment and with the use of the material requisites of wellbeing.' (_Principles of Economics_ [8th ed.; London: Macmillan & Co., 1920], p. 1.) Cannan gave a broad interpretation to material welfare, and he explicitly included cultural activities, such as concerts, as contributors to material welfare. Lionel Robbins, in his criticism of Cannan's definition, mistakenly interprets it as excluding orchestral concerts from material welfare. (_An Essay on the Nature and Significance of Economic Science_, pp. 5-6.)

[4] A distinction between 'positive economics' and 'normative economics' will, however, be considered in a later section.

[5] Cf. Sir Dennis Robertson, _Lectures on Economic Principles_ (London: Staples Press, 1957), Vol. I, p. 6.

predictions that flow from economic hypotheses, which have to be tested in the light of historical experience. Historical events are the result of many influences and it is difficult to isolate the effects of the factors specified in an economic hypothesis. If the results confirm the hypothesis, this may be owing to accidental factors; and if they do not, it could be argued that the hypothesis was correct but because of special circumstances the results appear contradictory. It should not be surprising that under these conditions economics contains many unverified and conflicting hypotheses.[6] For example, the hypothesis could be that the imposition of wage and price controls would lead to lower investment. The Canadian experience of declining investment following the adoption of such a program in October 1975 does not necessarily confirm this hypothesis because of the effects of other events, such as the slowdown in the world economy and the uncertainty about the country's future caused by the election of the Parti Québécois in the Province of Quebec on November 15, 1976.

Another problem with the scientific aspect of economics relates to the observations that precede the formulation of hypotheses: these observations are affected by the observer. There are no economic 'facts' without theories. Gunnar Myrdal has written: 'Facts do not organize themselves into concepts and theories just by being looked at; indeed, except within the framework of concepts and theories, there are no scientific facts but only chaos. There is an inescapable *a priori* element in all scientific work. Questions must be asked before answers can be given. The questions are an expression of our interest in the world, they are at bottom valuations. Valuations are thus necessarily involved already at the stage when we observe facts and carry on theoretical analysis, and not only at the stage when we draw political inferences from facts and valuations.'[7] This is a problem we must face as best we can by trying to describe events in as objective a way as possible, with all descriptions being checked against possible alternative ways of relating the same events.[8]

---

[6] Joan Robinson contrasts the opportunities for decisively testing hypotheses in the natural and social sciences with the observations that 'in the social sciences, first, the subject-matter has much greater political and ideological content, so that other loyalties are also involved; and secondly, because the appeal to "public experience" can never be decisive, as it is for the laboratory scientists who can repeat each other's experiments under controlled conditions; the social scientists are always left with a loophole to escape through—"the consequences that have followed from the causes that I analysed are, I agree, the opposite of what I predicted, but they would have been still greater if those causes had not operated." . . . So economics limps along with one foot in untested hypotheses and the other in untestable slogans.' *Economic Philosophy* (Harmondsworth, Middlesex: Penguin Books, 1964), pp. 27-8.

[7] Gunnar Myrdal, *The Political Element in the Development of Economic Theory*, trans. by Paul Streeten (Cambridge, Mass.: Harvard University Press, 1954), p. vii.

[8] Cf. Robinson, *Economic Philosophy*, pp. 18-19.

Our definition makes clear that economics is concerned with only part of human welfare. Even though a particular policy might improve material welfare, it might be judged to be detrimental to welfare as a whole. For example, the existence of a particular nation-state, and its independence, might be judged by its citizens to be of great importance, and they might decide to adopt policies that *decrease* their material welfare because they increase the nation's security. Various measures to protect defence-oriented industries, shipping, etc., have often been presented as promoting a nation's security. Similarly, policies that would promote material welfare might be opposed on moral grounds. For example, there could be opposition to government-run lotteries—even though it might be agreed that more funds would be made available this way for, say, the support of hospitals—on the grounds that the national promotion of gambling would be injurious to the characters of individuals in society.[9]

One final point about our definition of economics should be noted. Economics is concerned with individuals and groups in societies. It is thus not a universal subject whose findings are valid for all times, places, and societies. An important element in any analysis is a statement of the social system that is being analysed. This book is concerned with the activity of individual units in a modern capitalist economy. Non-agricultural production is largely carried out by many firms directed and controlled by private interests and their activities are co-ordinated by a *market system*. 'A market is a pattern of regular, recurrent exchange relations between units of economic decision . . . Meeting in the market, the various units match their offers and bids, their supplies and demands, against each other.'[10] The success of firms, their ability to survive and grow, depends on their ability to sell their outputs in markets at prices that are at least high enough to cover their expenses of production (the cost of labour, materials, and the maintenance of their means of production). Firms try to increase their activity in those areas where they expect to more than cover their costs. They are always concerned about the state of markets in which they buy and sell. There are markets not only for the goods produced, but also for labour and land.[11] Thus the prices for labour services and land might be affected by

---

[9] For a discussion of situations where policies that affect economic welfare in one way affect welfare as a whole in another, see A.C. Pigou, *The Economics of Welfare* (4th ed.; London: Macmillan & Co., 1932), Chapter I.

[10] O. Lange, 'The Scope and Method of Economics', *Review of Economic Studies*, Vol. 13 (1945-6), p. 26.

[11] For an interesting analysis of the social dislocations caused by the extension of free markets to labour and land that accompanied the Industrial Revolution, see Karl Polanyi, *The Great Transformation: The Political & Economic Origins of Our Time* (Boston: Beacon Press, 1957).

conditions of demand and supply and individuals and groups might try to manipulate these conditions wherever possible so as to improve their positions.

There are other types of economic systems in which markets play a much more limited role, and they might even be prohibited in some areas. For example, in feudal society land and labour services could not be sold. Labour services were owed to feudal lords in return for rights to cultivate land, and the movement of labourers out of their home areas was prohibited in order to ensure that this labour was obtained. In this type of society, markets existed on a very limited scale. It is also possible to conceive of a *command or planned society* in which economic activity is largely regulated in accordance with a plan developed by some centralized authority. Orders are sent down to managers of plants telling them what to produce, where to obtain their inputs, and where to ship the final product. The plan generally specifies each plant's annual output, its target for the year, as well as the inputs that will be made available for this purpose; the socialist countries of Eastern Europe make extensive use of commands of this type. There are no pure market or pure command systems. So-called market economies limit the scope of markets in some areas of economic activity, while markets are to be found in command societies.

1.3 Economics and scarcity

There are limits to the material well-being of people in a society in a particular time period because of the scarcity of resources, and economics is thus very much concerned with the allocation of these scarce resources. People experience various wants that can be placed in categories, such as food, clothing, shelter, education, entertainment, social prestige, religious and national feelings, etc. These wants result from biological needs, but the particular forms they take are also very much affected by the society in which people live. They can be satisfied directly or indirectly by means of appropriate objects that are called *goods*—such as bread, wheat, meat, cattle, machinery, land, coal, oil, etc.—and by the use of the *services* of objects or persons, such as transportation, housing, teachers, actors, etc. Wants are satisfied directly when goods (e.g. bread) or services are consumed by individuals and they are satisfied indirectly when the goods (e.g. wheat) or services are used to produce goods and services that are then consumed by individuals. These goods and services are the *resources* available for the satisfaction of human wants. Some, such as air in a country setting, might be so plentiful that all wants dependent on them can be fully satisfied. Others, such as land, minerals, housing services, exist in quantities that are not sufficient to satisfy all wants: they are said to be *scarce.* Changes in demand and/or supply of a particular resource might make it scarce—or enable it to satisfy all wants fully. The constraints placed on the material welfare of people by the scarcity of resources is an ever-present theme in economics; indeed, some economists have included the scarcity of resources in their definitions of the discipline.[12]

1.4 Economic models

Economic analysis makes use of models. An *economic model* is a set of assumptions concerning some aspects of economic reality. A model is constructed, i.e. these assumptions are made, in an attempt to understand the forces at work in an economy. The implications of these assumptions are deduced using logic and mathematics. The model arrives at certain conclusions with respect to the economic phenomena it is designed to study; that is, it leads to hypotheses about reality. A model is, and must be, unrealistic, since it leaves out many of the elements that operate in actual economies. Nevertheless, if it is a good model it provides the key to understanding reality. The only way to make sense of reality is by simplifying and redrawing it to some sort of order, by abstracting what appear to be the main elements at work before studying their effects. This is not an easy task, there are no hard-and-fast rules for model building, and the dangers are many. A model may abstract from important elements of reality and thus be misleading, rather than provide insights and understanding.

In spite of the very obvious dangers this method of simplification is necessary, but great care must be taken that the simplifications used are legitimate.[13] For these purposes a legitimate simplification is defined as one whose results will essentially remain the same when some of the complexities of the real world are introduced. A relaxation of the severity of the assumptions, e.g. the introduction of more elements, leads only to a complication of the analysis rather than to an overturning of the conclusions. An economic theory can ideally be tested by checking its predictions against observations. However, as we noted in Section 1.2, there are many problems in obtaining from history the data that can decisively test economic hypotheses. Whenever possible a theory should be tested by

---

[12] Lange's definition of economics as 'the science of administration of scarce resources in human society' ('The Scope and Method of Economics', p. 19) falls into this category, as does that of Lionel Robbins: 'Economics is the science which studies human behaviour as a relationship between ends and scarce means which have alternative uses.' *An Essay on the Nature and Significance of Economic Science*, p. 16.

[13] James S. Duesenberry has observed that 'Knowing how to simplify one's description of reality without neglecting anything essential is the most important part of the economist's art.' *Business Cycles and Economic Growth* (New York: McGraw-Hill, 1958), pp. 14-15.

checking its predictions, but the assumptions on which a theory is based also provide an indirect test of the validity of the theory.[14] The presentation of economic theory in this book will try to specify the assumptions on which the analyses are based. In addition to the standard textbook analyses, alternative approaches that have greater empirical support will also be considered.

1.5 Positive and normative economics

Economists try to understand what is occurring in economies; they also try to devise policies to influence economic events. Their discipline can be viewed as consisting of two parts: *positive and normative economics.* Positive economics can be defined as a body of systematized knowledge concerning *what is,* while normative economics tries to develop criteria for *what ought to be.*[15] Positive economics is concerned with the description of economic events and the formulation of theories to explain them. It tries to follow scientific principles and devise 'objective tests' of these theories. Myrdal's warning (Section 1.2) about the inescapable *a priori* element in all scientific work should not be forgotten, but ethical judgements have a much stronger role in normative economics than they do in positive economics, where a much wider range of agreement is possible. Some economists have even suggested that all questions of what ought to be should be left to moral and political philosophy, with economics being restricted to positive studies.[16] This book is largely concerned with positive economics, but in the final chapter there will be a brief examination of theoretical welfare economics that tries to establish principles for judging the desirability of alternative economic situations.

1.6 Microeconomics and macroeconomics

Economic theory deals with micro and macro questions. *Micro* questions are such things as: What determines the relative prices of commodities, such

---

[14] This view differs from that of Professor Milton Friedman, who has argued that theories should be tested solely by their predictions without reference to the reality of the assumptions. ('The Methodology of Positive Economics', *Essays in Positive Economics* [Chicago: University of Chicago Press, 1953], pp. 3-43.) For a thoughtful criticism of Friedman's position see Eugene Rotwein, 'On "The Methodology of Positive Economics"', *Quarterly Journal of Economics*, Vol. 73 (November 1959), pp. 554-75.

[15] ' . . . a *positive science* may be defined as a body of systematized knowledge concerning what is; a *normative* or *regulative science* as a body of systematized knowledge relating to criteria of what ought to be, and concerned therefore with the ideal as distinguished from the actual.' John Neville Keynes, *The Scope and Method of Political Economy* (4th ed.; New York: Kelley & Millman, 1955), pp. 34-5. (Italics in the original.)

[16] This is the opinion of Robbins, *An Essay on the Nature and Significance of Economic Science*, pp. 147-51.

as steak and bread? What determines the behaviour of individual units (firms and households) in the economy? What determines a firm's rates of output and employment of labour? *Macro* questions are concerned with the behaviour of the economy as a whole. What are the major influences on the rates of output and employment in the economy? What is the relation between total consumption expenditures and total incomes? Why do economies experience cyclical variations in economic activity? As economics has developed and become more complex, it has become common practice to distinguish between microeconomic and macroeconomic theory. This distinction is useful for many purposes, since the focus of a particular study might be on either micro or macro questions, but care should be taken not to treat these two areas of inquiry as self-contained. The answers to micro questions (e.g. the relative prices of commodities) might be affected by the overall level of activity in the economy, while macro questions cannot be adequately handled without an understanding of micro behaviour.

This book is concerned with microeconomics and is therefore an introduction to only part of economic theory. The discussion of theories of income distribution in Chapter 15 makes clear that distribution cannot be considered fully without the explicit introduction of macroeconomics. Similarly only some aspects of the determination of the rate of interest are noted in Chapter 16, since a full treatment would require consideration of the theory of money and the general level of activity in the economy. One of the ways in which this book differs from the standard textbooks on price theory is in not assuming that the economy is necessarily at a full-employment equilibrium.[17] In fact short-term changes in the relative prices of broad categories of commodities are related to changes in the level of activity in the economy. This follows from the distinction made between the methods of price determination for primary and manufactured goods. Prices of primary goods are much more susceptible to short-term changes in demand than are the prices of manufactured goods that are largely determined by costs of production, because of the conditions under which they are produced and sold.[18]

---

[17] For example, Professor Hirshleifer writes: ' . . . microeconomics concentrates mainly upon equilibrium states of particular markets, presuming an equilibrium of the market system as a whole.' *Price Theory and Applications* (Englewood Cliffs, N.J.: Prentice-Hall, Inc., 1976), p. 17.

[18] This distinction was made by Michal Kalecki, *Selected Essays on the Dynamics of the Capitalist Economy 1933-1970* (Cambridge, Eng.: Cambridge University Press, 1971), p. 43.

1.7 Neoclassical economic theory

The dominant approach to economic theory in capitalist economies is neoclassical economic theory. Development of this theory began around 1870 with the writings of William Stanley Jevons (1835-82) in England, Carl Menger (1840-1921) in Vienna, and Léon Walras (1834-1910) in Lausanne, although some of the elements in this approach can be found in earlier writings. There have been many developments and refinements in this theory over the years as large numbers of highly talented and carefully trained people have turned their attention to economics. The basic approach, however, is still the same. Neoclassical economic theory concentrates on the determination of relative prices and the allocation of scarce resources under the assumption that consumers try to maximize utility (or, more generally, they are assumed to act rationally) and firms try to maximize profits. Neoclassical theory examines these questions under the assumption of general equilibrium in all markets, and full employment of labour in particular.

John Maynard Keynes, in his influential book *The General Theory of Employment, Interest and Money,* argued that this basic assumption of neoclassical theory[19] relegates it to a special case, with the general case in a capitalist economy being one of unemployment: 'A monetary economy . . . is essentially one in which changing views about the future are capable of influencing the quantity of employment and not merely its direction.'[20] Economists working in the neoclassical tradition have taken refuge in the so-called 'neoclassical synthesis', which assumes that governments can and do adopt policies to maintain full employment under non-inflationary conditions. A prominent supporter of this approach has seen it as validating ' . . . the classical assumption that monetary phenomena can be treated as a "veil" over the operation of real economic forces. This assumption was the focal point of the Keynesian Revolution; but with the success of that revolution, especially in obtaining governmental commitment to the objective of maintaining full employment, it is reasonable once again to use that assumption as the basis for analysis.'[21]

A critical examination of the neoclassical synthesis is beyond the scope of this book, but it can be observed that current economic problems that feature both unemployment and inflation make it clear that both governments and market economies may fail to maintain full employment. The

---

[19] He referred to it as the classical theory.
[20] John Maynard Keynes, *The General Theory of Employment, Interest and Money* (London: Macmillan & Co., 1936), p. vii.
[21] Harry G. Johnson, *The Theory of Income Distribution* (London: Gray-Mills Publishing Ltd., (1973), Preface.

microeconomic analysis in this book does not assume full employment.

This book will be largely devoted to a presentation of the standard neoclassical techniques of analysis, giving due attention to the assumptions on which they are based. Neoclassical theory can provide useful insights into the operation of particular sectors of the economy when the assumptions on which it is based are legitimate simplifications of the reality being analysed. For example, the markets for agricultural commodities can be usefully examined with neoclassical techniques, and such applications will be presented in this book. In addition, we will present some alternative approaches to neoclassical economic theory that pay more attention to the social relations in an economy and to the requirements of an analysis dealing with historical time.

1.8 Summary

Economics has been defined as the subject concerned with the material welfare of individuals and groups in societies. Its interest and importance lie in its ability to provide insights into the appropriateness of policies to be pursued by private or governmental bodies in order to achieve economic ends. Economists follow the scientific method of induction and deduction in formulating their theories, and they try to test them by comparing their predictions with actual events. Their inability to conduct controlled experiments means that there are conflicting hypotheses favoured by different groups that have not been shown to be false. Economics is permeated with value judgements because of its intimate concern with matters of public policy. Positive economics, which attempts to understand how the economic system works in practice, is distinguished from normative economics, which is concerned with judging the desirability of changes in the economic system. Microeconomic theory, the subject of this book, analyses the behaviour of individual units, while macroeconomics focuses on the behaviour of the economy as a whole. For the most part the standard neoclassical techniques of analysis will be presented, but some alternative approaches will also be examined.

SUGGESTED READINGS

Lange, O. 'The Scope and Method of Economics'. *Review of Economic Studies*, Vol. 13 (1945-6), pp. 19-32.

Marshall, Alfred. *Principles of Economics*. 8th ed. London: Macmillan & Co., 1920. Book I.

Myrdal, Gunnar. *The Political Element in the Development of Economic Theory*. Translated by Paul Streeten. Cambridge, Mass.: Harvard University Press, 1954.

Polanyi, Karl. *The Great Transformation: The Political & Economic Origins of Our Time*. Boston: Beacon Press, 1957.

Robbins, Lionel. *An Essay on the Nature and Significance of Economic Science*. 2nd ed. London: Macmillan & Co., 1935.

Robertson, Sir Dennis. *Lectures on Economic Principles*. London: Staples Press, 1957. Vol. I, Chapter I.

Robinson, Joan. *Economic Philosophy*. Harmondsworth, Middlesex: Penguin Books, 1964.

2

THEORY OF EXCHANGE: DEMAND AND SUPPLY

2.1 Introduction

Our examination of the standard tools of economic analysis begins with a consideration of the theory of exchange in perfectly competitive markets, which form a special category of markets. Within this category a distinction can be drawn between *spot* and *forward* markets.

The adjective *spot* is used for markets in which the transactions that occur require current delivery of the products being bought and sold. For example, in spot markets for wheat, buyers purchase the right to receive immediate delivery of the quantities of wheat specified in their contracts. The adjective *forward* is used for markets in which contracts for future deliveries (or *futures*), at specified terms, are bought and sold. For example, there are forward markets for wheat in which individuals could, in June 1977, buy and sell contracts for delivery of specified quantities of wheat in May 1978. These buyers might have made such transactions even if they had no intention of accepting delivery of wheat. Similarly sellers might have no intention of supplying wheat on that date. The existence of forward markets makes it possible for both groups to arrange other transactions, before the May 1978 delivery date, that cancel their obligations under the original transactions. This chapter will be concerned only with spot markets, though there will be some consideration of forward markets in Chapter 3.

The orderly functioning of competitive markets is made possible by a group of traders or merchants who hold stocks of the commodities and are prepared to buy and sell these goods at terms that are responsive to market conditions. As their perceptions of market conditions change, they adjust the prices at which they are prepared to trade. This tends to happen in response to changes in their stocks of commodities that are brought about by differences in the quantities they can buy and sell at their established prices. Market conditions are represented in the economic analyses of perfectly competitive markets by demand and supply curves. Theoretical treatments of this subject ignore the role of the specialist traders (who facilitate the operation of specific markets) in order to focus attention on the role of market conditions. In this book the analyses of markets will be conducted mainly at this level of abstraction. Any study of actual markets, however, would have to include a consideration of the behaviour, and the rules governing the conduct, of the specialist traders.

Each set of demand and supply curves is defined for a particular market, and for a particular period of time. The shapes of these curves and their positions depend partly on the length of the period covered by the analysis. In the case of supply curves, the possibility, if the time period is long enough, of producing different rates of output of the commodity would affect their positions and slopes. For example, if the time period is a week, the total quantity of the commodity available for sale will in most cases be fixed by decisions made in earlier time periods. However, if the time period is a year, the total quantity available in that year might also be affected by production decisions made in that time interval in response to expected prices. This ability to affect the quantities currently available, in response to current prices, is reflected in the slope and position of the supply curve. Demand curves are also affected by the length of the interval of time for which they are drawn. A longer interval allows potential buyers to investigate alternative sources of supply more thoroughly, and to adjust their habitual patterns of behaviour.

In this chapter demand and supply curves and their properties are examined in order to indicate their uses and limitations. Their derivation from assumptions about individual behaviour and technology, etc., will be dealt with in later chapters.

2.2 Exchange and the division of labour

One avenue through which economic growth has taken place has been exchange—such as the buying and selling of goods and the hiring of labour services. It provides opportunities for gain in two ways:

(i) Exchange makes specialization in production feasible. A community in a market system is not required to produce everything it needs, since goods can be obtained in exchange for items on which the productive efforts of its members are concentrated, or with the incomes they earn by working for others. This specialization increases the total amount and varieties of goods available to the communities that are part of a market system because there are increasing returns to scale in many areas of production. (This will be explained in more detail in Section 8.13.) The cost per unit of output is lower the larger the rate of output (at least until some upper limit is reached) for which appropriate provision has been made.

(ii) Exchange also makes possible a better distribution of any particular combination of goods. It will be illustrated later that it is very probable that individuals or groups will be better off if they can trade some of their original endowments of goods for other goods, even if the total amounts of the goods available to the groups are unchanged.

The first factor, the specialization in production for which exchange is a necessary and sufficient condition, is the more important. Its role in allowing societies to prosper and grow was recognized by the earliest economic theorists. It received classic expression in Adam Smith's *Wealth of Nations* (1776). Smith stated that the opportunity for specialization—or the division of labour, as he called it, which is made possible by exchange—enabled labour to be more productive. 'The greatest improvement in the productive powers of labour, and the greater part of the skill, dexterity, and judgement with which it is anywhere directed or applied, seem to have been the effects of the division of labour.' He goes on to give his famous example of pin-making:

> . . . a workman not educated to the trade of pin-maker (which the division of labour has rendered a distinct trade), nor acquainted with the use of the machinery employed in it (to the invention of which the same division of labour has probably given occasion), could scarce, perhaps, with his utmost industry, make one pin in a day, and certainly not make twenty. But in the way in which this business is now carried on, not only the whole work is a peculiar trade, but it is divided into a number of branches, of which the greater part are likewise peculiar trades. One man draws out the wire, another straightens it, a third cuts it, a fourth points it, a fifth grinds it at the top for receiving the head; to make the head requires two or three distinct operations, etc., . . .[1]

Smith proceeds to count eighteen different operations and estimates that through this division of labour the output per labourer is about 4,800 pins per day per man, while if working alone a labourer's output would almost certainly not exceed 20. He believed that the effect would be similar in all trades and that this advantage was due to three circumstances, made possible by the division of labour: (i) improved dexterity; (ii) saving of time in moving from one operation to the next; (iii) application of machinery. He stated that this division of labour gave rise to differences of talent more important than the natural differences and rendered these differences useful.

---

[1] Adam Smith, *The Wealth of Nations* (The Modern Library ed.; New York: Random House, 1937), p. 4.

It is important to keep this advantage of exchange in mind. Without the possibility of exchange, or with greater restrictions on this possibility, the types and quantities of goods available in modern societies would be very different. This relationship between varieties and volumes of goods, and exchange, goes both ways. The development of new goods and technical possibilities for producing more goods extends both the opportunities for exchanges and the manner in which they are carried out.

2.3 Definition of a market

Exchange in capitalist economies takes place in a *market*. Economists use the term 'market' not to denote any particular market-place in which things are bought and sold, but for a location, or set of locations, in which buyers and sellers of a particular commodity are in regular communication. Different locations are welded into one market by the potential and actual transfer of transactions from one place to another. Buyers try to make their purchases at the lowest net cost to themselves, while sellers try to obtain the highest prices for their goods. In some markets—for example, foreign-exchange markets—the transactions of groups of specialist traders play an important role in the maintenance of consistent prices in different locations. These traders are called *arbitrageurs*. The activity of buying a particular commodity in one location and simultaneously selling it in another, because the price is lower in the former, is called *arbitrage*.

In deciding whether to buy in one part of the market or in the other, a rational buyer considers not only the prices in each of these locations but also other costs incurred in obtaining the commodity. These other costs might arise because of the need to transport the commodity, or because of other barriers to trade, such as tariffs. Some commodities, whose costs of transportation relative to their prices are high because of their bulk or perishability, have local markets, while other commodities have national and even international markets. Improvements in communications and transportation facilities extend markets to cover great distances. In recent years, commodities that previously had only local markets have experienced substantial changes in the extent of their markets; for example, fresh fruits and vegetables are now traded in national and international markets. In-stitutional changes that alter tariffs and other trading arrangements can also affect the size of the markets for particular items by opening up or eliminating the possibility of trade in these items between different areas.

Goods that have wide markets satisfy certain general conditions. They must be capable of being easily and exactly described, so that they can be bought and sold by persons at a distance from one another, and also at a distance from the commodities. Cotton, wheat, and iron satisfy these conditions. Samples that are truly representative can be taken from the lots offered for sale; moreover, they can even be graded by an independent authority according to their quality. There are many manufactured items— ladies' dresses, shoes, etc.—where these conditions do not hold: individual buyers or their representatives must judge the quality of the goods offered for sale. They may still have very wide markets, however, because they can bear a long transport. Their prices are high enough relative to their costs of transportation to make their movement between distant points economically feasible. Goods such as bread and cement do not satisfy these conditions; their markets are therefore much narrower than those for, say, wheat and iron.

2.4 How large is a market?

The number of locations covered by a particular market is not always easy to determine. The geographical extent of a market is frequently a contentious issue in antitrust cases. (The judicial finding in the Canadian Western Sugar Case, referred to in Section 13.2, turned on the question of whether the relevant market was a national one or whether it was only regional.)

There is a *commodity* as well as a *geographical* dimension to a market. It can be said to cover items that are similar, even though they may differ in some respects. The importance of the differences between items is a matter of judgement and can be subject to dispute. For example, the 1975 antitrust suit brought by the United States Justice Department against the International Business Machines Corporation (IBM)—and still in progress in 1978—raised questions about the appropriate market. The government defined the relevant market as the general-purpose electronic-data-processing-systems market; this included only those companies that put together and sold computer systems covering hardware, software, and services. IBM maintained that the government's definition was artificial and that the relevant market was a much broader one, consisting of all the firms involved in providing items for electronic-data processing. Thus a major issue in this trial is the question of the relevant market.

In the theoretical models to be presented here, the market will be assumed to be defined unambiguously. Nevertheless one should keep in mind the essential vagueness about the boundaries of a particular market in any application of the analysis. Economic theory indicates the criteria to be used in defining a market, but the drawing of actual market boundaries is not an exact science. When economic analysis is used for policy purposes in this area, it is important to be aware of the difficulties in drawing boundaries around markets. There is no good substitute, in all applications, for a thorough knowledge of the institutional features of markets and of their historical development.

2.5 Perfectly competitive markets

Markets have been classified into four major categories: perfectly competitive, monopolistically competitive, oligopolistic, and monopolistic. Attention will be focused in this chapter on perfectly competitive markets. (The other categories will be introduced in Chapter 9.)

Perfectly competitive markets will be defined here as those in which the following two conditions are satisfied:

(i) *There are large numbers of buyers and sellers. The proportion of the total market transactions carried out by any single participant must be very small, so that each buyer or seller separately has a negligible influence on values in the market.*

(ii) *The commodity is homogeneous. Each unit of this commodity is identical to every other unit and buyers and sellers are indifferent, given the price, about whom they buy from or sell to.*

In most theoretical analyses the level of abstraction is such that the activities of specialist traders or merchants are ignored. The buyers referred to in the definition of perfectly competitive markets are consumers of the commodity; the sellers are producers. The analysis proceeds as though the consumers and producers deal directly with each other rather than through the intermediation of merchants.

The introduction of merchants would complicate the analysis, without changing the general nature of the conclusions, if certain conditions were met. These complications would arise because there might be two (or even more) markets for the same commodity in a particular location, with differences in prices. One of these markets would comprise producers as sellers, and merchants as buyers, while in another market the merchants would be sellers and the consumers would be buyers. The differences in prices in these markets represent the gross-profit margins of the merchants, who perform wholesaling and retailing functions. They buy in large quantities, resell in smaller units, and maintain stocks of the commodity. In addition, some of the participants in a market might be speculators who buy and sell the commodity, even though they are not consumers, producers, or merchants for that commodity. They believe, or hope, that they can anticipate future price movements and that as a consequence their buying and selling activities will result in profits. They are particularly active in forward markets.

Economic analyses of markets that abstract from the activities of merchants leave out much of the detail of actual market operations. They ignore the differences between selling and buying prices, which provide the merchants' gross-profit margins. The general conclusions derived from a theory of perfectly competitive markets are not sensitive to this omission if merchants individually cannot act to change their gross-profit margins. Their buying and selling prices tend to move together in response to market conditions. It is often reasonable, therefore, to consider the effects of these conditions directly, without reference to merchants.

2.6 Full knowledge of current market conditions

In markets where the two necessary conditions for a perfectly competitive market are satisfied, there is very little scope for individual buyers and sellers to affect the prices at which they buy or sell. They have therefore often been referred to as *price takers*. Their decisions relate to the extent of their purchases or sales at the market price. However, there may be some differences in the prices at which different transactions are made in a given period of time, if market participants lack full knowledge of the terms at which others are prepared to make transactions. For example, if some buyers are not well informed about market conditions, an astute or lucky seller may be able to sell some of his goods at higher prices than those obtained by others. This might occur even though all sellers were selling a homogeneous commodity.[2]

For all transactions in a perfectly competitive market to occur at a single price in a specified period that is long enough to allow for many individual transactions, all participants must know the general market conditions sufficiently well to predict accurately the price that will 'clear the market'. A *market-clearing price* will be defined as the price at which the quantity purchasers want to buy in a particular period is equal to the quantity suppliers want to sell. When this market-clearing price is generally known, buyers will refuse to pay a higher price, since they know that their demands can be met at the lower market-clearing price. Similarly sellers will refuse to accept a price lower than the market-clearing price because they can sell all they wish at that price. (When transactions are made through merchants, this 'single market-clearing price' should be interpreted as composed of two prices that differ by the merchants' profit margins. The higher price is used for their sales to buyers, and the lower price is used for their purchases from sellers. At these prices the stocks of the commodity remain unchanged; merchants' sales in the period are equal to their purchases. An example of

---

[2] For an interesting report on a classroom experiment with a perfectly competitive market where the student-participants did not have full knowledge of market conditions, see V.L. Smith, 'An Experimental Study of Competitive Market Behaviour', *Journal of Political Economy*, Vol. 70 (April 1962), pp. 111-37.

this price range in a well-developed market is the difference between the buying and selling prices of jobbers in stock exchanges. A jobber specializes in a particular class of securities and is always prepared to supply brokers with, or to buy from them, any one of the securities in which he deals.)

Thus a third condition must be added to ensure a single market-clearing price in perfectly competitive markets. It can be stated as follows:

(iii) *All participants must have full knowledge of the price at which market demand is equal to market supply in the particular time period.*

This condition will ensure that all transactions take place at the market-clearing price. At this price there will be no unsatisfied buyers or sellers. All who want to sell can sell as much as they want, and all who want to buy can buy as much as they want. It is important to note that this full knowledge with respect to market demand and supply is assumed to hold only for the present. The views that these buyers and sellers now have of future market conditions may be mistaken, even though condition (iii) is satisfied.

2.7 Pure and perfect competition

The adjective 'perfect', as applied to a market, originally referred to the tendency for a single price to hold for all transactions in a particular period of time. Alfred Marshall, for example, used it in this way: 'Thus the more nearly perfect a market is, the stronger is the tendency for the same price to be paid for the same thing at the same time in all parts of the market.'[3] Over time, however, the term *perfect competition* has come to have very broad connotations. In addition to the three conditions given above, it also assumes perfect knowledge on the part of market participants of all relevant present and *future* economic and technological data, perfect mobility of resources, etc.[4] In a reaction to the many possible attributes of 'perfection' covered by perfect competition, E.H. Chamberlin introduced the concept of *pure competition*,[5] using it to describe markets where the two necessary conditions for perfectly competitive markets are satisfied. He does not refer explicitly to condition (iii), but since his analysis deals only with market-

---

[3] Alfred Marshall, *Principles of Economics* (8th ed.; London: Macmillan & Co., 1920), p. 325.
[4] See, for example, Edwin Mansfield, *Microeconomics: Theory and Applications* (2nd ed.; New York: W.W. Norton & Co., 1975), pp. 234-5.
[5] He wrote of 'pure competition' that 'It is a much simpler and less inclusive concept than "perfect" competition, for the latter may be interpreted to involve perfection in many other respects than in the absence of monopoly. It may imply, for instance, an absence of friction in the sense of an ideal fluidity or mobility of factors such that adjustments to changing conditions which actually involve time are accomplished instantaneously in theory. It may imply perfect knowledge of the future and the consequent absence of uncertainty.' E.H. Chamberlin, *The Theory of Monopolistic Competition* (6th ed.; Cambridge, Mass.: Harvard University Press, 1950), p. 6.

clearing prices, presumably it too is satisfied under pure competition. Thus the term 'perfectly competitive market' as used in this book will in general be synonymous with pure competition. It will always be made clear whether full knowledge of current market conditions is assumed in any examination of these markets.

The large numbers of buyers and sellers in perfectly competitive markets means that entry into these markets in either one of these capacities must be relatively easy. Over time there can be substantial changes in the participants in these markets in response to changes in market conditions.

Economists analyse the behaviour of perfectly competitive markets with the aid of *demand and supply schedules*. However before considering them, it is important to distinguish between stock and flow concepts.

2.8 Stock and flow concepts

Economic activity always occurs at some point or period of time. The length of the time period used in economic analysis depends on the particular problem being studied—it can be a week, a month, a year, etc. In each of these time periods the analysis can be concerned with *stocks* or *flows*. The term *stock* refers to the quantity of a particular item in some specific period of time and is measured in units of the commodity. An example of a stock is the quantity of wheat held in Canadian grain elevators on December 31, 1977. Wealth is another example of a stock. An individual's wealth in a particular year would be equal to the value of his assets less the value of his debts in that year and is measured in units of currency. The term *flow* refers to the time rate of change in the quantity of a particular item in some specific time period. Income is a flow; it is measured as a time rate in some particular period. For example, an individual's income in a particular year could be $2,000 per month. The rate of sales of a commodity is also a flow. For example, sales of cars in the United States in the period May 1-10, 1975 were at a daily rate of 18,005 cars.

A stock demand for a particular item refers to the average quantity that individuals want to hold of the item in the specified time period, while a stock supply refers to the quantity they are holding. Flow demand and supply are related to these desired and actual holdings of the item and also to the expected consumption and production of this item during the particular period being examined. (These holdings of commodities are referred to as inventories.) Flow demand refers to the time rate at which individuals intend to purchase the commodity in order to provide for their consumption in the particular period and to move toward their desired inventories: it is the time rate of intended purchases in that period. Flow supply refers to the time rate at which the item is offered for sale in the period: it is the time rate of intended sales. (Actual purchases and sales in any period must be the same by definition, but intended purchases and sales might differ.)

When we deal with flow demand and supply in this book it will be important to keep in mind that these flows are affected both by the stocks actually held and by the desired stocks.

2.9 Demand schedules and curves

A market demand schedule indicates the relationship between the desired time rate of purchase of a commodity and its price. This schedule provides information about the time rate of demand at alternative prices for the commodity, in the particular market in the specified period of time, assuming that each of these prices was ruling for the full time period. All other factors that might affect the individuals' demand for this commodity —e.g. tastes, incomes, prices of other goods, expectations of future conditions—are assumed to be fixed during the time period under consideration. To illustrate, consider the hypothetical demand for apples in Montreal for a given period, say a specific month. This hypothetical schedule is set out in Table 2.1 for selected prices and is drawn in Figure 2.1. The flow demand is expressed as an average weekly rate for the specified month. Even though the demand schedule shown in Table 2.1 provides information only on demand at selected prices, it is common practice to interpolate between these points and smooth out the demand curve as shown in Figure 2.1.

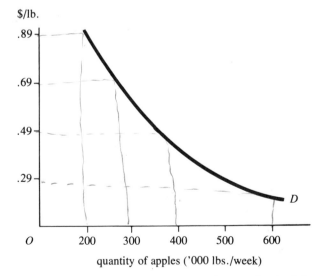

FIGURE 2.1 *Average weekly rate of demand for apples in Montreal in a specific month*

TABLE 2.1 *Demand for apples in Montreal in a specified month*

PRICE IN SPECIFIC MONTH $/lb.	QUANTITY DEMANDED IN SPECIFIC MONTH ('000 lbs.)/week
$0.89	200
0.79	230
0.69	260
0.59	300
0.49	345
0.39	410
0.29	510
0.19	620

In Chapter 5 various methods of deriving demand curves and the standard justifications for the shape drawn will be presented in detail, but certain observations can be made here on the factors that can affect the position and shape of these curves. Their values have been assumed constant in order to concentrate on the relationship between the price of a commodity and the quantity demanded. Before considering these factors, it should be noted that two implicit assumptions have been made to permit treatment of the apple market as perfectly competitive with a single demand curve. It has been assumed that an apple is a distinct commodity, different from other fruits, and that all apples are considered by potential market participants as homogeneous, no matter what type they may be. There is no distinction here between eating or cooking apples or between different kinds of eating apples, e.g. Delicious, McIntosh, or Granny Smith, etc.

In drawing the demand curve in Figure 2.1 it has been assumed that:

(i) The market, Montreal, has some definite geographical extent, with some fixed population having access, if it desires, to the Montreal apple market in the specified month.

(ii) The stocks of apples or of other goods held by potential purchasers, which may affect the demand for apples in the specific month, are given.

(iii) Tastes of individuals, as they might affect demand for apples, are assumed to be constant during the specified period.

(iv) Money incomes of all potential purchasers are assumed to be constant during the specified period.

(v) Prices of other commodities are assumed to be constant during the specified period.

(vi) Potential purchasers have some more-or-less definite expectations of what market conditions—in particular, prices for apples and other commodities—will be in future time periods.

These factors, whose values affect the position of the demand curve for apples in Montreal, are examples of parameters. A *parameter* is an element that affects the variables being studied, and whose value is constant in the particular case considered. The parameter may take on different values in other cases.

The demand curve for apples in the Montreal market would be different from that drawn in Figure 2.1 if any of the above parameters had different values from those that went into determining the position of that curve. For example, if the population with access to the Montreal apple market were larger in the specified month, other things being equal, the demand curve would be further to the right (at each price more apples would be demanded). While if the prices of other fruits were lower, other things being equal, the demand curve for apples would lie to the left of its position in Figure 2.1 (at each price fewer apples would be demanded). However, if the prices of certain other commodities—for example, prepared pie-crusts—were lower, the demand curve for apples could be further to the right.

Expectations of future conditions play a role in determining purchases. These expectations are more important the greater the scope for storing the item purchased. Storage makes it possible for current consumption to be met, if necessary, out of inventories, or for current purchases to provide for future consumption. If, for example, potential buyers expect future prices of apples to be higher (e.g. because they are higher in this period than they were in the previous period), they might want to purchase more in the present in order to anticipate future needs. Conversely, when future prices are expected to be lower, current consumption can exceed current purchases, with the difference representing a reduction in inventories. The extent to which expectations can influence current demand can also be affected by other characteristics of the good. If current consumption is a substitute for future consumption, purchases might be postponed if future prices are expected to be lower and increased when future prices are expected to be higher.

2.10 Price elasticity of demand

The demand curve in Figure 2.1 relates quantities of apples demanded, measured in '000 lbs. per week, to its price, quoted in dollars per pound. If the quantities of apples were measured in different units, the curve that conveyed the same information could look very different. For example, if the price was still quoted in dollars per pound but the quantities were measured in 100 lbs. per week, so that in the diagram the distance on the abscissa that previously measured 1,000 lbs. now only indicated 100 lbs., then the curve would be much flatter. It would appear to indicate that demand was more responsive to differences in price than is shown by Figure 2.1. This is one reason why it is useful to have a measure of the responsiveness of quantity demanded to price differences that is independent of the units of measurement. Such a measure also has the great advantage of allowing comparisons of the degree of responsiveness of demand to price for different commodities—e.g. between apples and radios, or beef and potatoes, etc.

Marshall developed the concept of *elasticity* to deal with the responsiveness of demand to price. It is a very general concept and can also be used to summarize the functional relationships between other variables. Elasticity can be defined, generally, as *the relative difference in the dependent variable divided by the relative difference in the independent variable*. (The difficulty with units is eliminated by dealing only with 'relatives'. They are equal to the differences divided by the appropriate levels. The units of measure appear in both numerators and denominators and are thus cancelled, leaving pure numbers.) The term 'elasticity' has a physical analogy. A spring is considered elastic if it can be readily compressed by a certain amount of force placed on it and springs back and expands sharply when this force is diminished. One of the 'forces' influencing the quantity demanded of a particular commodity is its price: a higher price 'squeezes' the quantity demanded to a lower figure. The extent to which the quantity demanded would be lower when the restraining force is stronger—that is, when price is higher—is measured by the price elasticity of demand.

In a demand schedule the quantity demanded is taken to be the dependent variable, with the price as the independent variable. Therefore the price elasticity of demand for a commodity (η_D) is equal to the relative difference in quantity demanded, divided by the relative difference in price. That is,

$$\eta_D = \frac{\Delta q}{q} \div \frac{\Delta p}{p} = \frac{p \Delta q}{q \Delta p} \qquad {}^{6}$$

The derivation of values for the price elasticity of demand is illustrated in Table 2.2.

The ranking of elasticity values according to size is done on the basis of their numerical (or absolute), rather than their algebraic, values. That is, a price elasticity of −3.0 is greater than a price elasticity of −2.0 (the number 3 is greater than the number 2), since it indicates a greater responsiveness of demand to differences in price. The dividing line between 'high' and 'low' values of price elasticity of demand is taken to be −1.0, the elasticity value numerically equal to one. Demand is considered to be 'elastic' on those

---

[6] The price elasticity of demand can be defined, using the notation of calculus, as

$$\eta_D = \frac{p}{q} \frac{dq}{dp}, \quad \text{where} \quad \frac{dq}{dp} = \lim_{\Delta p \to 0} \frac{\Delta q}{\Delta p}$$

TABLE 2.2 *Price elasticity of demand*

RELATIVE PRICE DIFFERENCE ($\Delta p/p$)	RELATIVE QUANTITY DIFFERENCE ($\Delta q/q$)	PRICE ELASTICITY (η_D) ($\Delta q/q \div \Delta p/p$)
-.01	.01	-1.0
-.01	.03	-3.0
-.01	.005	-0.5

parts of demand curves where the price elasticity of demand is numerically greater than one, and 'inelastic' on those parts where the price elasticity of demand is numerically less than one. (An equivalent way of classifying price elasticities would be to use the absolute value of the elasticity, written as $|\eta_D|$, rather than the numerical value.)[7]

2.11 Price elasticity and total expenditure

The reason for choosing an elasticity value numerically equal to one as the dividing line between 'elastic' and 'inelastic' demands lies in the relationship between the price elasticity of demand and total expenditure. If the price elasticity of demand has a value numerically equal to one, the total expenditure on the commodity in question will be the same at two distinct prices that differ slightly. When demand is elastic, total expenditure is higher when the price is lower, and lower when the price is higher. For inelastic demands the reverse situation holds. Total expenditure is lower when the price is lower, and higher when the price is higher. This relationship can be derived as follows:

Let Δp be the (slight) difference in price; Δq the corresponding difference in quantity. The difference in expenditures (ΔE) at the two prices can be expressed as:

$$(p + \Delta p)(q + \Delta q) - pq = p\Delta q + q\Delta p + \Delta p\Delta q$$

Neglecting the second order of 'smalls' (the product of Δp and Δq, which is very small relative to $p\Delta q$ and $q\Delta p$), this expression reduces to $\Delta E = p\Delta q + q\Delta p$. This term is positive, zero, or negative, as $p\Delta q + q\Delta p \gtreqless 0$, or

$$p\Delta q \gtreqless -q\Delta p \qquad \qquad (1)$$

---

[7] The price elasticity of demand is often defined in textbooks to be equal to *minus* the relative difference in quantity divided by the relative difference in price. See, for example, Mansfield, *Microeconomics*, p. 59. This practice is not followed here because it obscures the generality of the elasticity concept. Some elasticity terms would then be defined without a change in sign, while others are defined with such a change. The relationship between average and marginal curves (derived in Chapter 9) would also appear in two forms rather than as a single general relation.

To obtain an elasticity expression on the left-hand side of this relation, both sides should be divided by $q\Delta p$. If Δp is negative, this operation will reverse the inequality signs. Therefore,

$$\text{for } \Delta p < 0, \Delta E \gtreqless 0 \text{ as } \frac{p\Delta q}{q\Delta p} \lesseqgtr -1, \text{ that is as } \eta_D \lesseqgtr -1$$

This expression is in terms of algebraic values; $\eta_D < -1$ means that numerically, elasticity is greater than unity (e.g. -3 is numerically greater than -1 even though -3 is algebraically less than -1). When demand is elastic, a lower price results in a higher total expenditure; when demand is inelastic, the total expenditure will be lower when the price is lower. If Δp is positive, there is no change in the inequality signs in expression 1 above when both sides are divided by $q\Delta p$:

$$\text{for } \Delta p > 0, \Delta E \gtreqless 0 \text{ as } \frac{p\Delta q}{q\Delta p} \gtreqless -1, \text{ that is as } \eta_D \gtreqless -1$$

If demand is inelastic, total expenditure on the commodity will be higher when the price is higher. If demand is elastic it will be lower when the price is higher.[8]

This relationship between the price elasticity of demand and differences in total expenditure is illustrated in Table 2.3 for four price-elasticity values.

TABLE 2.3 *Relationship between price elasticity of demand and difference in total expenditure at different prices*

PRICE ELASTICITY (η_D)	PRICES COMPARED $/Unit of X		CORRESPONDING QUANTITIES Units of X ('000s)/week		CORRESPONDING EXPENDITURES $ (000's)/week	
	a	b	a	b	a	b
−2.0 (elastic)	5.00	5.05	100	98	500	494.9
−0.4 (inelastic)	5.00	5.05	100	99.6	500	502.98
−3.0 (elastic)	10.00	9.90	200	206	2000	2039.4
−0.8 (inelastic)	10.00	9.90	200	201.6	2000	1995.84

NOTE: The price elasticities of demand in this table are 'point' estimates of elasticity, with the values listed under *a* used to form the price and quantity relatives.

2.12 The geometrical derivation of the price elasticity of demand

At a particular point on the demand curve the price elasticity of demand can also be estimated geometrically. This procedure will first be illustrated for a straight-line demand curve, such as RT in Figure 2.2.

---

[8] These results can be obtained using calculus:

$$E = pq, \quad \frac{dE}{dp} = \frac{pdq}{dp} + q, \quad \text{or} \quad \frac{dE}{dp} = q\left(\frac{pdq}{qdp} + 1\right). \quad \frac{dE}{dp} \gtreqless 0 \text{ as } \frac{p}{q}\frac{dq}{dp} \gtreqless -1.$$

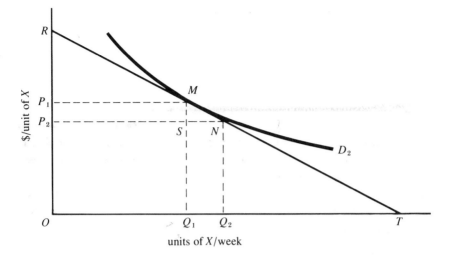

FIGURE 2.2 *Quantity demanded of commodity X in a specific period*

The point on the demand curve at which the price elasticity is to be estimated is M (the price is OP_1 and the quantity is OQ_1 at this point). If the price were slightly lower, and equal to OP_2, the quantity demanded would be OQ_2, and the corresponding point on the curve would be N. The price elasticity of demand at point M, given by the definition $\Delta q/q \div \Delta p/p$, is $SN/OQ_1 \div MS/OP_1$, which can be rewritten as $SN/MS \cdot OP_1/OQ_1$. Triangles MSN and MQ_1T are similar and $OP_1 = -MQ_1$.

$$\text{Therefore} \quad \frac{SN}{MS} = \frac{-Q_1T}{OP_1} \quad \text{and } \eta_D = \frac{-Q_1T}{OQ_1}$$

We have now derived one of the expressions for the elasticity of the demand curve RT at point M. Two equivalent expressions can be derived by manipulating the similar triangles RP_1M and MQ_1T. These two expressions for the price elasticity of demand at point M are:

$$\frac{-TM}{MR} \quad \text{and} \quad \frac{-OP_1}{P_1R}$$

The price elasticity of any demand curve at a point is the product of two values: the slope of the curve with respect to the *price axis* and the ratio of price to quantity. This relationship enables us to extend the geometric method of estimating the elasticity of a linear demand curve to non-linear demand curves. For example, in Figure 2.2 the elasticity of demand of the curve D_2 at point M can be estimated geometrically by first drawing a tangent to the curve at that point. This tangent is the straight line RT. We have just seen that the elasticity of this line at point M can be expressed by the ratio $-TM/MR$, which must be equal to the price elasticity of the demand curve D_2 at point M, since M is common to both RT and the curve D_2 and the values for their slopes are the same at this point by construction.

2.13 Point elasticity and the elasticity of a curve

It should be noted that we have been discussing the price elasticity of demand at a particular point on a curve. As the mathematical expression for the elasticity of demand makes clear, the value for the elasticity depends on the slope of the curve and the ratio of price to quantity at the point where the calculation is made. In general, therefore, the value for the elasticity of a demand curve will vary with the point chosen on the curve for the calculation of elasticity. The elasticity values for linear demand curves that touch both price and quantity axes range from minus infinity, for the points where the curves touch a price axis, to zero for the points where they touch the quantity axis. Two such curves, AB and FG, are illustrated below.

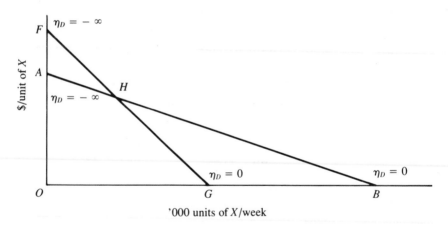

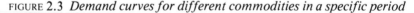

'000 units of X/week

FIGURE 2.3 *Demand curves for different commodities in a specific period*

Three categories of demand curves — illustrated in Figure 2.4 — have the same values for price elasticity at all their points. Curves of the type (i) are linear and parallel to the quantity axis; they have an elasticity value of minus infinity throughout. They are called *perfectly elastic* curves. Curves that are linear and perpendicular to the quantity axis, represented by curve (ii) in Figure 2.4, have a price elasticity value of zero at all points. They are called *perfectly inelastic* curves. If a curve is a rectangular hyperbola (that is, if it has the property that the rectangles formed by drawing per-pendicular lines to the two axes from points on the curve all have the same

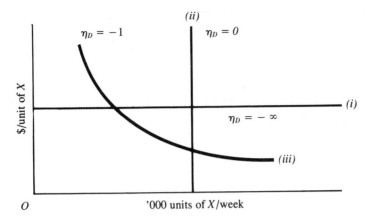

FIGURE 2.4 *Demand curves for different commodities in a specific period*

area), then it has a price elasticity value of minus one throughout. The curve labelled (iii) in Figure 2.4 is a rectangular hyperbola. The areas of the rectangles under that curve represent the total expenditures on the commodity and are the same at different points (prices). Although it is not possible to characterize precisely the degree of elasticity of curves at all points, except in these special cases, it is not uncommon in the literature to find comparisons of the degree of elasticity of different curves. This procedure is acceptable if the context makes clear the points, or range of points, on the different curves that are being compared. For example, if the elasticity of curves AB and FG in Figure 2.3 are compared for point H, or for points close to H, then the demand curve AB can be described as being more elastic than the demand curve FG. Since both have elasticity values ranging from 0 to $-\infty$, it is obvious that many points on these curves can be found where the price elasticities of those on FG are greater than those on AB. In order to avoid any misunderstanding, the areas of comparison should be specified when statements are made about the relative elasticities of different curves. As a general rule, and unless otherwise stated, we shall compare the elasticities of curves that intersect at their points of intersection.

2.14 Arc elasticity

The elasticity formula we have been using assumes that the difference in prices used for the elasticity calculation (Δp) is very small. It provides us with an estimate of the *point elasticity* of demand. When the difference in prices between the two positions on the demand curve is not small, the elasticity value calculated from this formula is very sensitive to the choice between the two price and quantity pairs. A single value for elasticity can be obtained in such cases by estimating the *arc* elasticity of demand. Average values for price and quantity are used to form the ratios required to calculate the price elasticity.

If the two prices are p_1 and p_2, and the corresponding quantities are q_1 and q_2, then the formula for the arc elasticity (η_D arc) can be written as:

$$\eta_D \text{ arc} = \frac{\Delta q}{(q_1 + q_2)/2} \div \frac{\Delta p}{(p_1 + p_2)/2} = \frac{\Delta q}{\Delta p} \cdot \frac{p_1 + p_2}{q_1 + q_2}$$

where $\Delta p = p_2 - p_1$ and $\Delta q = q_2 - q_1$.

The use of the arc elasticity formula may be illustrated by a numerical example. The two pairs of values for prices and quantities are: $p_1 = \$10$ per unit and $q_1 = 1,000$ units per day; $p_2 = \$12$ per unit and $q_2 = 800$ units per day. Δq is thus equal to -200 units per day and Δp is equal to $\$2$. When the appropriate values are substituted in the equation for arc elasticity, we have

$$\eta_D \text{ arc} = \frac{-200}{2} \times \frac{22}{1800} = \frac{-11}{9}$$

The sensitivity of the point elasticity measure to the choice of base values to form the price and quantity relatives can be illustrated by this example. If the (p_1, q_1) values are used, then we obtain

$$\eta_D = \frac{-200}{2} \times \frac{10}{1000} = -1.0$$

If the (p_2, q_2) values are used, then we obtain

$$\eta_D = \frac{-200}{2} \times \frac{12}{800} = -1.5$$

2.15 Income and cross elasticity of demand

Elasticity is a very general concept; it can be employed, as the definition in Section 2.10 makes clear, wherever there is a functional relationship between variables. For example, the quantity demanded of a commodity depends not only on the price of that commodity but also on the incomes of consumers. A quantitative measure of this dependence is provided by the *income elasticity* of demand, which is equal to the relative difference in the quantity demanded divided by the relative difference in income. This elasticity may be expressed in symbols as:

$$\eta_{x \cdot y} = \frac{\Delta Q_x}{Q_x} \div \frac{\Delta Y}{Y}$$

where $\eta_{x \cdot y}$ is the income elasticity of demand for commodity X; Q_x is the quantity of X demanded; Y is money income; and ΔQ_x and ΔY are the differences in the quantity demanded and income respectively in the two situations compared.

The values for the income elasticity of demand may be positive or negative. Higher incomes for consumers, other things being equal, could be associated with either a higher or lower demand for particular goods. Goods are said to be *superior* (or normal) when the demand for them is higher when incomes are higher. Goods are said to be *inferior* when the demand for them is lower when incomes are higher. Superior goods can be further subdivided into necessaries and luxuries. Necessary goods are those for which the income elasticity of demand is positive but small, while luxuries are goods for which the value for the income elasticity of demand is greater than one. The proportionate increase in the quantities demanded of luxury goods is greater than the proportionate increase in income.

The quantity demanded of a particular commodity also depends on the prices of related commodities, a relationship that can be represented for each of these commodities by the *cross elasticity* of demand. This elasticity is equal to the relative difference in the quantity demanded of one commodity divided by the relative difference in the price of another commodity. In symbolic form it may be written as:

$$\eta_{x_1 \cdot x_2} = \frac{\Delta Q_{x_1}}{Q_{x_1}} \div \frac{\Delta p_{x_2}}{p_{x_2}}$$

$\eta_{x_1 \cdot x_2}$ is the cross elasticity of demand for commodity X_1 with respect to the price of commodity X_2. Q_{x_1} is the quantity demanded of X_1; p_{x_2} is the price of commodity X_2; ΔQ_{x_1} and Δp_{x_2} are the differences between the quantities of X_1 demanded and the price for X_2 respectively in the two situations compared.

The values obtained for the cross elasticity of demand are a reflection of the relationship between the two commodities. If the two goods are *substitutes* (if they are viewed to some extent as alternatives)—as in the case of beef and pork—the cross elasticity of demand will be positive. A higher price for beef, given the price of pork, would increase the quantity demanded of pork. If the two goods are *complements* (if the consumption of one is directly related to the consumption of the other)—as in the case of automobiles and tires—the cross elasticity of demand will be negative. A higher price for automobiles would be associated with a lower demand for tires. If two goods are unrelated, their cross elasticity of demand will be zero.

2.16 Analysis of comparisons and changes
The different points on a demand curve represent alternative positions, each

of which is appropriate for a particular price for the commodity given the same values for all the other parameters. This curve thus enables us to compare the differences in quantities demanded due to any specified difference in price *all other things given*. In order to explain the effects on quantities demanded of *changes* in price, a demand curve must be supplemented by information on (i) whether these changes affect the values of the parameters; and (ii) the length of time available for the adjustment to the change in price. The comparison of two situations, which is provided by any two points on a demand curve, is not the same thing as the tracing of a movement from one to the other.[9] In particular a change in price might affect the expectations concerning future prices and thus the position of the demand curve. A change in the price of this commodity might affect the prices of related commodities: this would also affect the position of the demand curve.

Economics textbooks distinguish between 'movements' along a demand curve and 'shifts' of the curve.[10] The former is concerned with the comparison of different positions on the same curve, the latter with the comparison of different curves. This distinction is a useful one, but care must be taken not to be misled by the terminology into thinking that changes through time are being considered. The difference between these two concepts can be illustrated by considering Figure 2.5. D_1D_1 is a reproduction of the demand curve in Figure 2.1, while D_2D_2 represents a different demand curve, one that shows a higher quantity of apples demanded at each price.

The D_1D_1 curve in Figure 2.5 shows that at a price of $0.59 a pound the average weekly demand for apples in the specified month would be 300,000 lbs., while if the price were $0.49 a pound this demand would be 345,000 lbs. A 'movement' along a demand curve consists of a comparison of these two quantities and their corresponding prices. But this does *not* necessarily indicate what would happen to the quantity of apples demanded in the specified time period if the price changed in that period from $0.59 to $0.49 a pound. In order to know the effect of such a change in price, it would be necessary to determine its effects on expectations, on other prices, and on the time it takes purchasers to respond to differences in the values of these factors.

'Shifts' in the demand curve are said to occur if the values for at least one

---

[9] The importance of this methodological rule, which emphasizes that time must be treated seriously and that an analysis of comparisons should not be confused with an analysis of changes, is stressed in Joan Robinson, *Exercises in Economic Analysis* (London: Macmillan & Co., 1960), p. v.

[10] See, for example, Mansfield, *Microeconomics*, p. 59.

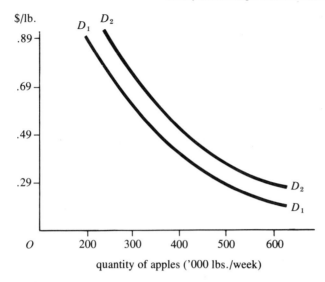

FIGURE 2.5 *Two demand curves for apples in Montreal in a specific month*

of the parameters affecting demand is different. For example, in Figure 2.5 the demand curve D_2D_2 would be the appropriate curve if the good were a superior good and if the incomes of consumers were greater than the incomes underlying curve D_1D_1. The two curves indicate only what the differences in the quantities demanded of the particular commodity would be if incomes were different. An analysis of the effects of changes in income would require a consideration of the effects of these changes on the values of the other parameters, and of the time available for individuals to adjust to the changed circumstances.

2.17 The price elasticity of demand and the passage of time

The nature of a commodity is an important determinant of its price elasticity. If it is considered to be a necessary part of the standard of living of consumers, and if there are no very close substitutes, the price elasticity of demand will be low. The quantities of this item demanded by consumers will be relatively constant, even though its price differs, because they consider its consumption necessary and that this need cannot be satisfied in other ways. The degree of commodity classification will also affect these elasticity values. They will, in general, be higher for narrowly defined goods than for those that have a much broader coverage because they are more likely to have close substitutes. For example, the demand for spinach is more elastic than the demand for green vegetables; the demand for green vegetables is more elastic than the demand for all vegetables, etc. Another

factor affecting the price elasticity of demand is the proportion of consumers' budgets accounted for by the commodity in question. The larger
this proportion, the greater the effect of a difference in price on the consumers' abilities to purchase this commodity, since this difference affects
the purchasing power of their incomes. This factor will be examined in some
detail in Chapter 5.

The length of time consumers have to adjust to any differences in price is
also a very important determinant of the value for the elasticity of demand.
The longer this time period, the larger the price elasticity. Time is required
not only to change habitual patterns of behaviour but also to make the
physical changes that are often necessary before substitution can be made.
For example, the price elasticity of demand for oil in one month is less than
it is over three years. The quadrupling of world oil prices in 1973 has
demonstrated that the price elasticity of demand for this item over a short
period is low. However, it has set in train many attempts to expand the
supply of alternative fuels and to develop methods of making more efficient
use of oil and its products. As these efforts bear fruit, the demand for oil
will become lower than would otherwise be the case. This will be reflected in
a larger numerical value for the estimates of the price elasticity of demand
for oil.

Different assumptions about the time available for adjustment to different prices would lead to different demand curves for a particular good,
even though the values for the parameters listed in Section 2.9 are the same.
Two such curves are drawn in Figure 2.6. It is assumed that in previous
periods the purchasers expected the price of the good in this period to be
equal to P_1, and they made their other arrangements on that basis. Thus the
two curves have a common point at this price. The curve labelled D_s shows
the quantities that would be demanded at other prices for this good if
purchasers were faced with a different price at the beginning of the month

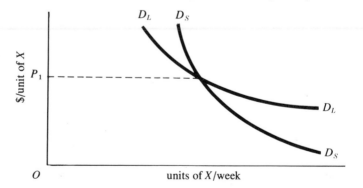

FIGURE 2.6 *Demand curves for commodity X in a specific month*

and only had this month in which to adjust their patterns of expenditure. The D_L curve, on the other hand, assumes that they had a longer period of time, say a year, in which to adjust to a different price. It is thus more elastic than D_s.

2.18 Supply schedules and curves

Supply schedules can be constructed for commodities sold in perfectly competitive markets. A flow-supply schedule shows the time rate at which quantities of a particular commodity would be offered by sellers at alternative prices for that commodity. This schedule is defined for a particular market in the specified time period and is based on the assumption that in each of the alternative situations the price is constant for the full time period. In a perfectly competitive market an individual seller cannot by his own independent actions affect the terms at which he sells. The supply schedule is therefore independent and distinct from the demand schedule in this market.

To illustrate, consider fictitious data on the supply of apples to the Montreal market in a specific month. (All apples are assumed to be identical from the point of view of the sellers.) The total stock of apples available to potential sellers in that month is assumed to be fixed.

TABLE 2.4 *Supply of apples in Montreal in a specific month (fictitious data)*

PRICE IN SPECIFIC MONTH $/lb.	RATE AT WHICH QUANTITY SUPPLIED IN SPECIFIC MONTH ('000 lbs./week)
0.89	430
0.79	400
0.69	380
0.59	360
0.49	345
0.39	310
0.29	270
0.19	220

The relationship indicated by this supply schedule—the quantity supplied is larger the higher the price—is typical of such schedules, but it need not always be so. Under certain circumstances to be considered in Chapter 11, there may be an inverse relationship between price and quantity supplied. For the present these schedules will be assumed to follow the pattern shown in Table 2.4. The supply schedule for apples in Table 2.4 can be represented by a supply curve, as in Figure 2.7.

The position and shape of this supply curve are affected by many factors.

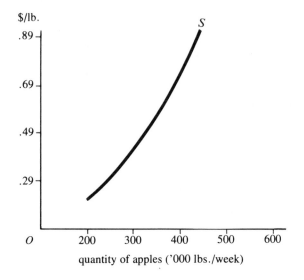

FIGURE 2.7 *Supply of apples in Montreal in a specific month*

They include (i) the stocks of apples available to potential sellers in the Montreal market in the specific month; (ii) the expected prices for apples in this and other markets in future periods; (iii) costs of storage and transportation; (iv) expected prices for apples in this specified period in other areas to which apples from Montreal could be shipped, or from which apples could be shipped to Montreal; (v) expectations held in the past concerning prices for this commodity in the present; (vi) the costs of producing apples in the recent past. The last three factors would affect the facilities and resources available for producing, shipping, and storing apples for the Montreal market. For example, the facilities available for the production, shipment, and storage of apples to Montreal would tend to be greater if, some time in the past, higher prices for apples were expected to be ruling in Montreal over a period that contained the specified month. More facilities would be reflected in the position of the supply curve, which would lie further to the right than the position shown in Figure 2.7. The quantities sellers would be able and willing to sell at any particular price, all other factors given, would be greater.

When supply curves are used to help explain current prices, one should always keep in mind the dependence of the quantity supplied in a specified period on expectations about future prices held in the past and the present. The importance of expectations on the position of the supply curve and on prices is illustrated by the following extract from the *New York Times* (December 5, 1971).

By land, by sea and by air—but mostly by sea—the heroin pours into the country. Last week, here and abroad, the traffic pattern was a study in confusion.

In New York, the 59-day dock strike ended as longshoremen returned to work under a court order; and suddenly, within hours, the critical shortage of heroin on the city's streets had eased. It was as though a magic wand had been waved—and it had.

The heroin pushers had initially reacted to the strike-caused shortage much as other kinds of merchants have been known to react when the demand for their products outstripped the supply: they cut quality and raised prices. And they built up a reserve in the expectation that the strike would continue and the prices, which had in some instances more than tripled, would keep soaring. With the strike's end, police said, the heroin merchants released their reserve supply. And the city's 150,000 addicts—nearly half the nation's total—suddenly were able to make their connections even before the new waterborne supplies hit the market.

2.19 Price elasticity of supply

A supply curve contains information about the responsiveness of quantity supplied to differences in price; it is based on a functional relationship between these two variables. A measure of the degree of this responsiveness at various points on the curve can be provided by the *price elasticity of supply* (η_s). This is equal to the relative difference in quantity supplied divided by the corresponding relative difference in price. Its sign depends on the sign of the slope of the supply curve, and it is therefore positive for upward-sloping curves. The elasticity of a supply curve at a particular point can be estimated geometrically. The method used is demonstrated for the linear supply curve BS in Figure 2.8.

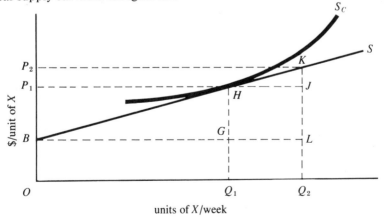

FIGURE 2.8 *Quantity supplied of commodity X in a particular market in a specific period*

The point on the curve at which the elasticity of supply is to be estimated is H. The price at this point is OP_1 and the quantitiy is OQ_1. If the price were slightly higher, at OP_2, the corresponding point on the curve would be K, and the quantity would be OQ_2. From its definition we know that the elasticity of supply (η_s) is equal to $\Delta Q/Q \div \Delta p/p$. The values for point H are used to form the price and quantity relatives. From Figure 2.8 we see that $\Delta Q = Q_1 Q_2$, which can be written as HJ, while $\Delta p = P_1 P_2$, which can be written as JK. When these terms are substituted in the equation for the price elasticity of supply, we have:

$$\eta_s = \frac{HJ}{OQ_1} \div \frac{JK}{OP_1} = \frac{HJ}{JK} \cdot \frac{OP_1}{OQ_1}$$

Note that triangles HKJ and BHG are similar and $OQ_1 = BG$, $BP_1 = GH$.

$$\therefore \quad \frac{HJ}{JK} = \frac{BG}{GH} = \frac{OQ_1}{BP_1}$$

$$\therefore \quad \eta_s \text{ at point } H = \frac{OQ_1}{BP_1} \cdot \frac{OP_1}{OQ_1} = \frac{OP_1}{BP_1}$$

That is, the elasticity of supply at a particular point on a linear supply curve is equal to the ratio of the price at that point divided by the difference between the price and the value of the intercept of this linear supply curve and the ordinate. In general, the value for the price elasticity of a supply curve will differ for different points on the curve. However, there are certain regularities for linear supply curves. If, as in Figure 2.7, the linear supply curve cuts the ordinate at a positive value, the elasticity of supply at all points on the curve has a value greater than one. If the linear supply curve (when extended, if necessary) cuts the ordinate below the origin, then the value for the elasticity of supply is less than one at all points. Finally, if the curve cuts the ordinate at the origin, the elasticity value is equal to one at all points.

These relationships are illustrated in Figure 2.9. The linear supply curve labelled S_1 has unit elasticity at all points because when extended it goes through the origin. The price elasticity for all points on the curve S_2 is greater than one, but this value is smaller the further a point is from the origin. All points on S_3 have elasticity values of less than one, but for any two points on this curve the one further from the origin has the larger value. The range of possible price elasticity values for a linear supply curve is more restricted than it is for a linear demand curve. As we saw in Section 2.13, the latter can have elasticity values both numerically greater and smaller than one at different points.

If a supply curve is parallel to the abscissa, it has an elasticity value of

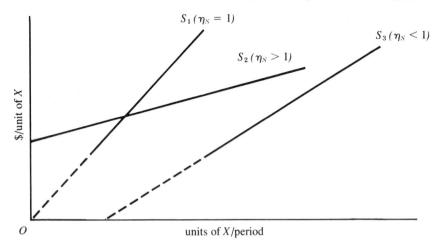

FIGURE 2.9 *Supply curves for a particular commodity in a specific period*

infinity at all points; if it is perpendicular to the abscissa, it has a value of zero at all points.

A geometrical estimate of the price elasticity at a particular point for a non-linear supply curve is readily obtained by finding the elasticity for the tangent to that curve at this point. For example, in Figure 2.8 the elasticity of the supply curve S_c at point H is equal to the elasticity at that point of the tangent to the curve BS. The price elasticity of supply is equal to the product of the slope of a curve and the corresponding ratio of price to quantity. Point H is common to both curves and both have the same slope at that point.

When the difference in the prices being compared is not small, then an *arc elasticity* of supply is a more appropriate estimate of the responsiveness of quantity to price than is a point elasticity estimate. The considerations and procedures here are similar to those dealt with in the discussion of the elasticity of demand. The value for the arc elasticity of supply is obtained by using the average of the quantities supplied and the average of the prices as the bases for the quantity and price relatives.

2.20 Supply curves and the passage of time

The supply curve for a particular commodity is very much affected by the amount of time suppliers are assumed to have to adjust to differences in the price of their good. If this time is too short to allow for any change in the current rate of producing the item, the potential supply is limited by the existing stocks and the current rate of production of this item. If, in addition, the commodity is perishable and cannot be stored for possible future sale, then the supply curve will be perfectly inelastic. If it can be stored, then the quantity offered for sale in this period will be dependent on expectations of prices in future periods and the supply curve need not be perfectly inelastic. Supply curves based solely on existing stocks and on a predetermined rate of production are called *market-period supply curves*. A curve of this type is labelled S_m in Figure 2.10. (The supply curve for apples drawn in Figure 2.7 is a market-period supply curve for a storable good and is thus not perfectly inelastic.)

The greater the time available for producers to adjust to differences in price, the greater the elasticity of supply. If this period of time is long enough to allow for changes in the rate of production from existing plant and equipment, the supply curve will be more elastic than the market-period supply curve. Changes in the rate of production will enable sellers to offer larger quantities at higher prices, while smaller amounts will be available at lower prices. Supply curves based on time periods long enough to alter the rate of production from existing facilities are called *short-period supply curves*. A curve of this type is labelled S_s in Figure 2.10. If it is assumed that the facilities available for production (as well as the rate of production with these facilities) are what producers would choose to have at each price, then the supply curve would be still more elastic. Curves of this type are called *long-period supply curves* and are represented by the curve labelled S_L in Figure 2.10.[11]

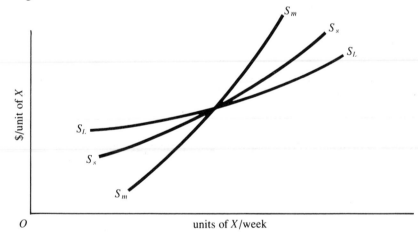

FIGURE 2.10 *Three supply curves with different assumptions about the time available to adjust to the differences in price*

[11] Short- and long-period supply curves are derived in Chapter 11. It is shown there that long-period supply curves may be horizontal or even negatively sloped.

2.21 Equilibrium price and quantity

Demand and supply curves have been developed to help in the analysis of price determination in perfectly competitive markets. If it is assumed that the commodity market under examination is perfectly competitive, with full knowledge on the part of all participants of current market conditions, then these curves can be used to determine the actual price for the commodity in a very straightforward manner. This will be illustrated with the fictitious demand and supply curves for apples in the Montreal market, which are redrawn in Figure 2.11.

Given the assumptions and the curves in Figure 2.11, the price for apples in the Montreal market in the specified month will be $0.49 per pound and the quantity exchanged per week will be 345,000 lbs. These values are given by the point of intersection of the demand and supply curves. The price of $0.49 per pound is the only possible market price when full knowledge of current market conditions is assumed. At all other prices the quantity demanded would differ from the quantity supplied. If a higher price were quoted, sellers would want to sell more than buyers would want to purchase at that price. Since this circumstance is known (because the analysis assumes full knowledge of the price at which total demand is equal to total supply), then purchasers would refrain from buying at that price because they would know that they could make all their purchases at a price of $0.49. Similarly for a lower price: buyers would want to purchase more than sellers would want to sell at that price. With full knowledge of this situation, individual sellers would not sell at a price below $0.49.

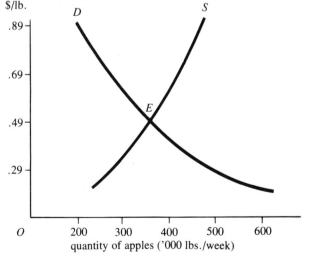

FIGURE 2.11 *Demand and supply curves for apples in Montreal in a specific month*

The price of \$0.49 per pound clears the Montreal apple market in the period under consideration. At that price every buyer can purchase as much as he wants, and every seller can sell as much as he wants. The total amount buyers want to purchase is equal to the total amount sellers want to sell. \$0.49 per pound is the *equilibrium price*, and 345,000 lbs. per week is the *equilibrium quantity*. Point *E* in Figure 2.11 represents the *equilibrium market position*.

2.22 Equilibrium defined as a position of rest

Great use is made in economic theory of the concept of equilibrium, even though it can be applied only to a limited class of situations. It has been used in economics to mean at least two things: a *position of rest* for the values of certain variables,[12] or for a situation in which the individual units being studied are in their *chosen positions*.[13] A position may be characterized as being an equilibrium position according to one of these definitions, while it may not be an equilibrium position according to the other.

If the criterion of rest is employed, *equilibrium simply means a position of rest. This is a position in which, given the values of the parameters, there is no tendency for the values of the variables under consideration to change in the period studied.*

Point *E* in Figure 2.11 represents a position of 'rest' in the sense that, given the values for the parameters that determine the particular demand and supply curves, there would be no net forces at work tending to change a price of \$0.49 per pound (and a quantity of 345,000 lbs. per week) *in this specific month.* This does not necessarily mean that this price and quantity would be unchanged over time—that is, over a sequence of months. More information than is given by the curves drawn in Figure 2.11 would have to be provided before the behaviour of price over time could be determined. Only if conditions were *stationary* would a particular equilibrium position

---

[12] For example, Bent Hansen has thus defined it in *A Survey of General Equilibrium Systems* (New York: McGraw-Hill, 1970): 'The concept of economic equilibrium has been taken from classical mechanics . . . It is loosely defined as a state wherein the forces that operate on a point (or body) "cancel each other out" . . . we can say that if we have an economic model that explains certain variables, and if there is no tendency for these variables to change, given the data of the model, then the system of variables is in equilibrium' (pp. 3-4). This is the definition of equilibrium given in textbooks; see, for example, Jack Hirshleifer, *Price Theory and Applications* (Englewood Cliffs, N.J.: Prentice-Hall, Inc., 1976), p. 19.

[13] For example, J.R. Hicks has written: 'The static economy . . . is in a state of equilibrium when all the "individuals" in it are choosing those quantities which, out of the alternatives available to them, they prefer to produce and to consume . . . The alternatives that are open are set in part by external constraints . . . But they are also set in large part by the choices made by other "individuals".' *Capital and Growth* (Oxford: Clarendon Press, 1965), pp. 15-16.

be one of rest over time. Stationary conditions mean that there would be no changes in the values of the parameters over time.

2.23 Equilibrium defined as a chosen position

With the chosen-position criterion, *equilibrium means a position in which the individuals make all the transactions they would choose to make in the specified time period, given the values for the parameters of the system.*

According to this definition an individual is in equilibrium when he is making the best of the situation facing him. Given the market price, he is making all the transactions he wants to make at that price. Of course chosen transactions referred to in the definition may be zero for some individuals. For example, given the market price of a commodity, some individuals might choose not to make any purchases.

In Figure 2.11 point E is also a position of equilibrium when the chosen position criterion is used. All the buyers and sellers are making all the transactions they wish to make at \$0.49 per pound. Under these circumstances this is the only price for which this is true. At a higher price, sellers would want to sell more than buyers would want to purchase, and vice-versa for a lower price.

Both definitions of equilibrium indicate point E as the equilibrium position in this example; however, they may give different categorizations in more complex models. For a position of rest to be a chosen position, it is necessary for forces to be at work that change market values until a chosen position is reached. These forces exist in the hypothetical example of the Montreal apple market because of the assumption of full knowledge of current conditions in that market, which ensures that all transactions will take place at a single price. In other cases the forces leading to the chosen position in this market may not operate, and the market may come to rest at values where not all of the individuals are in a chosen position. This situation is exemplified in the conclusion of Keynes that there may be involuntary unemployment in equilibrium in a capitalist economy in the absence of governmental intervention. He was using the definition of equilibrium as a position of rest for the variable (employment) under consideration when he argued that even though employment was less than the supply of labour at the prevailing real-wage rate, there may be no net tendency for employment to increase because the changes that may occur in the labour market in response to this situation would be offset by their effects in other markets.[14] There has been unnecessary confusion in

---

[14] John Maynard Keynes, *The General Theory of Employment, Interest, and Money* (London: Macmillan & Co., 1936), Chapters 2 and 19.

economics about this analysis because the two definitions of equilibrium were not distinguished. It is often assumed that a position of rest *must* be a chosen position.[15]

The chosen-position definition of equilibrium will be used in this book unless otherwise specified. It is important to note that there is nothing normative about equilibrium—it is a descriptive term for one possible market outcome. Even though each individual is 'making the best of the situation facing him', the results may be judged unsatisfactory. They are 'the best' only in a relative sense, given the constraints under which the individuals operate. These constraints may produce equilibrium values that are judged by many to be inequitable. For example, the equilibrium price for apples in Figure 2.11 may be too low to enable apple producers to earn more than a subsistence level of income. Attempts to interfere with the operation of perfectly competitive markets for these and other reasons will be considered in the next chapter.

2.24 Summary

This discussion of exchange has introduced some concepts that play an important role in economic analysis. In order to ensure that they are used properly, it is important to know the assumptions on which they are based. The demand and supply curves presented here are defined for perfectly competitive markets. These are markets for homogeneous products in which the number of buyers and sellers is very large, with each individual having a negligible effect on market price. Even though the terms 'movements' and 'shifts' are commonly used in dealing with demand and supply curves, it has been emphasized that analyses described in this way are not examining changes through time. The term 'movement' refers to a comparison of points on a demand or supply curve, while the term 'shifts' refers to a comparison of positions for the curves. The distinction between analyses concerned with comparisons and those tracing changes over time will be stressed in this book.

Elasticity is a very general concept and its particular forms have useful roles in economic theory. They provide a convenient summary of the quantitative relationships between dependent and independent variables, and references to elasticities will keep recurring in the remaining chapters of this book.

Equilibrium and deductions based on equilibrium comparisons occur frequently in economic analysis. The treatment of equilibrium here has been

---

[15] See, for example, Don Patinkin, *Money, Interest, and Prices* (2nd ed.; New York: Harper & Row, 1965), p. 323.

very formal to emphasize its theoretical nature. Actual market values need not be the same as the equilibrium values, and possible differences between the two will be indicated throughout this book.

SUGGESTED READINGS

Boulding, Kenneth E. *Economic Analysis*. Vol. I: *Microeconomics*. 4th ed. New York: Harper & Row, 1966. Chapters 2, 3 and 7-10.

Marshall, Alfred. *Principles of Economics*. 8th ed. London: Macmillan & Co., 1920. Book III, Chapter IV, and Book V, Chapters I and II.

Robinson, Joan. *Exercises in Economic Analysis*. London: Macmillan & Co., 1960. Pages 153-7.

Robinson, Joan and John Eatwell. *An Introduction to Modern Economics*. London: McGraw-Hill, 1973. Pages 146-53 and 161-5.

Smith, Adam. *The Wealth of Nations*. The Modern Library ed. New York: Random House, 1937. Book I, Chapters I-III.

EXERCISES

1. (a) What do you think would be the effect on the demand curve for beef products of an increase in the price of pork? Why?

(b) What do you think would be the effect of higher income on the demand curve for T-Bone steaks? Why?

2. The demand schedule for commodity X is shown in part in the following table:

PRICE ($/unit of X)	QUANTITY DEMANDED ('000 lbs. / week)
8	50
9	45
10	40
11	34

(a) Calculate the point elasticity of demand at a price of $9 when the price is increased by $1.

(b) Calculate the arc elasticity of demand for the price interval $9-$10.

3. (a) You are told that when the price of X is reduced (from $20 to $19), the total expenditure per week is increased (from $200,000 to $228,000). Is the demand for this product, in this price range, elastic or inelastic?

(b) Give a reason for your answer and calculate the elasticity of demand from the data supplied.

4. Assume that the demand and supply schedules for Canadian No. 1 Northern wheat in the Winnipeg Grain Market on a particular day were:

PRICE ($/bu.)	DEMAND ('000 bu./day)	SUPPLY ('000 bu./day)
1.25	350	190
1.40	330	220
1.50	320	250
1.60	310	270
1.75	295	295
1.90	280	320
2.00	245	350

(a) What is the equilibrium price?

(b) What is the equilibrium quantity?

(c) Would you expect all trades that day to take place at the equilibrium price? Why?

(d) Assume that these demand and supply schedules were repeated each day for a month. Would you expect the prices on the last day of trading in that month to differ from the average of prices on the first day of trading in that month? Why?

5. A trade unionist, who was on the Board of Directors of the Sydney Opera House, complained that prices of tickets to opera performances were set at too high a level for 'working-class' families.

(a) What do you think the effects would be of, say, reducing the price of tickets by 50 per cent (with the government increasing its subsidy to the Opera House to keep its revenues unchanged)?

(b) Would such a policy have any 'distributional' implications?

6. In a study prepared in 1976 by the Charles River Associates the short-run price elasticity of demand for aluminum in the United States was estimated to be –0.066, and the long-run price elasticity to be –0.319.

(a) Why do these price elasticities differ?

(b) The price of aluminum was increased in the United States by 6 per cent in the spring of 1977. If the above estimates of the price elasticities of demand are correct, what effect would this price change have on the demand for aluminum?

7. Per-capita coffee consumption in the United States during the first three months of 1977 was reported to have dropped to 3 pounds from 3.6 pounds during the same period in 1976. Retail prices of coffee were 81 per cent higher in the former period than they had been in the latter.

(a) Calculate the price elasticity of demand on the basis of this data.

(b) Why might this not be a good estimate of the price elasticity of demand for coffee?

3

SOME APPLICATIONS OF DEMAND AND SUPPLY ANALYSIS

3.1 Introduction

The demand and supply curves that were introduced in the previous chapter are of assistance in understanding the forces at work in certain types of markets. With this understanding, economic policies can be formulated to produce results that are judged to be more desirable than those that would occur in their absence. To apply demand and supply analysis correctly, however, it is important to be aware of the assumptions on which it is based. Demand and supply curves were defined for perfectly competitive markets in which there are large numbers of buyers and sellers dealing in homogeneous commodities. This analysis, therefore, finds its main application in markets in which these conditions are at least approximately satisfied. Markets that tend to meet these requirements are those for primary commodities—the products of agriculture, mining, forestry and fishing. Thus agricultural policy is one important area for the application of demand and supply analysis.

Before studying applications, however, it is important to be aware that theory often tries to analyse *changes* by making *comparisons* between different equilibrium positions. Valuable insights into the factors causing changes can sometimes be obtained in this way. Nevertheless, one should always keep in mind the distinction between an analysis based on comparisons of alternative positions and one that handles changes through time.

3.2 Effects of a specific tax

The comparisons of equilibrium positions to be found in the literature of economics can be illustrated by the demand and supply curves in Figure 3.1. The differences between the two supply curves is due to a difference in the

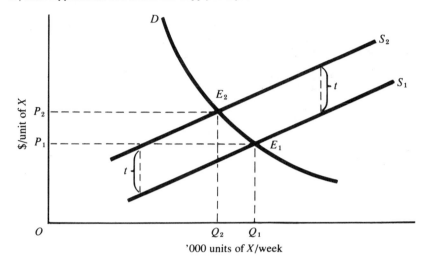

FIGURE 3.1 *Equilibrium positions for commodity X in a specific period with and without a specific tax of $t per unit*

value for one of the parameters. There is a specific tax on the commodity of $t per unit for S_2 but none for S_1. For each quantity supplied, S_2 is thus $t above S_1.

We saw in Chapter 2 that a supply curve indicates the relationship between the rates at which sellers are prepared to supply the commodity and its price. The alternative prices referred to for this purpose are the prices received by the sellers. If they must pay a specific tax to the government, the price to the buyers must be higher by the amount of the tax for any particular quantity of the good supplied. For example, sellers were prepared to supply a quantity of OQ_1 per week at a market price of $$OP_1$, but after the imposition of the tax a market price of $$(OP_1 + t)$ is required. This does not mean, however, that the equilibrium price would necessarily be higher by $t. If, as in Figure 3.1, the equilibrium quantities exchanged differ in the no-tax and tax situations, the market price in perfectly competitive markets might differ by less than the tax.

Given the size of the tax, the differences in equilibrium prices and quantities depend on the values for the elasticities of the demand and supply curves in the area where they intersect. Special cases are illustrated in Figure 3.2 where the effects of a specific tax are concentrated either on equilibrium price or quantity. It can be seen from panels A and B that if the demand curve is perfectly elastic, or if the supply curve is perfectly inelastic, the equilibrium prices will be unaffected by the tax. The equilibrium quantity will also be unchanged with the inelastic supply curve, but it will be lower

Some Applications of Demand and Supply Analysis | 49

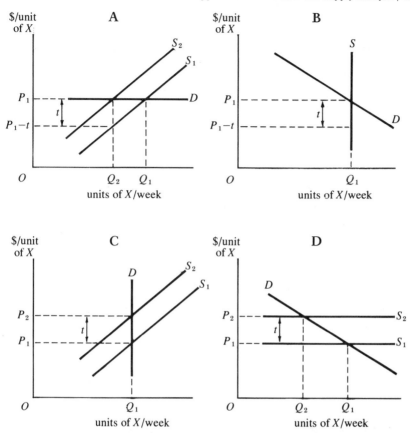

FIGURE 3.2 *Illustrations of the effects of a specific tax on a commodity, sold in perfectly competitive markets, in special cases where equilibrium price or quantity is the same*

with the perfectly elastic curve. Panels C and D show the two situations in which the equilibrium price is higher by the full amount of the tax. This result requires either a perfectly inelastic demand curve or a perfectly elastic supply curve. With the former the equilibrium quantity is unchanged, while with the latter it is lower.

In all but these four special cases, both equilibrium price and quantity will differ when situations with and without a specific tax are compared. The values for these differences in prices and quantities depend on the elasticities of the demand and supply curves. For any given supply curve (which is not perfectly elastic or inelastic) the difference in quantity is greater (and the difference in price is smaller) the more elastic the demand curve. For any given demand curve (which is not perfectly elastic or inelastic) the differences in both equilibrium quantity and price are greater the more elastic the supply curve.

The shapes of the demand and supply curves depend, as we have seen in Chapter 2, on the length of time that market participants have to adjust to differences in prices (as well as on the characteristics of the goods), but time enters into this analysis only in this indirect manner. The comparison of equilibrium positions does *not* indicate how the values of the variables being studied change *in time* from one equilibrium position to another. The time required and the path followed depend on the information available to individuals and on their ability to adjust their activities to bring them in line with the changed circumstances. Their experience of non-equilibrium positions, and in particular the changes in their expectations, may produce oscillations in market values around the equilibrium prices and quantities (see Section 3.14) and may also alter the equilibrium. For example, the imposition of a specific tax and the lower price received by sellers may lead to the expectation of *further* decreases in price and cause many producers to abandon this market as soon as they can disengage themselves from their commitments. With this change in market participants and production facilities, the equilibrium position will also change.

3.3 Partial and general equilibrium analysis

The foregoing examination of the equilibrium effects of a specific tax on a commodity whose market is perfectly competitive is an example of *partial equilibrium* analysis: one part of the economic system is examined in isolation from all other parts. In the two situations compared, the only differences in equilibrium price are for the commodity X. The prices of all other commodities are assumed to be the same in all the comparisons. However, there is a further relationship between markets that should be made explicit: changes in one market will tend to change prices in related markets as well.

The imposition of a tax on commodity X, and the higher price for this commodity that may result, will generally affect the demands for other commodities. (They may also be affected by the uses the government makes of this tax revenue.) The quantities demanded of goods that are substitutes for X will tend to be higher and the quantities demanded of goods that are complements for X will tend to be lower. These shifts in the demand curves for other goods, caused by the tax on X, will alter their equilibrium prices. With different prices for other commodities, there will be a different position for commodity X's demand curve. The impact of differences in the prices of other commodities might also influence the position of the supply curve for X. Thus the equilibrium prices in the tax and no-tax situations could differ substantially from the values shown in Figure 3.1 after all adjustments in other commodity markets are made. Before any policy conclusions are drawn from partial equilibrium analysis, it should be modified to handle the possible effects on the results obtained of repercussions in related markets.

The method of analysis explicitly dealing with the full interdependence of the economic system is called *general equilibrium* analysis. It would clearly be desirable to employ this method whenever possible. The virtue of this approach, however, is also its vice. The number of variables to be considered may be so numerous that the analysis becomes very formal and mathematical. The system must be described in terms of a large number of equations, and the economic analyst does not get much beyond the stage of checking that the number of unknowns in the model is equal to the number of equations. In a world where there are many commodities and elements of production, it is necessary to try and combine some aspects of both partial and general equilibrium analysis. A possible compromise would allow for the interdependence of closely related goods without making the analysis completely general. This would correct some of the more serious defects of a partial equilibrium approach without overloading the analysis.

3.4 Applications of demand and supply analysis

Perfectly competitive markets are idealized representations of the markets for primary commodities, which are produced by different types of productive organizations. Some are mainly produced by peasant smallholders—for example, cocoa; some by relatively large farmers—for example, wheat or beef cattle; some by relatively small corporations—for example, tea; and some by very large corporations—for example, copper. Other commodities are produced by a mixture of organizations—for example, coffee by smallholders, substantial farmers, and very large family concerns; cotton by smallholders and also in large plantations.[1] Even though there are these differences in the way production is organized and in the methods of marketing different commodities, there are certain similarities that make them amenable to the same type of analysis. Different units of a particular primary commodity, or of a certain category of the commodity (e.g. No. 2 Ordinary Hard Kansas City wheat), are homogeneous, and the numbers of buyers and sellers in world or important regional markets are usually large. There may not be full knowledge of current market conditions on the part of all market participants, but the

---

[1] J.W.F. Rowe, *Primary Commodities in International Trade* (Cambridge, Eng.: Cambridge University Press, 1965), pp. 13-27.

presence of specialist traders, who are prepared to carry out arbitrage operations, ensures that prices at which transactions occur in a single market (in a given time period) are very similar. Demand and supply curves can be used to summarize the factors determining prices and quantities in these markets in the absence of either governmental intervention or combined action by market participants. Even if there is governmental or combined action, however, demand and supply analysis may still be useful as a starting point for the study of these markets. It can indicate some of the problems that the government policy makers, or the market participants who are acting together, must overcome.

The money incomes received by workers and the owners of resources (land and capital) engaged in the production of primary commodities are dependent on factors that influence output and prices. These factors include the weather and demand conditions for the commodity. In certain cases to be discussed below, producers might be worse off as a group the higher their output. Professor Joan Robinson has vividly described such a situation in terms of the case of the 'farmer who hanged himself in the expectation of plenty'.[2] There may be few alternative uses for many of these resources and the costs of switching to some other activity or location may be substantial.[3] In addition, the real incomes of producers of natural commodities—that is, the purchasing power of their money incomes—depend on the prices of other commodities. The markets for these manufactured commodities are not perfectly competitive and the prices of manufactured goods may follow a path quite different from that of the prices of primary commodities. Producers of primary goods may try to obtain government assistance to improve the levels of their real incomes through the maintenance of some 'proper' or 'normal' relationship between the prices of their output and the prices of the goods they purchase.

3.5 Agricultural prices and government policies

We will now look at some of the ways in which the prices of agricultural goods can be increased by governmental action. The policies examined make clear that it is not enough for a government to decree a higher price; total demand and total supply must somehow be equated at that price. In the following examples all the supply curves reflect average weather conditions in each year. It is also assumed, for the purposes of this examination, that the farmers' expectations of prices for the year, when they

---

[2] Joan Robinson, *Exercises in Economic Analysis* (London: Macmillan & Co., 1960), p. 138.
[3] Economic analyses based on a comparison of equilibrium positions do not examine the movement from one position to the other and ignore these costs.

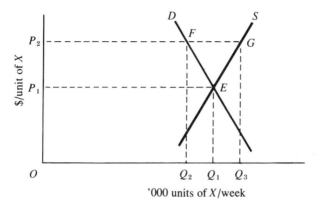

FIGURE 3.3 *Demand and supply curves for agricultural commodity X, in a particular market, for a given year*

make their production decisions for that year, are correct and borne out by events.

The demand and supply curves for a particular agricultural commodity, X, in a particular market are drawn in Figure 3.3. These curves show the quantities, expressed as weekly rates, that would be demanded and supplied at alternative prices in a given year. The supply curve is very inelastic; it reflects a situation where the resources available for the production of this commodity in a particular year do not have satisfactory alternative employment opportunities. Even if the prices that producers expect to receive are low, such prices do not appreciably diminish the resources used and the quantities they plan to produce and sell. Similarly, when prices are expected to be high in the year, very few resources can be switched that year into the production of this good. For the purposes of this illustration, let us assume that in the absence of governmental intervention, market conditions are expected to remain unchanged over a series of years. If the equilibrium price OP_1 is considered to be too low—e.g. because the incomes the producers would obtain from this price are too low—the government may be persuaded to try to raise the price.

Let us assume that the government is convinced that a higher price, OP_2, is appropriate in the circumstances and tries to make it the market price. For any such attempt to be successful over time, it would be necessary for the government to influence either the quantity demanded or the quantity supplied or both. Three possible lines of action will be discussed here. One makes use of quotas, the second employs price supports, while the third involves deficiency (or subsidy) payments. Each of these methods represents one way in which the market price of an agricultural good can be increased, but actual governmental policies might use some combination of these or other methods.

3.6 Quotas

Limits may be placed on the amounts each of the suppliers can sell. For example, if a price of OP_2 were considered to be appropriate in the circumstances, each individual's sales quota for the specific time period could be such that the total amount supplied was equal to OQ_2 and the market clearing price would then be OP_2 rather than OP_1. This policy should shift the effective supply curve to the left and it is represented in Figure 3.4 by the vertical line HS_Q. The intersection of this perfectly inelastic supply curve with the demand curve is at point F. The quotas imposed do not permit the farmers as a group to supply quantites larger than OQ_2. Their *desired* supply curve, however, is still the curve labelled S in Figures 3.3 and 3.4, and the difference between the quantities the farmers are permitted to supply and what they would want to supply creates tensions and may cause distortions in this market.

The incomes of suppliers would be higher under this policy if the demand curve were price inelastic in the range EF. Joan Robinson's 'farmer who hanged himself in the expectation of plenty', mentioned above, assumed (on the basis of past experience) that the demand for the commodity he was producing was price inelastic, and that other farmers would also have large crops. The result of these larger crops in this case would be not only lower prices but also lower total incomes.

A quota system is made effective by placing legal restraints on sales that

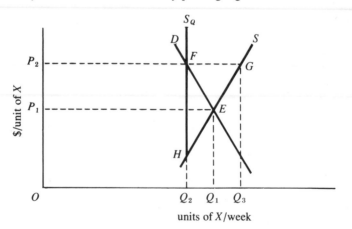

FIGURE 3.4 *Application of a quota system for the agricultural commodity shown in Figure 3.3*

are made without a permit. Producers of the commodity hold permits that specify the quantities that each may sell in the particular period. The total of these quantities is constrained by the need to ensure that the total quantity supplied is equal to the total quantity demanded at the desired price. Possession of such a permit thus allows an individual to obtain an income from the production and sale of a particular commodity. Therefore a policy of quotas creates valuable 'rights': each 'right' allows the owner to sell specific quantities of a commodity whose output is restricted in order to make production profitable. These rights may be negotiable. Even if their transfer is legally prohibited, a black market in them may spring up. An individual who has less of the good to sell than his quota may agree, for a consideration, to market part of the output of another producer as though it were his own.

These quotas may be given to individual producers or they may be assigned to the farms. For example, the supply of fluid milk to the Montreal market comes only from farms with quotas. Anyone who wants to start supplying milk to this market must first purchase a farm with a quota. The prices of such farms are consequently higher than the prices of farms that have no quota but are similar in every other way. A confidential government document prepared in 1977 by the Department of Consumer and Corporate Affairs in Canada[4] estimated that the right to produce broiler chickens in Ontario was worth between $4 and $7 per bird per year. If the minimum efficient level of production for a family farm is assumed to be 50,000 birds per year, then with an average value of $5.50 per bird for the right to market birds, $275,000 is added to the capital cost of producing broiler chickens.

A variation of this method for raising the price of the agricultural commodity is to place restrictions, not directly on the amount that can be sold, but on the number of acres individual producers can use for the production of the particular commodity. The effect of this policy on prices is not as predictable as fixing the total quantity to be sold, since farmers may be able to increase output per acre in an attempt to counter acreage restrictions.

An example combining both quotas and acreage restrictions can be found in the arrangements for the production of flue-cured tobacco in Ontario in the 1960s. Only a limited number of farms had rights to grow and market tobacco. They were assigned by the producer-controlled Ontario Flue-Cured Tobacco Growers' Marketing Board, which was created under provincial legislation to handle all tobacco grown in Ontario. There were

---

[4] This document was quoted in the *Montreal Star*, April 16, 1977, p. A-1.

approximately 2 million acres of good tobacco-growing land in the proper climatic zones in Ontario, compared with about 300,000 acres that were owned by farms with tobacco rights. The basic acreage rights for each such farm was about 45 per cent of its total acreage. Each year the Marketing Board further established the percentage of the basic acreage that could be used for growing tobacco. This percentage, applied to all farms, depended on the Board's estimate of market conditions. It varied from 60 per cent in 1963 to 100 per cent in 1967. Attempts to increase output per acre partly to overcome acreage restrictions are indicated by the increase in yields of 50 per cent per acre in the period 1959 to 1967.

The rights were associated with farms, and were transferred to new ownership only when the farms were sold; they could not be bought and transferred from one farm to the other, as in the case of some other schemes (e.g. fluid milk quotas in Ontario). Since growing tobacco, under existing conditions, was much more profitable than possible alternative uses of the land, the price of land with tobacco-growing (and marketing) rights was much higher than that of comparable land without such rights. It has been estimated that the market value of an acre of tobacco rights was in the $1,800 to $2,700 range in 1965. The owners of farms that were given rights when restrictions were imposed obtained substantial capital gains. Those who bought farms with rights in the interval faced higher costs because of the higher cost of acquisition. (A reversal of this system of restriction would have had substantial impact on the price of land with rights and on the financial position of the owners.) In this case, government policy created capital gains for some, which were absorbed into the economic system as costs of production.[5]

Not only has government policy affected conditions in the tobacco market, it has also had effects on other markets. The limitation on acreage that can be devoted to tobacco has increased the land available for other crops. This has tended to increase the quantities supplied of these other agricultural goods, and to decrease their prices. As we indicated in Section 3.3, a full treatment of the implications of this policy would thus require a more general study than the partial equilibrium approach underlying the curves in Figure 3.4. Government policy has affected the distribution of

[5] See D.R. Campbell, 'The Economics of Production Control: the Example of Tobacco', *Canadian Journal of Economics*, Vol. 2 (February 1969), pp. 115-24. The same pattern was found in the United States where the supply of tobacco was regulated by granting 'allotments' to grow tobacco only to certain specific acres. The value of such an allotment in the period 1954-7 in North Carolina and Virginia was estimated to be in the $900-$2,500 range per acre. See F.H. Maier, J.L. Hedrick, and W.L. Givson, Jr, *The Sale Value of Flue-Cured Tobacco Allotments* (Agricultural Experimental Station, Virginia Polytechnic Institute), Technical Bulletin No. 148 (April 1960).

income among farmers. It has created a privileged position for those who were qualified to receive marketing rights: those without such rights must either pay for them or use their land to grow less profitable crops. The distribution of income between those engaged in agriculture and others in the economy has also been affected as a result of the quota system. The higher money income received by tobacco farmers has been at the expense of consumers, who paid higher prices for tobacco products.

3.7 Price supports

A price-support scheme is another method that could raise the price to OP_2 in the situation depicted in Figure 3.3. These demand and supply curves are redrawn in Figure 3.5 to illustrate the operation of a price-support program. To make this method effective the government must purchase the commodity in order to support the price it wants to establish. In this example there is a difference between what farmers want to supply and what consumers are willing to buy at that price. The government must therefore enter the market and purchase this difference. Under the conditions that determine the curves in Figures 3.3 and 3.5, the government must buy FG units per week over the year. The weekly cost to the government of these purchases is equal to the area of the rectangle Q_2FGQ_3.

If a price-support program is to be effective over time, then the quantities of the commodity purchased by the government must not be allowed to reappear in the market or to affect private trading arrangements. This requirement could be met by the destruction of the government's purchases of this commodity, or by its disposal in some other, completely separate markets for it. It could also be met by storage of the commodity, as long as

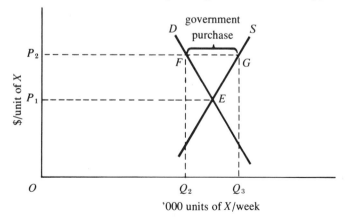

FIGURE 3.5 *Application of a price-support program to the agricultural commodity shown in Figure 3.3*

this action did not lead to expectations that it would eventually be resold in this market. Of course a change in expectations would affect the position of the demand and supply curves and would thus alter the amounts of the commodity the government would have to purchase to maintain a price of OP_2. For example, the demand curve would be shifted to the left if the buyers expected that the government would be forced to resell some of its holdings, or at least slow down its rate of purchases in the face of the large surpluses it was storing. Changes in expectations could also affect the supply curve. If the government-support policy was expected to be continued, and other crops were not supported to the same extent, in future years the supply curve would shift to the right as more acres were devoted to this crop. Over-supply could become an increasingly serious problem.

From the point of view of farmers, government purchases of the commodity are preferable to a policy based on quotas. Their incomes will be higher with price supports because of higher sales. Under the conditions depicted in Figure 3.5, sales under price supports would be at the weekly rate of OQ_3 rather than at the quota rate of OQ_2. The higher cost to the government of a price-support scheme, even when the demand and supply conditions were unchanged over the years, would make it difficult for the government to continue such a program. Pressures would arise to combine this policy of supporting prices with some form of quotas to limit the quantity of the commodity being produced.

There were many price-support schemes in the United States in the post-war period, but the large surpluses that resulted in many cases led to changes in policy. Price-support programs were combined with acreage restrictions: they were made available only for crops in which the farmers accepted acreage limitations. However, a decrease in the number of acres cultivated is not the same thing as a decrease in the size of the crops raised, even with average weather conditions. The concentration of efforts and resources on a smaller number of acres, aided by technological changes over time, can go a long way in maintaining the size of crops.

Recognition must be given here, as in all cases, to the interdependence of different markets. The markets for other commodities would be affected if the land taken out of cultivation for one commodity was used to produce other crops. An attempt was made in the United States in 1957 to eliminate this type of cross-effect by the introduction of a 'Soil Bank' program: the government made acreage payments to farmers for keeping land out of cultivation.

The benefits received by a farmer from a price-support program depend on his circumstances. Farmers with larger crops receive more, since the subsidy is based on a per-unit of sales. Thus a complete analysis of any of these programs must also study their effects on the distribution of income among farm units of different sizes, as well as between farmers and other segments of the economy. With farming being made more profitable than it otherwise would be, these programs might also affect the movement of resources into and out of agricultural activity.

3.8 Deficiency payments

The government can increase the price received by producers by means of a system of deficiency payments or subsidies. This method and its financial cost to the government can be illustrated by Figure 3.6. If the government guarantees a price to the producers of OP_2, they would want to supply the commodity at a weekly rate of OQ_3 over the year. This quantity would fetch only a price of OP_3 on the market, as shown by the point on the demand curve that corresponds to this quantity. In order to make the unit payment received by producers equal to OP_2, the government must pay them $\$P_3P_2$ per unit supplied. The weekly financial cost of such a scheme to the government would be equal to the amount of the subsidy per unit of the commodity multiplied by the amount of sales per week. This value is shown by the area of the rectangle P_3P_2GH in Figure 3.6.

Under a system of deficiency payments, market prices would be lower (because of the absence of government purchases) than under a price-support program, even though the total revenues of producers would be the same. If governments use this policy they must be prepared to pay out sums that may be very large, and for which there is no offsetting provision of goods. Governments may try to keep down the cost of such a program by combining it with production limits, requiring farmers to sell only limited amounts through approved marketing outlets.

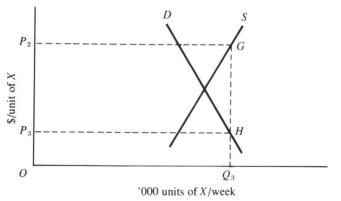

FIGURE 3.6 *Application of deficiency payments for the agricultural commodity shown in Figure 3.3*

A policy of deficiency payments was used extensively in the United Kingdom (UK) before its entry into the European Economic Community (EEC). Market prices for many agricultural commodities in the UK were effectively world prices, since imports of these goods were permitted without duties or other constraints. Domestic farmers were guaranteed higher prices and the differences were made up by the deficiency payments. In the EEC, on the other hand, price-support programs along the lines discussed in the preceding section are in force. They are reinforced by various restrictions against lower-cost imports.

One of the conditions for the entry of the United Kingdom into the European Economic Community was the acceptance of the common agricultural policy. Many commentators expressed the fear that one of the results of entry would be higher market prices for agricultural commodities in the UK, since the EEC price supports were above world prices. These fears were not realized in the period immediately following the UK's entry into the EEC in 1973 because of the rapid rise in world agricultural prices at that time.

3.9 Other agricultural policies

The three types of market intervention listed above do not exhaust the possibilities open to governments to influence the prices of natural commodities. Governmental policies may combine these elements in different ways or incorporate other features. In Canada there are many marketing boards to control specific products in specific regions (e.g. fluid milk, tobacco, fruit, eggs). They may do no more than attempt to bring about 'orderly marketing' of whatever output their members deliver. The activity of some boards, for example, is restricted to storing non-perishable produce to keep it off the market during periods of seasonally low prices. Others may not even go this far, limiting themselves to bargaining for the best selling price for that season. Dairy boards, as well as the Ontario Flue-Cured Tobacco Board mentioned above, have more scope to influence prices. They can also practise price discrimination if they feel it increases the revenues of their members. For example, milk for fluid use is sold at a price that is almost twice the price of milk that is sold for manufacturing purposes.

The United States law that dealt with crop price levels in 1975 provided for both deficiency payments and price-support loans for some commodities, and price supports alone for others. The price guaranteed for wheat was $2.50 a bushel, for corn $1.87 a bushel, and for cotton 40 cents a pound. If market prices had fallen below these levels, the government would have made up the difference with direct payments to farmers. As an alternative, if farmers chose to withhold their output from the market when prices were low in the expectation of higher future prices, they could obtain loans from the government by using their crops as security. The 1975 law provided loan levels of $1.37 a bushel for wheat, $1.10 a bushel for corn, and 34 cents a pound for cotton. A majority of members in Congress found the guarantees too low and passed a bill to increase target prices. It was vetoed by President Ford.[6] Some agricultural leaders were reported to be urging farmers to cut back planting in order to prevent prices from declining drastically. This type of appeal is not usually successful because it is not in the interests of any one farmer voluntarily to restrain his production. In any case it does not appear to have had much effect on the 1975 crops. One farmer, commenting on the planning of crops, observed: 'It is human nature for farmers to produce more hoping that the other fellow won't.'[7]

Dairy products are eligible in the United States for price supports. Price-support levels are calculated with respect to parity. A 'parity' price for a particular commodity is one that preserves a supposedly fair relationship between this price and farmers' costs.[8] Dairy-product prices were supported in 1975 at a level corresponding to 80 per cent of parity.

3.10 Setting of maximum prices

The applications of demand and supply analysis presented up to this point have all involved cases where governments tried to raise prices received by producers. Governmental intervention may also be forthcoming when the prices that would be established in the market are judged to be too high—as in wartime, when supplies are restricted. A situation where the supply curve has shifted to the left is illustrated in Figure 3.7. The market price that

---

[6] The setting of price-support levels is a politically charged act. Prices of many agricultural commodities thus reflect political as well as economic forces. President Ford reversed his stance on the levels he was prepared to accept when the 1976 Democratic presidential candidate, Jimmy Carter, came out for higher target and support prices. When he became President, Carter in his turn proposed levels below those Congress wanted to impose. See, for example, 'House Farm Panel Votes Compromise on Price Supports', *New York Times*, April 29, 1977, p. D11.

[7] This illustrates the difficulty of appeals to voluntary individual restraint when there are large numbers. Changes in the production (or consumption) of any one individual would have negligible effects on the market, and unless others act in a similar manner, there would be a loss to the individual exercising restraint. Conversely, if all others exercise restraint, then the individual who does not gets an additional benefit. For example, if others decrease production and the price increases, then the farmer who maintains production benefits from the higher price on his unchanged output.

[8] For a discussion of parity prices, see Geoffrey S. Shepherd, *Agricultural Price Analysis* (5th ed.; Ames, Iowa: Iowa State University, 1963), Part VI.

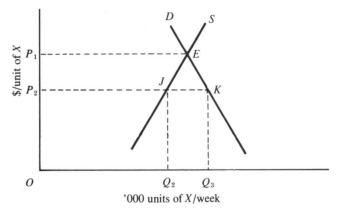

FIGURE 3.7 *Illustration of a price-control scheme for a commodity sold in a perfectly competitive market*

would result in the absence of governmental intervention would be OP_1, and it is considered to be too high.

If the government wants to establish OP_2 as the maximum price, it must find some way to eliminate the excess demand at this price. In Figure 3.7 this excess demand is equal to Q_2Q_3 units per week, and the government may introduce a system of rationing to eliminate its effects on the market. Rationing represents a change in the conditions required for a purchase to be made. Price is also a form of rationing, but if it is not permitted to rise sufficiently to limit demand to available supply, additional measures must be introduced. For example, purchasers might be required to provide a ration coupon as well as the price of the good. The number of these coupons issued by the government can be limited to correspond to the quantity of the good expected to be available at the controlled price.

Rationing schemes have been successful in special circumstances where their need has been generally recognized. However, there are many administrative costs in setting up and operating such programs. The control of perfectly competitive markets is not easily accomplished. 'Black markets', in which the good is sold without coupons and at prices much higher than the official prices, will tend to flourish. Attempts to prevent the spread of these illegal markets would involve increasing government regulation.

3.11 Instability of prices
Governments have intervened in the markets for primary commodities not only because of concern over the levels of prices but also to limit the wide fluctuations in prices that occur when these markets are uncontrolled. Even with a variety of programs that afford some protection to producers, it is

not difficult to find many examples of substantial fluctuations in the prices of these commodities, over both short and longer periods. Table 3.1 gives some examples.

Prices of commodities with perfectly competitive markets may be subject to substantial fluctuations because of changes in the positions of demand and supply curves. The extent of the fluctuations is also affected by the shapes of these curves. Both demand and supply curves for primary commodities are inelastic with respect to price in the short term—say up to six months or a year. Consumer demand for most foodstuffs has a low price elasticity over this time period. There is also a low price elasticity of demand

TABLE 3.1 *Cash (spot) prices of some primary commodities over a seven-year period*

DATE	SUGAR (Raw, N.Y. $/lb.)	COCOA (Accra, N.Y. $/lb.)	COPPER (N.Y. $/lb.)	TIN (N.Y. $/lb.)	COFFEE (Brazilian, N.Y., $/lb.)	WHEAT (No. 2 Ord. Hard KC, $/bu.)
April 27, 1970	.08	.31	.60	1.88	.53	1.46
April 23, 1971	.08	.27	.53	1.70	.44	1.54
March 24, 1972	.09	.28	.53	1.82	.46	1.57
August 25, 1972	.09	.36	.51	1.82	.59	1.86
October 27, 1972	.09	.38	.51	1.80	.58	2.11
January 26, 1973	.09	.37	.53	1.79	.58	2.63
June 22, 1973	.10	.76	.60	2.17	.67	2.57
July 27, 1973	.11	.91	.60	2.48	.69	3.33
August 24, 1973	.11	.78	.60	2.41	.70	5.15
September 28, 1973	.11	.86	.60	2.40	.70	4.98
January 25, 1974	.14	.66	.68	3.05	.69	5.74
February 22, 1974	.20	.79	.68	3.83	.72	6.02
March 29, 1974	.17	1.05	.68	4.03	.74	4.25
April 19, 1974	.20	1.12	.68	4.53	.74	4.03
August 2, 1974	.32	1.09	.86	4.26	.68	4.21
September 30, 1974	.32	1.08	.86	4.21	.64	4.31
December 13, 1974	.45	.85	.73	3.55	.69	4.76
March 6, 1975	.30	.83	.64	3.70	n.a.	3.70
September 29, 1975	.16	n.a.	.64	3.18	.94	4.25
April 28, 1976	.16	.93	.71	3.61	1.35	3.50
December 29, 1976	.10	1.55	.65	4.24	2.20	2.70
April 28, 1977	.12	1.93	.71	4.86	3.20	2.44
August 29, 1977	.11	2.39	.60	5.41	2.00	2.31
November 10, 1977	.11	n.a.	.60	6.26	1.85	2.67

SOURCE: *Wall Street Journal.* NOTE: The coffee is designated as Santo 4s until February 24, 1975, and then as Brazilian. The quoted price for copper is the producers' price. All prices are rounded to the nearest cent.

in the short period for most raw materials, which often comprise a relatively small proportion of the total costs of manufactured goods. Although higher prices for raw materials will be reflected in higher prices for manufactured goods, the total demand for these goods may not be appreciably affected. Thus the effects of higher or lower prices of raw materials on their demand may be very small over short periods when demand conditions for manufactured goods are unchanged.

The reasons for the low price elasticity of supply of primary commodities, over fairly short periods, vary as between commodities. In the case of annual crops, the value for this elasticity is limited because acreages cannot be changed until sowings are made for next year's crops. There is, perhaps, slightly more scope in the variation of output from tree crops. The current rate of output can be changed somewhat in response to a change in price. Rubber trees, for example, can be tapped more or less intensively; similarly, the degree of plucking of tea leaves can be varied, etc. Mining operations can also be adjusted in the short run through overtime operations if prices are high, or through a reduction in activity if they are too low. However, the scope for profitable changes of this kind is usually limited.

As a result of this short-term inelasticity of demand and supply curves, wide fluctuations in price can result from relatively minor variations in one or other of these curves. The effects of shifts in demand and supply curves on equilibrium prices are illustrated in Figure 3.8. These shifts are associated with sharp differences in equilibrium prices because of the shapes of the curves. In panel A, the differences in equilibrium prices are due to shifts in the supply curve, while in panel B it is the demand curve that has

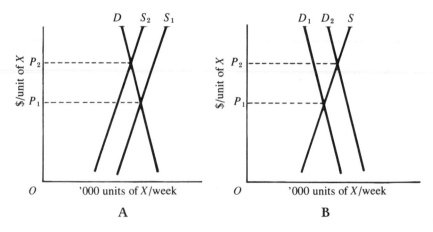

FIGURE 3.8 *Demand and supply curves for primary commodity X*

shifted. For a given shift in one curve, the difference in price is greater the more inelastic the other curve.

Among the factors determining the positions of these demand and supply curves are expectations of future conditions, as we discussed above. These expectations may be affected by the experience of changing prices, leading to further shifts in these curves and thus to further changes in price. For example, if prices have been rising, expectations of further price increases may lead merchants and final consumers to want to increase their stocks of the commodity. They might want to do so not only to anticipate their future consumption needs, but also as a speculative venture. If the price of a commodity increased in line with expectations, they would be able to resell at a profit what they did not need for their own purposes. The expectations of future price increases thus shift the demand curve to the right, raising the price higher than it would be in the absence of this change in expectations. The change would also tend to shift the supply curve to the left, with exporting merchants trying to increase stocks, producing further upward pressures on prices. Conversely, a change that resulted in lower prices may lead to further declines if the initial fall led to expectations of further changes in the same direction. Market participants in actual economies make decisions in situations where future and even present conditions are unknown. Changes in factors determining the supply of primary commodities occur frequently and are often reinforced by changes in demand. As their effects can be exaggerated by speculative activity, equilibrium positions are rarely achieved or maintained.

Fluctuations in prices over a longer term (say, five years) occur because of changes in final demand and in production facilities. Large changes in the price of a primary commodity, maintained for some time, can lead to substantial changes in the quantities demanded. The values for the elasticity of demand over long periods of time may be large. There would be a new demand curve for this good in a later period, owing to induced changes in tastes and/or to the development of substitutes. These changes would tend to be irreversible—a return to the earlier price would not result in a return to the old demand curve. In a study of primary commodities, J.W.F. Rowe gives the following examples of shifts in demand curves over time due to price changes:

> . . . when coffee prices rose very high in 1954, consumption in the U.S.A., the largest market, dropped by nearly one-fifth as housewives stretched a pound of coffee to make 60 instead of 40 cups. Consumers soon got used to this weaker brew and there has so far been little return to the old standard. This sort of occurrence is most likely to affect commodities which have competitive substitutes. If the price of natural rubber were to rise above a

certain level, manufacturers would soon substitute synthetic rubber. When tin was scarce during World War II, the use of substitute metals was much increased, and the post-war demand for tin did not recover its pre-war level even when the price became moderate or cheap for several years . . .

Similarly, a period of sustained low prices may surely bring about a more or less lasting increase in demand. Of this sisal is a good example, for its low price during most of the inter-war period, and in the latter part of the 1950's, was undoubtedly of great benefit in its competition with manilla and other fibres as the raw material for agricultural twines, ropes and string.[9]

More recent examples can readily be found. The development of 'high-fructose corn sweeteners', which was spurred on in part by the high prices for sugar in 1974 and 1975, has seriously affected the demand for sugar. The sugar industry is hard put to defend itself against the inroads of high-fructose corn sweeteners because domestic and international protective measures would only provide a price umbrella under which fructose producers could further expand their markets.

Longer-term fluctuations in commodity markets are also due to shifts in the supply curves as a result of substantial changes in price that are maintained, or are expected to be maintained, over time. Producers respond by changing their investment in productive facilities, for example by planting more trees (or cutting some down) in the case of tree crops such as coffee and rubber, or by exploiting new reserves (or closing down some of their operations) in the case of mineral production. Since future conditions are unknown, and are affected by the behaviour of others, these changes in capacity can be either excessive or inadequate. It is therefore not surprising that, over time, the prices of primary commodities are subject to considerable fluctuations.

3.12 Commodity agreements

The instability of prices for primary commodities, and the sharp downward movements that may occur, create serious economic difficulties for their producers. These goods are often produced in so-called underdeveloped economies that are very dependent on export earnings from them. It is not possible for individual countries to control these prices, or even to guarantee reasonable prices to their domestic producers. They have to look to inter-governmental or international agencies for assistance.

Many attempts have been made to establish international control schemes in order to stabilize the prices of primary commodities at reasonable levels. These schemes try to take into account the interests of producing as well as consuming countries, and representatives of both meet to agree on target

---

[9] Rowe, *Primary Commodities in International Trade*, pp. 73-4.

prices and general policies. Various devices have been used to try to bring about the desired results. They include guaranteed prices, or a range of prices; production quotas for each participating country; and provisions for buffer stocks to limit price fluctuations, etc. In principle these programs are not unlike the national agricultural policies discussed above, but they are more difficult to set up and operate because of the many national interests that have to be reconciled.[10]

3.13 Expectations and the supply of agricultural products

The analysis of agricultural policies has proceeded under the simplifying assumption that the expectations farmers held when they were planning their production turned out to be correct. However, in a changing world (an accurate description of conditions for agricultural products in general), expectations often turn out to be mistaken. Farmers may increase the acreage sown with a particular crop in the expectation of high prices only to find at harvest time that bumper crops have resulted in low prices. Forward markets can provide some protection. At the time they plant a crop producers can purchase a contract to sell specified quantities of the commodity at the current price for delivery after the harvest. For example, farmers trying to decide between planting corn or soybeans in the spring of 1977 could have used the December 1977 futures prices for these commodities, and their expected yields per acre, to estimate expected gross returns per acre. The futures price for corn delivered in December 1977 was

---

[10] For a survey of some of these schemes, see Rowe, *op. cit.* An interesting analysis of the International Tin Agreement, is found in G.W. Smith and G.R. Schink, 'The International Tin Agreement: A Reassessment', *Economic Journal*, Vol. 86 (December 1976), pp. 715-28. It is argued in this article that the Tin Agreement has only marginally reduced the instability of prices and producer incomes. A much more important souce of stability has been the United States government's transactions for its stockpile of tin.

The problems faced in trying to reach international commodity agreements are illustrated in the following news story from the *New York Times*, May 27, 1977:

SUGAR MEETING IN GENEVA UNABLE TO DRAFT A PACT

Geneva, May 26 . . . Major sugar consumer and producer countries failed today after a six-week effort to draft an international pact to stabilize the price and availability of the commodity.

The conference, convened by the United Nations, is to recess tomorrow after deciding on arrangements for a new attempt to reach an accord later this year if this appears feasible.

The major stumbling block proved to be the size of the stocks to be accumulated in times of plenty as a buffer against rising prices when sugar production failed to meet demand and how the cost of storing the stocks should be shared.

The United States had hoped to make the projected pact the cornerstone of its sugar policy after having abandoned the special accords it had with a number of producing countries for insuring the needs not met by domestic producers. The last attempt to negotiate an accord to stabilize trade in sugar collapsed in 1973, when agreement could not be reached on a range within which importers and exporters would attempt to hold prices.

$2.60 per bushel, and the expected average yield was 87 bushels per acre.[11] Thus the expected gross return per acre for corn was approximately $226 if it was sold in the forward market. The expected yield of soybeans was 26 bushels per acre, the December futures price was $7.30; thus the estimated gross return per acre from soybeans was approximately $195 per acre. The costs of growing these crops also differ, with corn requiring more fertilizer, insecticide, herbicide, and other chemicals. The farmers would have to balance these various factors in reaching their decisions. Even though they could settle the price at which they would sell their crop before they planted, they would still have to bear the uncertainty over the amounts grown, since actual and expected yields may differ. As they usually do not sell all their expected crops forward, they stand to gain by higher prices when their crops are ready for market—or stand to lose with lower prices.

The process of forming expectations is very complex. Certainly past experience is an important element in this process, but history never repeats itself precisely. Expectations that turn out to be incorrect can lead to cyclical variations in prices. This possibilitiy will be discussed in the next section.

3.14 Cobweb phenomena

Mistaken expectations when decisions are made about the crops to be raised may lead to fluctuations in market prices. The following analysis of some of the possible effects of such expectations will be simplified by assuming that the commodity is perishable and that it cannot be stored from one crop year to the next. (The general nature of the conclusions will not be affected by allowing for the storage of the commodity.) The rate at which the commodity can be supplied in a particular period thus depends only on production in that period. Production in one period is assumed to be determined by decisions made in the previous period. Expectations of market conditions in the succeeding period play a crucial role in these decisions. People act, and can only act, on the basis of expectations because time is required before decisions can be implemented and the results of these decisions are available. There is therefore no way in which they can avoid making an estimate, implicitly or explicitly, of conditions for the immediate future. In the example that follows, the quantity supplied in a particular time period is based on decisions about the scale of production taken at the end of the previous period. These decisions are dependent on the expectations held about the level of price at the end of the next period when

---

[11] The data for this example come from 'Decision for Farmers—What to Plant', *New York Times*, April 11, 1977, p. 47.

the crop is available for sale. To see what this may entail, it is assumed that expectations are based solely on present experience. The expected price for the next period is equal to the current price.

Under this formulation the quantity supplied in period t is a function of price in period $t - 1$. This relationship can be written as $S_t = S(P_{t-1})$, where S_t is the weekly rate at which the commodity is supplied in period t, and P_{t-1} is both the price in period $t - 1$ *and* the expected price in period t.

This functional relationship is based on three assumptions: (i) supply in time period t depends on decisions made in time period $t - 1$; (ii) supply decisions in time period $t - 1$ are based on the expected price in period t; (iii) the price expected to rule in period t is the actual price in period $t - 1$. The parameters determining this supply function are assumed to have constant values over a series of periods. The demand curve used here shows the relationship between quantity demanded and price in a particular time period. It can be written symbolically as $D_t = D(P_t)$. For our present purposes it is useful to look at the demand curve as presenting the prices at which the different quantities, placed on the market by supply decisions taken in the past, can be sold. In other words, it indicates the 'demand prices' for various quantities.

The equilibrium price and quantity for the demand and supply curves drawn in Figure 3.9 are given by the co-ordinates of point E. Not only would the market be cleared at this price but the producers' expectations would turn out to have been correct and their production decisions justified by events.

If the quantity supplied in period t (determined by decisions taken in

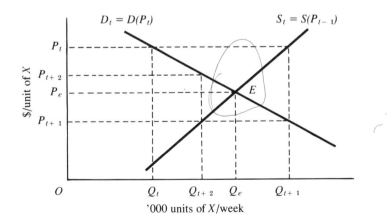

FIGURE 3.9 *Demand and supply of commodity X in specified periods in a particular market*

period $t - 1$) differs from Q_e, the price ruling in that period differs from the equilibrium price. Given the assumptions on which this analysis is based, there would not be a direct move to the equilibrium price in the next time period. For example, assume that the quantity supplied in period t is Q_t. The price in period t would be higher than P_e as shown in Figure 3.9. With no change in supply conditions or behavioural patterns, the quantity supplied in period $t + 1$ would be larger than Q_e. This pattern would then be reversed in period $t + 2$, etc.

If the underlying conditions are unchanged over time, with the demand and supply curves drawn in Figure 3.9 the market prices and quantities will converge to the equilibrium values. Other patterns can also be derived. If the numerical value of the slope of the demand curve is greater than the slope of the supply curve, when both are referred to the quantity axis, the market values will steadily diverge over time from the equilibrium values. If the numerical values of the slopes of the two curves are equal, the market values will move in a regular cycle around the equilibrium values, maintaining in absolute terms their initial distance from these values.

When the price and quantity lines continue to be traced out as indicated in Figure 3.9, what is called a *cobweb* pattern is formed around the equilibrium position. Analyses of the movements of prices and quantities when supply is wholly determined by prices in an earlier period, and the conditions for converging, diverging, or regular cycles, are described by the *cobweb theorem*. This states that if the slope of the demand curve with respect to the quantity axis is numerically smaller than the slope of the supply curve, the price will converge over time to its equilibrium value. Conversely, if the slope of the demand curve is numerically greater than the slope of the supply curve, the price will move further away from its equilibrium value. If the numerical values of the slopes of the demand and supply curves are the same, the price will follow a regular pattern around its equilibrium value.

The above analysis of cobweb phenomena has been carried out under very severe assumptions. It is not reasonable to assume that the underlying conditions determining demand and supply curves would remain unchanged over a period of years, especially in the face of substantial divergences between actual and expected prices. Low prices would lead to the bankruptcy of some producers, changing the number of participants and the position of the supply curve. There may even be some change in the way expected prices are estimated. The cobweb patterns are therefore unlikely to develop very far on the basis of unchanged demand and supply curves. Theorems about conditions that lead to constant, converging, or diverging cobwebs are thus not of much interest. What is of interest is the existence of a tendency for fluctuations in prices to appear and for deviations from equilibrium to be maintained over time.

3.15 Hogs, potatoes, and cobweb phenomena

Cobweb phenomena have been observed for some agricultural commodities. For example, movements in the prices of hogs and potatoes have sometimes followed a cobweb pattern. (The term *hog-cycle* is occasionally used to refer to this phenomenon.) In our consideration of agricultural policies the artificial nature of our assumption of average weather conditions each year should not be overlooked when the possible causes for the initiation or termination of a cobweb phenomenon are considered.

The very low prices received by farmers for the United States potato crop of 1974 is an example of the low point of a cobweb movement that was given a sharp impetus by poor weather conditions. Violent storms in the Northeast during the summer of 1972, and bad weather in Idaho, reduced the potato crop to 296 million hundredweight as compared to 319.4 million in 1971. The following year drought served to keep the crop below average at 299 million hundredweight. The prices for potatoes in these years were high and farmers responded by substantially increasing the acreage sown with potatoes. Their efforts, aided by more favourable weather conditions, resulted in the production of 340 million hundredweight in 1974—a record high. Prices dropped sharply in the manner predicted by our demand and supply analysis. The growers' cash price for Maine potatoes in May 1974 was about 13 cents a pound, while at the end of March 1975 it had fallen to less than 2 cents a pound. This level was well below the estimated average cost of production of potatoes.[12]

Such variations in the prices of potatoes are brought on by mistaken expectations as well as by variable weather conditions. They show that when particular expectations are held in common by many competing producers, the actions taken by them may lead to a disappointment of these expectations. In making this point, Professor B.S. Keirstead noted: 'This was brought to my attention when I was talking with a group of farmers in Prince Edward Island. Potato prices had been disappointing and all but one had . . . reduced potato acreage drastically. I asked this one neighbour, who has the name of being the most prosperous farmer in the community, why he had not done so. His reply showed a very shrewd perception of the cobweb theorem. He had learned he said, by long experience that when pork prices fell and his neighbours killed off their sows, that that was the

---

[12] The data for this paragraph were obtained from 'Depression-Level Prices Hit Potato Farmers', *New York Times*, April 4, 1975, p. 43.

time to increase pig production. By the time the new litters were ready for fattening, prices were back to a profitable level. He believed the same thing would be true of potatoes. His shrewdness was ordinarily justified by events.'[13]

3.16 Speculation and spot markets

The applications of demand and supply analysis examined in the preceding sections have been concerned with spot markets for commodities. In these markets buyers obtain the right and obligation to receive immediate physical possession of the commodity specified in the sales contract. Purchases may be made on these markets, as was mentioned above, not only to meet current consumption or production needs, but as a speculative venture as well. If individuals expect the price of a commodity to rise in the future, they may buy it currently in order to resell it later. When spot markets are used in this way, speculators must incur not only the risk of being mistaken in their expectations but also the costs involved in storing the goods they have purchased until the time for their resale.

Speculative activity occurs because some individuals expect spot prices in the future to differ from current prices and they buy (or sell) the commodity in order to profit from the expected difference in prices. Speculation has a tendency to iron out fluctuations of prices over time, if the speculators take a correct view of the average around which price fluctuations will occur. Sellers will allow their stocks of a commodity to be drawn down when they believe that the actual price is above the normal price that will be shortly re-established. Conversely, when they believe that current prices are too low, they will allow their stocks to increase. This line of behaviour will tend to bring actual prices closer to what are considered to be normal prices. If, however, speculators are mistaken about the normal level of price, or if they are largely guided in their decisions by the movement of prices—i.e. buying when they are rising and selling when they are falling—then their actions will increase the fluctuations in prices.

Speculation may be important in many commodity markets. It is also very important in foreign-exchange and real-estate markets.

3.17 Speculation and forward markets

The scope for speculative activity is greatly increased by the existence of *forward* or *futures* markets. In a *forward market* it is possible to buy and sell standardized contracts for delivery of a particular commodity at some future dates. For example, in the London cocoa market, cocoa can be

---

[13] B.S. Keirstead, *An Essay in the Theory of Profits and Income Distribution* (Oxford: Basil Blackwell, 1953), p. 24.

bought and sold for well over a year in advance. In July of a particular year it would be possible to make transactions in contracts that call for delivery in July, September, and December of that year, and for delivery in March, May, July, and September of the following year. These contracts can be purchased or sold by making deposits—only a small fraction of the money that would be required if the deliveries specified in the contract were made—with specialist dealers (brokers) in these markets.

Commodities with these forward markets usually satisfy certain conditions that are related to those required for perfectly competitive markets. They must be susceptible to accurate grading as to quality so that what is being bought and sold over time is clear to all participants in these markets. They must also be capable of being stored from at least one crop year to the next. Supplies of these commodities must be relatively inelastic to changes in price over short periods of time (say, up to six months or a year). If they are not, substantial changes in quantities supplied in response to price changes will greatly increase the risks in speculative activity.

The development of these markets is inhibited by monopolistic control of the commodity, since in this case speculation becomes a gamble over what the monopolist would do. Governmental intervention in commodity markets introduces a type of monopolistic control, and this can limit the scope of these markets. However, well-developed futures markets exist for many commodities such as wheat, corn, soybeans, and cotton, even though governments try to support prices in various ways. These markets are also to be found for non-ferrous metals, both on the London Metal Exchange and the New York Commodity Exchange, even though a substantial amount of production is accounted for by a few large firms.

Speculators in forward markets do not intend to hold their contracts to maturity because this would require them to take delivery of the commodity or to supply it. They usually plan to cancel out their obligations under the contracts before the delivery date by engaging in offsetting transactions. For example, if an individual had bought a contract in the Chicago market in July 1977 for the purchase of soybeans to be delivered in November 1977, he could effectively cancel this obligation to accept delivery by purchasing at a later date a contract to sell the same quantity of soybeans in November 1977. If his expectations of an increase in the price of soybeans for delivery in November 1977 turned out to be correct, then the price at which he was to buy the soybeans would have been lower than the price at which he was to sell them. This difference in price (multiplied by the scale of the transaction) provides the reward for acting on expectations that turn out to be correct. Losses would occur if the speculator misjudged the market and was forced to sell at a lower price than the one specified in his buying contract.

The purchaser of a forward contract who holds it to maturity can enforce delivery of the commodity at the date, and on the terms specified in the contract. By this means, prices for present delivery (spot or cash prices) tend to be kept in line with prices for future delivery (futures prices). If futures prices are much higher than the spot price, forward markets can be used for arbitrage operations over time. It would pay an individual to sell for future delivery and then concurrently to buy the commodity on the spot market, and to store it until the delivery date. As long as the futures price exceeds the spot price by more than his carrying and interest costs, he makes profits from this arrangement. Transactions of this type would tend to keep futures prices from exceeding spot prices by much more than the relevant carrying and interest costs. There is no similar limit to the extent to which futures prices may fall below current prices. Future delivery cannot be used to meet current consumption or production needs, except to the extent allowed for by the drawing down of current stocks of the good.

3.18 Hedging and forward markets

The existence of forward markets, and the roughly parallel movement of spot and futures prices, allow individuals to hedge. *Hedging* is undertaken by those who are committed, independently of the existence of forward markets, to produce a commodity, to sell it, or to use it as a raw material in the manufacture of another good. They engage in forward transactions to reduce the risks to them of changes in prices between the time they undertake a commitment and the time it is completed. For example, if a merchant's purchase and subsequent resale of a commodity are separated by three months (owing to transportation, rate of turnover of stock, etc.), he can hedge against a price change by selling in the forward market for delivery about four months hence at the same time that he makes the spot-market purchase. At the end of three months, when he sells the commodity he purchased originally, he also buys a futures contract for purchase about one month forward to cancel his earlier futures sale. Since spot and futures prices tend to move together, any losses on the original spot transaction due to a fall in price over the three months will tend to be made up by the profits from the pair of futures contracts.[14] The price received for the four-months forward sale would be greater than the price he would have to pay later for

---

[14] Although these two prices tend to move together, the difference between them may fluctuate. When it does, hedging does not eliminate all price risks. For example, if in the case illustrated in Table 3.2 the difference between the futures and the spot price had increased by 5 cents, then the profit in the forward market would have been insufficient to offset the loss in the spot market. Conversely, if the difference had decreased by 5 cents, the profit in the forward market would have more than offset the loss in the spot market.

the one-month forward purchase that cancels it. A numerical example is given in Table 3.2.

TABLE 3.2 *Hedging*

SPOT	DATE	FORWARD
Merchant buys 10,000 units of a commodity at $1.00/unit	*March 15*	Merchant purchases a futures contract to sell in July 10,000 units at $1.10/unit
(The market price for this commodity declines over the next three months.)		
Merchant sells 10,000 units of the commodity at the equivalent price* of $0.80/unit	*June 15*	Merchant purchases a futures contract to buy in July 10,000 units at $0.90/unit
Loss in spot market, $0.20/unit		Profit in forward market, $0.20/unit

* The equivalent price is his selling price less his normal gross margin required to cover his retailing expenses.

Hedging protects against the risk of price changing in an adverse manner, but it also eliminates the profits that would accrue from a rise in spot prices. For the example in Table 3.2, the profits in the spot market due to rising prices from March to June would be cancelled out by the losses on the two forward contracts. In this way the risk of losses on price changes are shifted onto speculators who, in an uncertain world, are prepared to take the risks of price changes in a quest for profits. In so doing they provide an insurance service to merchants, producers, and manufacturers.

When merchants and manufacturers do not maintain a fully hedged position, they expose themselves to risks of loss. For example, it was reported in the *Montreal Gazette* of January 22, 1975, that a wholly owned subsidiary (Cartier Sugar Ltd.) of a large retail grocery chain (Steinberg's Ltd.) had incurred an inventory loss of approximately $2.8 million, after taxes, for the twenty-four weeks ending January 11. This loss was attributed to 'Cartier's inability to maintain a fully-hedged position while world sugar prices rose to unprecedented levels.'

There have also been cases where manufacturers, or their employees on behalf of the firms, took speculative positions. A celebrated example is that of forward-market dealings in 1973 by the cocoa buyer for the British chocolate company, Rowntree Mackintosh. The company lost over £32 million in this venture. Instead of limiting himself to hedging operations, selling in the forward market the quantity being purchased in the spot market, the buyer sold much larger quantities in the expectation that futures prices would fall. As these prices rose, contrary to his expectations, he sold ever-larger quantities in order to recoup his losses. But the break in prices did not occur until after the company had to cover its position by buying at much higher prices. The company's need to buy contracts to cancel those purchased earlier by its agent forced up prices even higher.

An example of the use by farmers of forward markets for hedging purposes is found in a *New York Times* article. About 75 per cent of the farmers in Maine were said to hedge part of their crop in the forward market for potatoes. The experience of one farmer who hedged is reported as follows:

> 'He sold November 1974 potato futures last year at 7 cents a pound and March 1975 futures at 10 cents a pound, covering about one-third of his harvest. As prices declined he sold another third of his crop, by means of futures, at 5 cents for November 1974 delivery and 8 cents for March 1975 delivery. The remaining one-third he sold to a processor for 4 cents a pound.
>
> 'As the contracts reached delivery dates with prices much lower, he merely bought in his contracts at a large profit and then delivered his potatoes locally at current prices ranging down to less than 2 cents. Cash prices did not concern him because he had hedged at much higher levels. Thus the farmers who gained price protection for at least part of their crops have working capital to plant anew this year. Those who did not may become victims of the 1974-75 potato depression year.'[15]

3.19 Summary

This chapter has discussed some of the applications of demand and supply curve analysis. These curves have been defined for perfectly competitive markets and are particularly useful in analysing markets for primary commodities. Their role was illustrated in the brief examination of some types of agricultural policies designed to raise prices. They can be used to indicate the problems that must be solved if these policies are to be successful.

The chapter also included a preliminary consideration of economic methods. The use of comparisons of equilibrium positions to analyse the effects of changes in the values of the parameters, and the limitations of this approach, were noted. (These issues will be examined further in the next chapter.) The discussion of the effects of the imposition of a specific tax on a commodity was used to demonstrate the need to supplement a partial equilibrium analysis with some considerations of repercussions in other markets. Expectations of future conditions have an important influence on

---

[15] 'Depression-Level Prices Hit Potato Farmers', p. 43.

current prices and on the movements of prices over time. Their role was emphasized by the example of cobweb phenomena and the discussion of speculation and forward markets.

SUGGESTED READINGS

Boulding, Kenneth E. *Economic Analysis*. Vol I: *Microeconomics*. 4th ed. New York: Harper & Row, 1966. Chapters 11 and 12.

Rowe, J.W.F. *Primary Commodities in International Trade*. Cambridge, Eng.: Cambridge University Press, 1965.

Shepherd, Geoffrey S. *Agricultural Price Analysis*. 6th ed. Ames, Iowa: Iowa State University Press, 1963.

EXERCISES

1. (a) Illustrate, using demand and supply curves, why weather conditions may lead to sharp fluctuations in the prices of agricultural commodities from season to season in the absence of government intervention.

   (b) Assume that the government is interested only in stabilizing price. What policy should it follow? Would there be any need for storage facilities and the holding of stocks?

2. The government believes that the price received by farmers for a particular commodity would be too low if it did not intervene. Compare the effects on (i) price, (ii) quantity purchased by consumers, (iii) gross incomes of suppliers, and (iv) financial cost to the government of two programs. One is a price-support program. The other guarantees the same price to the farmers by making deficiency payments but allows the market price to settle at the level at which private demand is equal to private supply. (Assume that the goods purchased by the government under the price-support program are disposed of at zero cost.)

3. Consider two situations in which the supply curves are the same: straight-line curves with slopes of 1,000 bushels per dollar per bushel for supply. The demand curves are also straight-line curves and have the same slopes (100 bushels per dollar per bushel), but one of the demand curves lies further to the right; it is greater by 1,100 bushels at each price. What will be (a) the difference in price and (b) the difference in the quantity produced or consumed in the two situations?

4. It has been observed over the past year that, although the price of a particular commodity has increased, the quantity purchased has also increased. Would this lead you to conclude that the market demand curve for this commodity was upward sloping? How would you explain this observation?

5. The price of a commodity is $1. Compare the results of (a) a specific tax of 10 cents and (b) a 10-per-cent *ad valorem* tax on the quantity produced and on the consumers' and suppliers' prices. Why do the results differ? Under what circumstances would they be the same?

6. Assume that the supply of a commodity coming into the market depends on the last period's price, while demand is a function of the current price. An equilibrium position is disturbed by a downward permanent shift in demand. What is the effect of this change on price and quantity? Describe the possible time paths of price and output.

7. A government had a price-support program for potatoes but finally abandoned it because of the very large purchases it had to make. The year after the announcement that the program was being abolished and was not being replaced by any other form of government intervention, the price of potatoes reached very high levels even though weather conditions were favourable for the growing of potatoes. What reasons might explain the high price?

8. 'Land speculators' are often blamed for increases in the price of land.

(a) What effect do you think they have on the price of land over a fairly long period—say, twenty to thirty years?

(b) Assume that in a particular economy land speculation is prohibited. All residential land is divided into blocks of the same size, and no one can own more than one block for his or her house. What do you think the pattern and level of land prices would be in this economy over, say, 30 years, as compared to one that was identical in every other way (population, rate of growth of population, general level of income, attitude to home ownership and 'space', availability of residential land, etc.) except that land speculation was permitted?

(c) Do you think that land speculation has any effect on the distribution of income?

4
STATICS, DYNAMICS AND THE STABILITY OF EQUILIBRIUM

4.1 Introduction*

This chapter is concerned with methods of economic analysis and the ways in which attempts are made to handle the effects of changes through time in the values of the parameters.

In the previous chapters attention has been focused on the equilibrium values for a particular commodity and market in a specified period. This time period was a month in the apple-market example in Chapter 2 and a year in the agricultural examples in Chapter 3. Each set of demand and supply curves used to summarize market conditions for a commodity in one of these time periods was based on particular values for the parameters affecting its demand and supply. The starting point, the fundamental building block, for all economic analyses is some specified period of time, with constant values for all the parameters. It is important, however, to trace the effects of changes in these parameter values over time because the economies to be analysed are subject to such changes. Two general approaches have been employed for this purpose: *statics* (which includes *comparative statics*) and *dynamics*. The more developed and frequently used method is that of statics. There is general agreement that a method of dynamic analysis would be more appropriate for many of the questions that economic theory tries to answer, but the complexities of such an approach have not been mastered, except in very simple applications with very restrictive assumptions.

---

* This is a more difficult and technical chapter than the preceding ones and may be omitted in the initial reading of this book.

4.2 Statics and comparative statics

Static analysis is concerned solely with the equilibrium values of the variables of interest in the specified time period. The values of the parameters are assumed to be constant during this period. Its length depends on the particular problem being analysed by this method. In some analyses it is very short, with the consumption and production flows in the period being small in relation to the available stocks of the commodity; while in others it is very long, with the average stocks held during the period comprising only a small fraction of total production. For example, if the period is a week and the commodity is wheat, the stocks will be large relative to production and consumption; but if the period is a year, the production and consumption flows could be much larger than the average stocks held during the year. Static analysis can be employed in both these cases to try to explain the level of prices. When the time period is a week, the demand and supply curves are greatly influenced by the opinions of traders about the levels of consumption and production over longer periods. It is these opinions, and the consequent expectations of future prices, that determine the current equilibrium prices. With a period of a year, however, the demand and supply curves are very much influenced by the production and consumption flows in that year, which have an important role in the determination of equilibrium prices.

Static analysis is often employed for periods that are much longer than a year—sometimes long enough for investment to be undertaken and completed so that new production facilities become available for use. This extension of the time period of static analysis raises serious problems if it is to be applied to changing economies, since this analytic method is based on constant values for the parameters during the whole of the period. For lengthy periods, static analysis is appropriate for stationary states and not for those subject to changes. In a *stationary state*, the values of the parameters are constant over time. The general conditions of production, consumption, distribution, and exchange are unchanged. A stationary state does not resemble the modern economies we want to understand, but it is the starting point for much of standard economic analysis. With static analysis an indirect attempt is made to allow for the effects of change by comparing the equilibrium values for alternative assumptions about the values of the parameters. This method is called *comparative statics*. When the time period of the analysis is long, alternative stationary states are compared.

The demand and supply curves in Figure 4.1 can be used to illustrate the method of comparative statics and its limitations. The initial position of equilibrium is at E_1. This point is determined by the values for the fun-

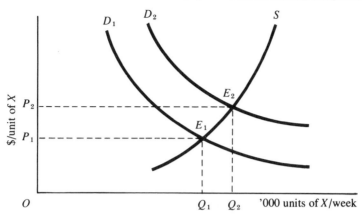

FIGURE 4.1 *Alternative equilibrium positions for commodity X in a specific year*

damental conditions (tastes, incomes, prices of other commodities, expectations, etc.) that fix the demand curve D_1 and the supply curve S. If tastes differed and the commodity were considered to be more desirable, as indicated by the demand curve D_2, the new equilibrium position would be at E_2. The effects on equilibrium values of this difference in tastes, all other factors given, is indicated by a comparison of points E_1 and E_2. However, this comparison is not a complete analysis of the effects of a *change* in tastes, even when the partial equilibrium approach adopted in Figure 4.1 is justified. (As we saw in Section 3.3, a partial equilibrium approach assumes that there are no repercussions from other markets that might be affected by this change.)

Comparative statics analysis, since it encompasses only *differences*, cannot by itself shed light on the effects of changes in the values of the parameters. Information about the adaptation to changes in values must be added to the analysis. It is necessary to determine whether, starting from equilibrium at point E_1, a change in tastes as reflected in the new position of the demand curve will lead to the new equilibrium point E_2. All the comparative statics anlaysis in Figure 4.1 can show is that E_2 is the new position of equilibrium if the only difference in the two situations is the assumed difference in tastes.

If the initial position is at E_1 and tastes change and shift the demand curve to D_2, then OP_1 is no longer the equilibrium price. Buyers and sellers want to exchange different quantities at that price and the movement of price over time will depend on how individuals respond to this change in conditions and on their expectations of conditions in the future. For example, if conditions had been stationary for a long period, then expectations would have been based on this experience. The changes in tastes and current price would be disturbances that could also affect prices in subsequent periods because of their effects on expectations. Transactions might also occur at more than one price because it would take time for the market participants to obtain knowledge of the new market clearing price. The assumption of full knowledge of current market conditions is not very convincing soon after a change has occurred. A complete analysis of the effects of changes in the values of the parameters should thus try to take into account the effects of these changes on expectations, and the time required for market participants to obtain knowledge of the new circumstances. The experience of an initial change might also affect the values of the parameters in subsequent periods because of its influence on expectations and the opportunities and actions of individuals. Those who employ static analysis have tried to make it more appropriate for the analysis of change by also considering the stability of equilibrium.

4.3 Stability of equilibrium

The analysis of the *stability of equilibrium* tries to determine whether, given that market and equilibrium values differ at some point, there is a tendency for these differences to disappear with the passage of time. An equilibrium position is said to be *stable* if the net effects of the forces at work, when the market being examined is not in equilibrium, are such as to return the market values to the equilibrium values.[1] It is said to be *unstable* if the net effects are such as to increase the difference between market and equilibrium values. If there is no tendency for the difference between the market and equilibrium values to change, then equilibrium is said to be *neutral*.

We shall consider two alternative conditions for examining the stability of equilibrium in order to illustrate the procedures used. These conditions describe the net effects of the forces at work on prices and quantities when market values differ from equilibrium ones. The market being examined is perfectly competitive, but there is not full knowledge of equilibrium prices; thus market and equilibrium values may diverge after a disturbance. The first condition, which is called the *Walrasian stability condition*, states that if, at a given price, the quantity demanded is greater than the quantity supplied, then the price will be increasing. If the quantity demanded is less

---

[1] Local and global stability are also distinguished. An equilibrium position is said to be locally stable if, after a *small* initial deviation from equilibrium, market values return to this position. It is said to be globally stable if, after *any* deviation from equilibrium values, market values return to the equilibrium position. An equilibrium position may be locally stable even though it is not globally stable.

than the quantity supplied, then the price will be decreasing. The price will be unchanged if the quantity demanded is equal to the quantity supplied— that is, if the market price is equal to the equilibrium price. According to this condition, disequilibrium is reflected initially by changes in price. The Walrasian condition can be written symbolically as:

(i)   For given P, ΔP has the same sign as $(Q_D - Q_S)$.

The other condition, which is called the *Marshallian stability condition*, assumes that the initial response to disequilibrium conditions comes from changes in the quantity supplied. It states that if the price that purchasers are willing to pay (the demand price, D_p) for the quantity currently being supplied is greater than the price required to bring forth this supply (the supply price, S_p), then the quantity supplied will be increasing. This quantity will be decreasing if the demand price is less than the supply price, and it will be constant if the two prices are equal. In the latter case, the quantity supplied is the equilibrium quantity. The Marshallian condition can be written symbolically as:

(ii)   For given Q, ΔQ has the same sign as $(D_p - S_p)$.

These two conditions may lead (as is shown below) to different conclusions about the stability of equilibrium. They assume different responses to non-equilibrium situations. The decision about whether to use the Walrasian or Marshallian condition for the analysis of the stability of equilibrium depends on whether it is more appropriate to consider variations in prices or in quantities as the leading forces when the particular market is not in equilibrium. The length of the period for which the demand and supply curves are defined is one of the factors affecting this choice. A longer period is generally required for changes in the quantities produced than is required for changes in prices; thus the second condition would be more appropriate the longer this time period. In the examples that follow, both conditions are used for illustrative purposes.

4.4 Examination of the stability of equilibrium

The use of the Walrasian and Marshallian conditions for determining the stability of equilibrium can be illustrated with the aid of the demand and supply curves in Figure 4.2.

The equilibrium position for the two curves in Figure 4.2 is stable under both conditions. If the market price is greater than OP_e, then according to the Walrasian condition this price will be decreasing, since the quantity demanded is less than the quantity supplied. If this condition correctly describes the forces at work out of equilibrium, then the price will continue

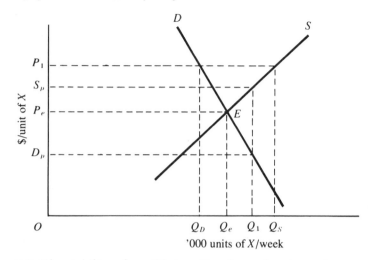

FIGURE 4.2 *The stability of equilibrium (i)—demand and supply curves for commodity X in a specific period*

to fall until the difference between the quantities demanded and supplied is eliminated. A movement towards the equilibrium position would also be deduced from the Marshallian condition. If the rate at which X is being supplied is greater than Q_e, then the demand price for this larger quantity, as determined from the demand curve, is smaller than the supply price. It thus follows that the rate of supply would be decreasing until the equilibrium quantity was supplied. Similarly it could be shown that a market price lower than the equilibrium price, or a rate of supply lower than the equilibrium quantity, would in these cases release forces that tended to establish equilibrium values. All positions of equilibrium, for situations in which the demand curves are negatively sloped and the supply curves are positively sloped, are stable according to both conditions.

If any credence is to be placed in a comparative statics analysis, it is important that the equilibrium positions considered be stable. Only then will it be possible to state that a change in one of the parameter values, which produces a new equilibrium position, will be accompanied by a movement towards that position. Questions concerning the time required for such a movement to be completed, or the sequence of non-equilibrium values, would still be left open. If the equilibrium positions are unstable or neutral, then changes in the values of the parameters will not be followed by a movement towards the new equilibrium positions.

Figure 4.3 depicts a situation where equilibrium is unstable according to the Marshallian condition. The initial position of equilibrium is at point E. If the rate at which the commodity is being supplied is OQ_1, then the supply

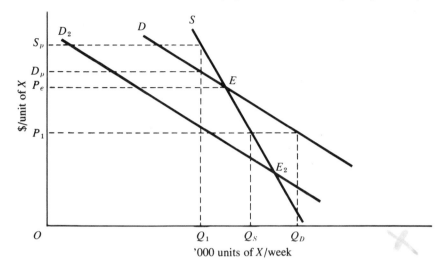

FIGURE 4.3 *The stability of equilibrium (ii)—demand and supply curves for commodity X in a specific period*

price exceeds the demand price. According to this condition, producers will respond by decreasing the rate at which they supply the commodity. In doing this, however, they will be moving *away* from the equilibrium position, not towards it. If this condition correctly explains the net effect of the forces at work when the market is not in equilibrium, then comparative statics would not give any indication of the direction of change of the variables of interest. For example, if tastes changed and the new demand was the curve D_2, with the supply curve unchanged, then quantities and prices would not move from E to E_2 but to the left of point E.

The equilibrium position shown in Figure 4.3, however, is stable according to the Walrasian condition. If the price is, say, less than the equilibrium price, the quantity demanded will exceed the quantity supplied, as shown for OP_1. The price will be increasing and thus moving in the direction of the equilibrium level P_e. If the new demand curve is D_2, and the supply curve is unchanged, then prices will move towards the new equilibrium level at point E_2 if the Walrasian condition correctly describes the forces at work when the market is not in equilibrium.

Figure 4.4 shows a situation in which the conclusions drawn from these two conditions for examining stability are reversed. Equilibrium is stable according to the Marshallian condition, but it is unstable according to the Walrasian. If the Marshallian condition correctly describes the forces at work when the market is not in equilibrium, then comparative statics would indicate the direction of change in actual values when the parameter values

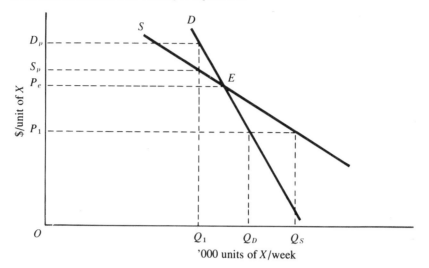

FIGURE 4.4 *The stability of equilibrium (iii)—demand and supply curves for commodity X in a specific period*

are changed. However, if the Walrasian condition describes the net effects of the forces at work when equilibrium is disturbed, then comparative static analysis could not indicate even the direction of change of market values when parameters change.

4.5 Limitations of standard stability analyses

The standard methods used to try to determine the stability of equilibrium, such as those examined in the preceding section, are mechanical. Expectations and the passage of time are ignored. When equilibrium is disturbed, it is assumed that the experience of non-equilibrium situations does not affect the positions of the demand and supply curves. In particular, the experience of changing prices does not change the expectations about future conditions. For example, when equilibrium is judged to be stable, after an accidental disturbance that raises the price, it is said that there is a tendency for the price to fall and move towards an unchanged equilibrium level. Movement, however, is something that takes place in real, historical time, and each pair of demand and supply curves refers only to a particular *slice* of time—e.g. a week, a month, a year, etc. There is no time in Figures 4.2 to 4.4 other than a representation of demand and supply conditions for this particular slice of time. They cannot be used to trace a movement over a series of such slices, or during this particular period of time if the initial price is not the equilibrium price, without additional assumptions concerning such things as the formation of expectations, the holdings of stocks, and the possible changes over time in the values for the parameters.[2]

Even when it is known that market values begin to move towards their equilibrium levels, a comparative statics analysis might need further supplementation. Information concerning the time required for this movement to be completed might also be important. If this interval of time is long, then the process of adjustment may itself change the values of some of the parameters. For example, technology may change over a long period of adjustment as firms try to adapt to adverse conditions. In this case the static method that assumes constant values for the parameters may be inappropriate, since the new equilibrium position will have changed before it can be reached. The nature of the path taken by market prices from one equilibrium position to the other may also be of interest, but it would not be revealed without a separate study, since the standard stability analysis does not provide any detailed information about this path.

4.6 Dynamic analysis
Dynamic analysis is concerned with the process of change in the values of the variables of interest in any time period. It thus encompasses many things. It could be concerned, for example, with the time path of weekly prices for a commodity in a particular year after the news of extreme weather conditions has changed expectations about the size of the year's crop. This type of analysis would require the sorting out of intricate relationships. Changes in expectations on receipt of news about crops tend to change current prices, which in turn react on expectations. Dynamic analysis should also be employed in an investigation of the rates of change of output in a particular economy over an interval of time as technology, investment, and population change. Dynamic analysis leaves the stationary world of static analysis, with its unchanged values for the parameters, including given expectations of the future, and its focus on equilibrium values. It tries to represent events happening in real, historical time in which the future is not known; expectations about future events are based on past experience and conventions that to the market participants may not be very trustworthy guides, even though they are the best available. The complexities of a fully fledged dynamic analysis are such that economists have used comparative statics to deal with problems that are dynamic, or else they have used very simple dynamic models that depart only to a small extent from static analysis.

---

[2] Cf. Joan Robinson and John Eatwell, *An Introduction to Modern Economics* (London: McGraw-Hill, 1973), pp. 161-5.

Theories of economic growth are examples of dynamic analysis, since continuing changes in the size of the labour force, technology, productive capacity, etc., over time are an essential part of the story. The classical economists and Marx were concerned with the factors determining the growth and development of economies over time. This development could not be explained without reference to historical changes.

One way in which the problems posed by changing economies have been made amenable to detailed analysis has been by assuming that the rates of change in the values of the parameters have been constant over time. This permits the economic theorist to concentrate on equilibrium values within the framework of dynamic analysis. Another method of simplification has been to break up the full time interval of analysis into single periods. It is assumed that the parameter values are constant in each of these periods, although they differ in successive periods owing to changes occurring over intervals that are at least one period in length. The equilibrium values are determined in each of these periods and are then linked to obtain the rates of change in these values. This 'Temporary Equilibrium Method'[3] is a partial method of dynamics—or rather a mixture of statics and dynamics because of its concentration on equilibrium values in each of the time periods and its neglect of the process of change and adjustment within them.

4.7 Alternative definitions of dynamic analysis

The literature contains many definitions of the terms 'statics' and 'dynamics'.[4] One that is widely used, proposed by Ragnar Frisch,[5] defines static models as those in which the values of the variables in the time period of the analysis depend only on the values of other variables and the parameters in that same time period. A dynamic model, according to this definition, is one in which the values of the variables in one period are related to the values of some of the variables, or to the values of some of the parameters, in another period.

In most cases this definition would provide the same classification of models as the ones given in the previous sections. However, there is an ambiguity in Frisch's definition. It is not clear how *current* expectations of

---

[3] John Hicks, *Capital and Growth* (Oxford: Clarendon Press, 1965), Chapter VI. Hicks attributes this approach to Erik Lindahl.
[4] A survey of some of the different meanings given to these terms is found in an essay by Fritz Machlup, 'Statics and Dynamics: Kaleidoscopic Words', *Essays in Economic Semantics* (Englewood Cliffs, N.J.: Prentice-Hall, Inc., 1963), pp. 9-42.
[5] Ragnar Frisch, 'On the Notion of Equilibrium and Disequilibrium', *Review of Economic Studies*, Vol. 3 (1936), pp. 100-5.

future prices are to be treated. If they are considered to be current values, then the analyses in which they appear could be classified as static; but if they are considered to be values for future periods, then the analysis would be classified as dynamic. Frisch's definition has been interpreted in the latter way, and the only expectations consistent with a static model according to it are those concerning current values.[6] However, according to the definition given in this book, constancy of the values for the parameters, even though they include expectations of future events, and concentration on equilibrium values are the decisive criteria for statics analysis.

R.F. Harrod has defined statics and dynamics to correspond with his approach to the theory of economic growth. He bases the distinction between these two modes of analysis on the assumptions made with regard to the presence of changes in the values of the parameters: 'In economic Statics we take certain fundamental conditions to be given and known, the size and ability of the population, the amount of land, tastes, etc., and these are deemed to determine the values of certain unknowns, the rates of output per annum of each of the various goods and services, the prices of the factors and of the goods and services. In Dynamics, on the other hand, the fundamental conditions will themselves be changing, and the unknowns in the equations to be solved will not be rates of output per annum but increases or decreases in the rates of output per annum.'[7]

Harrod's definitions would classify some analyses as static that would be considered dynamic by the definitions in this book. For example, both cobweb phenomena and the analysis of the stability of equilibrium would be listed as static by Harrod, since the market demand and supply curves are assumed to be unchanging over time.

This discussion of alternative definitions of statics and dynamics should make clear that the particular designation given to a model reflects the somewhat arbitrary nature of any method of classification. The quality of a particular analysis is unaffected by the label attached to it. The term static should not be taken as derogatory, nor the term dynamic as indicating worthiness. For example, Keynes's theory of employment would be considered a static analysis by the definition in Section 4.2. He concentrated on the factors determining the level of employment and output in a particular short period with given productive capacity and technical knowledge.[8] But

---

[6] Erich Schneider, *Pricing and Equilibrium* (London: George Allen & Unwin, 1962), Chapter III.

[7] R.F. Harrod, *Towards a Dynamic Economics* (London: Macmillan & Co., 1948), p. 4.

[8] The equilibrium level of employment in his model is, as mentioned in Section 2.23, a position of rest rather than a chosen position.

this analysis is clearly taking place in historical time and uncertain expectations about an unknown future have a crucial role. Theories that would be classified as dynamic, on the other hand, may be useless as guides to the formation of economic policy when they include, for example, the assumption of perfect foresight on the part of all market participants.

4.8 Stationary states

A stationary state is one where the fundamental conditions in the economy are constant over time. In this economy, births and deaths cancel each other and the age distribution and the size of the population are constant. There can be no net saving in the aggregate, since this would imply net investment (the accumulation of capital) and thus a change in productive capacity. No net saving in the aggregate is consistent with saving by some people (e.g. in particular age groups) and dissaving by others (e.g. retired workers) as long as the saving and dissaving balance each other. Technical knowledge is also unchanged over time; there are no new inventions or new products.

Stationary states provide the appropriate framework for static analysis when the time period of the analysis is long, since the fundamental conditions are constant over time by definition. For the classical economists (e.g. David Ricardo), stationary states had a different role; they represented possible terminal points (and very undesirable ones!) for capitalist economies, rather than a setting for their economic analyses. A stationary state would be reached in their models when the growth in population, in conjunction with a fixed amount of land and the cessation of technical progress, led to a marginal product of labour and capital so low that after payment of the subsistence wage rate, the return on capital was insufficient to permit accumulation to occur.

4.9 Absence of a full knowledge of future conditions

Explicit recognition of the absence of a full knowledge of market conditions in the future is particularly important for the analysis of price movements over time. The present period stands between a past that cannot be changed and a future that cannot be known. Events may have disappointed expectations for some people, and turned out better than expected for others. The underlying conditions may change through the action of factors external to the market (e.g. wars), or because the actual market results are such that future participation in the market is affected. For example, if the prices in a particular market are very low, resources may be withdrawn from the provision of goods to this market; if they are high for some time, new resources may be drawn in and substitute products may be developed.

Any analysis that treats movement through time in terms of a sequence of equilibrium values is in great danger of being misleading. Firms and individuals are in a particular position in the present as a result, in large part, of decisions taken in the past. When these decisions were made they did not know what present conditions would be like, and their actions were unlikely to be those they would have chosen if they had had full knowledge of present conditions. Participants might be in equilibrium with respect to the range of choices they can make in the particular period, but not with respect to all the choices that determine the present position. Dissatisfaction with some aspects of their present position might affect their actions in the future. For example, a firm's rate of utilization of its plant in one year may be appropriate in the circumstances, but the firm might wish that its plant in that period were of a different size and change its investment.

4.10 Tranquillity and steady states
A market where everything has been the same long enough for equilibrium to have been established, and where it is confidently expected to continue in the same condition in the future, may be said to be dwelling in a state of *tranquillity*.[9] For the market to remain in this state, the pattern of prices taken in conjunction with technical conditions must be such that the producers of each commodity can continue producing at the same rate in each period. They base their decisions on expectations of future events that turn out to be correct because of the tranquil nature of the market.

A state of tranquillity is very unlike life. Chance fluctuations in supply due to weather, new methods of production, shifts in demand, etc., may prevent the achievement of an equilibrium position or may disturb one. Actual prices are likely to differ from the equilibrium prices in periods when such disturbances occur. The difference between expectations and actual events caused by a disturbance may itself create divergences from a tranquil path.

A dynamic state that resembles tranquil situations is one in which the values for the fundamental conditions are changing at a steady rate. Here it is the rates of change that are constant over time and not the values.[10] *Steady states,* in which the rates of change in values of the parameters are constant, can provide the setting for very simple dynamic analyses. Changes of this type are not inconsistent with the maintenance of equality between actual and equilibrium prices over time. For example, assume that population and real income have been increasing at a steady rate and that

---

[9] Joan Robinson, *Exercises in Economic Analysis* (London: Macmillan & Co., 1960), p. 153.
[10] A stationary state can be treated as a special type of steady state with the rates of change in all the values equal to zero.

suppliers have learned about this steady rate of growth in demand through experience, and base their production and investment decisions on it. Assume also that technical progress has been occurring at a steady rate in this industry, allowing more to be produced now at a given cost than was possible in the past. These steadily changing conditions are similar to tranquil conditions as long as they continue at the same rate over time. The future is not known, but the market participants find that their expectations are justified if they project the experienced rates of change into the future.

4.11 Steady-state models and comparative dynamics

Steady-state models are dynamic models with the special features of constant rates of change in the values of the parameters and in the equilibrium values of the variables. The method of *comparative dynamics* compares the equilibrium values for steady-state models that exhibit different rates of change for one of the fundamental conditions. There may be a difference, for example, in the rates of population growth in two economies. In the economy with the lower population growth, wage rates may be growing at a faster rate; thus there appears to be an inverse relationship between population growth and wage rates. However, this apparent relationship must be handled with extreme caution. With comparative dynamics, as with comparative statics, the analysis can shed light only on the effects of *differences* and not of *changes*.

Each economy in a steady-state model has its own past history of development. A change in the rate of growth of population in the economy with the higher rate, so that it is now equal to that in the economy with the lower rate, does not make the two economies identical. In this example, the change to a lower rate of population growth in one economy does not mean that it will follow the time path of wages in the other economy, which has had the lower rate of population growth for a long period of time. The fall in the rate of population growth may result in disappointed expectations and a fall in the rate of accumulation, resulting in still lower wages. The method of comparative dynamics must be supplemented by an investigation of the forces at work out of equilibrium before it can deal with changes in the rates of change of the parameter values.

4.12 Equilibrium and causal models

Much of standard economic theory consists of equilibrium models, where equilibrium is defined as a chosen position. (See Section 2.23.) In these models, market conditions are summarized in functions or curves, such as the demand and supply curves for perfectly competitive markets. Attention is then concentrated on the sets of values that satisfy all these functions, which are given by the intersections of these curves. If the initial position is not one of equilibrium, it is often assumed that equilibrium is stable, with the system quickly moving to equilibrium. The standard examinations of the stability of equilibrium, such as those discussed in Sections 4.3 and 4.4, are rather mechanical. The conclusions reached turn on the relative values of the slopes of the curves. These values are sometimes chosen so that, given the assumed rule for the forces at work when the system is not in equilibrium, equilibrium is stable. For example, if the Walrasian condition is chosen, the only situations considered are those in which demand curves are negatively sloped and supply curves are positively sloped, as in Figure 4.2; or where a negatively sloped supply curve cuts a negatively sloped demand curve from above, as in Figure 4.3. If the Marshallian condition is considered to be appropriate, and the theorist believes that the market being analysed is stable, then only the sets of curves similar to those in Figures 4.2 and 4.4 are admissible.

Such analyses of the stability of equilibrium do not give an important role to expectations. The effects of disturbances that may lead to changes in expectations and to further shifts in the curves are ignored, even though they may be important in actual economies. For example, if the equilibrium position E for commodity X in Figure 4.2 is disturbed because of a temporary drop in supply, and the price is higher than OP_e, the experience of this price increase might change expectations. Even though the factors leading to the temporary decrease in supply may no longer be present, there may not be a return to the initial equilibrium position. The change in expectations not only alters demand and supply curves because it is one of the factors determining the position of these curves, but it might result in action that affects the values for the other parameters as well. For example, new investment might be undertaken in industries producing substitute products if an increase in the price of X is mistakenly judged to be more than a temporary disturbance. This could have long-term effects on the demand for commodity X and the initial equilibrium position would no longer be relevant. To deal with questions of this kind, causal rather than equilibrium models are required.

A *causal* model deals with a particular situation on a particular date. In addition to the technical and physical data, the initial position contains the state of expectations of all participants. These expectations may be based on past experiences or traditional beliefs or both. The model works out what is going to happen next to the variables of interest. These results, which may be such as to fulfil or disappoint the expectations previously held, will have repercussions on the subsequent behaviour of the individual participants. Causal models are worked out in actual historical time and observe the restrictions imposed by historical processes. The present is a moment in time that separates a past that cannot be changed from a future that is unknown.[11]

Keynes developed a causal model in his *General Theory of Employment, Interest and Money* and stressed this in his reply to reviewers of his book.[12] He emphasized the importance of investment in determining the level of employment and output, and the unreliability of the factors on which it depends, 'since it is they which are influenced by our views of the future about which we know so little.'[13] Keynes accused classical economic theory, which concentrates on full employment situations, 'of being itself one of these pretty, polite techniques which tries to deal with the present by abstracting from the fact that we know very little about the future.'[14] By contrast he felt that not only is our knowledge about the future uncertain, but 'about these matters there is no scientific basis on which to form any calculable probability whatever.'[15]

In causal models the technical and physical data that determine production possibilities in the present are the results of actions taken in the past. Decisions in the present then determine the degree of utilization of these inherited facilities (the rates of output of different commodities), as well as the future provision of production facilities for an unknown future. A model based on this step-by-step approach through time need not be characterized at any moment by equilibrium values, since changes in fundamental conditions and continued uncertainty about future conditions may prevent them from being reached.

A causal model may, however, reach an equilibrium position if conditions in the economy being analysed are tranquil, or if they are changing at a steady rate. Such a position will have the characteristics of the solution for an equilibrium model, with the difference that in a causal model it is a special case. It is the result of very favourable circumstances that permit self-fulfilling expectations, and these circumstances must be spelt out to get the result. *An equilibrium position in a causal model will be stable if, when a disturbance occurs, there is a return to the equilibrium position.* For this to happen, the market participants must have a clear view of the appropriate equilibrium values so that their actions, when not in equilibrium,

[11] Joan Robinson, *Essays in the Theory of Economic Growth* (London: Macmillan & Co., 1964), pp. 22-35.

[12] John Maynard Keynes, 'The General Theory of Employment', *The Quarterly Journal of Economics* (1937). Reprinted in *The Collected Writings of John Maynard Keynes* (London: Macmillan & Co., 1973), Vol. XIV, pp. 109-23.

[13] *Ibid.*, p. 121.

[14] *Ibid.*, p. 115.

[15] *Ibid.*, p. 114.

move the system toward these values and do not alter them. Consideration of stability would thus involve more than just an examination of the relative values of the slopes of curves. An explicit statement of the formation and process of change of expectations is crucial to the analysis.

This introductory book is devoted to a presentation of equilibrium models because they, rather than the more difficult causal models, form the basis of economic analysis.

4.13 Summary

Many important concepts have been defined and examined briefly in this chapter. They include statics, dynamics, the stability of equilibrium, the distinction between causal and equilibrium models, and the notion of a steady state. These terms and approaches to economic theory have been considered at this point in the book to emphasize that there are limitations to many of the standard tools of economic analysis that introductory books such as this one must, in the absence of better methods, present. One can obtain a better understanding of the points raised here after acquiring some familiarity with the tools of economic analysis and their applications.

SUGGESTED READINGS

Hayek, F.A. 'Economics and Knowledge'. *Economica*. Vol. 4 (February 1937). Reprinted in *L.S.E. Essays on Cost*. Edited by James M. Buchanan and G.F. Thirlby. London: Weidenfeld & Nicolson, 1973. Pages 43-70.

Hicks, John. *Capital and Growth*. Oxford: Clarendon Press, 1965. Part I.

Knight, F.H. 'Statics and Dynamics'. *The Ethics of Competition and Other Essays*. London: George Allen & Unwin, 1935. Pages 161-83.

Marshall, Alfred. *Principles of Economics*. 8th ed. London: Macmillan & Co., 1920. Book V, Chapters III and V.

Schneider, Erich. *Pricing and Equilibrium*. London: George Allen & Unwin, 1962. Chapter III.

5

THE THEORY OF CONSUMER BEHAVIOUR

5.1 Introduction

The theory of consumer behaviour, focusing attention on the relationship between man and economic goods, has played a central role in the neoclassical approach to economics, which explains market prices for commodities on the basis of the interaction of demand and supply curves. Market prices influence the direction of activity of producers since, if they are expected to remain relatively unchanged, they give some idea of the rewards that may be obtained from the utilization of productive resources in different activities. The demands for most goods can be traced directly or indirectly to the decisions of individual consumers or households, and some supply curves—for example, the supply of labour services—are also viewed as being determined by the choices of individuals.

Individual consumers are assumed to be rational in their actions—'rational' in this context meaning that the choices made in some particular period are consistent. This chapter will present three ways of deducing the general shapes of demand curves from this assumption. The method of *revealed preference* assumes only that the choices are consistent. The *ordinal utility* approach is based on the assumption that an individual's choices are made on the basis of an ordinal ranking of the available alternatives. (The revealed preference and ordinal utility approaches are logically equivalent.) Our examination of the theory of consumer behaviour will begin with the *cardinal utility* approach, which was historically the first of these three methods used to deduce the shape of demand curves. A cardinal utility function not only provides an ordering of alternatives; it also gives numerically comparable estimates of the intensities of preferences.

Individual preferences, which form the basis of the neoclassical approach to demand, are assumed to be unchanged over the period of the analysis. They are very much affected, of course, by social influences and attitudes, and by the availability of particular types of goods in the particular society. For example, the strong preference in some Asian countries for rice, rather than other types of starchy foods, is a reflection of the relative availability of this food, which over the years has conditioned tastes. In modern economies the numbers and varieties of particular commodities change as producers try to find sales for the items they can produce. Producers not only try to tailor products to satisfy consumers' preferences; they also try to change these preferences so that their particular commodities will be purchased. This double-sided relationship between preferences and the availability of goods is a continuing feature of modern industrial societies. The emphasis placed by firms on market research and sales promotion is evidence of this.

The traditional analysis of consumer behaviour presented here is carried out at a very abstract level, and dynamic aspects of consumer demand are not considered. Our analysis concentrates on equilibrium positions: the consumer has full knowledge of his opportunities and is assumed to make the best of them in the light of his given preferences.

The preferences indicated by the utility functions presented here, and the choices to be made, are concerned with bundles of goods and services. However, these commodities may not give satisfaction directly and may have to be combined or prepared in some way. In order to enjoy goods, time for preparation and consumption is often required. Individuals are constrained in their choices not only by the money they have to spend, given the prices of the commodities, but also by the time they have available to make use of these commodities in order to obtain satisfaction from them. (Unless there is time to cook a steak, the satisfaction derived from the purchase of raw steak would, for most people, be very limited indeed!) The time constraints on an individual's choices will be ignored in the following analysis.

The money the individual has to spend on commodities in the particular period is assumed to be known. No light is shed by the analysis presented here on the important problem of how much of the individual's total financial resources in the period is to be spent on commodities and how much is to be retained as assets.

5.2 Cardinal utility functions
Utility functions indicate the extent to which different bundles of commodities satisfy individual wants. Such functions are said to be *cardinal utility* functions if the numbers assigned to different bundles indicate the

intensity of preferences as well as the preferential ordering of bundles. For example, if the function represented by the symbol U(. . . .) is a cardinal utility function for a particular consumer, the numbers it assigns to alternative bundles of goods have significance for that individual's choices beyond the preferential ordering of the bundles. The amount of utility the individual derives in a particular period from the consumption of the bundle containing x_1 units of X, y_1 units of Y, and z_1 units of Z can be written as $U_1 = U(x_1, y_1, z_1)$. The utility obtained from an alternative bundle of these goods—for example, x_2, y_2, z_2—consumed in the same time period can be written as $U_2 = U(x_2, y_2, z_2)$. The adjective 'cardinal' is given to this function because the differences between these two levels of utility can be compared to the difference between the utilities of any two other bundles, just as the difference between the cardinal numbers 9 and 7 can be said to be twice as great as the difference between 5 and 4. Differences in the utilities of bundles that differ only by small amounts in the quantities of one of the commodities are used to deduce the shape of demand curves.

Cardinal utility functions thus make it possible to measure utility, at least conceptually, in the same way that thermometers measure temperature or scales measure mass. However, they are only conceptual functions; we have no objective units of measurement for utility. The textbook device of using 'utils' for this purpose[1] (which goes back to the pioneer work of W.S. Jevons[2] on this subject) should not be allowed to obscure the absence of an objective unit of measure.

One final point about the term 'utility' should be noted. A utility function does not explain why, or how, an individual obtains utility from a particular collection of commodities. The analysis of utility is introspective. As Joan Robinson has stated: '*Utility* is a metaphysical concept of impregnable circularity; *utility* is the quality in commodities that makes individuals want to buy them, and the fact that individuals want to buy commodities shows that they have *utility*.'[3] Maximization of satisfaction is often taken to be synonymous with the maximization of utility, but this should not be taken to imply that utility is derived only from acts that result in selfish pleasure. The broad scope of utility maximization has been emphasized by Jerome Rothenberg: 'Thus, rationalization of human choice in terms of utility maximization does not assert that individuals are motivated

[1] E.g. Edwin Mansfield, *Microeconomics: Theory and Applications* (2nd ed.; New York: W.W. Norton & Co., 1975), pp. 33-4.
[2] W.S. Jevons, *The Theory of Political Economy* (4th ed.; London: Macmillan & Co., 1930). This book was first published in 1871.
[3] Joan Robinson, *Economic Philosophy* (Harmondsworth, Middlesex: Penguin Books, 1964), p. 48. (Italics in the original.)

by pleasure or avoidance of pain. Utility may not even bear on pleasure or pain in a particular choice situation; other goals may be more important than either, where they do appear. Furthermore, it does not assert that individuals are selfish as opposed to altruistic. One's concern for others is as much a part of one's utility function as one's concern for oneself.'[4]

5.3 The principle of diminishing marginal utility

The values a cardinal utility function gives for alternative bundles of goods are reflections of the tastes of the individual. It is assumed that his tastes are such that, although larger quantities consumed of a particular commodity will give rise to larger levels of utility, the difference in levels of satisfaction for equal differences in quantities consumed will be smaller the larger the quantities. For example, consider two alternative baskets of commodities to be consumed over identical periods of time. These baskets are the same, except that in one there are 20 units of commodity X and in the other there are 30 units. The assumption about tastes means that the addition of one unit of commodity X to the first basket will add more to the individual's satisfaction than the addition of one unit of X to the second basket—a relationship that is given formal expression in the *principle of diminishing marginal utility*. Although it is usually described in terms of changes, this principle is concerned with a comparison of different positions. It states that the *marginal utility*—the addition to total utility for a small unit addition to consumption of a particular commodity—declines as larger amounts of that commodity are consumed. The positions compared are the same in every other respect—in particular tastes, the quantities consumed of other commodities, and the time period of consumption. This principle is based on the belief that all our appetites for goods are capable of satisfaction and that the attraction of additional units steadily diminishes when tastes are unchanged.

It should be noted that the assumption of constant tastes has an important role in the principle of diminishing marginal utility.[5] This principle

---

[4] Jerome Rothenberg, 'Values and Value Theory in Economics', *The Structure of Economic Science*, ed. by Sherman Roy Krupp (Englewood Cliffs, N.J.: Prentice-Hall, 1966), p. 228.

[5] Marginal utility and the principle of diminishing marginal utility can readily be represented in the notation of calculus. If the utility function is $U(x_1, y_1, z_1)$, when quantities x_1, y_1, z_1 of the commodities X, Y, Z, respectively, are consumed, then the marginal utility of $X(MU_x)$ is represented by the partial derivative,

$$\frac{(\partial U)}{(\partial X)} X = x_1; Y = y_1; Z = z_1$$

Diminishing marginal utility is indicated by the condition that the second (partial) derivative is negative, i.e. by $\frac{\partial^2 U}{\partial X^2} < 0.$

would not necessarily be applicable to goods for which a basic change in the consumer's attitude occurs with consumption—for example, drugs. It is put forth as the basis for an explanation of consumer behaviour in a market in situations where the individual's tastes are assumed to be unchanged.

5.4 The marginal utility of money

The translation of the principle of diminishing marginal utility into a downward-sloping demand curve faces some difficulties. As we have seen, this principle is expressed in terms of differences in utilities that are not directly observable and have no units of measure. A demand curve, on the other hand, is a relationship between measurable items: the quantity demanded of a commodity and its price. It is possible to move from the assumption of diminishing marginal utility to a downward-sloping demand curve if the price an individual is prepared to pay for an additional unit of a commodity can be related to the (marginal) utility he expects to receive from the additional unit. This price can serve as a proxy for expected marginal utility if assumptions are made about the values for the marginal utility of money in different situations.

The method to be presented here for the derivation of an individual's demand curve from a cardinal utility function is based on the approach of Alfred Marshall. He assumed that in all the comparisons made, a monetary unit of purchasing power (e.g. a dollar) has the same utility for the particular individual. The individual is rational and the choices he makes maximize his utility, subject to the given constraints. He would thus buy an additional unit of the commodity if he expected to gain more utility from it than the utility he gave up in money to obtain it; he would not buy an additional unit if the utility equivalent of the money were greater than the expected utility from a unit of the good. The maximum amount of money an individual is willing to pay for an additional unit of a commodity can thus serve as an index of the amount of utility he expects to derive from the consumption of that additional unit. Since it is assumed that the marginal utility of money is constant, a difference in the amount of money an individual is prepared to pay for additional units indicates a difference in the expected utility of consumption (and not in the utility measure of money).

Marshall's use of a money measure of utility was an attempt to avoid the difficulties associated with the immeasurable concept of utility. It also served to mask differences between expected satisfaction from a particular amount of consumption and the actual amount of satisfaction derived from it. Marshall noted: 'It cannot be too much insisted that to measure directly, or *per se*, either desires or the satisfaction which results from their fulfillment is impossible, if not inconceivable. If we could, we should have two accounts to make up, one of desires, and the other of realized satisfaction. And the two might differ considerably . . . But as neither of them is possible, we fall back on the measurement which economics supplies, of the motive or moving force to action: and we make it serve, with all its faults, *both* for the desires which prompt activities and for the satisfactions that result from them.'[6]

It is important to be clear about the meaning Marshall gave to the marginal utility of money. Money in this context represented general purchasing power or income; he did not assume that there was a commodity 'money' whose marginal utility was constant. *The assumption of a constant marginal utility of money was used for the derivation of demand curves for commodities on which an individual spent only a small part of his income.* Differences in the price of any one of these commodities, with money income constant, would not appreciably affect an individual's purchasing power. Marshall thus felt justified in assuming that under such circumstances any differences in the marginal utility of money would be negligible.[7]

5.5 Cardinal utility and the derivation of an individual's demand curve

The derivation of an individual's demand curve from a cardinal utility function proceeds in a straightforward manner, given the assumption of a constant marginal utility of money. Use is made of the *marginal demand price*, which is defined as the maximum amount an individual is ready to pay for an additional unit of the commodity. It is a money measure of the expected utility from the consumption of an additional unit of the commodity in the specified time period. We know from the principle of diminishing marginal utility that the larger the amount of a good a person is consuming, the smaller the amount of money, other things being equal, he will be willing to pay for an additional unit. The marginal demand price would thus be lower when larger quantities of the commodity are consumed. Fictitious figures for the marginal demand price of tea that follow this pattern are given in Table 5.1

The individual consumer is assumed to be rational and to spend his

---

[6] Alfred Marshall, *Principles of Economics* (8th ed.; London: Macmillan & Co., 1920), p. 92, n.l. (Italics in the original.)

[7] Marshall did not subscribe to the belief that the utility derived from purchasing power was independent of its quantity. He felt that the principle of diminishing marginal utility was valid for income as well as for individual goods. In two situations that differ only with respect to the level of the individual's income, the marginal utility of money would be lower in the situation with the higher income. To illustrate this point, Marshall noted that a clerk with an annual income of '£100 a year will walk to business in a heavier rain than the clerk with £300 a year'. *Ibid.*, p. 95.

TABLE 5.1 *Individual's marginal demand prices for the consumption of tea in a specific year*

CONSUMPTION OF TEA	MARGINAL DEMAND PRICE
(one-quarter lb. units/week)	*($/one-quarter lb. of tea)*
1	2.50
2	2.00
3	1.40
4	0.90
5	0.60
6	0.30

money in a manner that maximizes his utility. In the situation represented in Table 5.1 this is equivalent to purchasing a quantity of tea in the specified time period that equates his marginal demand price to the market price of tea. For example, if the price of tea were $1.40, the consumer would purchase and consume 3 units of tea, while if the price were $0.60 he would purchase 5 units. If in the latter case he purchased only 2 units of tea, he would be obtaining a money measure of utility equal to $4.50 (as shown by the sum of the marginal demand prices for the first 2 units) and paying a total of $1.20 for them. His net gain from this transaction would thus be equivalent to the utility represented by $3.30. He could do much better than this by following the rule of purchasing the quantity that equates his marginal demand price to the market price. If, under these conditions, he purchased 5 units, his total satisfaction would be $7.40 while his cost would be $3.00; thus the net gain would be $4.40. Purchasing 6 units, on the other hand, would reduce this net gain to $4.10. (The use of conventional terminology should be noted. Although the values in the right-hand column of Table 5.1 are money measures of *expected* marginal utilities, the language used here implicitly assumes that the satisfaction resulting from consumption is equal to that which was anticipated when the purchase was contemplated.)

When an individual is purchasing that quantity of a commodity at which the marginal demand price is equal to the market price, he is said to be at *equilibrium* with respect to the purchase of this commodity. Such a position satisfies the requirements for equilibrium contained in the definition presented in Section 2.23. It is the most advantageous position for the individual consumer with respect to the purchase of tea, given the values for the parameters. In this case these parameters are the consumer's tastes and money income, the prices of other commodities, as well as the market price for tea in the particular time period and his expectations about prices in future periods.

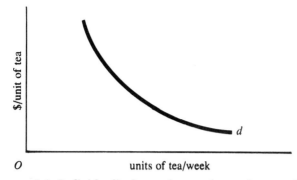

FIGURE 5.1 *Individual's demand curve for tea in a specific year*

The columns in Table 5.1 can be re-labelled and transposed to give the individual's demand schedule for tea. Market price (the independent variable) then replaces the marginal demand price at the head of one column and the quantity demanded (the dependent variable) becomes the heading of the other. The values in these columns provide the basis for drawing a demand curve as in Figure 5.1. All points on such a curve represent potential positions of equilibrium.

5.6 Marginal utilities and prices

It is customary to draw smooth demand curves of the type shown in Figure 5.1. This implies that the size of the units in which commodities can be purchased could be made as small as the individual desired; that is, the commodity is perfectly divisible. Given that all commodities were divisible in this way, an individual would be in equilibrium when the market price of each good he consumed was equal to his marginal demand price for that good. The equality between these two prices would be brought about by the decisions the individual made about how much to purchase of each good.

The marginal demand price for any good, since it is a money measure of the expected utility from consuming an additional unit, is equal to the expected marginal utility of that good divided by the marginal utility of money. These equalities can be written as:

$$P_{x_1} = MDP_{x_1} = \frac{MU_{x_1}}{MU_m} \quad ; \quad P_{x_2} = MDP_{x_2} = \frac{MU_{x_2}}{MU_m} ; \text{etc.}$$

P_{x_i} is the market price of the good X_i; MDP_{x_i} is the marginal demand price of the good X_i; and MU_m is the marginal utility of money.

It can readily be proved from these relations that, when an individual consumer is at equilibrium with respect to his purchases of all (perfectly divisible) goods, the ratio of the marginal utilities of any two goods consumed is equal to the ratio of their market prices.

Proof: MU_m is the same for both goods, and in equilibrium we have both $MDP_{x_1} = P_{x_1}$ and $MDP_{x_2} = P_{x_2}$; therefore,

$$\frac{MU_{x_1}}{MU_{x_2}} = \frac{P_{x_1}}{P_{x_2}}$$

An alternative way of expressing this equilibrium relationship, which allows it to be extended to cover many commodities, makes use of the ratio of the marginal utility for each good to its price. It can be written as:

$$\frac{MU_{x_1}}{P_{x_1}} = \frac{MU_{x_2}}{P_{x_2}} = \ldots = \frac{MU_{x_n}}{P_{x_n}} = MU_m$$

These equalities pertain only to goods purchased in equilibrium. Individuals, typically, do not purchase and consume all of the commodities available for sale. For those goods not purchased in equilibrium, the money measure of their expected marginal utility must be less than their price. Since the marginal demand price is this money measure, we can write:

$$MDP_{x_i} < P_{x_i} ; \quad \text{and therefore,} \quad \frac{MU_{x_i}}{MU_m} < P_{x_i}, \quad \text{or} \quad \frac{MU_{x_i}}{P_{x_i}} < MU_m$$

where *none* of commodity x_i is purchased at the specified market price.[8]

If a particular good is not perfectly divisible, the equilibrium condition for its purchase might involve inequality signs. (Inequality signs are also involved, as we have just seen, if none of the commodity is purchased.) At equilibrium, the money measure of the expected marginal utility of the last unit consumed may be greater than, or equal to, its price, while if an additional unit were consumed, this measure would become smaller than its price.

5.7 The law of demand
A method for the derivation of a demand curve from a cardinal utility function was presented in Section 5.5. The curve obtained was downward sloping. As a general rule economists expect that demand curves will have this shape. This expectation has often been formulated in terms of a *law of demand*. In Marshall's words: 'The greater the amount to be sold, the smaller must be the price at which it is offered in order that it may find purchasers; or, in other words, the amount demanded increases with a fall in price, and diminishes with a rise in price.'[9]

---

[8] The caution expressed in Section 5.4 concerning the use of the word 'money' in this context should be recalled. MU_m does not stand for the marginal utility of some commodity that acts as money. It is simply the equilibrium value of the ratios of the marginal utilities for all commodities consumed to their respective prices.

[9] Marshall, *Principles of Economics*, p. 99.

Marshall's law of demand may appear very reasonable, given his discussion of utility and rational consumer behaviour, but it is an assertion none the less. An individual's demand curve may not be downward sloping, even though the marginal utility of money is constant and there is diminishing marginal utility to consumption in the specified period. The principle of diminishing marginal utility assumes constant quantities of all other commodities, as well as constant tastes. Thus the inverse relationship shown in Table 5.1 between the quantity of the commodity consumed and the marginal demand price is a necessary consequence of these assumptions only if the quantities consumed of all other commodities are constant. On a demand curve, however, it is the prices of other commodities that are assumed to be constant, *not* the quantities consumed of these other commodities.[10] Further consideration of the problems of establishing the law of demand, and the reasons for exceptions to the law, will be given after the exposition of the ordinal utility approach to consumer behaviour.[11]

5.8 Ordinal utility functions
Economists prefer to arrive at a given result with as few assumptions as possible, both for aesthetic reasons and to limit the number of possible

---

[10] A downward-sloping demand curve for a commodity would follow unequivocally from the assumption of constant marginal utility of money and diminishing marginal utility for the commodity if the utility derived from the consumption of a commodity was independent of the quantities consumed of other goods. The assumptions of constant prices for all other goods and constant quantities consumed of these goods would come to the same thing in this case. Under these assumptions the price elasticity of demand for the particular commodity has a value of minus one (see the Exercises in this chapter). Marshall did not assume independent utilities in all his examples.

[11] Opinions differ about the parameter values Marshall assumed to be constant at all points on the individual's demand curve. Tastes were constant and so was income; but did this refer to money income or real income (purchasing power)? Prices of other commodities were constant; but did this refer to all other commodities or only to the prices of commodities that are related to the one examined? (Commodities may be related in two ways: as substitutes or complements; these terms were defined in Section 2.15.) If it is assumed that the prices of all other commodities and money income are constant, then the individual's real income (purchasing power) differs at different points on the demand curve because of the different price for the particular commodity. It is higher when the price is lower and vice versa. Both money income and real income, as well as the prices of related commodities, can be constant if differences in the prices of unrelated commodities are assumed to compensate, in terms of the purchasing power of the individual's money income, for the difference in the price of the commodity. In this latter case, Marshall's assumption of a constant marginal utility for money is consistent with his view that it depends on the individual's purchasing power. The advantages and disadvantages of these two positions will not be discussed further here. The individual demand curves drawn in this book are based on the assumption of constant money income, tastes, and the prices of all other commodities. For a discussion of alternative interpretations of the Marshallian demand curve, see Milton Friedman, 'The Marshallian Demand Curve', *The Journal of Political Economy*, Vol. LVII (December 1949), pp. 463-95.

objections to the applicability of the result. In the last forty years the cardinal utility approach to deriving demand curves has been replaced by a method (going back to Pareto and Edgeworth) that needs only an individual's preferential ordering of alternatives. For some applications, further information about the intensity of preferences is still required and resort is then made to cardinal utility functions. This happens, for example, when the choice is between alternatives whose outcomes are subject to risk and in analyses that make use of the concept of consumer's surplus (to be defined in Chapter 6). A function that provides only a preferential ordering of alternatives is called an *ordinal utility function*. With such a function we know which alternative is judged to be best or 1st; which is 2nd; which is 3rd, etc. On the basis of this ordering it is not possible, as it is with the numbers provided by a cardinal utility function, to compare the differences in utilities to be derived from the consumption of alternative bundles. The difference in utilities between the bundles shown to be 1st and 2nd may be very small, while the difference between the 2nd and 3rd bundles may be very large; but there is no way in which this can be known if the only information available consists of the ranking of these alternatives.

Ordinal utility functions are assumed to follow three basic rules. One of them states that more of any good is better than less; another that preferences are consistent; and the third rule is a substitute for the principle of diminishing marginal utility.

Rule (i). Non-satiation. If two commodity bundles differ only in the quantity of one of the goods, then the bundle with the larger amount is preferred.

Rule (ii). Consistency or transitivity. If bundle A is preferred to bundle B, and B is preferred to C, then any comparison of A and C with this ordinal utility function would also show that A is preferred to C.

Rule (iii). Principle of diminishing marginal rate of substitution. Marginal rate of substitution refers to the ratio of the differences in an individual's consumption of two goods that would leave his level of utility unchanged. Its value depends on the individual's tastes and on the amounts of the commodities he is consuming. If the marginal rate of substitution is diminishing, the amount of one commodity, Y, that an individual is prepared to give up for an additional unit of another, X, is smaller the larger the amount of X. As in the case of diminishing marginal utility, this principle is concerned with comparisons of different situations even though the language used often implies changes.

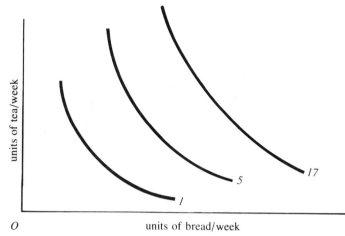

FIGURE 5.2 *Individual's indifference curves for combinations of tea and bread consumed in a specific period*

5.9 Indifference curves

An individual's preferences can be shown diagrammatically with the aid of indifference curves if the commodity bundles to be ranked consist of two goods. This procedure is illustrated in Figure 5.2. The two commodities are bread and tea. Each point in Figure 5.2 represents a possible bundle of goods, and the amounts of bread and tea in each bundle are equal to the co-ordinate values of the point. An ordinal utility function assigns a magnitude to each bundle, indicating the level of utility to be obtained from its consumption. (The differences between these magnitudes have no significance, of course.) The curve joining all points representing bundles that give the same level of utility is called an *indifference curve*.

If the commodities can be purchased in units that can be made as small as we wish—in other words, if these goods are perfectly divisible—then the indifference curves are smooth. It was assumed in drawing the curves in Figure 5.2 that bread and tea were perfectly divisible. Even if commodities were not divisible in this way, it might still be possible to find many points in diagrams such as Figure 5.2 that represent bundles of commodities to which the individual gives the same ranking. The lines joining these points, however, would not be smooth; and the intervals on such lines, between these points, would not indicate alternatives that were available for individual choice.

5.10 Properties of indifference curves

Indifference curves have certain properties that can be derived from the basic rules that ordinal utility functions are assumed to observe. These properties are four in number and concern the relations between different curves, their slopes, and their shapes.

1. *An indifference curve that lies further from the origin joins points representing a combination of goods that provide a higher level of utility.* This property follows from the non-satiation rule for ordinal utility functions. More of at least one of the goods can be provided by points on the higher indifference curve. In order to establish the relative distance of two curves from the origin, a ray is drawn from the origin to the curves and the distances are measured along this ray. This is indicated in Figure 5.2 by the labelling of indifference curves. Higher numbers are used for curves that are farther away from the origin along any ray. (It is important to keep in mind that the differences between these numbers have no significance because the underlying utility function is ordinal.)

2. *Indifference curves have a negative slope.* This property is again a consequence of the assumption of non-satiation. An increase in one of the goods must be compensated for by a decrease in the other if the individual is to be kept to the same level of utility.

3. *Indifference curves never touch or intersect.* This property is a consequence of the combination of the non-satiation and consistency requirements. If two indifference curves touched at a point, or intersected, it could be shown that if the consistency rule held, the non-satiation rule would be violated.

Consider Figure 5.3 where two indifference curves are drawn so that they touch and may cut if extended. Compare point *A* on one of the curves with point *C*, the point common to both. By definition the utility magnitudes assigned to *A* and *C* are the same. Take a point *B* on the second curve,

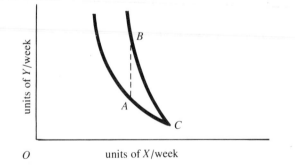

FIGURE 5.3 *An illustration of indifference curves that violate the rules for ordinal utility functions*

which has the same amount of X as the bundle represented by point A. This point lies directly above A (it has more of Y). Since B and C are on the same curve, they must have the same preference ranking, and, according to the consistency rule, B must have the same ranking as A. But this contradicts the non-satiation rule, which requires that B be preferred to A, since it has more of one of the commodities and the same amount of the other commodity. Thus if both rules hold, indifference curves cannot touch or intersect.

4. *Indifference curves are convex to the origin.* The convexity of an indifference curve means that the numerical value of its slope declines as one goes through points representing bundles with larger and larger quantities of X and smaller and smaller quantities of Y. This property is derived from the principle of diminishing marginal rate of substitution. *The marginal rate of substitution of X for Y (or, in our notation, MRS_{xy}) is defined as the difference in Y required to compensate the individual for a small unit difference in the quantity of commodity X he consumes.* Its value is equal to the numerical value of the slope of the curve at the point being considered. The assumption of a diminishing marginal rate of substitution thus means that the numerical value of the slope of an indifference curve will be lower the greater the quantity of X (and the smaller the quantity of Y) indicated by this point.

This property is illustrated in Figure 5.4. If the amount of X is increased from 10 to 11 units, the amount of Y must be decreased from 20 to 18 units if the individual is to remain on the same indifference curve. Thus the slope of the indifference curve at point A is approximately equal to minus 2 units of Y per unit of X. However, if the amount of X is increased from 21 to 23, the amount of Y must be decreased from 11 to 10 units. Then the slope of

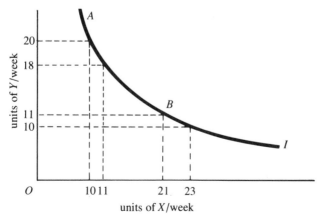

FIGURE 5.4 *Diminishing marginal rate of substitution*

the indifference curve at point B is approximately equal to minus 1/2. Its numerical value is smaller because of the assumption of a diminishing marginal rate of substitution.

In the derivation of demand curves from ordinal utility functions, the principle of diminishing marginal rate of substitution plays the same role as the principle of diminishing marginal utility for the derivation of demand curves from cardinal functions. It leads to the strong presumption that demand curves will be downward sloping.

5.11 Cardinal utility and the marginal rate of substitution

One way to visualize an ordinal utility function is as a device for extracting information on the preferential ranking of alternatives from the set of cardinal utility functions that provide the identical ordering of all alternatives. As an ordinal utility function uses these cardinal functions only to rank alternatives, it does not matter which cardinal function is used. All of these cardinal utility functions give the same value for the marginal rate of substitution, since this rate can be expressed as a ratio of marginal utilities.

In order to verify this statement, assume that one of the cardinal utility functions in the set is used to derive the two marginal utilities. We know that if we go from one point on an indifference curve to an adjacent point on the same curve, with more of X and less of Y, the level of utility must be the same. The difference in total utility resulting from a small unit difference in X is equal to this difference in X multiplied by the marginal utility of X and must be offset by the compensating difference in utility from Y. This compensating difference is equal to the difference in the amount of Y consumed multiplied by the marginal utility of Y. Therefore the ratio of the differences in the quantities of Y and X (which is equal, under these circumstances, to the marginal rate of substitution) must be equal to the ratio of their marginal utilities. The marginal rate of substitution is equal to the numerical value of the slope of the indifference curve. Thus the ratio of marginal utilities must be the same, no matter which of the eligible cardinal utility functions is used for this purpose.[12]

---

[12] The relation between the marginal rate of substitution and marginal utility can be shown using calculus. Along an indifference curve, $\Delta X \cdot MU_x + \Delta Y \cdot MU_y = 0$, where ΔX is very small ($\Delta X > 0$); MU_x and MU_y are the marginal utilities of X and Y, measured by a particular cardinal utility function at specific values of X and Y on the indifference curve.

Therefore, $\dfrac{-(\Delta Y)}{\Delta X} = \dfrac{MU_x}{MU_y}$

The value for the marginal rate of substitution is invariant to the choice of a cardinal utility function to measure the marginal utilities of X and Y (*as long as the same function is used for both X and Y*), since it is equal to a ratio of marginal utilities and the units of measurement

5.12 The elasticity of substitution

The shapes of the indifference curves depend on the individual's tastes and the characteristics of the goods. Indifference curves with some curvature, such as those drawn in Figure 5.2, are based on the assumption that the two goods are substitutable. These curves are derived from non-lexicographic functions, which make it possible to substitute one good for another in order to achieve any particular level of utility. (With *lexicographic functions*, preferences are dominated by the amounts consumed of a particular commodity. It is not possible to compensate for a loss of some of the dominant commodity with more of any other good. An illustration of such a function is to be found in the problems at the end of this chapter.)

If the consumer considers the two goods to be perfect substitutes, the indifference curves are straight lines. The numerical value of the slope of such an indifference curve indicates the ratio in which these two commodities are perfect substitutes. (The value for this slope could be made equal to minus 1 by an appropriate choice of units of measurement for the two goods.) Indifference curves for perfect substitutes are illustrated in panel A of Figure 5.5. These curves are not convex because the principle of diminishing marginal rate of substitution does not apply here. This consumer does not distinguish between these two goods when they are available in the appropriate proportions. (For example, two nickels and one dime are perfect substitutes for making a 10¢ purchase in a store.)

If the two commodities are perfect complements—that is, if the satisfaction derived from the consumption of one depends entirely on the concurrent availability of the other in some proper proportion—then the indifference curves will be right-angled as drawn in panel B of Figure 5.5. For this consumer, these two commodities are of interest only if they are consumed together in the proportions indicated by the slope of the line OG.

For the individual concerned, the degree of substitution between the two goods can be represented by the *elasticity of substitution* of the indifference

---

cancel out. For example, let the two cardinal utility functions be denoted by $U(X, Y)$ and $\phi(U(X, Y))$, where $\dfrac{d\phi}{dU} > 0$, showing that an increase in satisfaction is indicated by both, even though the units of measurement differ. With the first utility function, the marginal utility of X would be $\dfrac{\partial U}{\partial X}$, and of Y, $\dfrac{\partial U}{\partial Y}$. Therefore the marginal rate of substitution of X for Y would be equal to $\dfrac{\partial U}{\partial X} \Big/ \dfrac{\partial U}{\partial Y}$. With the second utility function, the marginal utility of X would be $\dfrac{\partial \phi}{\partial X} = \dfrac{d\phi}{dU}\dfrac{\partial U}{\partial X}$; and of Y, $\dfrac{d\phi}{dU}\dfrac{\partial U}{\partial Y}$. The marginal rate of substitution would be equal to $\dfrac{d\phi}{dU}\dfrac{\partial U}{\partial X} \Big/ \dfrac{d\phi}{dU}\dfrac{\partial U}{\partial Y}$, which reduces to the same term as before, $\dfrac{\partial U}{\partial X} \Big/ \dfrac{\partial U}{\partial Y}$.

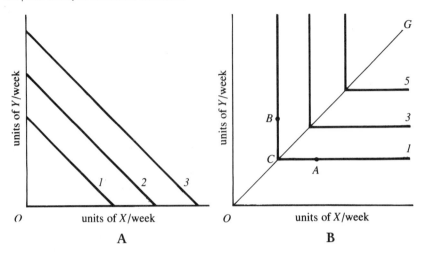

FIGURE 5.5 *Individual's indifference curves for consumption of perfect substitutes* (A), *and perfect complements* (B), *in a specific period*

curves. The elasticity of substitution between goods X and Y is equal to the relative difference in the ratio of the quantity of Y consumed to the quantity of X consumed, divided by the relative difference in the slope of the indifference curve.[13] The functional relation that is the basis for this elasticity has the ratio of the quantities as the dependent variable and the slope of the curve as the independent variable.

It can be readily deduced that the elasticity of substitution of the curves drawn in panel A of Figure 5.5 has a value of minus infinity. There can be a difference in the value for the dependent variable (the numerator is non-zero), even though there is no change in the value for the independent variable (the denominator is zero). A movement from one point on the curve to the other, changing the ratio of Y to X, does not alter the value for the slope of the curve, since it is a straight line.

The elasticity of substitution of indifference curves for perfect complements, such as those drawn in panel B of Figure 5.5, is equal to zero. Consider a small change in Y/X in the neighbourhood of point C, such as that from A to B. The numerator of the expression for the elasticity of

---

[13] This can be written as $\dfrac{\Delta(Y/X)}{Y/X} \div \dfrac{\Delta\left(\dfrac{dY}{dX}\right)}{\dfrac{dY}{dX}}$ where X and Y represent the quantities consumed

of the two goods; $\Delta(Y/X)$ is the change in the ratio of their consumption; $\dfrac{dY}{dX}$ is the value for

the slope of the indifference curve; and $\Delta\left(\dfrac{dY}{dX}\right)$ is the change in the value for this slope.

substitution would be positive. The value for the denominator—i.e. the change in value for the slope of the indifference curve—is infinite. (The value for the slope at point A is zero and at B is infinite.)

Indifference curves with some degree of curvature, such as those drawn in Figure 5.2, have a value for the elasticity of substitution in the range minus infinity to zero.

5.13 A consumer's best choice

A consumer's demand curve shows alternative positions of equilibrium. At each point the individual is making the best of the situation facing him. Indifference curves can be used to indicate a consumer's best choice in a particular situation. It is assumed that only two commodities, X and Y, are available for purchase and consumption. His indifference curves, three of which are drawn in Figure 5.6, reveal his preferential ordering of commodity bundles composed of different amounts of these two goods.

In this exercise the individual's money income is fixed at the rate of M per period, and it is assumed to be completely spent on these two commodities. The constraints on the consumer's purchases in this period are determined by his income (he does not borrow) and the prices of the two commodities. For example, the maximum weekly rate of purchases of good Y in this period is calculated by dividing the price of Y into his total weekly income. In Figure 5.6 this amount is represented by the quantity OF (equal to M/P_y) shown on the ordinate. Similarly $OG(=\$M/P_x)$ is the maximum weekly rate of purchase of X in the period. The line FG in Figure 5.6 shows all the combinations of the two commodities that would just exhaust the consumer's total income, given the prices for the two commodities. If we use the lower-case letters x and y to stand for quantities purchased of X and Y respectively, the equation for the line FG is $M=xP_x + yP_y$. The line FG will be referred to here as the consumer's *budget line* (it has also been called an *income line* and a *consumption possibility line*). The numerical value of its slope is equal to the ratio of the prices of the two goods—that is, P_x/P_y. This conclusion follows directly from the equation for the budget line, but it can also be obtained by noting that the numerical value of the slope of the budget line is equal to OF/OG. We know that $OF = M/P_y$, and $OG = M/P_x$; therefore their ratio is equal to P_x/P_y.

The consumer whose situation is represented in Figure 5.6 can choose any point on the budget line FG. His best choice, the one that gives him the most satisfaction, depends on his tastes. These are represented in the diagram by the indifference curves. Consider point H; it lies on the line FG and is therefore attainable. But is it his best choice? The answer is no, because by choosing points on FG that lie to the right of H he could reach indifference

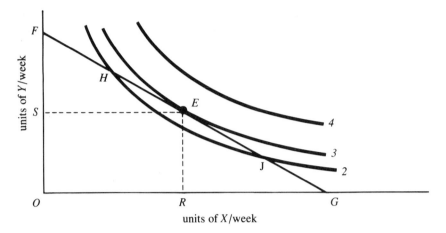

5.6 *Individual's indifference curves and budget line in a specific period*

curves representing higher levels of satisfaction. Similarly point J is not his best choice; points on FG to the left of J lie on higher indifference curves. The consumer's best choice in these circumstances is point E, and the indifference curve labelled 3 is the highest he can reach. Point E represents a position of equilibrium for this consumer, meeting all the requirements of our definition of equilibrium in Section 2.23. At this point the consumer would be making the best of the situation facing him, given the values of the parameters (his tastes, money income, the prices of the commodities, and his expectations).

The equilibrium position in Figure 5.6 is one in which positive quantities of both commodities are purchased and the budget line is tangent to the indifference curve at the equilibrium point. It can then be deduced that the marginal rate of substitution of X for Y is equal to the ratio of their two prices. As we have seen in Section 5.10, the numerical value of the slope of an indifference curve is equal to the marginal rate of substitution of X for Y; while the slope of the budget line is equal to the price of X divided by the price of Y. At point E the budget line and the indifference curve are tangent; thus at that point the marginal rate of substitution of X for Y must be equal to the price of X divided by the price of Y. (This can be written as $MRS_{xy} = P_x/P_y$.)

The equality of the marginal rate of substitution and the ratio of prices is not, however, a necessary condition for equilibrium. In the situation depicted in Figure 5.7 the individual's money income and the price of Y are assumed to be the same as in Figure 5.6, but the price of X is much higher. His budget line is FK and point F lies on the highest indifference curve he

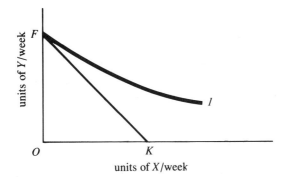

FIGURE 5.7 *Individual's indifference curve and budget line in a specific period*

can reach. In these circumstances he consumes only good Y in equilibrium. At this equilibrium position the marginal rate of substitution of X for Y is less than the ratio of the price of X to the price of Y. (This can be written as $MRS_{xy} < P_x/P_y$.)

A consumer's demand curve for commodity X shows the quantities of X he would choose to buy at different prices in situations where there are many commodities for sale. Before deriving a demand curve with the aid of indifference curves, we will show how these curves can be used to represent situations in which there are more than two goods. This demonstration may be difficult to grasp, and the following section may be omitted if the student is prepared to accept that sums of money can be used to represent all other commodities as a group when their prices are unchanged. Money-per-week thus replaces units-of-commodity-Y-per-week on the ordinate. The consumer is assumed to be faced with choices between combinations of commodity X and sums of money to be spent on other goods.

5.14 Indifference curves when there are many goods

Even though indifference curves are drawn in two dimensions, they can be used for situations where there are many commodities if the prices of all but one of the commodities remain in fixed proportions. The commodities whose relative prices are unchanged can be treated as a composite commodity. For example, assume that there are three commodities, X_1, X_2, and X_3, and the prices of the last two, P_2 and P_3, are in fixed proportion in all the indifference map comparisons. A composite commodity X_c, can be constructed from X_2 and X_3 by using their relative prices to combine them. This is then measured in the units of the commodity whose price is in the denominator of the price ratio. For example, the quantity of X_c, measured in units of X_2, is equal to $X_2 + P_3 X_3/P_2$, and its price is equal to P_2. The price ratio P_3/P_2 is constant by assumption; therefore any change in the consumption of X_2 or X_3 will change the quantity consumed of X_c, the composite commodity.

If the analysis is concerned primarily with the purchase of a commodity outside the composite group, the composite commodity can be treated as a single commodity. For example, if in Figure 5.6 the consumption of X is to be analysed, the commodity measured on the ordinate could be a composite commodity. Different points on the indifference diagram show different combinations of X and this composite commodity. However, they provide no information on the relative proportions of the constituent elements of this commodity at different points in the diagram. It is clear that even with P_3/P_2 given, a constant value for $X_2 + P_3X_3/P_2$ can be obtained with many different sets of values for X_2 and X_3.

Sums of money can be used to indicate the quantities of the composite commodity if it is assumed that the absolute prices (and not only the relative prices of the commodities that make up the composite) are the same in all the comparisons. For example, in Figure 5.8 money and X are the two commodities. Each point on the diagram represents a combination of the good X and money.

Of course the composition of the goods that make up this composite commodity may not be the same, even though the money spent on it is unchanged. This composition would vary with differences in the amounts of commodity X in the bundles being examined. For example, in Figure 5.8 the bundles represented by points A and B differ in that the amount of X is greater in bundle B. The amount of money spent on other goods is the same in both bundles, but the quantities purchased differ because of the difference in the individual's consumption of commodity X. In the B bundle more would be spent on goods that are complements of X (goods whose

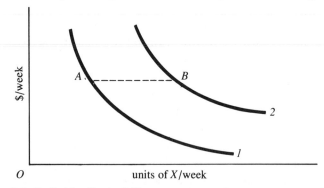

FIGURE 5.8 *Individual's indifference curves between commodity X and money spent on all other commodities in a specific period*

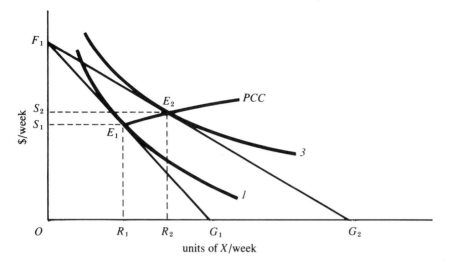

FIGURE 5.9 *An individual's alternative equilibrium positions, corresponding to different prices in a specific period*

attractiveness to the consumer is higher because of the larger quantity of X) and less on those that are substitutes (goods whose attractiveness to the consumer is lower because of the larger quantity of X).

5.15 Derivation of an individual's demand curve

In order to derive a demand curve for a particular commodity, it is necessary to consider situations that differ only with respect to the price of that commodity. In Figure 5.9 the budget line F_1G_1 depicts a situation in which the individual's money income is equal to $\$OF_1$ and the price of commodity X is equal to OF_1/OG_1. The budget line F_1G_2 also shows the same money income, but the price of X is lower. This price is equal to OF_1/OG_2. If F_1G_1 is the individual's budget line, then his equilibrium position is at point E_1. At this point—which lies on the highest indifference curve he can reach, given his budget constraint—he consumes OR_1 units of commodity X and spends $\$OS_1$ on all the other commodities. His total weekly expenditure on X in the period is equal to $\$S_1F_1$.[14] This individual's

---

[14] It is possible to deduce the degree of price elasticity of the demand curve for a commodity, in any price range, from the shape of the price-consumption curve in the interval covered by this price range. In Figure 5.9, for example, the upward-sloping price-consumption curve between points E_1 and E_2 shows that the total expenditure on the commodity X is smaller at the lower price ($\$S_2F_1$ is less than $\$S_1F_1$). As was shown in Section 2.11, total expenditure on a commodity is smaller at a lower price when the price elasticity of demand for a commodity is numerically smaller than unity. So this individual's demand curve for commodity X in the price range OF_1/OG_1 to OF_1/OG_2 has a price elasticity value numerically less than one.

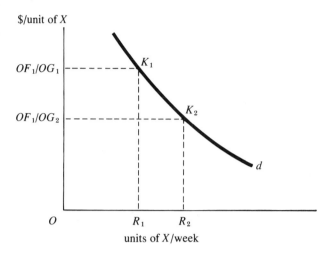

$/unit of X

OF_1/OG_1

OF_1/OG_2

K_1

K_2

d

O

R_1

R_2

units of X/week

FIGURE 5.10 *Individual's demand curve for commodity X in a specific period, based on data shown in Figure 5.9*

equilibrium position with the budget line F_1G_2 is at point E_2. He would consume a larger quantity of X (OR_2 per week) and spend more on other goods ($\$OS_2$ per week). The curve joining all points such as E_1 and E_2, which are the equilibrium positions for alternative prices of commodity X—given his tastes, expectations, money income, and prices of other goods—is called a *price-consumption curve*. The co-ordinates of the points on this curve, and the slopes of the corresponding budget lines, contain all the information required to draw a demand curve such as the one depicted in Figure 5.10.

Point K_1 on the demand curve in Figure 5.10 corresponds to point E_1 (on the indifference curve *1*) in Figure 5.9. It shows that a quantity of OR_1 units of commodity X per week would be demanded when the price of X is equal to OF_1/OG_1 and money income is $\$OF_1$ per week. Similarly, point K_2 corresponds to point E_2. If it is assumed that the individual would purchase a different quantity of commodity X for even a small difference in its price, then both the price-consumption curve and the demand curve would be continuous. They are so drawn in Figures 5.9 and 5.10.

The procedures illustrated in Figure 5.9 for dealing with the effects on the consumer's behaviour of different prices for a particular commodity provide a full explanation of the way in which an individual's demand curve can be derived from indifference curves. However, they do not give any justification for drawing the demand curve with the negative slope shown in Figure 5.10. The reader should be sure that a price-consumption curve that goes up and to the left with higher prices can be obtained without violating any of the four basic properties of indifference curves presented in Section 5.10. The demand curve implicit in such a price-consumption curve would have a positive slope in the price range corresponding to this portion of the price-consumption curve: a smaller quantity of the commodity would be purchased at a lower price.

Economists have maintained that demand curves for commodities are generally downward sloping. This assumption is based on the expected relative values of two effects of a price difference. One of these, the *substitution effect*, always leads to more being demanded at a lower price, while the other, the *income effect*, may lead to less being demanded at a lower price. These two aspects of a price difference will be considered in Section 5.17.

5.16 Income-consumption curves

In the derivation of an individual's demand curve in Section 5.15 it was assumed that the amount of money the individual spends on commodities in this period is invariant to differences in the price of the commodity. This sum can be either his total income for the period or his budget for commodity expenditures. His commodity budget in a particular period differs from his income in that period when he saves or dissaves. The analysis presented here is not designed to explain the individual's saving decisions, and it will be assumed that his budget is equal to his total money income in the period examined. Thus the terms 'budget' and 'income' will be used interchangeably.

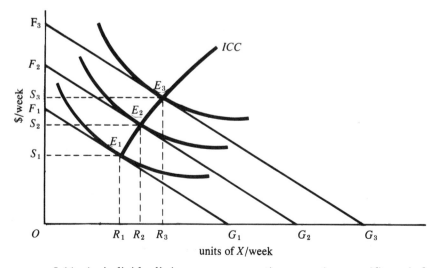

FIGURE 5.11 *An individual's income-consumption curve in a specific period*

Three budget lines, and the corresponding positions of equilibrium, are shown in Figure 5.11. They differ only with respect to the amount of money the individual has to spend on the commodity. If this is equal to OF_1 per week, and the price of X is equal to the slope of the line OF_1/OG_1, then the equilibrium point is E_1. Points E_2 and E_3 can be derived in a similar manner. The slopes for the three budget lines are the same because the price of commodity X is assumed to be the same.

The curve joining all points representing equilibrium positions—in which the price of the commodity is the same, but money incomes differ—is called an *income-consumption curve*. E_1, E_2, and E_3 in Figure 5.11 are three points on such a curve. Income-consumption curves may have a variety of shapes, and a particular curve may have both positive- and negative-sloping segments. The shape of the curve will reflect the characteristics of the good, the extent and nature of possible substitutes, the individual's tastes, and his purchasing power.

A commodity is said to be a *superior* good if, when two situations differing only in money income are compared, the quantity demanded of the commodity is higher in the situation with the higher income. (Commodities for which this relationship holds have also been called *normal* goods.) A commodity is said to be an *inferior* good if the quantity demanded is smaller the larger the consumer's income. However, the classification of particular goods into superior or inferior categories is not absolute. A commodity may be superior within one income range and inferior in a higher income range.

The relationship between quantities demanded of commodities and incomes has often been illustrated by *Engel curves*, which show the relation between expenditures on particular commodities and total incomes. They are estimated from data provided by budget studies, which are concerned with the commodity breakdown of expenditures by households with different incomes. The data consist of estimates for a cross-section of households at one point in time rather than for a particular household at different points in time.

Superior goods are often classified in two ways, depending on the values for their income-elasticity of demand. If their income-elasticity is much smaller than one, they are called *necessaries*. The higher the individual's income, the smaller the proportion of income spent on these goods. Goods with an income-elasticity greater than one are called *luxuries*. The higher the individual's income, the larger the proportion of income that is spent on these commodities. (The income-elasticity of demand for inferior goods is negative by definition.)

5.17 Income and substitution effects

Different prices for a particular commodity can be interpreted as affecting a consumer's behaviour in two ways—since his purchasing power as well as the prices of this commodity relative to the prices of other commodities will differ—and their effects can be separated conceptually. The *substitution effect* is the difference in quantity demanded because of a difference in price, the purchasing power remaining unchanged. The *income effect* is the difference in the quantity demanded due to the difference in purchasing power. In economic analysis three methods have been used to divide the effect of a difference in price into income and substitution effects. One of these, the cost-difference method, will be presented here. The other two— the compensating-income variation and equivalent-income variation methods—will be examined in the following chapter in connection with applications of utility analysis. They are based on estimates of the differences in money income required to enable the individual to attain the same level of satisfaction when price differs.[15]

5.18 Cost-difference method for separating income and substitution effects

The *cost-difference method* estimates the difference in purchasing power due to a difference in price by calculating the difference in the cost of a specific basket of commodities at the two sets of prices.

Two situations that differ only in the price of commodity X are compared in Figure 5.12. The two budget lines are $F_1 G_1$ and $F_1 G_2$ and the corresponding equilibrium positions are at points E_1 and E_2. The difference in the quantity of X purchased—$R_1 R_2$ units per week—is due to the difference in price and is called the *price effect* (price-consumption curves and demand curves are based on the price effect). This can be viewed as being made up of two components: a substitution effect and an income effect. *The substitution effect is the difference in purchases of the commodity due to a difference in price, with 'income' constant. The income effect is the difference in purchases due to the difference in 'income' resulting from the difference in price.* When the cost-difference method for separating income and substitution effects is employed, the constant 'income' in the definition

---

[15] The cost-difference method was first presented by E.E. Slutsky in 'On the Theory of the Budget of the Consumer', *Giornale degli Economisti*, Vol. 51 (July 1915), pp. 1-26. This article has been reprinted in The American Economic Association, *Readings in Price Theory* (Homewood, Ill.: Richard D. Irwin, 1952), pp. 27-56. The compensating and equivalent-income variation methods can be found in J.R. Hicks, *Value and Capital* (2nd ed.; Oxford: Clarendon Press, 1946).

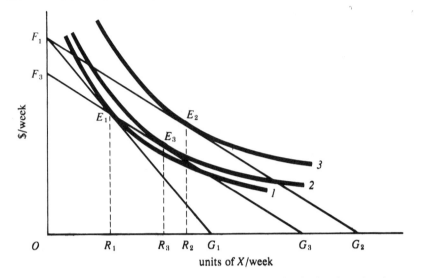

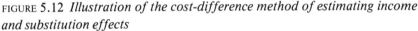

FIGURE 5.12 *Illustration of the cost-difference method of estimating income and substitution effects*

of the substitution effect means constant purchasing power in terms of a particular basket of goods.

The separation of a price effect into an income and substitution effect will be illustrated by using as the basis of comparison the basket of goods purchased in equilibrium at the higher price. This basket is represented in Figure 5.12 by point E_1. Its co-ordinates show the amount of X, and the money spent on other goods, when the price is equal to OF_1/OG_1. If the price of X were lower, as shown by the numerical value of the slope of the line F_1G_2, then this basket would cost less. This difference in cost can be shown geometrically by drawing a line through point E_1 that is parallel to the line F_1G_2. This new line is F_3G_3, and the distance F_3F_1 indicates the difference in the cost of purchasing this basket at the two prices. Point E_1 is common to both the original budget line F_1G_1 and the constructed budget line F_3G_3. This means that the purchase of the basket of goods represented by this point exhausts an income of $\$OF_1$ if the price is equal to OF_1/OG_1; it also exhausts the lower income of $\$OF_3$ if the price is equal to OF_1/OG_2. It is in this special sense that the two budget lines F_1G_1 and F_3G_3 are said to indicate the *same* purchasing power. They do so only with respect to the basket of goods that corresponds to their point of intersection.

If F_3G_3 were the budget line, the individual would choose the basket of goods represented by point E_3 rather than the basket indicated by point E_1. E_3 lies on a higher indifference curve; it is the highest indifference curve he can reach with this budget line. With the two lines F_1G_1 and F_3G_3 having the same purchasing power, the difference between their equilibrium positions (points E_1 and E_3) must be due to the substitution effect of the price difference. In this case the substitution effect increases the quantity demanded of X from OR_1 to OR_3, or by R_1R_3 units per week.

The substitution effect always increases the quantity demanded of the good whose price is lower, because the indifference curves are assumed to be downward sloping and convex to the origin. Budget lines such as F_3G_3, which show a lower price for commodity X and go through the initial equilibrium position for the higher price, must cut the initial indifference curve from below. A budget line constructed in this way must be tangent to an indifference curve at some point to the right of E_1 (or it touches the highest indifference curve it can reach to the right of E_1). This point of tangency represents a basket with a larger quantity of the good whose price is lower.

Points E_3 and E_2 are the equilibrium positions for the budget lines F_3G_3 and F_1G_2 respectively. These lines show the same price for commodity X but different incomes. The difference in the quantity of X demanded in these two positions can thus be appropriately called an income effect. In Figure 5.12 this income effect is positive: the equilibrium position for the budget line with the higher income has a larger quantity of the good being considered. However, this positive result may not generally hold. If the good is an inferior good, the income effect of a lower price will result in a smaller quantity of the good being demanded.

This breakdown of the price effect into two components is done only for analytical purposes. It does not imply that a consumer calculates the substitution and income effects of a price change in order to decide on his appropriate response: there is no path running from E_1 to E_2 to E_3 that the consumer follows. This analysis simply tries to provide some insight into a consumer's optimal choices in different price situations and allows for a precise statement of the conditions that give rise to the negatively sloped demand curve.

Income and substitution effects can also be estimated if the equilibrium position corresponding to the lower price is used as the basis for comparison. In Figure 5.12 this position is represented by point E_2 on the budget line F_1G_2. To estimate the substitution effect it would now be necessary to construct a budget line that has the same purchasing power as F_1G_2 with respect to the basket of goods at point E_2, even though the price of X is higher. This budget line would be drawn through point E_2 and the value for its slope would be equal to OF_1/OG_1, which is the higher price. The equilibrium position on this constructed budget line would lie to the left of point E_2 because of the convexity of the indifference curves. The substitution effect thus acts to lower the quantity demanded of the good whose price is higher. (It is left to the reader to complete and illustrate the analysis.)

5.19 Indifference-curve analysis and the law of demand

The presumption that an individual's demand curve is downward sloping— i.e. more is purchased of a good when its price is lower—is based on the operation of the substitution effect. This acts to increase the quantity demanded of the good whose price is lower. In order to determine the total effect of a lower price, it is necessary to allow for the income effect. If the commodity being considered is a superior good, the individual's demand curve for this good will be negatively sloped as a consequence of both the income and substitution effects. His purchasing power will be higher as a result of the lower price and he will demand more of this superior good. In the case of an inferior good, however, the income effect of a lower price decreases the quantity demanded of this good. The individual's demand curve will have a negative slope only if the substitution effect outweighs the income effect. For inferior goods, therefore, demand curves are negatively sloped only if the substitution effect of a lower price is greater than the numerical value of the income effect.

It should be noted that there is nothing in the basic assumptions about consumer behaviour made in this chapter that precludes either an upward-sloping demand curve or a curve with an upward-sloping portion. If a good is inferior, and if, between two prices, the income effect outweighs the substitution effect, then a smaller quantity will be purchased at the lower price. Goods with this attribute are called *Giffen goods*. They have been named after Sir Robert Giffen, a statistician with the British Board of Trade in the late nineteenth century who, on the basis of budget studies for working-class families, pointed out that the lower the price of bread, the lower the consumption of bread by these families. Bread was a very important item in their diets and accounted for a substantial portion of their total income. It was also an inferior good. An increase in the price of bread thus made them sufficiently poorer that the income effect outweighed the substitution effect and they consumed more bread.

Economists have followed Marshall in recognizing that there may be Giffen goods, and also in making the judgement that 'such cases are rare'.[16]

5.20 Theory of revealed preference

In the indifference-curve analysis of consumer behaviour we have gone

[16] Marshall, *Principles of Economics*, p. 132.

from assumptions about an individual's preferences to an investigation of his optimal choices in different circumstances. This analysis has resulted in predictions about a rational consumer's market response to differences in the price of a commodity that may also be arrived at by reversing the order of preferences and choices. This alternative method, first developed by Paul Anthony Samuelson,[17] is based on the assumption that choices reveal preferences. An individual chooses a particular basket because he prefers it to the other alternatives available to him at that time. These *revealed preferences* are then used to deduce the sign of the substitution effect of a price difference. There is no conflict between this approach and the one based on ordinal utility functions. Both have been shown to be logically equivalent and both imply the same restrictions on consumer behaviour.[18]

The revealed preference approach makes use of the supposition that a consumer purchases one set of items rather than another for one of two reasons. Either he prefers the first set, or it is cheaper than the second. If he chooses set A, when B, C, etc. are no more expensive, then the statement is made that A has been *revealed preferred* to the others (or the others are *revealed inferior* to A). The following assumptions are then made to arrive at smooth demand curves.

(i) The consumer will never behave in so inconsistent a manner that set A will be revealed preferred to B and that B will simultaneously be revealed preferred to A.[19]

(ii) Each set of goods is chosen in one, and only one, price-income situation.

The standard results of the theory of consumer behaviour—in particular, the direction of the substitution effect—can now be readily obtained. If the individual chooses point E_1 when his budget line is F_1G_1, the basket of goods represented by point E_1 is revealed preferred to all others represented by points on F_1G_1 or between this line and the origin. This means that with a lower price of X, and a budget line (F_3G_3) that includes point E_1, the individual would choose a basket with a larger quantity of X, such as that represented by point E_3 in Figure 5.13. By assumption (i) he would not choose any point on the line segment F_3E_1, since all points on that segment

---

[17] Paul Anthony Samuelson, *Foundations of Economic Analysis* (Cambridge, Mass.: Harvard University Press, 1948), pp. 107-17.

[18] H.S. Houthakker, 'Revealed Preference and the Utility Function', *Economica*, Vol. 17 (May 1950), pp. 159-74.

[19] This is known as the *weak axiom of revealed preference*. The strong axiom, which was used by Houthakker to derive an indifference map from hypothetical choices, ensures transitivity of revealed preferences. It states that if A is revealed preferred to B, which is revealed preferred to C . . . which is revealed preferred to S, then S must never be revealed preferred to A.

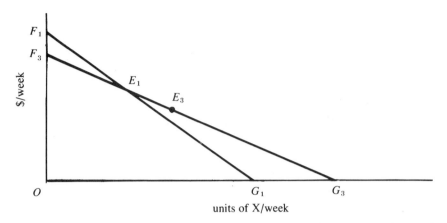

FIGURE 5.13 *Budget lines and points representing alternative price and income situations, and the individual's choices in a specific period*

have been revealed inferior to point E_1; by assumption (ii) (which brings in continuity) he would choose a point other than E_1, such as E_3. More of the good whose price is lower is thus in the chosen basket. The substitution effect on the quantity demanded of a good whose price is lower is positive. It can readily be shown by this same procedure that the substitution effect of a higher price is negative.

In order to move from this conclusion to the individual's demand curve it is necessary to add the income effect of a price difference to the substitution effect. The procedure followed is similar to the cost-difference method discussed in Section 5.18. The initial budget line is F_1G_1. The constructed budget line that goes through the initial equilibrium point (E_1) and has a numerical value for its slope equal to the lower price is F_3G_3. The equilibrium position for this lower price, given the individual's level of income $\$OF_1$, will lie on a budget line (*not* drawn in Figure 5.13) that starts at F_1 and has a slope equal to that of F_3G_3. The equilibrium position on this third budget line will tend to show a higher quantity of X purchased than the point E_1 because of the substitution effect. Exceptions to the rule of a negatively sloped demand curve will occur here, as they do with indifference curve analysis, only if a good is inferior *and* the income effect outweighs the substitution effect (i.e. for Giffen goods).

5.21 Aggregation of individual demand curves

Analyses of price determination such as those in Chapters 2 and 3 make use of market demand curves, which show the total quantities demanded, at alternative prices, by all those with access to a particular market. An important element in market demands is the demand of consumers. The

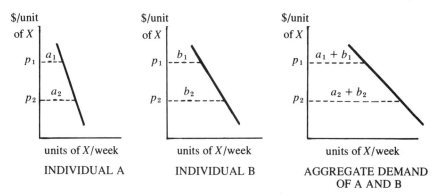

FIGURE 5.14 *Illustration of horizontal summation of individual demand curves to obtain aggregate demand for a particular commodity in a specified period*

aggregate demand of individual consumers[20] can be obtained directly from their demand curves by a process of horizontal summation if it is assumed that the equilibrium choices made by each individual are independent of those made by others.

Horizontal summation is illustrated in Figure 5.14. At any specified price, the quantity shown by the demand curve for the group is the sum of the quantities each of the individuals would buy at this price. Individual A's demand is not affected by B's demand; therefore the two demand curves may be added together to obtain their joint demand. If these demands were not independent (as in the cases to be examined in Section 5.23), they could not be added together in this way.

5.22 Individual and market demand curves and expectations
In the theory of consumer behaviour, economists are not trying to say anything useful about the behaviour of any particular individual, whose actions may be dominated by motives peculiar to himself. What they are trying to explain is the behaviour of the whole market. Their assumption of 'rational' behaviour means that it will be observed 'on the average' and not necessarily in any particular case. If two situations are compared that differ only in the price of the commodity, and individual choices are independent, then the quantity demanded by the group as a whole will be larger in the situation with the lower price (Giffen goods excepted). To move from these demand curves for groups of consumers to the market demand curves displayed in Chapters 2, 3, and 4, it is necessary to consider the effects of

---

[20] This may not be the only element in these demand curves. Merchants, speculators, and even governments may have a strong influence on market demands in particular periods.

different types of expectations and the activities of firms, merchants, and speculators.

For the derivation of individual demand curves it was assumed that the individual's expectations about future conditions were unaffected by current prices. Expectations of future prices were the same at all points on the demand curve even though currect prices were different. When this is not the case, the demand curves (even for non-Giffen goods) may deviate from the standard downward-sloping curves. For example, if a higher price results in expectations of still higher prices in the future, the quantity demanded may increase. This tendency will be particularly strong if the good can be stored at costs that are not in excess of the expected increase in future prices. The demand by merchants and speculators would also be affected by their expectations of future prices, which could be influenced by changes in prices. The market demand curves calculated from observed data might thus show departures from the standard slope even though all individual demand curves, if derived under the assumptions of the theory of consumer behaviour, would be downward sloping.[21]

5.23 Bandwagon, snob, and Veblen effects

A key assumption underlying the method for obtaining aggregate demand curves through horizontal summation, as illustrated in Figure 5.14, is the independence of individual demand curves. If they were not independent, the procedure for arriving at these aggregate demand curves would be more complex. The demand for a good is said to be subject to *bandwagon effects* when an individual's demand for it is higher because others are also consuming it. Conversely, *snob effects* are said to be present when an individual's demand for the commodity is lower than it would otherwise be because others are buying this commodity.[22]

When individual demands are interdependent there are many demand curves for an individual, given the values of the usual parameters. Each of these curves corresponds to a particular value for an additional parameter, which is the quantity of the good purchased by other consumers. For example, in panel A of Figure 5.15, the curve labelled Q_1 shows the

---

[21] The estimation of demand curves from data on market transactions is also subject to the *identification problem*. A transaction represents a sale as well as a purchase, and special conditions have to be satisfied to enable the demand curve to be distinguished (or identified) from the data. For an early statement of this problem, see E.J. Working, 'What do Statistical "Demand Curves" Show?', *Quarterly Journal of Economics*, Vol. 41 (1927), pp. 212-35. Reprinted in The American Economic Association, *Readings in Price Theory*, pp. 97-115.

[22] This terminology and an analysis of the resulting demand curves are to be found in H. Leibenstein, 'Bandwagon, Snob and Veblen Effects', *Quarterly Journal of Economics*, Vol. 64 (May 1950), pp. 183-207.

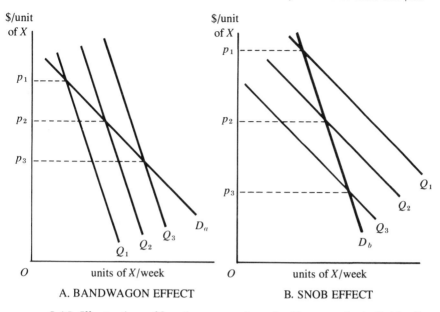

FIGURE 5.15 *Illustration of bandwagon and snob effects on the individual's demand for a particular commodity in a specified period*

quantities of X the consumer would purchase at alternative prices given the total quantities, Q_1, purchased by all other consumers. The curve labelled Q_2 lies to the right of Q_1, and Q_3 lies still further to the right, since these points represent increasingly larger quantities purchased by others. For the purpose of deriving an aggregate demand curve for the commodity exhibiting bandwagon effects, the relevant demand curve is D_a. This is more elastic than curves that would be derived under the assumption of fixed purchases by other consumers. A lower price increases the quantity demanded not only through the price effect but also as a result of larger purchases by others in response to this lower price. Thus there is an augmentation of the price effect by a bandwagon effect.

In panel B of Figure 5.15 the commodity is more attractive to the individual the smaller the quantities purchased by others. His demand curve, when others purchase the larger quantity Q_2, lies to the left of his demand curve when the smaller quantity Q_1 is purchased. This leads to a less elastic demand curve for this snob commodity than would be the case if demands were independent. A lower price that increases the purchases of others makes the commodity less appealing to the individual. The snob effect thus acts as a counterweight to the price effect of a difference in price.

Aggregate demand curves can be obtained in both these cases by summation of individual demand curves, such as D_a and D_b, that take into account the interdependence of consumer choices. For goods with snob values, this total demand curve would still be downward sloping even though it was tilted to the right.

Some goods may be purchased for *conspicuous consumption*; that is, their high prices make them suitable for purposes of display. Preferences here are positively related to price rather than to the consumption of others. Demand curves in these cases display a *Veblen effect*.[23] The quantity demanded is higher at a higher price than it would otherwise be because the higher price makes the commodity better for purposes of conspicuous consumption. This effect may be strong enough to cause portions of a demand curve for this type of good to be upward sloping.

5.24 Comparison of the three methods for deriving demand curves

The cardinal utility, ordinal utility, and revealed preference methods for deriving demand curves all reach the same result. The individual's demand curve for a particular commodity at a particular period will be downward sloping, subject to one possible exception. This would occur when the good is inferior *and* the income effect outweighs the substitution effect. The substitution effect is more easily isolated and the possible combinations of income and substitution effects can be shown more clearly with the indifference curve and revealed preference methods than with the cardinal utility approach. There is also some difference in the assumptions underlying these methods, and this difference affects their potential application.

The Marshallian version of the cardinal utility method requires that it be considered reasonable to assume that increments in utility derived from particular things are both intrinsically and practically measurable. Comparisons of differences in the sums of money individuals are prepared to pay for different bundles of commodities indicate the differences in utilities they expect to derive from their consumption. In deciding whether to make a particular purchase, the individual compares the marginal utility he expects to obtain from the good with the marginal utility of the money he must pay for it. With this approach the marginal utility of money is available for the individual to help judge the merits of individual transactions. But the marginal utility of money is not available for the ordinal utility and revealed preference methods since marginal utility can be derived only from a cardinal utility function. The ordinal utility and revealed preference methods assume that when an individual is faced with a special

[23] This effect is named after Thorstein Veblen, who discussed conspicuous consumption in his *Theory of the Leisure Class* (New York: Modern Library, 1934), Chapter IV. This book was first published in 1899.

opportunity to buy a particular good, his decision will be made after a consideration of all the possible different bundles of goods he might purchase with his income.

If the theory of consumer behaviour is to be used to try to predict the effect of differences in the price of a commodity, it is not necessary to introduce the notion of utility. The revealed preference approach is sufficient for this purpose. For many problems in welfare economics, however, it is necessary to obtain some estimate of the values individuals place on alternatives. Notions of cardinal utility underlie many cost-benefit analyses.[24] Cardinal utility functions have been constructed to help analyse choices among alternatives whose outcomes are uncertain.[25]

The cardinal utility, ordinal utility, and revealed preference methods for deriving demand curves are all based on the assumption of rational behaviour: a consumer's choices are assumed to be consistent and to reflect his preferences. They all lead to the conclusion that interference with a free market choice of individuals is undesirable.

5.25 Criticisms of the theory of consumer behaviour

A persistent critic of the theory of consumer behaviour is John Kenneth Galbraith, who advocates sending 'to the museum of irrelevant ideas the notion of an equilibrium in consumer outlays which reflects the maximum of consumer satisfaction.'[26] The basis for his criticism is the belief that consumers' tastes in modern industrial states are largely created by the sellers through advertising. Even these created tastes may not be satisfied by the goods purchased because individuals are often poorly informed about the qualities of these goods. Galbraith has stated that 'if an individual's satisfaction is less from an additional expenditure on automobiles than from one on housing, this can as well be corrected by a change in the selling strategy of General Motors as by an increased expenditure on his house.'[27] From this position Galbraith criticizes the operation of the doctrine of consumer sovereignty. 'A doctrine that celebrates individuality provides the cloak for organization . . . It is not the individual's right to buy that is being protected. Rather, it is the seller's right to manage the individual.'[28]

Such a criticism makes it clear that there are discrepancies between market conditions and the assumptions used to derive demand curves in the

---

[24] See Section 6.12.

[25] J. von Neumann and O. Morgenstern, *Theory of Games and Economic Behavior* (2nd ed.; Princeton: Princeton University Press, 1947), Chapter 1.

[26] J.K. Galbraith, *The New Industrial State* (Boston: Houghton Mifflin, 1967), p. 223.

[27] *Ibid.*, p. 225.

[28] *Ibid.*, pp. 226-7.

preceding sections. Consumers may not have full knowledge of the alternatives facing them; their choices at any particular moment may be largely due to habitual behaviour rather than to the consequence of a careful consideration of alternatives. Their tastes can be influenced by advertising and show more frequent changes than is assumed in the theory of consumer behaviour. However, the basic thrust of the theory of consumer behaviour is rather robust. It appears to explain market behaviour even though the assumptions on which it is based do not have exact counterparts in reality. The habitual behaviour of consumers in making purchases is not necessarily irrational. Shopping around has its costs, in time if nothing else, and it might not be wise to reconsider one's pattern of choice each time purchases are to be made. On the basis of this theory, however, substantial changes in prices can be expected to bring about changes in purchases. This prediction appears to be in agreement with observed behaviour. For example, the very large increase in the price of sugar in 1974 led to increased purchases of substitute products such as honey and was one of the important factors in the substantial increase in the price of soft drinks during the same period, the demand for which suffered a sharp fall. Even automobiles provide a counter-example to Galbraith's extreme position. The United States automobile manufacturers misjudged the extent of demand for their output in the fall and winter of 1974. Their rates of production exceeded their rates of sales and this resulted in an increase in their inventories. They turned to short-term price reductions, in the form of price rebates, as the method for selling off their excess inventories. An increase in advertising expenditures was not considered to be an effective method for raising the rate of sales of automobiles. However, advertising was extensively used to inform potential customers of price rebates, which were to be valid for only a limited period.[29]

This defence of the theory of consumer behaviour should not be taken to imply that the consumer can always fend for himself in the market-place. Many of the items purchased by an individual are bought only infrequently and he may not be in a position to judge quality from past experience. The results of product testing by groups such as the Consumers' Union indicate that many products are purchased because individuals are not sufficiently aware of product qualities. Consumers may also have difficulty in comparing the prices of different goods. Modern packaging techniques, with their proliferation of sizes and shapes, make it difficult for buyers to

---

[29] For an interesting examination of search costs for buyers and sellers, and an explanation of the dispersion of prices under changing conditions, see George J. Stigler, 'The Economics of Information', *Journal of Political Economy*, Vol. 69 (June 1961), pp. 213-25.

determine unit prices. In some countries laws have been passed that require the posting of unit prices and the standardization of package sizes in order to make it easier for consumers to evaluate the alternatives facing them.

5.26 Summary

This chapter has shown how economic theorists have deduced the shapes of individual demand curves. In presenting the theory of consumer behaviour it has also introduced techniques of analysis that have many applications elsewhere in economic theory.

The consumer, the centerpiece of this analysis, was assumed to be rational and to act on the basis of tastes that, even though they were conditioned by historical, social, and cultural factors, change only slowly over time. The consumer was assumed to be very knowledgeable about the technical characteristics of the goods he was purchasing. The utility he expected to get from these goods was in fact what he obtained from them. His choices were deduced in situations where fundamental conditions were constant over time. He expected conditions, and prices of commodities in particular, to remain unchanged over time.

The pure theory of consumer behaviour is obviously very abstract. It leaves out many of the factors that influence purchases in actual markets. These include the fashioning of tastes by sellers; lack of knowledge on the part of many consumers of the qualities and unit prices of the goods they are buying; constantly changing conditions with respect to products, prices, and incomes—all of which make it impossible for consumers to know all the options available to them. However, the predictions obtained from such a theory do seem to have general applicability. Changes in prices generally lead to changes in purchases that follow the lines predicted by this theory.

SUGGESTED READINGS

Galbraith, J.K. *The New Industrial State*. Boston: Houghton Mifflin, 1967. Chapters 18 and 19.

Green, H.A. John. *Consumer Theory*. Harmondsworth, Middlesex: Penguin Books, 1971.

Hicks, J.R. *Value and Capital*. 2nd ed. Oxford: Clarendon Press, 1946.

Marshall, Alfred. *Principles of Economics*. 8th ed. London: Macmillan & Co., 1920. Book III, Chapters 1, 2, and 3.

Robertson, D.H. *Lectures in Economic Principles*. London: Staples Press, 1957. Vol. 1, Chapters 4, 5, and 6.

Robinson, Joan. *Exercises in Economic Analysis*. London: Macmillan & Co., 1960. Pages 120-31.

EXERCISES

1. Let $MU_x = 500/q_x$, and $MU_m = 2$, where MU_x is the marginal utility of commodity X; q_x is the rate of consumption of commodity X, in a specified period; and MU_m is the marginal utility of money for a particular individual where his tastes, income, and prices of other goods are constant. Derive this individual's demand curve for commodity X.

2. Show that the demand curve derived in Question 1 always has a price elasticity of demand value of minus one. What is the critical assumption underlying the statement of Question 1 that ensures this result?

3. A family spends all its income on two composite commodities, 'food' and 'clothing'.

(a) Illustrate, using indifference curve analysis, its equilibrium position, assuming given prices for these two items and a given money income. What is the equilibrium relationship between the marginal rate of substitution of food for clothing and the prices of these two items?

(b) Would there be any difference in the quantities purchased of these two commodities if their prices and the family's money income were all double their assumed values in (a)? Why?

(c) What can you infer about the nature of the family's demand function from your answer to (b)?

4. Do you agree with the following statements? (Give your reasons.)

(a) A consumer's income elasticities of demand for the commodities he buys cannot all be less than unity.

(b) A consumer's demand curve for at least one of the commodities he is purchasing must be downward sloping.

5. The *London Financial Times* of May 26, 1974 reported that shrinking domestic and export markets had forced Italian apple and pear farmers to destroy thousands of tons of fruit. Domestic sales were said to have been hit by the rising cost of living.

What would you infer, on the basis of this report, about the price and income elasticities of demand for apples and pears in Italy?

6. (a) Derive an income consumption curve, using indifference curve analysis, for a commodity that is 'inferior', at least in one income range. Indicate this range.

(b) Derive an income consumption curve using indifference curve analysis for a commodity that is 'normal', at least in one income range. Indicate this range.

7. (a) Derive an individual's demand curve for commodity X using indifference curve analysis.

(b) If this demand curve had been inelastic in the range of prices used to illustrate its derivation, how would this be reflected in your indifference map diagram?

8. An individual is at equilibrium consuming a positive amount of commodity X when its price is P_x. Show, using indifference curve analysis, his new equilibrium position if the price were cut in half to $1/2P_x$. Distinguish between income and substitution effects.

9. Draw indifference curves and budget lines to illustrate the following three situations in a specified period.

(a) Given the individual's money income and the price of tea, no tea is bought.

(b) With the same money income but with the price of tea one-half its level in (a), some tea is bought.

(c) With the price of tea as in (a) and money income twice its level in (a), some tea is bought.

10. Prove the following propositions for special situations where it is assumed that the marginal utility derived from each commodity is independent of the amount of the other commodity consumed.

(a) If the marginal utility of Y is constant, all indifference curves will have equal slopes at a given value for X.

(b) Assuming diminishing marginal utility, more of both commodities will be purchased when income rises.

11. Draw indifference curves for a 'Giffen good', the demand for which is higher at a higher price. Illustrate this property by showing the equilibrium positions for two different prices. Distinguish between income and substitution effects. Does the substitution effect have the expected sign?

12. Draw indifference curves between money (to be spent on other commodities) and a commodity X. Assume that the price for this commodity in the specified period is such that the consumer would choose to purchase a positive quantity of X. Determine the total amount of money the consumer would be willing to pay for the privilege of buying this equilibrium quantity of X in the specified period rather than doing without it entirely.

13. A farmer has a single crop, potatoes, for the support of his family. He consumes some and sells the remainder to obtain income to spend on other goods. Assuming a given price for potatoes, and given prices for all other

commodities, illustrate his equilibrium position using indifference curve analysis. Specify the quantity of potatoes he (and his family) consumes and the quantity he sells. Then take a higher price for potatoes, with all other prices unchanged, and obtain the new equilibrium position.

14. Only two commodities are available, bread and ale. Adam is a complete dipsomaniac with an ungovernable passion for ale. Bread has its uses for him, but his desire for ale is such that its quantity is the dominant factor in all his choices. On the basis of this information, construct Adam's preference map for these two commodities. (This type of preference map reflects a *lexicographic* or *lexical* ordering.)

6

APPLICATIONS OF UTILITY ANALYSIS

6.1 Introduction

Utility analysis has been used to provide a theoretical basis for the examination of many practical problems. A few of these applications will be examined briefly in this chapter.

The first concerns cost-of-living indexes. In order to make clear the issues involved, however, it is necessary to introduce two additional methods for breaking down a price effect into income and substitution effects: the *compensating-income variation* and *equivalent-income variation* methods. With these approaches the change in purchasing power due to a change in price is estimated by the difference in the amount of money required to reach a particular level of utility. Thus they both differ from the cost-difference method, which makes use of the difference in the cost of purchasing a particular basket of goods.

6.2 The compensating-income variation method

This is based on an estimate of the change in income required to maintain the initial level of utility when the price of a commodity is changed. In Figure 6.1 the initial equilibrium position is at point E_1 on indifference curve *1*. Money income is equal to $\$OF_1$, the initial price of X is equal to OF_1/OG_1, and the budget line is F_1G_1.

Assume that the price of X is reduced, with the new price being equal to OF_1/OG_2. This individual could now achieve the same level of utility as at E_1 even if his income were reduced. The compensating-income variation of a price decrease is the maximum reduction in income that would still permit him to reach the initial level of utility. It is equal to $\$F_4F_1$ for the case illustrated in Figure 6.1. This amount is estimated by drawing a budget line that is both parallel to F_1G_2 (to reflect the new price) and tangent to indifference curve *1*. This line is labelled F_4G_4 in Figure 6.1. The individual

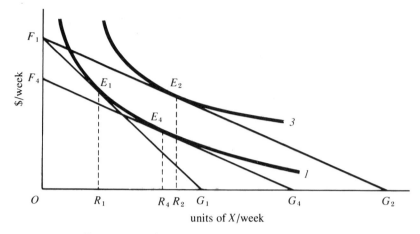

FIGURE 6.1 *Illustration of the compensating-income variation method of estimating income and substitution effects when the higher-priced situation is the point of reference*

could reach indifference curve *1* at point E_4 with a money income of $\$OF_4$ if the price of X were equal to $OF_4/OG_4(=OF_1/OG_2)$.

Both the budget lines F_1G_1 and F_4G_4 allow the individual to reach the same level of utility; they display, in this special sense, the same purchasing power. The difference between the two equilibrium positions on these lines is due solely to the difference in the two prices. The substitution effect of the decrease in price is thus equal to R_1R_4 units of X per week—a quantity that is equal to the difference in the commodity X purchased in the two equilibrium positions. The income effect of the lower price is obtained with this method by comparing the equilibrium positions on the budget lines F_4G_4 and F_1G_2. The price of X is the same in both cases, but the income is higher in the latter. The income effect is equal to R_4R_2 units of X per week. X is a superior good for this individual, at least in the income range considered.

The equilibrium position and level of utility in the lower-price situation could have been used as the reference point for calculating the compensating-income variation. In this case we would be deriving the income and substitution effects of a price increase. The initial position would be at point E_2 in Figure 6.1, with the budget line F_1G_2, and the new position would be at point E_1. The compensating-income variation would be the increase in income required to compensate the individual for the higher price of X. This increase can be estimated by constructing a budget line that is tangent to indifference curve *3* and has the same slope as F_1G_1 (the price is the same for both). This line is drawn in Figure 6.2 and is labelled F_5G_5. Its

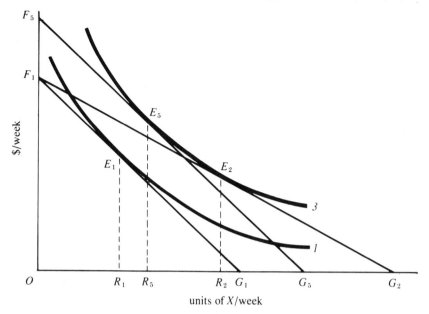

FIGURE 6.2 *Illustration of the equivalent-income variation method of estimating income and substitution effects when the higher-priced situation is the point of reference*

point of tangency with the indifference curve E_5 lies above and to the left of E_2 because of the convexity of the indifference curve. Both the budget lines F_1G_2 and F_5G_5 allow the individual to reach the same level of utility even though the price of X differs. The decrease in the quantity of X, when E_5 is compared with E_2 (R_2R_5 units of X per week), is equal to the substitution effect of the price increase. The income effect of this price increase is equal to R_5R_1 units per week.

6.3 The equivalent-income variation method

The *equivalent-income variation* of a price change is the change in income that will permit a consumer, when he is constrained to trade at the initial price, to reach the level of utility he can attain at the new price. It differs from the compensating-income variation in that it refers to the change in income required to allow him to reach the new level of utility at the initial price rather than to the change in income required to maintain the initial level of utility at the new price.

The budget lines F_1G_1 and F_1G_2 of Figure 6.1 are re-drawn in Figure 6.2. Assume that the initial price is equal to the numerical value of the slope of F_1G_1. E_1 and E_2 are the initial and new equilibrium positions respectively. If the individual could obtain X only at the initial price, then in order to reach indifference curve *3* his income would have to be higher than OF_1. This required increase in income (the equivalent-income variation of a price change from OF_1/OG_1 to OF_1/OG_2) is estimated by constructing a third budget line that is parallel to F_1G_1 and touches indifference curve *3* at E_5, which lies to the left of E_2 because of the convexity of the indifference curve. The equivalent-income variation of this price decrease is equal to $\$F_1F_5$ per week. An increase in income by this amount would permit the consumer to reach the higher indifference curve even if the price were higher. The estimate of the substitution effect on the quantity of X purchased, obtained by this method, is R_5R_2 units per week. The income effect of the lower price is R_1R_5 units per week.

This method for separating income and substitution effects can also be used when the price is increased. Assume that the initial budget line is F_1G_2 in Figure 6.1 and the new budget line is F_1G_1. The equivalent-income variation of this price increase is obtained by drawing a line that is both parallel to F_1G_2 and tangent to indifference curve *1*. The change in income that is equivalent to being required to purchase X at the new price is $\$F_1F_4$ per week. The income effect of this increase in price is R_2R_4 units of X per week and the substitution effect is R_4R_1 units of X per week.

6.4 A comparison of the three methods for estimating income and substitution effects

In this chapter a price effect—the difference in the quantity purchased of a particular commodity at different prices with the values for the parameters unchanged—has been split into income and substitution effects in two ways. A third way, the cost-difference method, was presented in Section 5.18. Each method makes use of a different estimate of the change in purchasing power resulting from a change in price. However, it is possible to make a general statement about the relative values of these estimates for any particular price difference.

The compensating-income variation, when the higher price is assumed to be the initial price, is always equal to the equivalent-income variation when the lower price is assumed to be the initial price. Both the compensating-income variation of a price decrease and the equivalent-income variation of a price increase were estimated with the aid of Figure 6.1: the same numerical value $\$F_4F_1$ was obtained in both cases. The converse also holds, of course. The compensating-income variation, when the lower price is assumed to be the initial price, is always equal to the equivalent-income variation when the higher price is the initial price. Figure 6.2 was used to obtain the estimate $\$F_1F_5$ in these two cases.

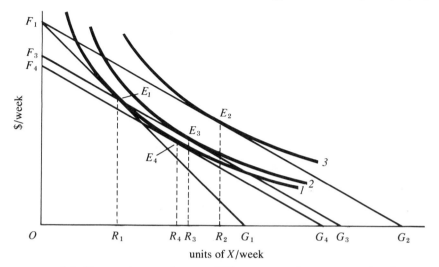

FIGURE 6.3 *Comparison of cost-difference and compensating-income variation values when the higher-priced situation is used as a point of reference*

The compensating-income variation for a given price difference is always greater than the corresponding cost-difference when the higher price is assumed to be the initial price. Even if the cost-difference amount is subtracted from the consumer's income, he could still reach a higher indifference curve (indifference curve *2* in Figure 6.3) as long as he could trade at the lower price. This would not be the case if the compensating-income variation were subtracted from his income. We know from its definition that the consumer could reach the initial level of utility only by trading at the lower price for *X*. (E_1 and E_4 lie on the same indifference curve.) $\$F_4F_1$ in Figure 6.3 is greater than F_3F_1. The reverse relation applies when the lower price is the initial price. The cost-difference measure is greater than the compensating-income variation when we move from a lower to a higher price. This is illustrated in Figure 6.4. The cost difference of the change in price from OF_1/OG_2 to OF_1/OG_1 is equal to $\$F_1F_6$ per week for this individual, while the compensating-income variation would be equal to the smaller value, $\$F_1F_5$ per week.

Each of the three methods for distinguishing between income and substitution effects is describing a hypothetical 'path' between two points (E_1 and E_2). The information contained in the assumptions about the given situations and the consumer's behaviour relates only to these points, each of which is an equilibrium position for particular values of the parameters. The hypothetical paths between these points are presented to provide an

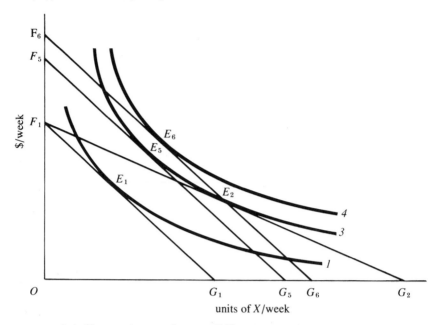

FIGURE 6.4 *Comparison of cost-difference and compensating-income variation measures when the lower-priced situation is used as a point of reference*

insight into a consumer's optimal choice in different price situations. As each method gives a different value for the income effect, the sizes of the substitution effects differ. However, the direction of the substitution effect is always the same no matter which method is used, or which commodity is examined, because of the assumption of a diminishing marginal rate of substitution that results in convex indifference curves. This effect is always positive when the price is decreased and negative when the price is increased. The substitution effect provides the theoretical underpinning for drawing an individual's demand curve for a commodity with a negative slope.

6.5 Cost-of-living indexes

A *cost-of-living index* is a measure of the difference in the cost of achieving a given level of utility when prices differ. It can be calculated for the two price situations shown by the budget lines in Figure 6.5. If the individual's initial money income is equal to OF_1 per week, and the price of X is equal to the numerical value of the slope of F_1G_2, then the individual's equilibrium position is point E_2. He reaches a level of utility represented by indifference curve *3*. If the price of X were higher, as shown by the slope of

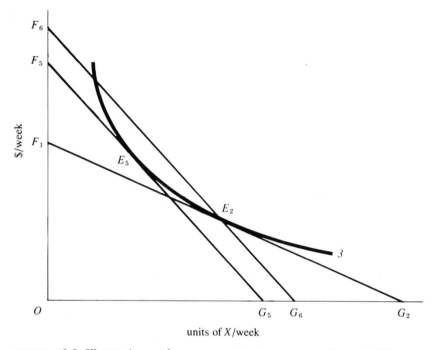

FIGURE 6.5 *Illustration of compensating-income and cost-difference methods of estimating the difference between the consumer's cost of living in two price situations*

the line F_5G_5, it would cost the individual more money to reach indifference curve *3*. With the higher price equal to the numerical value of the slope of the line F_5G_5, his money income would have to be OF_5 per week to enable him to achieve this level of satisfaction.

The ratio of OF_5 to OF_1 (multiplied by 100) is thus the cost-of-living index for this individual when the price is increased. If it is desired to protect this individual's 'standard of living'—i.e. to adjust his money income to enable him to maintain the same level of utility even though the price of commodity X is higher—then an additional F_1F_5 per week should be paid to him.

The practical application of this principle is hampered by lack of information on the indifference curves of individuals. In the absence of this knowledge there is no way of calculating precisely the ratio of OF_5 to OF_1. In lieu of such a calculation, the costs of purchasing a basket at the two sets of prices are often compared and used to estimate this ratio. The cost of purchasing the initial basket of goods shown by point E_2, when the price is increased to OF_5/OG_5 (= OF_6/OG_6), is equal to OF_6. The *fixed-basket* price index, which is obtained by comparing the cost of purchasing a given basket of goods at two sets of prices, is equal to OF_6/OF_1 (multiplied by 100). An adjustment of the individual's income by this factor will over-compensate for the increase in price. F_1F_6 is the cost-difference of the price increase, which is always greater, as we saw in the previous section, than the compensating-income variation.

With the lower price situation as a reference point, employment of a fixed-basket price index overestimates the extent to which the individual's cost of living is higher when prices are generally increasing. It does not allow for the substitution between commodities that will occur in the consumer's chosen basket because of changes in relative prices. It is left as an exercise for the reader to show that the decrease in the cost of living is underestimated by this index when the price is decreasing over time and the basket chosen at the higher price is used to calculate the index. (Hint: When the price is decreased, the cost-difference is smaller than the compensating-income variation.)

6.6 Price indexes over periods of time

Price indexes are usually constructed to compare changes in the cost of living over time. If the basket purchased in the earlier time period is used to construct the index, it is called a *Laspeyres index*. The bias in this type of index can be deduced from our discussion in the preceding section. If prices have been generally increasing over time but at different rates so that relative prices have also changed, then such an index overestimates the increase in the cost of living. Individuals would respond to the changes in relative prices by substituting goods whose relative prices have fallen. A different combination of goods would be purchased to achieve the initial level of satisfaction and its cost would be increased by *less* than the cost of the initial basket. Conversely, if prices are generally decreasing, then the Laspeyres index underestimates the decreases that have occurred in the cost of living. The changes in relative prices would again lead individuals to purchase baskets of goods that contained relatively more of the goods whose prices have decreased at a faster rate. They would achieve the initial level of satisfaction with a combination of goods whose cost had decreased by more than the cost of the initial basket of goods.

The analysis of cost-of-living indexes in Section 6.5, which was based on an assumption of fixed tastes, might not be realistic when different time periods are considered. If the individual's tastes have changed over the time periods covered by the comparison, then of course the statements made about the bias in these indexes (as estimates of changes in the cost of living) need not apply. To take an extreme example: if an individual's cost of living goes up even though prices are generally lower in the later period, this could be because his tastes have changed and the higher-priced commodities now appear more desirable to him and the lower-priced ones less so.[1]

If the basket purchased in the current period is used to construct the index, it is called a *Paasche index.* Its value is equal to the ratio of the present cost of this basket to its cost at the prices of some earlier period (multiplied by 100). The biases with this index are the reverse of those with a Laspeyres index. The basket currently being purchased reflects present prices. If prices have been generally increasing (but with some differences in the rates of increase), then the comparison of the cost of this basket at present prices and its cost at the prices prevailing in some earlier period would understate the increase in the cost of living. Conversely, with generally falling prices the Paasche index exaggerates the decrease in the price level.

6.7 The Consumer Price Index

Movements in price indexes are well publicized when prices are increasing. One index that receives special attention is the Consumer Price Index (CPI), which is often used to adjust money-wage rates and pension payments. It is a Laspeyres-type index. The fixed basket whose changing cost is calculated is obtained from a survey of expenditures of a target group of families in a base year. These families satisfy certain size and income constraints and are located in specific geographical locations. The reference dates for prices and quantities purchased may differ—e.g. for Canada the price reference date for the CPI is now 1971—but the quantities in the basket are based on purchases in 1967. In that year the target group of families for the Canadian CPI lived in cities with populations of 30,000 or more, had family sizes from two to six persons and an annual income in 1967 in the \$4,000-to-\$12,000 range.[2]

In the above discussion of the Laspeyres index it was pointed out that the index would lead to an overestimation of the increase in an individual's cost of living. This result followed from the definition of the index; the assumption of the same tastes for the individual in the two price situations;

---

[1] In order to calculate a fixed basket index it is necessary to obtain prices for the same commodities in the time periods being compared. Because of changes in the types and qualities of commodities purchased, price statisticians face many problems in obtaining comparable price series over time to construct their indexes. They make use of various devices to adjust for changes in the availability of commodities. See Ethel D. Hoover, 'The CPI and Problems of Quality Change', *Monthly Labor Review* (November 1961), pp. 1175-81.

[2] *The Consumer Price Index for Canada (1971=100).* Revision based on 1967 expenditures, 62-539. (Ottawa: Statistics Canada, June 1973.)

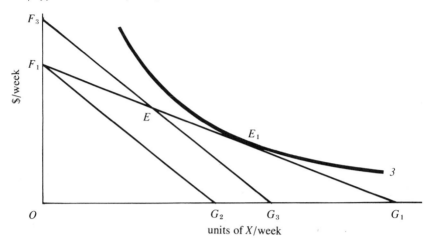

FIGURE 6.6 *Illustration of bias in the estimated change in an individual's cost of living, in a specified period, if a basket of goods relating to a group's purchases is used for the index*

and the convexity of indifference curves. If the individual consumer's income were adjusted by this index, we would say that he had been over-compensated for the higher price. However, if the Laspeyres index is based on the average purchases made by a *group*, adjustment of this particular individual's income by the index value may result in his being insufficiently compensated for the higher price. This could occur if his tastes differ from the average for the group. In Figure 6.6, point E_1 represents the equilibrium position for the individual in the base period, while point E represents the average basket of goods purchased by the target group for the Laspeyres index. The individual has a stronger preference for commodity X. The value for this index, when the price in the later period is equal to the slope of the line F_1G_2, is OF_3/OF_1 (multiplied by 100). It is clear from Figure 6.6 that since F_3G_3 lies everywhere below indifference curve *3*, the adjustment of this individual's income by this index will only partially compensate him for the higher price in the later period.

6.8 Definition of substitutes and complements

The cross-elasticity of demand presented in Section 2.15 has been used to define *substitutes* and *complements*. According to this criterion, two goods are said to be complements if the relative difference in the quantity demanded of one good divided by the relative difference in the price of the other (all other prices being the same) is negative. They are said to be substitutes if this cross-elasticity of demand is positive. These definitions of substitutability and complementarity can be called *gross* definitions because they involve income as well as substitution effects. Goods that are classified according to these definitions can thus be called *gross substitutes* or *gross complements*. Alternatively the definitions of substitutability and complementarity may consider the effects on the quantity demanded only after allowance has been made for the compensating-income variation of the price change. They can then be called *net price* definitions.

Two goods are said to be *net price substitutes* if a lower price for one good will, after suitable variations in money income to allow the consumer to reach the same level of satisfaction, result in a lower demand for the other good. (The reader should satisfy himself that if there are only two goods, and there is some degree of curvature to the indifference curve and the initial equilibrium position is one where both goods are consumed, these two goods must be substitutes.) Two goods are said to be *net price complements* if a lower price for one good will, after suitable variations in money income to allow the consumer to reach the same level of satisfaction, result in a higher demand for the other.

The data that is available to economists often relates to situations where there are price differences without suitable income differences. In such cases use is made of the cross-elasticity of demand to distinguish between substitutes and complements. The classifications obtained from the two sets of definitions may differ. For example, good X may be a substitute for good Y according to the *net* price definition but be a complement under the *gross* price definition. The cross-elasticity of demand for X with respect to Y may be negative because good X is a superior good and the income effect of a lower price for Y (increasing the demand for X) outweighs the substitution effect of this difference on the demand for X.

6.9 Edgeworth-box diagrams and the gains from exchange

The potential for gains from the exchange of a fixed endowment of goods can be shown by indifference curves when they are arranged in what is called an *Edgeworth-box diagram*. The size of the diagram illustrated in Figure 6.7 is determined by the amounts of the commodities jointly held by the two traders. The quantity of commodity X held by individual A is shown by the distance to the right of O_A and his holdings of Y by the distance above O_A. Individual B's holdings of X are shown by the distance to the left of O_B and his holdings of Y by the distance below O_B. It is assumed that in the absence of trade the two individuals would be at point C in the lower-right-hand corner of this box, with A having only X and B only Y.

Both individuals can improve their positions—i.e. reach higher levels of

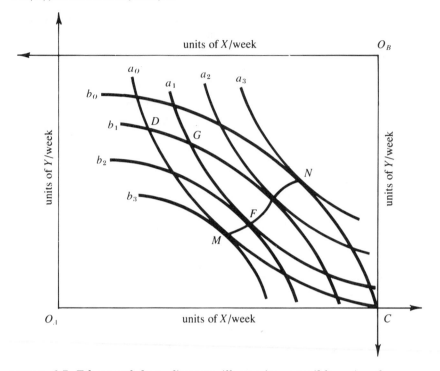

FIGURE 6.7 *Edgeworth-box diagram illustrating possible gains from exchange when there are two traders in the market (bilateral exchange or monopoly) in a specific period*

utility—if they trade some of their commodity for the other good. The pre-trade levels of utility are represented by the indifference curves a_o and b_o, and any trade that takes them into the area enclosed by these curves will be advantageous to both. Exchanges that place the two individuals·in positions such as G, where indifference curves for both intersect, can be shown to be non-optimal. They could be made better off by moving to some other point. For example, both individuals would be better off than at G if the exchange placed them inside the area enclosed by the two indifference curves that intersect at G. Points such as F, where the indifference curves are tangent, represent optimal exchange in the sense that it is not possible to improve the level of utility of one of the market participants without loss to the other. The curve MN, joining all points with this property in Figure 6.7, is called a *contract curve*.

The closer the trading position to point M, the greater individual B's share of the fruits of the exchange. On the basis of the information given in

Figure 6.7, it is not possible to predict the terms of the exchange when there are only two traders, one on each side of the market. This market situation is one of *bilateral monopoly*. The bargaining strengths and skills of the two participants will play a role in determining their final positions, which may lie on the contract curve. A necessary condition for this to happen is that the utility functions of the two individuals be independent, meaning that each individual's level of satisfaction depends only on the goods he consumes. An individual would thus be prepared, after due consideration was given to maintaining his bargaining position, to allow changes in tentative terms of trade that improved the position of the other, as long as the goods he would acquire at least maintained his level of utility.

6.10 Edgeworth-box diagrams and competitive equilibrium

An Edgeworth-box diagram can also be used to show the equilibrium position, under certain assumptions, if the market considered is perfectly competitive. In Figure 6.8 there are large (and equal) numbers of individuals with initial endowments of commodities X and Y. All those with X have identical tastes and the same endowments (they are called A-individuals). Similarly all those with endowments of Y have identical tastes and endowments (they are called B-individuals). The total amount of X available per week in the period is equal to $O_A C$ units, and the total amount of Y per week is equal to $O_B C$ units. Figure 6.8 shows some of the indifference curves for the two sets of individuals.

In this market the individual does not consider that he can have any effect on the market price. He will determine his transactions—the amount of X he will offer in exchange for a unit of Y—in light of the ruling terms of trade between the two commodities. CA is the offer curve for the A-individuals. It shows the amounts of commodity X they would exchange for the indicated quantities of Y at different terms of trade between the two. For example, if the price of X in terms of Y is given by the numerical value of the slope of the line CT_1, then the A-individuals would be prepared to give up CF_1 units of X in order to obtain CG_1 units of Y. The offer curve, CB, for the B-individuals is defined in a similar manner. The equilibrium position, where these offers are consistent, is determined by the intersection of the two offer curves, which must intersect on the contract curve MN, since at their point of intersection an indifference curve for each group must be tangent to the price line that goes through this point. The two indifference curves must therefore be tangent to each other at this point. The equilibrium position in Figure 6.8 is at point E and the equilibrium terms of trade are given by the slope of the line CT_e.

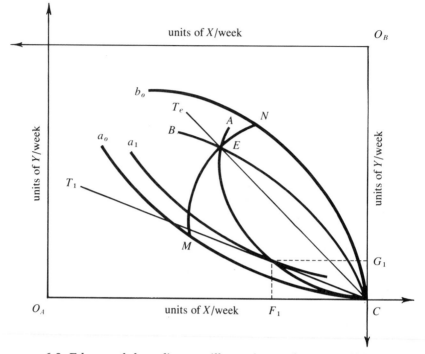

FIGURE 6.8 *Edgeworth-box diagram illustrating exchange equilibrium in a perfectly competitive market in a specific period*

6.11 Monopoly and non-optimality in exchange

An Edgeworth-box diagram can also be used to show that the formation of a monopoly on one side of the market will lead to an equilibrium position that is not on the contract curve. Not only does the group that acts as a monopolist gain at the expense of the group acting independently, but there is also an *efficiency loss*. This means that the equilibrium position is non-optimal and that it would be possible to find, under different arrangements, a position in which both groups would be better off.

To illustrate this point, assume that all the B-individuals act as a group. This is equivalent to assuming that there is a monopolist controlling commodity Y who faces a large number of identical individuals who sell X and purchase Y and act independently on the basis of whatever market price is facing them. Their market responses to different prices are shown by the A-offer curve in Figure 6.8, which is also reproduced in Figure 6.9. If it is assumed that the monopolist knows the position of this curve, then it is possible to determine the terms of trade that will maximize his utility in the given situation. His best position is at point K in Figure 6.9, the point of tangency of A's offer curve and a B indifference curve, and the terms of

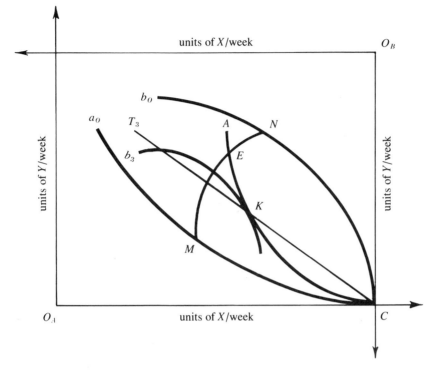

FIGURE 6.9 *Edgeworth-box diagram illustrating exchange equilibrium, in a specific period, in a market controlled by a monopolist*

trade set by the monopolist are equal to the slope of the line CT_3. The level of utility for an A-individual is higher at K than it would be in the absence of trade, but it is lower than the level of utility he could reach in a perfectly competitive market (that is, at point E). B-individuals have improved their positions by acting together as though they were a monopolist at the expense of those on the competitive side of the market. There has also been an efficiency loss. Point K is not on the contract curve, and points could be found at which both A and B could be better off.

6.12 Consumer's surplus

As we saw in Section 6.9, exchange between individuals makes it possible for them to reach higher levels of utility. The concept of *consumer's surplus* has been introduced to indicate a consumer's gain from the availability of a commodity on specified terms.

Alfred Marshall illustrated the concept of consumer's surplus by comparing the individual's marginal demand price for different quantities with

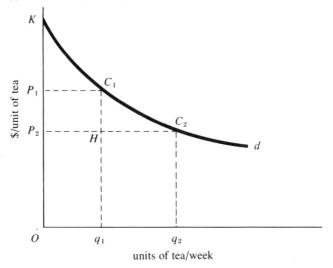

FIGURE 6.10 *Individual's demand curve for tea in a specific period*

the market price at which he could purchase tea.[3] The values in Table 5.1 (Section 5.5) will be used to demonstrate his approach. This individual would be prepared to pay up to $2.50 per quarter-pound of tea for the first quarter-pound, up to $2.00 for the second, up to $1.40 for the third, up to $0.90 for the fourth, and up to $0.60 for the fifth. With a market price of $0.60 he would be in equilibrium purchasing five quarter-pound units of tea. He would pay the same price for all five units even though he would have been prepared to pay higher prices for all but the last unit. He would have been prepared to pay $2.50 for the first unit; thus his gain, or con-sumer's surplus, from paying $0.60 for it would be the equivalent of $1.90. The money estimates of his gains from the other three units would be $1.40, $0.80, and $0.30. The total money measure of his consumer's surplus from being able to buy tea at $0.60 per quarter-pound would thus be $4.40 per week.

Marshall further indicated how an estimate can be obtained geometrically from the demand curve. Consider an individual's demand curve for tea, as drawn in Figure 6.10. Assume that his expenditure for tea accounts for only a small proportion of the total consumer's income. (The difference in his marginal utility of income when he purchases tea at different prices can thus be ignored.) At a price of OP_1, he would purchase Oq_1 units of tea at a total cost of $\$OP_1C_1q_1$. As we saw in Section 5.5, when the demand curve was derived following Marshall's method, each point on this curve indicates the

---

[3] Alfred Marshall, *Principles of Economics* (8th ed.; London: Macmillan & Co., 1920), p. 125.

money-measure of the expected addition to total utility from the consumption of that unit of the commodity. The addition of all these expected increments to total utility for Oq_1 units of tea provides a money-measure of the expected utility from the consumption of this quantity of tea. This money-measure exceeds the cost to the individual of his purchase by an amount equal to the area P_1KC_1. This is a money-measure of the consumer's surplus arising from the opportunity of purchasing tea at a price of OP_1.

It is also possible to estimate in this way the gain in utility of being able to trade at a price lower than OP_1. For example, assume that the price is lowered to OP_2. A money-measure of the utility obtained by consuming Oq_2 of tea is $\$OKC_2q_2$. The net gain when the consumer can purchase this quantity at a price of $\$OP_2$ per unit is $\$P_2KC_2$. The corresponding gain when he is purchasing Oq_1 units at a price of $\$OP_1$ is $\$P_1KC_1$. The consumer's surplus, arising from the opportunity to buy at the lower price, is thus equal to the area $\$P_2P_1C_1C_2$ ($= \$P_2KC_2 - \$P_1KC_1$).

This Marshallian method of estimating consumer's surplus is based on the quantity the individual would purchase at the market price with his money income. Two other estimates can be obtained using the compensating and equivalent-income variations. The 'compensating' estimate is the maximum sum the individual would be prepared to pay for the option of purchasing the good at the market price. The 'equivalent' estimate is the

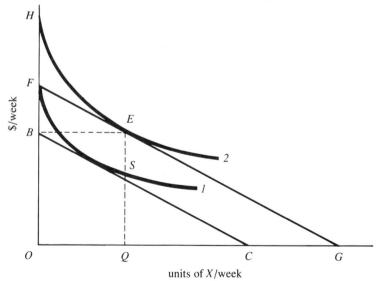

FIGURE 6.11 *Indifference curves illustrating three ways of estimating consumer's surplus*

sum the individual would consider equivalent to the opportunity of purchasing the good at the market price. These two estimates, along with Marshall's, are illustrated by the indifference curves in Figure 6.11.

With a money income of $OF per week and a market price of $OF/OG, the individual would be at equilibrium at point E on indifference curve 2. If this good were not available he would be at point F on indifference curve 1. This individual would be just as well off at point S on indifference curve 1, where he is paying an additional $SE for the OQ units of X. Marshall's estimate of consumer's surplus is $SE per week. The compensating income estimate is $BF per week, which is greater than Marshall's estimate because the individual is not constrained to purchase OQ units. A payment of $FH per week would be equivalent to the opportunity of purchasing X with the budget line FG.[4]

Consumers' surplus is an interesting and deceptively simple concept. From the advantages of exchange, it follows that the total amount consumers pay for a good is not a measure of the total utility they expect to derive from its consumption. It is tempting to try to build on this insight and to obtain an estimate of the benefits that will accrue to consumers as a group from the availability of a particular good. Such an estimate could then be compared with the costs of providing the good. Estimates of total consumers' surplus are obtained by calculating the appropriate areas from market demand curves along the lines indicated by our measures for consumer's surplus in Figure 6.10.

The idea of consumers' surplus was first introduced in 1844 by a French engineer, Jules Dupuit, who wanted to estimate the benefits derived from bridges,[5] and it is an important element in present-day studies of the costs and benefits of projects such as the building of highways, bridges, the provision of recreational facilities, etc. However, there are many problems to be faced in estimating consumers' surplus in any practical application. The aggregate demand curve must be estimated, and strictly speaking the use of the area under a market demand curve for the estimation of consumers' surplus requires the assumption that the same sum of money represents the same utility for all individuals whose demands contribute to this curve. Since Marshall's time at least, economists have been aware that

---

[4] In this case, since the good is a superior good, the equivalent income estimate of consumer's surplus, FH, is greater than the compensating income estimate, BF. For inferior goods the compensating income estimate is greater than the equivalent income estimate. E.J. Mishan, *Cost-Benefit Analysis* (2nd ed.; London: George Allen & Unwin, 1975), pp. 416-19.

[5] Jules Dupuit, 'De la mesure de l'utilité des travaux publics', *Annales des Ponts et Chaussées* (2nd series, VIII, 1844). Translated by R.H. Barback as 'On the Measurement of the Utility of Public Works', *International Economic Papers*, Vol. 2 (1952), pp. 83-110.

'the same sum of money represents different amounts of pleasure to different people.'[6] But they tend to follow Marshall in according equal utility significance to equal sums of money. Marshall justified this practice with this statement: 'On the whole however it happens that by far the greater number of the events with which economics deals, affect in about equal proportions all the different classes of society; so that if the money measures of the happiness caused by two events are equal, there is not in general any very great difference between the amounts of the happiness in the two cases.'[7]

6.13 Summary

This chapter has examined some of the applications of utility analysis. A cost-of-living index was defined and compared with the fixed-basket indexes that can be calculated from available data. Indifference curves were used to indicate the gains from exchange, and the Edgeworth-box diagrams employed for this purpose showed how a monopolist would likely improve his position if he were facing a large number of buyers. Consumers' surplus estimates the money value of the availability of a good and is an important element in cost-benefit studies.

SUGGESTED READINGS

Marshall, Alfred. *Principles of Economics*. 8th ed. London: Macmillan & Co., 1920. Book III, Chapter VI.

Mishan, E.J. *Cost-Benefit Analysis*. 2nd ed. London: George Allen & Unwin, 1975. Chapter 7.

Vickrey, W.S. *Microstatics*. New York: Harcourt, Brace & World, 1964. Chapter 3.

---

[6] Marshall, *Principles of Economics*, p. 128.
[7] *Ibid.*, p. 131.

7

THE THEORY OF PRODUCTION

7.1 Introduction

The theory of production plays a key role in economic analysis. It is important in considering possibilities for economic growth; it provides the basis for most theories of distribution; and it is used in the derivation of cost curves. Production can be viewed as dealing with the technical relations between inputs and outputs. The term can also be used in a broader sense to cover the social relations of production; that is, the relations between the groups involved in production. In a capitalist economy the two main groups are capitalists and workers. In this chapter the term 'production' will be used in the narrower sense of the technical relations between physical inputs and outputs. Attention will be focused on providing a basis for the derivation of cost curves for individual units of production.

Production can be represented as a relationship between flows of outputs (i.e. rates of output of particular commodities) and flows of inputs (i.e. rates of input of particular elements of production) during a specified period. This relationship is a technical one between *physical quantities* of different items per unit of time. The values obtained for the rates of outputs, given the rates of inputs, depend on the technical characteristics of the inputs and outputs; the operating knowledge of those directing the production activity; and the extent to which that knowledge is reflected in the rates of outputs.

Two approaches to production will be discussed. The first is based on assumptions that are consistent with empirical estimates of cost curves. The second is the standard neoclassical approach, which is an important element in the neoclassical theory of distribution. This approach is more formal and emphasizes the substitutability between inputs; however, at crucial points in the analysis it treats as physical quantities items that can be aggregated only in value terms.

156

7.2 Elements and factors of production

The production of a commodity requires contributions from elements of production. Economists often classify these elements into three categories, each of which is called a *factor of production*. They are land, labour, and capital. *Land* includes all elements of production that are a gift of nature, such as the earth's surface, air, rain, and natural resources. The *labour* category includes the mental and physical efforts of human beings in productive activities. The term *capital* is used to cover all the produced elements of production; it includes capital equipment of all kinds, work in progress, and raw materials that have been produced, etc. Capital differs from land and labour in that it is produced in response to purely economic motives, while land cannot be produced and the supply of labour depends on the size of the population, which is affected by social and economic factors. The various capital items can be bought and sold and used in whatever ways seem appropriate to those owning them, but labour itself cannot (in a non-slave society) be bought and sold in the manner of capital goods, even though labour services can be hired.

There are cases where the distinction between these three factors tends to become blurred. For example, land on which crops are grown is not only a gift of nature but is also partly a produced means of production: before it can be used for production, the land has to be prepared in various ways— cleared and drained, for example. Some of the mental and physical abilities of human beings have also been produced, as a result of education and training. The term *human capital* is sometimes employed to emphasize the produced nature of human elements of production.

7.3 Production and time

The measure of the required time of production for a particular commodity depends on what is taken to be the beginning and the end of the production process. The beginning occurs when the transformation of inputs in the producing unit (the plant) begins; the end is when the commodity moves from the plant to the purchaser.[1]

---

[1] Some of these inputs are themselves part of the outputs of other production processes, and the time of production may be extended to include the time required to produce them as well, and then the time required to produce their inputs, etc. The time measure of production obtained in this way is called the *period of production*. This term is associated with the Austrian economist E. von Böhm-Bawerk (1851-1914). It was introduced to emphasize the role of time in capitalist production and to indicate the degrees of capital-intensity of different methods of production. The term *time of production* (or production period) used here differs from the Böhm-Bawerkian period of production. The former deals only with the time required for the completion of a specific production process in a plant that results in an article that is available for sale.

The time of production for a commodity produced by an industrial process will thus be related to the operation of a plant that is suitable for its production. For agricultural commodities, this time of production is determined by climatic conditions: it is equal in length to the time required to grow the crop, with given land, seeds, fertilizers, agricultural implements, and labour.

7.4 Production functions

The rates of output of the products (and waste) over their time of production depend on the rates of the inputs of all the elements of production. This technical relationship, when presented in functional form for a given state of technology, is called a *production function*. It can be written as the function H connecting inputs and outputs,

$$Q + W = H(G, I, M; L, R, \bar{K})$$

The letters represent the vectors of values for specified types of inflows or outflows over the time of production at the completion of the production process. Q is the commodity level of output; W stands for the waste products emanating from the production process (part of the output along with the desired products); the elements of production that are transformed in the production process either come from nature and are represented by G (e.g. air, water, space for buildings) or are the outputs of other production processes and are represented by I; M represents the inflows of elements that are used for maintenance of capital equipment. Inputs that reappear at the end of the production process essentially unchanged are L, labour; R, land; and $\bar{K}$, capital equipment (buildings as well as machines). Many elements of production may be represented by each of these symbols. Two examples follow: if more than one commodity is produced, the rates of output of all the commodities are denoted by the elements in the vector Q; if many different types of labour are employed, they are all represented by L.[2]

It is customary in economic theory to make use of a less general form of the production function than the one presented above. Inputs obtained from nature without cost, and the output of waste, are usually ignored; these factors are sometimes treated separately under the heading of *externalities*. (See Section 7.21.) It is this more restricted form of the production function that will be examined in this chapter and will subsequently provide the basis for the discussion of plant cost curves. The restricted function is a partial statement of the production process, however, and the general form of the production function is required for an

---

[2] This presentation of the production function is based on Nicholas Georgescu-Roegen, 'The Economics of Production', *American Economic Review*, Vol. 60 (May 1970), pp. 1-9.

understanding of important policy issues such as pollution. Before proceeding with our examination of the production function, the concept of the Marshallian short period, the basic unit of time in our discussion of production, must be introduced.

7.5 The short period

The *Marshallian short period* is a period of time in which the *plant* used for production can be assumed to be fixed, even though the demand for the plant's services may change. By 'plant' we mean the buildings or area in which productive activity is carried on, and it includes as well most items of capital equipment and some of the labour inputs involved in managerial, supervisory, and maintenance tasks.[3] The plant that is available to the firm for production, in a particular short period, is the result of investment decisions made and carried out some time in the past. The rates of output from the given plant can be altered by varying the rates of employment of elements of production—such as production workers, raw materials, and energy—whose availability to the firm in this short period is not completely determined by decisions and commitments made in the past.

For many purposes it is useful, and not unrealistic, to assume that there is an upper limit to the possible rates of output from a particular plant. This maximum rate is called the *capacity rate*, and output in any period is often reported as a percentage of the capacity rate of output.[4] It is determined by the nature and quantities of the elements of production and the state of technical knowledge. The capacity rate of output is not necessarily the maximum that is physically possible from the plant; but it is the highest rate that can be produced, using standard operating procedures, at average costs that are not much higher than those for lower rates of output.[5]

---

[3] Alfred Marshall wrote: 'To sum up then as regards short periods. The supply of specialized skill and ability, of suitable machinery and other material capital, and of the appropriate industrial organization has not time to be fully adapted to demand; but the producers have to adjust their supply to the demand as best they can with the appliances already at their disposal.' *Principles of Economics* (8th ed.; London: Macmillan & Co., 1920), p. 376.

[4] For example, production in the primary aluminum industry in the United States in the spring of 1975 was reported as being about 75 per cent of capacity. Council of Wage and Price Stability, Staff Report, *Aluminum Prices 1974-75* (Washington, D.C., Sept. 1976), p. 121.

[5] 'Businessmen generally seem to think of plant capacity with full-crew operations at some given standard, usually a level of achievement attained a number of times in the past and somewhat short of maximum conceivable output under ideal conditions with full-crew operations. It is the output for which the plant and equipment were designed, assuming some "normal" rate of efficiency and the regular number of shifts. That is the concept used here. Admittedly it is not as exact as one would desire. Presumably plant capacity so defined would vary somewhat with operating conditions such as the quality of materials, the product mix, and the extent to which maintenance is temporarily deferred.' Richard A. Lester, 'Equilibrium of the Firm', *American Economic Review*, Vol. 39 (March 1949), p. 478, n. 3.

The short period is defined analytically as the period that is so short that changes in the plant or in its productive capacity would be very small and can be neglected; yet it is long enough that output from the plant can be varied in response to changes in demand. It is these features rather than any definite period of time that distinguish a short period. The length of actual time represented by this analytically defined short period depends on the amount of time required to change significantly the productive capacity of the unit being analysed. With this information it is possible to give the short period an actual time dimension—e.g. a month, a quarter of a year, etc.—in which production and changes in production rates can occur. Marshall gives 'a few months or a year' to indicate the length of time he thought was involved in the concept of a short period.[6]

7.6 Variation of the rate of output in a short period

With the time span of a Marshallian short period a firm may, as we saw above, change the degree of utilization of its plant by varying the employment of some of the elements of production. (The maximum degree of utilization is reached when the plant is operated at full capacity.) The interval of time required to change the rates of input of the variable elements of production is thus relevant for production decisions.

Keynes uses the term *daily* to stand for the shortest interval of time after which the firm is free to revise its decisions about the degree of utilization of its plant. He calls this 'the minimum effective unit of economic time'.[7] Here, as with the short period, the length of time covered by the term 'daily' depends on particular circumstances. The nature of the capital equipment may affect the time required to vary the degree of utilization; blast furnaces, for example, cannot be brought into or taken out of production very readily. Trade-union agreements and government legislation may also affect the time required before employment may be decreased. But even with these complications, the concept of some minimum time required to vary the degree of utilization of a given plant is a useful one. In general, this minimum unit of time is shorter than a 'short period'; it takes less time to change the degree of utilization of a plant than to change its capacity.

The minimum interval of time required for a change in the rate of output will be called a *week* throughout this book. The production rates to be presented and compared will thus be the average weekly rates of output over particular short periods. Similarly, the quantities of the variable inputs of

---

[6] Marshall, *Principles of Economics*, p. 379.
[7] John Maynard Keynes, *The General Theory of Employment, Interest and Money* (London: Macmillan & Co., 1936), p. 47, n. 1.

production will be the average weekly rates of their employment in the production process.

7.7 The short-period production function

The short-period production function for a particular commodity expresses the technical relationship between the rate of output and the rates of input of the variable elements of production, given the size of the plant and technical knowledge. This function can be indicated by

$$x = f(v_1, v_2, \ldots, v_n; \overline{K})$$

In this expression, x is the weekly rate of output of commodity X in the specified short period; v_i ($i = 1, 2, \ldots n$) is the weekly rate of input of the *ith* element of production (e.g. a particular raw material of specified quality, or a particular type of labour) in that period; $\overline{K}$ is a *vector* whose elements represent the values for items of equipment, buildings, supervisory or other kinds of fixed labour input (that is, $\overline{K}$ indicates all the elements of the given plant). Each unit of a particular variable productive element, V_i, is assumed to have fixed technical characteristics and to be physically homogeneous. Its rate of input can be expressed in physical units (e.g. weight or volume) per week. The symbol $\overline{K}$ represents many heterogeneous elements and cannot be expressed in such a simple fashion.

The production function is anchored to a particular technology, which is reflected in the technical characteristics of the plant and in the way it is operated in the specified time period. This function specifies the maximum rate of output that can be obtained in a given period from any specified rates of input for the variable elements of production; that is, production is assumed to be technically efficient.[8] Technical efficiency can also be expressed in terms of the rates of input required to produce a particular rate of output. Production is technically efficient if it is not possible to produce the specified rate of output with less of any one of the inputs, given the values for the others.

It should be noted that the assumption of given technical knowledge in the statement of a production function may be mistaken because the operating knowledge of those employed in a plant may be increased by their experience of producing this particular type of product. Improved technical knowledge is often obtained through experience, or 'learning by doing'. Learning by doing has been observed when firms start producing new

---

[8] Harvey Leibenstein—in 'Allocative Efficiency vs. "X-Efficiency"', *American Economic Review*, Vol. 56 (June 1966), pp. 392-415—has argued that empirical studies often show that production is *not* technically efficient.

products or when they operate new plants. After they have produced the first units, they are able to reduce the time required for production and thus reduce their direct unit costs. A 'learning curve' that estimates the effect on efficiency of total experienced output has been estimated for the Airframe Industry.[9] In certain cases it has been found that the direct cost of the *2nth* item is 80 per cent of the cost of the *nth* item. Thus the direct cost of the 20th airframe of a particular design would be 80 per cent of the direct cost of the 10th airframe. In the following analysis, however, we will make the standard assumption that production functions are based on a given state of technical knowledge.

7.8 The services obtained from a plant in the short period

Although the size of the plant is fixed in the short period, the *services* provided by the plant depend on the rates of input of the variable elements of production. For example, a particular machine may be capable of operating at a constant level of efficiency for twenty-four hours a day, thirty days at a time, before requiring a day's maintenance. But this machine may be operated only 40 hours a week if the plant is worked on a single-shift basis for five days a week. Overtime operation of the plant, or the introduction of a second shift, would obviously increase the services provided by the machine in the short period. The production function, whose functional form depends on technology and the technical charac-teristics of all the elements that make up the fixed plant, thus indicates what the plant is capable of producing. What is actually produced depends on its *degree of utilization*, and this is determined by the rates of input of the variable elements of production.

Another aspect of the services that can be obtained from a given plant can be illustrated by considering the two general ways in which production may be organized. Production processes may be handled *in line*, as in a factory, with the processes started at different times being in various stages of completion at a given time. Alternatively they may be handled *in parallel*, with the different processes all starting at about the same time. All would be roughly at the same stage of completion at a given time, as in agricultural production where climatic conditions do not permit factory methods of operation in most lines of output. (However, factory methods have been introduced in some areas—for example, in the production of broiler chickens and eggs.) Production in line makes it possible to increase the amount of services obtained from equipment. If a particular item of capital

[9] H. Asher, *Cost-Quantity Relationships in the Airframe Industry*, R-291 (Santa Monica, Calif.: The RAND Corporation, 1956).

equipment (a plough, for example) is required only at a particular stage of the production process, then it must be idle a large part of the time when the production processes are handled in parallel. In a factory, on the other hand, since the stage of production in which a particular item of capital equipment is required keeps reappearing, the time during which it is idle can be substantially reduced.

7.9 The short-period marginal product of labour

Many of the variable inputs are complements within the given plant in any particular short period; that is, an increase in the rate of output generally requires an increase in the rates of input of the other variable inputs, as well as an increase in the rate of input of labour. Whenever attention is focused on the relationship between changes in output and changes in the input of labour, estimates of labour productivity are obtained that reflect the effects of changes in the input not only of labour but of other elements of production, such as raw materials, machine services, electricity, etc. We shall define the *short-period marginal product of labour* as the difference in the rate of output due to a small increase in the rate of input of labour *and* its co-operating inputs.[10]

Any particular plant usually employs different kinds of labour, with different degrees of skill and specialization. The heterogeneity of labour means that all measures of labour productivity must use index-number measures for the input of labour.[11] Relative wage rates are generally used to obtain a measure of total employment from data on the rates of input of different types of labour.[12] Workers in a plant may be divided into two broad categories according to their roles within a plant: direct production workers, whose employment varies with the planned rate of production, and those who are only indirectly involved with production and are considered to be overhead labour. The distribution of labour between these two categories depends on the nature of the product and the plant and on the

---

[10] In Section 7.13 this short-period marginal product of labour is distinguished from the marginal product concept used in neoclassical analysis, which is concerned with the difference in the rate of output when *only* the rate of input of one element of production is higher.

[11] Output from a plant is often heterogeneous, and index-number measures must thus be used for output as well.

[12] This approach was followed by Keynes in order to define 'the quantity of employment'. 'For, in so far as different grades and kinds of labour and salaried assistance enjoy a more or less fixed relative remuneration, the quantity of employment can be sufficiently defined for our purpose by taking an hour's employment of ordinary labour as our unit and weighting an hour's employment of special labour in proportion to its remuneration; i.e. an hour of special labour remunerated at double ordinary rates will count as two units.' *The General Theory of Employment, Interest and Money*, p. 41.

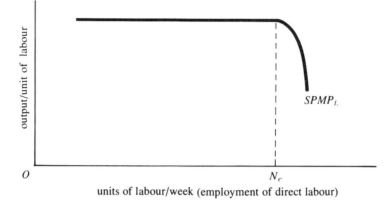

FIGURE 7.1 *Short-period marginal product of labour in a particular plant*

rate of utilization of the plant.[13] If the output per unit of direct labour is constant for rates of output up to normal productive capacity, then the short-period marginal product of labour will follow the curve shown in Figure 7.1. Normal productive capacity is reached when the weekly employment of direct labour is equal to ON_c. The results obtained from empirical estimates of cost curves are consistent with the assumption of a constant short-period marginal product of labour, since they often report constant marginal costs for output up to productive capacity.[14]

It has been suggested that the short-period marginal product of labour increases up to capacity. Richard A. Lester has noted that 'Plants are ordinarily designed and equipped so that at (or possibly even slightly above) capacity operations there should exist the most efficient flow of materials,

---

[13] This distinction between direct production and overhead labour is often noted in empirical studies. It has also been argued that ' . . . a very large, and rapidly growing, proportion of employment is overhead employment. In manufacturing, for example, the proportion of total employees classified as "nonproduction" workers has risen from 16 per cent in 1947 to 26 per cent in 1962.' Charles L. Schultze, 'Uses of Capacity Measures for Short-run Economic Analysis', *American Economic Review*, Vol. 53 (May 1963), p. 302. The dependence of overhead employment on the structure of the plant is conveyed in the following statement made by Lynn Townsend, Chairman of the Board of Chrysler. Townsend was commenting on the need to reduce his company's overhead in the wake of the sharp reduction in automobile sales in late 1974. 'He said most of the reductions would come in the fixed cost category involving such positions as foremen, supervisors and factory managers. "They're in the plant that day whether the plant builds 300 cars or 600 cars, and it is this overhead that we are working structurally on reducing."' *New York Times*, Jan. 14, 1975.

[14] Marginal cost is the increase in total cost due to the unit increase in output (see Section 8.4). The findings from a large number of studies of cost functions are summarized in Edwin Mansfield, *Microeconomics: Theory and Applications* (2nd ed.; New York: W.W. Norton & Co., 1975), pp. 188-90. Mansfield notes that these studies find short-period marginal cost to be constant in the output ranges examined.

the most effective use of transport and other services, the best runs of a production item, and so forth. A general reduction in the scale of operations below capacity would usually mean more time on setup operations per unit of output with shorter runs, transfer and less effective distribution of personnel.'[15] Thus cyclical variations in the rate of output might lead to cyclical variations in labour productivity for this reason, or because overhead labour is included in the estimates of total labour inputs used to calculate productivity.[16] Since the employment of overhead labour is a constant in the short period, total labour productivity would increase with increases in output, even though the short-period marginal product curves were constant, as in Figure 7.1.

There is one further problem in using empirical estimates to infer the nature of the underlying production function. It relates to the difference between actual and equilibrium values. The curve drawn in Figure 7.1 is based on the assumption that the employment of direct labour is in the desired relationship to output; actual employment, however, may not be in the desired relation to actual output. The hiring and training of new workers is expensive, and it is in the firm's interest to retain a core of production workers in recessions, even though not all of them are needed to maintain the current rate of output.[17] The observed cyclical variations in labour productivity, therefore, might not be inconsistent with the short-period marginal product of labour curves of the type drawn in Figure 7.1, even if there is no overhead labour. Cost curves for plants with this characteristic will be examined in Section 8.4

7.10 Substitution between elements of production
The discussion of production in manufacturing plants has emphasized that many of the inputs are complementary, but this does not mean that the substitution of one input for another is not potentially important. Substitution is generally possible only after the passage of time, which allows for the construction and installation of new machinery, the training of workers, etc. The changes that permit substitution give rise to different

---

[15] Lester, 'Equilibrium of the Firm', pp. 478-9.
[16] Cyclical variations in labour productivity (increasing during a recovery period and falling during a contractionary period) have been widely observed. See, for example, U.S. Congress, Joint Economic Committee, *Profits, Profit Markups, and Productivity*, by Edwin Kuh, Study Paper No. 15, Study of Employment, Growth and Price Levels (Washington, D.C., 1960); and Edwin Kuh, 'Cyclical and Secular Labor Productivity in United States Manufacturing', *The Review of Economics and Statistics*, Vol. 47 (February 1965), pp. 1-12, and the references cited therein.
[17] Cf. Schultze, 'Uses of Capacity Measures for Short-run Economic Analysis', pp. 302-3.

short-period production functions. For example, coal is a potential substitute for oil as a plant's heating fuel. But before it can be substituted, the plant's heating equipment must be changed.

When investment decisions are being made, the expected *scale* of output is an important factor in the choice of plant. Plants with different productive capacities often have different types of capital equipment as well as different quantities of equipment. For low rates of output, plants with small productive capacities may be able to produce at lower unit costs than plants with large productive capacities. Conversely, for high rates of output the larger plants may have lower unit costs than the combination of smaller plants required to produce the same rate of output. The firm's expected rate of output would therefore be one of the factors in its investment choice.

The choice of a plant to be constructed (i.e. the choice of technique) is often presented in economic theory as taking place within the context of given technical knowledge. This approach can be misleading. Investment is often the means by which new technology is developed and made available. Technical change can be called *embodied* if it results from the introduction of new equipment or materials and *disembodied* if it results from improvements in operating knowledge. The short-period production functions introduced in this chapter are based on the assumption of given technology as well as given plant. Investment and technical changes give rise to new short-period production functions.

The substitutability of inputs often requires changes in technology, occurring over time as a result of the investment of skilled labour and resources and leading to new production functions, each of which reflects a new state of technical knowledge. If there are increases in the relative prices of some inputs, any analysis of the effects of these increases on their employment should take into account the time required to change plant and technology so that substitutions can be made that minimize the adverse effects of these increases.

7.11 The law of diminishing returns

In the early nineteenth century, David Ricardo introduced marginal analysis into economic theory in his consideration of agricultural production. According to this analysis, different quantities of labour (combined with agricultural implements, fertilizer, etc.) could be appropriately employed on a fixed amount of land. That is, it was considered feasible to vary the proportions in which labour and land were used to produce agricultural output. Ricardo and other classical economists enunciated the *law of diminishing returns* (or the law of variable proportions) to predict the effects of changes in these proportions. They believed that the increases in output resulting from the increased application of labour, appropriately equipped, to the fixed amount of land imposed by nature would eventually diminish.[18] The principle played an important role in their analyses of economic development and led to fears about the eventual cessation of economic growth—the establishment of a stationary state—because of the limits to the possible growth of supplies of food due to the fixed supply of land. (Diminishing returns to equal increments of labour were also expected, even when the area of land sown was increased, if the new land was of poorer quality than that previously cultivated.)

The law of diminishing returns, which implicitly assumes a given state of technology, can be formally stated as follows: *the increments in output resulting from equal increments in input of labour, with the quantity of land remaining constant, eventually diminish.* The increment in output resulting from a small unit increment in the quantity of equipped labour with land constant can be called the *marginal product of labour*. Thus the law of diminishing returns states that the marginal product of labour will eventually diminish. No formal proof for this proposition was offered by the classical economists; it was taken as self-evident—if it did not hold, then the world's food supply could be grown in a flower-pot! It should be noted that this law, or principle, is concerned with the comparison of marginal products for alternative positions. No statement is made in the law about the relative values of marginal products when the rates of input of labour are changing over time.[19]

7.12 Neoclassical production functions: introduction
Neoclassical production functions bear some resemblance to the classical economists' approach to agricultural production. They are based on the

---

[18] The first clear statement of the law of diminishing returns was made by Anne Robert Jacques Turgot (1729-81).

[19] Marshall's discussion of diminishing returns makes clear that this law is based on a comparison of alternative positions. He illustrated the notion of a return to a 'marginal dose of labour and capital' (his expression for equipped labour) with the following data on four plots of land of an acre each at an experimental station in Arkansas. The marginal product of equipped labour used to harrow the first time is equal to two and one-third bushels per acre. The marginal product of harrowing is only one and seven-twelfths bushels per acre if the land had already been ploughed twice and harrowed once. Marshall, *Principles of Economics*, p. 155, n. 1.

PLOT	CULTIVATION	CROP YIELDS, BUSHELS PER ACRE
1	Ploughed once	16
2	Ploughed once and harrowed once	18 1/3
3	Ploughed twice and harrowed once	21 2/3
4	Ploughed twice and harrowed twice	23 1/4

principle of substitution.[20] The substitutability of land for labour and capital (or equipped labour) in agricultural production has been extended to the substitutability between all elements in industrial as well as agricultural production. Diminishing returns, when some inputs are fixed, are a characteristic feature of neoclassical production functions.

There are serious problems with this extension of the classical approach. The emphasis on substitutability in the neoclassical production functions obscures the importance of the passage of time for the necessary changes in the plant's equipment before significant substitution can occur. An indirect attempt is made to allow for the passage of time by distinguishing between production 'in the short run' and production 'in the long run'. In the short run, at least one of the inputs cannot be varied, while in the long run all inputs can be varied. The short run can thus be identified with the short period where productive capacity is constant,[21] but the emphasis on substitutability, even in the short run, ignores the importance of the complementarity of inputs within a given plant. Inputs are more substitutable after a long run of time when plant and technology can be changed. The neoclassical emphasis on substitution has more justification for long-period analysis, but the neoclassical long-run production functions are appropriate only for stationary states, since they are based on the assumption of given technical knowledge.

Production functions express the technical relations between rates of output in physical units and rates of input of elements of production, also in physical units. Neoclassical economic theory includes capital as one of the factors of production in these functions, along with land and labour, even though capital cannot be measured in physical units. The various items of capital equipment can be measured in their own physical units, but there is no corresponding physical unit for aggregate capital. A money value for all the items of capital equipment can be obtained by using their prices, but there is no place for a value in a production function. The quantity of capital as a value input could change with any change in the set of prices for its constituent elements (even though all the items of physical capital

---

[20] *Ibid.*, p. 341.

[21] This identification may be inappropriate because of the vagueness of the term 'short run' as used in neoclassical economic theory. The neoclassical theory of production is not based on production with a given plant in a particular period of calendar time. Instead, the short run is a very elastic concept that is defined simply in terms of the inability to vary *all* the inputs. For example, Mansfield writes: 'Any time interval between one where the quantity of no input is variable and one where the quantity of all inputs is variable could reasonably be called the short run.' (*Microeconomics: Theory and Applications*, p. 168.) He goes on to note that he uses 'a more restrictive definition: we say that the short run is the time period so brief that the firm cannot vary the quantities of plant and equipment.' (*Ibid.*)

equipment that provide input services are unchanged) without any consequent change in output.[22]

The neoclassical economists treat capital in production functions as though it were land and pretend that it can be measured in physical units.[23] In Edwin Mansfield's widely used textbook, the author begins his discussion of production with labour and land as the two factors of production and notes that labour is measured in man-years and land in acres.[24] Capital then replaces land in his diagrams with the statement, 'In contrast to the previous diagrams, we assume that labour and capital—not labour and land—are the relevant inputs in this case,'[25] but Mansfield does not have any physical units with which to measure the 'quantity of capital' he purports to show in his diagrams.[26]

The presentation of neoclassical production functions in the following sections will avoid the use of aggregates as inputs. Only individual elements of production, each measured in their own physical units, will appear as inputs.

7.13 Neoclassical production functions: single variable input

The general features of the typical neoclassical production function can be illustrated by the case in which only one of the elements of production is variable. The weekly production rate of commodity X, over the period examined when the rate of input of the single variable element V_1 is v_1, is equal to x, where $x = f(v_1)$. This function, which is based on given technical

---

[22] Neoclassical production functions that use capital as an input have been subject to recurring criticism. For a review of recent literature on the subject, see G.C. Harcourt, *Some Cambridge Controversies in the Theory of Capital* (Cambridge, Eng.: Cambridge University Press, 1972).

[23] Professor Samuelson—in a paper written with W. Stolper ('Protection and Real Wages', *The Review of Economic Studies*, Vol. 9 [November 1941], pp. 58-73)—used two factors of production, capital and labour, although the reader was advised in a footnote that land could be substituted for capital 'because of the ambiguities involved in the definition of capital' (p. 62). In many of his other papers on international trade—for example, 'International Trade and Equalisation of Factor Prices', *Economic Journal*, Vol. 58 (June 1948), pp. 163-84—Samuelson used land and labour as his factors of production in production functions that had the same properties as those in which he had previously used capital and labour.

[24] Mansfield, *Microeconomics: Theory and Applications*, p. 133.

[25] *Ibid.*, p. 137.

[26] There is an aggregation problem in using land and labour as factors of production, since there are many different types of land and labour, but there are physical units that can be used as bases for combining them. For labour, the unit could be an hour of unskilled labour, with other types of labour being expressed as a multiple of this basic unit. For example, a man-hour of labour after a period of training could be equivalent to two man-hours of unskilled labour (see Footnote 12 for Keynes's approach to this problem). Similarly with land, the basic unit could be an acre of land with a specific quality of soil. There is no comparable physical basis for the aggregation of the wide range of items that are covered by the term 'capital'. Capital can be aggregated only in terms of values.

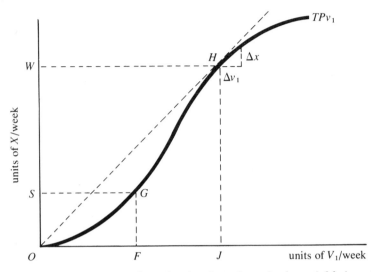

FIGURE 7.2 *Neoclassical production function: single variable input*

knowledge as well as on given amounts of fixed inputs,[27] is illustrated graphically in Figure 7.2. The variable element of production V_1 is assumed to be an essential ingredient for production. A positive rate of output can be obtained only if this element is employed at a positive rate. It can be shown that the shape of the total product curve (TP_{V_1}) reflects the relationship between the rates of input of the variable element and its marginal product. Neoclassical production functions are assumed to display increasing marginal products before diminishing marginal products are encountered (as in Figure 7.2).

With neoclassical production functions, the marginal product of a particular input is defined as the increase in total output due to a small unit increase *only in this variable input.* This concept should not be confused with the short-period marginal product of labour, defined in Section 7.9, or with the marginal product of labour used to illustrate the classical economists' law of diminishing returns. In both these cases complementary inputs were increased along with labour. The marginal product of V_1, at a particular value for the rate of input of this element, is obtained by dividing a small increment in the input into the resulting small increment in output. In Figure 7.2 the marginal product of V_1, when its rate of input is equal to OJ, is equal to the ratio of the increments Δx and Δv_1. The smaller the value

---

[27] Neoclassical production functions are conventionally written with fixed inputs incorporated in the form of the functions. This convention will be followed in this presentation: only the rate of input of the variable elements will be shown explicitly.

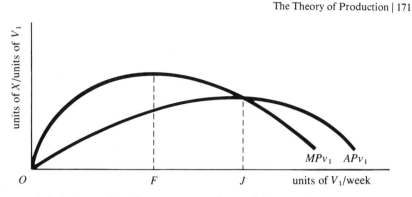

FIGURE 7.3 *Marginal and average product of input V_1 corresponding to the total product curve in Figure 7.2*

for Δv_1, the closer is the value for this ratio to the slope of the total product curve at point H. As this increment becomes very small, the marginal product is equal to the slope of the total product curve.[28]

The slope of the total product curve (and thus the marginal product of V_1 in the given situation) achieves its highest value at the point of inflexion of the curve (point G in Figure 7.2). This is the point where diminishing marginal products begin and the shape of the curve changes from being convex from below to being concave from below.

The *average product* of the variable input V_1 (denoted by AP_{V_1}) is defined as the rate of output divided by the rate of employment of this element. At any particular rate of input for this element, its average product is equal to the rate of output corresponding to that input rate divided by the rate of input. Given the total product curve, the average product for any rate of input can be derived by finding the slope of the line joining the corresponding point on the total product curve to the origin. For example, in Figure 7.2, if the quantity of the input is OJ units per week, the average product of V_1 is equal to the weekly rate of total output, JH, divided by the weekly rate of the variable input OJ. This value is equal to the slope of the line joining point H to the origin.

The average and marginal product curves that correspond to the total product curve in Figure 7.2 are shown in Figure 7.3. (Note that they cannot be drawn on the same diagram as the total product curve, since the units on the ordinates differ.) The marginal product curve lies above the average product curve for input rates less than OJ, because it has been assumed that

---

[28] The marginal product (MP_{V_1}) can be defined using calculus:

$$MP_{V_1} = \lim_{\Delta v_1 \to 0} \frac{\Delta x}{\Delta v_1} = \frac{dx}{dv_1} = f'(v_1)$$

there is a range of values for these rates in which increasing returns are experienced. When the marginal product curve is above the average product curve, the average product is rising, and vice versa. It reaches a maximum value for the rate of input that corresponds to the point where the marginal product curve intersects the average product curve from above. These relationships follow from the definition of the *marginal* and *average* curves (see Section 9.13).

7.14 Neoclassical production functions: two variable inputs

When it is assumed that there are two elements of production that can be varied, then isoquants are used to indicate the rates of output that would result from different combinations of rates of input for these elements.[29] *An isoquant is a line joining all points representing combinations of rates of input of the variable elements that produce a particular rate of output.* Production is assumed to be technically efficient. A set of isoquants is drawn in Figure 7.4. The isoquant labelled x_1 shows the various combinations of rates of input of V_1 and V_2 that produce a weekly rate of x_1 of commodity X. For example, weekly input rates of Ov_{11} units of V_1 and Ov_{21} units of V_2 would produce a weekly output rate of x_1 units of commodity X. Higher rates of output over the period could be obtained only if there were a higher rate of input for at least one of these elements. The isoquants are, in effect, 'production indifference' curves. They differ from the indifference curves dealt with in consumer theory in that output can be measured by a cardinal scale. Not only is it possible to indicate which of two levels of output is the higher, but the differences in these output levels can be compared with the differences between other output levels.

The shapes of the isoquants depend on the technical characteristics of the inputs and the technical knowledge used to combine them to produce the product. In neoclassical production functions it is generally assumed that, at least for some range of values for rates of inputs, there is partial substitutability between the elements of production. This assumption is reflected in the shapes of the isoquants drawn in Figure 7.4.

The scope for substitutability among particular types of machinery, raw materials, and labour may be very limited since machinery is often designed with particular, inflexible requirements. For example, in order to produce a particular rate of output, one man with a specific amount of training and technical skill may be required to tend three machines in an eight-hour day. During this period a specified amount of electrical energy would be required

---

[29] A more appropriate name for these curves would be *isoproducts*, since they show equal products, but the standard terminology will be used.

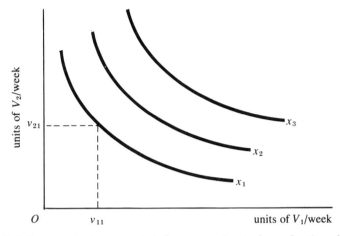

FIGURE 7.4 *Isoquants (x_1, x_2, etc.) for a neoclassical production function with two variable inputs*

to power each machine, and the amounts and quality of the raw materials required would be determined by the nature of the product and production process. An increase in the rate of input of only one of these elements would have no effect on output, since the necessary co-operating elements would be absent. In such cases isoquants would be of the right-angled type drawn in panel A of Figure 7.5.[30] The proportion in which these two elements can be usefully employed is equal to the value of the slope of the line *OF*. Increases in the rate of output would be reflected in equiproportional in-

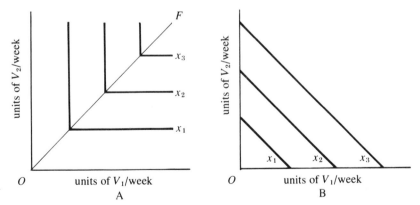

FIGURE 7.5 *Isoquants for variable inputs that are perfect complements* (A) *and perfect substitutes* (B)

---

[30] It was argued in Section 7.9 that production in industrial plants is characterized by this complementarity of inputs.

creases in the rates of input of the variable elements of production. They would also involve more intensive use of the elements in the fixed plant.

If the variable elements were perfect substitutes, the isoquants would be straight lines, as in panel B of Figure 7.5. The proportion in which they are perfect substitutes is equal to the value of the slopes of the isoquants. The units for measuring these elements can be chosen so that this value is numerically equal to one.

7.15 The marginal rate of technical substitution

The numerical value of the slope of an isoquant can be called (following the indifference curve terminology) *the marginal rate of technical substitution* (*MRTS*) of the two variable elements of production. The marginal rate of technical substitution of V_1 for V_2 (denoted by $MRTS_{v_1 v_2}$) is the difference in the rate of input of V_2 that will compensate for a very small difference in the rate of input of V_1.[31]

It can be deduced that the $MRTS_{v_1 v_2}$ is equal to the ratio of the marginal product of V_1 (MP_{v_1}) to the marginal product of V_2(MP_{v_2}). A small difference in the rate of input of V_1 (represented by Δv_1) will result in a difference in the rate of output equal to the product of this difference and the marginal product of V_1($=\Delta v_1 \cdot MP_{v_1}$). The same relation holds for V_2. If two adjacent points on an isoquant are compared, we know that the difference in the rate of output due to the difference in V_1 must be offset by the difference in the input of V_2. The following equation thus holds on an isoquant: $\Delta v_1 \cdot MP_{v_1} + \Delta v_2 \cdot MP_{v_2} = 0$. The numerical value of the slope of the isoquant can be represented by $-\Delta v_2/\Delta v_1$. It can be deduced from the above equation that the numerical value of the slope must be equal to the ratio of the marginal product, MP_{v_1}/MP_{v_2}.[32]

The assumption of some, but not perfect, substitutability among variable inputs (as in the middle range of the typical isoquants for neoclassical production functions drawn in Figure 7.4) means that the marginal rate of technical substitution of V_1 for V_2 is smaller, the larger the value for V_1. These isoquants exhibit a diminishing marginal rate of technical sub-

---

[31] This means that in the limit the increase in V_1 tends to zero; i.e. $lim\ \Delta v_1 \rightarrow 0$.

[32] The relationship between the marginal rate of technical substitution and the marginal products can be obtained more precisely with calculus. If the rate of output is x_1, then the isoquant is made up of those pairs of values for the rates of input of the elements of production that satisfy the equation $x_1 = f(v_1, v_2)$. The following relation holds for an equation of this type: $dx_1 = (\partial f/\partial v_1)dv_1 + (\partial f/\partial v_2)dv_2$. Along an isoquant $dx_1 = 0$, therefore $(\partial f/\partial v_1)dv_1 + (\partial f/\partial v_2)dv_2 = 0$, or $-(dv_2/dv_1) = (\partial f/\partial v_1)/(\partial f/\partial v_2)$. $-dv_2/dv_1$ is the numerical value of the slope of the isoquant and $\partial f/\partial v_1$ and $\partial f/\partial v_2$ are the marginal products of V_1 and V_2 respectively.

stitution among the two variable elements in this middle range. When these elements are perfect complements, as in panel A of Figure 7.5, it is not possible to derive the marginal rate of technical substitution between them in the production of this good. The marginal product for each element, taken separately, is equal to zero, and one cannot divide by zero. For perfect substitutes, as in panel B of Figure 7.5, the marginal rate of technical substitution is always equal to some number that is constant for all values of V_1. (This number can be made equal to one by choosing units of measure for V_1 and V_2 that make one unit of V_1 a perfect substitute for one unit of V_2.)

7.16 Elasticity of substitution

The elasticity of substitution, employed in Section 5.12 to indicate the degree of substitutability between goods for a consumer, can also be used for elements of production. The elasticity of substitution of a production function is equal to the relative difference in the ratio of rates of input of the two elements of production, divided by the relative difference in the slope of the isoquant. This can be written in symbols:

$$\sigma = \frac{\Delta\left(\dfrac{v_1}{v_2}\right)}{\dfrac{v_1}{v_2}} \div \frac{\Delta\left(\dfrac{MPv_1}{MPv_2}\right)}{\dfrac{MPv_1}{MPv_2}}$$

where σ is the elasticity of substitution and MPv_1/MPv_2 is equal to the numerical value of the slope of the isoquant, as we saw in the preceding section. Δ represents a very small difference that, in the limit, goes to zero.[33]

The results derived in Section 5.12 for the elasticity of substitution of products in ordinal utility functions carry over to production functions. In particular, the elasticity of substitution when isoquants are right-angled, as in panel A of Figure 7.5, is equal to zero. It is equal to minus infinity when elements of production are perfect substitutes, as in panel B of Figure 7.5. For production functions whose isoquants have at least some curvature, such as those drawn in Figure 7.4, the numerical value for the elasticity of substitution lies between zero and minus infinity. The greater the degree of substitutability, the higher the numerical value for σ. This value need not be constant for a particular production function; it may have different values for different rates of input of the elements of production.

---

[33] In the notation of calculus:

$$\sigma = \frac{-d\left(\dfrac{v_1}{v_2}\right)}{\dfrac{v_1}{v_2}} \div \frac{d\left(\dfrac{\partial f}{\partial v_1} \middle/ \dfrac{\partial f}{\partial v_2}\right)}{\dfrac{\partial f}{\partial v_1} \middle/ \dfrac{\partial f}{\partial v_2}}$$

7.17 Neoclassical production functions: many variable inputs

When the number of variable elements of production is greater than two, no new concepts are introduced into the analysis. It is no longer possible to display the production functions diagrammatically by means of isoquants and they must be handled algebraically. A function of this type can be written as $x = f(v_1, v_2, v_3, \ldots, v_n)$. The marginal rate of technical substitution between any two elements of production that are substitutable can still be defined. Its value would be equal to the ratio of the two marginal products (where these are non-zero).

7.18 Homogeneous production functions

Neoclassical production functions are often assumed to have the special property of *homogeneity*. A production function is said to be homogeneous for those situations where, when the rates of input of all the variable elements of production differ in the same proportion, the rate of output differs by some power of this proportion.[34] The property of homogeneity can be defined as follows: *A production function is homogeneous of degree γ if, when all the variable elements of production are changed in the same proportion λ, the rate of output is changed in this proportion λ raised to the power γ.*

This definition can be stated in symbols. The production function, $x = f(v_1, v_2, \ldots, v_n)$, is said to be homogeneous of degree γ if $\lambda^\gamma x = f(\lambda v_1, \lambda v_2, \ldots, \lambda v_n)$, where λ is a positive real number other than one.

If the value of γ is greater than one, the homogeneous production function is said to exhibit *increasing returns*. This means that a doubling of the rate of output can be obtained even though the rates of input of all the variable elements are increased in a smaller proportion. With a value of one for γ, the production function is said to exhibit *constant returns*. Doubling the rates of input for all variable elements would double the rate of output. A homogeneous production function is said to exhibit *diminishing returns* if the value of γ is less than one. In this case, something more than twice the initial rates of input is required to double the rate of output. Of course production functions may not be homogeneous.[35]

---

[34] A function is defined here as being homogeneous only with respect to the situations being compared. Some production functions might be generally homogeneous and display this property for all comparisons, while others may be homogeneous only for some comparisons.

[35] Homogeneity is defined following standard practice only with respect to the inputs shown explicitly in the statement of the production function. The elements that comprise the fixed plant have the same values in all the comparisons. The homogeneity of production functions is often defined in the economics literature in terms of the effects of proportional differences in the values for *all* the elements of production. If this practice is followed, then the analysis is concerned with *returns to scale*. They were referred to in Section 7.10 and will be discussed further in Chapter 8.

If a complete statement of the production function is available, it is easy to check whether it is homogeneous and, if so, its degree of homogeneity. Consider the following production functions where only the variable inputs are shown explicitly:

$$\text{(i)} \quad x = A v_1^\alpha v_2^\beta; \quad \text{(ii)} \quad x = A v_1^\alpha v_2^{1-\alpha}; \quad \text{(iii)} \quad x = \frac{A(v_1^2 + v_2^2)}{v_1^{1/2} \, v_2^{1/2}};$$

$$\text{(iv)} \quad x = A(v_1 + v_2) + B, \quad B \neq 0.$$

The characteristics of the plant and the state of technology on which these production functions are based are reflected in the values for A and B in the above expressions.

In order to determine whether a production function is homogeneous, the term λv_i should be substituted for v_i in the statement of the production function. The corresponding value for the rate of output can then be derived. If it is equal to some power of λ times the rate of output obtained when the input rates are at v_i, the function is homogeneous. For example, when these substitutions are carried out for production function (i) above, we have $A((\lambda v_1)^\alpha \ (\lambda v_2)^\beta) = \lambda^{\alpha + \beta} \ A(v_1^\alpha v_2^\beta)$. This function is homogeneous of degree $(\alpha + \beta)$. Similarly it can be found that (ii) is homogeneous of degree one, (iii) is homogeneous of degree one, and (iv) is not homogeneous because of the constant term.

If a production function with only two variable elements of production is homogeneous, then its degree of homogeneity can be illustrated diagrammatically. Assume that the initial position in Figure 7.6 is point G. The rates of the two inputs are v_{11} and v_{21}, and the corresponding rate of output is x_1. If the proportion of the two inputs (as represented by the slope of the line OF) is kept unchanged, a rate of output twice that of x_1 would require input rates of v_{12} and v_{22} (as indicated by the co-ordinates of point H). The slopes of the isoquants would be the same at points G and H as a result of the assumption of homogeneity. Their numerical values, as we have seen, depend on the ratios of the marginal products of the two elements of production. These are unchanged when a production function is homogeneous as long as the inputs are used in the same proportion.[36] The

---

[36] The following is a proof of this statement. The production function $x = f(v_1, v_2)$ is homogeneous of degree γ and can thus be written as $\lambda^\gamma x = f(\lambda v_1, \lambda v_2)$. If $\lambda = 1/v_2$, then this equality can be written as $x/v_2^\gamma = f(v_1/v_2, 1)$. It can be rewritten as $x = v_2^\gamma g(v_1/v_2)$, where $g(v_1/v_2) \equiv f(v_1/v_2, 1)$. The marginal product of $v_1(\partial x/\partial v_1)$ is equal to $v_2^{\gamma - 1} g'(v_1/v_1)$. The marginal product of $v_2(\partial x/\partial v_2)$ is equal to $\gamma v_2^{\gamma - 1} g(v_1/v_2) - v_2^{\gamma - 2} v_1 g'(v_1/v_2)$. The slopes of the isoquants (the marginal rates of technical substitution of V_1 for V_2) are equal to the ratios of the marginal products. Substituting, we find:
$$(\partial x/\partial v_1)/(\partial x/\partial v_2) = g'(v_1/v_2)/\gamma g(v_1/v_2) - (v_1/v_2)g'(v_1/v_2)$$
This expression is constant, given constant values for γ and the ratio of employment of the inputs (v_1/v_2).

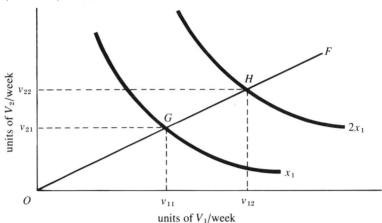

FIGURE 7.6 *Isoquants for a homogeneous production function*

degree of homogeneity of the production function can be determined by calculating the ratio v_{12} to v_{11}. If this ratio is equal to 2, then the production function is homogeneous of degree one; if it is greater than 2, the degree of homogeneity is less than one; while if it is less than 2, the degree of homogeneity is greater than one.

7.19 Linear production processes

In the consideration of production functions a distinction was made between the typical neoclassical functions that assume substitutability between elements of production and those that assume that they must be combined in fixed proportions within a particular plant. A special class of production functions has been postulated that displays *both* fixed proportions and substitutability. They are based on the assumption that there is a finite (and possibly a quite small) number of separate production processes that may be operated within a particular plant. For each of these processes there can be no substitution between the required elements of production: these elements can be usefully employed only in some fixed proportions. The variable elements used, as well as the proportions in which they are employed, may differ in different production processes. Input substitution may thus be achieved within a plant by changing the 'mix' of processes in operation.

Each of these production processes is assumed to display constant returns. This means that a process can be described by a statement of the rate of input for each element required to produce a unit rate of output. In order to produce twice the unit rate, twice the rate of input of each variable element is required. It is assumed that these processes can be combined linearly. That is, a unit rate of output can be obtained by using two processes at proportions of their unit rates of output that add up to unity.

For example, one process can be used at a rate that produces three-quarters of the unit rate of output, and the other can be used at a one-quarter rate. To emphasize their properties, these processes will be called *linear production processes*.

An example of a linear production process would be the production of a daily output of 100 units of commodity X and w units of waste from a set of elements of production that are combined in fixed proportions. For this rate of output it is necessary to have the services of a particular machine with given technical characteristics for eight hours a day; a certain number of kilowatt hours of electricity per day to provide power for the machine; a certain quantity of some raw material used up per day; and the daily employment of eight hours of labour with specified skill and experience to operate the machine. Since the process displays constant returns, a doubling of all these inputs would double the daily output to 200 units of commodity X and $2w$ units of waste. The daily production rate of 100 units of commodity X might also be possible with the same plant if another linear production process were employed. For example, an input of the services of another machine (available in the plant) for eight hours a day, with eight hours per day of labour with different skills, and daily quantities of kilowatt hours of electricity and raw materials—somewhat different than those required for the first process—could produce a daily output of 100 units of commodity X and w units of waste.

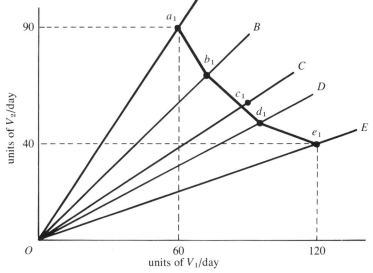

FIGURE 7.7 *Graphic representation of possible linear production processes with a given plant (source: Table 7.1). a_1, b_1, c_1, d_1, e_1 are the unit rates of output for the indicated process*

7.20 Technical efficiency and linear production processes

In the presentation of the neoclassical production function, it has been assumed that the function is *technically efficient*, meaning that the values obtained from the function are for the maximum rate of output that can be obtained from any combination of rates of inputs. In dealing with linear production processes, the same result can be obtained by working only with *efficient processes*. An efficient process is one in which a higher rate of output can be obtained only if there is a higher rate of input for at least one of the elements of production.

The representation of these processes and their manipulation are best handled algebraically. However, graphic illustrations of linear processes are possible if they are greatly simplified. They can illuminate the meaning of efficient processes and provide a comparison with the continuous isoquants of neoclassical production functions. In Figure 7.7, it is assumed that the production processes possible with the given plant need specify only two variable elements: the number of hours per day of service (v_2) obtained from a machine that can combine with labour in more than one way,[37] and the hours per day of labour with a particular skill (v_1). The electricity to power this machine is assumed to vary with the hours of service of the machine, and rates of input of the elements that are transformed in the production process are proportional to the rate of output and cannot be substituted one for the other. Output of waste will also be ignored; it is assumed that the plant can dispose of waste at zero cost to itself (the social cost of the waste disposal may very well not be zero!). The input requirements for the unit rate of output (taken to be a daily output of 100 units of commodity X) for five possible production processes are listed in Table 7.1 and shown graphically in Figure 7.7.

The ratio of the input of hours of machine services (v_2) to hours of labour (v_1) varies from a high of 1.50 for production process A to a low of 0.33 for production process E. The ratio of the inputs (v_2/v_1) for any process is shown by the slope of the ray through the origin representing the production process. For example, the ray OA represents production process A and the value of its slope is 1.50. Substitution between the two inputs can be achieved by operating a different mix of processes. If only process A is employed, then the ratio of hours of labour input to hours of machine service input is two to three. If another process, B, were employed as well as A to produce the same rate of output as obtained previously with A, then

---

[37] Although the linear-production-process approach sets limits on the substitutability usually assumed in neoclassical production functions, the assumption that inputs can be combined in more than one way in a given plant to produce a single product indicates that this approach is a member of the neoclassical family.

TABLE 7.1 *Linear production processes*
available with a particular plant

OUTPUT:	LINEAR PRODUCTION PROCESSES				
	A	B	C	D	E
Units of commodity X, produced in an eight-hour day. (Unit level)	100	100	100	100	100
INPUTS:					
Hours of labour of a specified skill, employed in an eight-hour day (v_1)	60	75	95	100	120
Hours of service from a particular type of machine, in an eight-hour day (v_2)	90	70	60	50	40
Ratio v_2/v_1	1.50	0.93	0.63	0.50	0.33

some labour services would be substituted for some machine services. Since the production processes considered here are linear, the production effects of combining processes can be readily calculated.

The unit rate of output can be obtained by combining the processes in such a way that the proportions of the unit rate, in which each process is operated, add up to one. For example, if process A is employed at one-seventh of the unit rate of operation and process B is employed at six-sevenths of the unit rate, then 100 units of commodity X per day will be produced (this is the unit rate). Incidentally, with this combination of the two processes the number of hours of labour and machine service would be the same (they would be equal to 510/7 hours).

The line $a_1b_1d_1e_1$ joining the points for the unit levels of operation of efficient processes is an isoquant. It differs from the isoquants for neoclassical production functions in not being a smooth convex curve. Its slope has a constant value between two processes, and this value changes when this curve comes to another efficient process. An angle is thus formed at points whose co-ordinates represent the proportion in which the elements are employed in an individual production process.

Production process C is not efficient and the point c_1, representing its unit rate of output, is not on the isoquant. This process is dominated by a combination of the processes B and D. (The reader should note that if only processes A, B, and C were available, production process C would then be efficient.) By combining processes B and D in the proportion 25:43, the ratio of the two inputs for the C process is obtained. The unit rate of output would be achieved using a daily rate of input of 90.8 hours of labour and 57.4 machine hours. This represents a saving of 4.2 hours of labour and 2.6 machine hours as compared to the requirement of process C at a unit rate. It can readily be seen from Figure 7.7 that only linear combinations of adjacent efficient production processes are themselves efficient. A line joining points representing efficient processes that are not adjacent lies above the rates of input that can also produce the same rate of output. The term *basic production process* is used to distinguish the efficient production processes—such as *A, B, D,* and *E* in Figure 7.7—that cannot be obtained from a linear combination of other processes.

The information provided in Table 7.1 (and the assumption of constant returns) allows us to draw in Figure 7.7 as many isoquants as desired. All these curves would have the same values for their slopes between each pair of rays representing the basic production processes. The isoquant for one-half the unit rate of output would start on OA at a point halfway along Oa_1, then join a point on OB halfway along Ob_1, etc. The greater the number of basic production processes available for the two elements, the more closely would the isoquant derived from them approximate the smooth isoquants for the standard neoclassical production functions. In order for there to be many basic production processes, the two individual elements of production must have technical characteristics that permit them to be used in many different proportions.

7.21 External effects of production

In the preceding sections a firm's rate of output has been assumed to depend solely on technical knowledge, the size and technical characteristics of its plant, and the rates of input of the variable elements of production. The firm's production possibilities with a given plant have been assumed to be independent of activity in other plants. This assumption may not be appropriate in some cases, and external effects of production must be recognized. If increases in the rates of production of others make it possible for the firm to produce a given rate of output with a lower rate of at least one of the inputs, then its production is said to be subject to *external technical economies*. Conversely, if increased rates of production in other plants require the firm to increase its rate of input of at least one of the variable elements in order to maintain its rate of output, it is said to be subject to *external technical diseconomies*.

These externalities may result from changes in the rates of production in plants belonging to the same industry, or in plants of other industries. In the former case they are said to be external to the firm but internal to the industry. In the latter case they are also external to the industry. An example of external technical economies that are internal to the industry would be the case of two firms mining coal from adjacent pits. If the rate of output for one is greater, so is the amount of water it is pumping out. This lowers the amount of water the neighboring mine must pump out in order to produce any particular rate of output. A similar case, but one that illustrates external diseconomies, would be that of oil firms tapping the same oil pool. The higher the rate of output of one firm, the higher the pumping costs to the other of maintaining a particular rate of output. An external economy that is often referred to relates to the production of honey and apples.[38] If the bees feed on apple blossoms, an increase in the number of apple trees would also increase the production of honey for beekeepers in their vicinity.

Robert Dorfman gives examples of two externalities that are external to the industry.[39] The Salton Sea in Southern California is a very productive inland fishery, in part because it is fed by water that has flowed through the heavily fertilized Imperial Valley and carries appreciable amounts of plant nutrients that help feed the aquatic life of the Sea. The larger the amounts of these beneficial nutrients that farmers employ in order to raise their outputs, the lower the unit costs for fishermen in the Salton Sea. They are benefiting from external economies. Dorfman's example of external technical diseconomies illustrates the problem of pollution due to the limited ability of the environment to absorb waste. Chesapeake Bay and the clam beds of Long Island Sound are being endangered by polluted waters from cities and industries of the East. The greater the production in these industries, other things being equal, the more difficult it is, and the higher the cost, to produce a given rate of output of oysters and clams. Fishermen in this region are thus subject to external technical diseconomies.

A firm may be subject to external economies from some sources and diseconomies from others. The net effect of these externalities may or may not be beneficial to the firm.

7.22 Summary

This chapter has provided the basis for the derivation of cost curves to be covered in the following chapter. Two approaches to the theory of production were examined. The first is consistent with empirical estimates of cost curves and was based on the assumption that the variable inputs in a particular plant tend to be complements. The short-period marginal product of labour was assumed to be constant up to the normal productive capacity of the plant. Production functions were defined for a Marshallian short period. It was assumed that the plant could not be significantly changed during this length of time, which was nevertheless long enough to

---

[38] J.E. Meade, 'External Economies and Diseconomies in a Competitive Situation', *Economic Journal*, Vol. 62 (June 1952), pp. 54-67.

[39] Robert Dorfman, *The Price System* (Englewood Cliffs, N.J.: Prentice Hall, Inc., 1964), pp. 139-40.

permit changes in the rate of utilization of the given plant. Substitution between elements of production usually occurs after the passage of time when investment can change the plants and thus the mix of elements they can employ.

Neoclassical production functions that assume that inputs are substitutable were also examined. They do not make explicit the importance of time in permitting substitution between inputs. They often use capital as a variable in production functions, even though as a value term it has no place in a technical relation between flows of inputs and outputs, which are expressed in physical units. Neoclassical production functions play a key role in the neoclassical theory of income distribution as well as in the derivation of cost curves.

SUGGESTED READINGS

Ayers, R.U. and A.V. Kneese. 'Production, Consumption, and Externalities'. *American Economic Review*, Vol. 59 (June 1966), pp. 282-97.

Brownlee, O.H. and John A. Buttrick. *Producer, Consumer, and Social Choice*. New York: McGraw-Hill, 1968. Chapters 2 and 3.

Gold, Bela. *Explorations in Managerial Economics—Productivity, Costs, Technology and Growth*. New York: Basic Books, 1971. Chapters 6 and 7.

Marshall, Alfred. *Principles of Economics*. 8th ed. London: Macmillan & Co., 1920. Book IV, Chapters I-III.

Phillips, Almarin. 'An Appraisal of Measures of Capacity'. *American Economic Review*. Vol. 53 (May 1963), pp. 275-92.

Salter, W.E.G. *Productivity and Technical Change*. Cambridge, Eng.: Cambridge University Press, 1960.

EXERCISES

1. Assume that the technical characteristics of a particular plant are such that only one production process can be employed. The plant contains a fixed number of machines, and the operation of each machine requires a specified number of units of labour, electrical energy, and raw materials. The degree of utilization of the plant can be increased until all machines are being operated to their fullest extent (as determined by their technical characteristics) by employing more labour to man the machines and by adding to the electrical energy and raw materials. The rates of output and input increase in the same proportion. In addition to this 'direct' labour, a certain rate of input of labour is required once the decision to operate the plant in the short period is taken, and this rate is independent of the degree of utilization of plant. Included in this category of 'overhead' or 'indirect' labour would be some of the supervisory and maintenance staff, quality control personnel, etc. Draw the short-period marginal product of labour for this plant. Draw the average product of labour. Why do these curves differ?

2. You are given the following table of values relating the rate of output of a particular agricultural commodity X to the rate of labour input (with appropriate agricultural implements) on a given area of land (the quantity of seed used is also constant).

RATE OF INPUT OF LABOUR (Man-years per year)	RATE OF OUTPUT (Units of X per year)
2	100
3	160
4	224
5	280
6	330
7	370
8	400
9	425

(a) Calculate the marginal and average product of labour at all the rates of input. (The marginal product of labour for the 8th unit is the addition to total output resulting from the addition of the 8th unit of labour.)

(b) After what rate of input do diminishing returns to the variable input appear?

(c) For what rate of input are the marginal and average products the same?

(d) Why must the slope of the average product curve be negative when the marginal product values are less than the average product values?

3. A careful study of the cultivation of corn in a particular region in a particular year found the marginal product of labour to be 500 bushels. When this area was restudied five years later, it was found that both more labour was employed on the land and its marginal product was 700 bushels. Weather conditions seemed to be equally favourable for the growing of corn in both years. Do these observations contradict the principle of diminishing returns? Give reasons for your answer.

4. The following *linear production processes* are possible in a particular plant.

	LINEAR PRODUCTION PROCESS		
OUTPUT:	A	B	C
Units of commodity X produced in an eight-hour day.	100	100	100
INPUTS:			
Hours of labour of a specified skill.	60	80	90
Hours of service from a particular multi-purpose machine.	90	75	60

(a) Are all these production processes technically efficient? Why?

(b) If processes A and B were the only two available, would they both be technically efficient? Why?

8
COSTS OF PRODUCTION

8.1 Introduction

The rate of output of a particular commodity can be expressed as a function of the rates of input of variable elements of production and of the size and nature of the available plant. The costs of producing this rate of output therefore depend on the costs associated with the employment of variable inputs and the availability of the plant. In a particular short period the plant is given, and the decisions with respect to that plant relate to its degree of utilization. All costs incurred because the plant is operated in a particular short period are called *variable costs*—they could be avoided by not operating the plant. This contrasts with other costs associated with the existence of the plant that are independent of the rate of output in the short period and that arise largely because of decisions and commitments undertaken in some earlier period. These are called *fixed costs*. As this distinction is useful when examining a firm's short-period decisions, plant costs will be divided into these two categories in the discussion that follows.

Expected total costs are important for investment or long-period decisions that determine the size and nature of the plants that will be available for production in future periods. A distinction will be made between *plant cost curves*, which relate to the operation of a particular plant, and *envelope cost curves*, which compare the costs with alternative plants.

The cost curves that receive empirical support will be presented first, and then cost curves will be derived, using neoclassical production functions.

8.2 Plant variable costs

The Marshallian short period was used in the previous chapter as the basic time period for the consideration of alternative rates of production. Plant and equipment as well as operating knowledge are assumed to be unchanged during this period, though the period is long enough to permit changes in the rate of utilization of the plant. This time period is also the basic one for the consideration of cost curves. Even though the plant is fixed, the rates of input of some of the elements of production can be varied, along with the services obtained from the plant's equipment. All costs arising from the utilization of a plant in a particular short period are called *plant variable costs*—they could be avoided by leaving the plant idle.[1] These costs include the costs of hiring variable inputs, the costs of the raw materials used up in the production process, and the loss in value of the plant's equipment due to its utilization. Some of these costs arise from monetary payments for elements of production, such as the payment for workers hired to operate the machines in the plant, while others reflect opportunities foregone. For example, if raw materials used in current production are obtained from the plant's inventories, their use will not require any current payments. However, the current value of these materials if they were sold is the *opportunity cost* of using them.[2] It is this cost that is part of the plant's variable costs.

Two categories of variable costs can be distinguished that correspond to the distinction made in Section 7.9 between direct and overhead (or indirect) labour. Costs that vary directly with variations in the rate of utilization of plant are called *direct variable costs*. They include the costs of hiring production workers, the costs of raw materials used in production, the costs of the electricity used to power the machines, and the loss in value of the equipment due to wear and tear. Costs that arise because the plant is operated in the particular short period, but that are constant for all positive rates of utilization, are called *indirect variable costs*. They include the costs of overhead labour and payments to managerial and supervisory personnel.

8.3 Plant fixed costs

The fixed costs for a plant in a particular short period are the costs that result from decisions and commitments made by the firm in some earlier period. They cannot be avoided by not operating the plant in this short

---

[1] They might also be called 'avoidable costs'. R.H. Coase suggested that this term would be more useful than the distinction between variable and fixed costs, since 'there is . . . good reason for thinking that categories of cost which vary for some changes in output do not vary for all changes of output.' 'Business Organization and the Accountant', in *L.S.E. Essays on Cost*, ed. by J.M. Buchanan and G.F. Thirlby (London: Weidenfeld & Nicolson, 1973), p. 100. The distinction between direct and indirect variable costs to be presented here does go some way to meet the problem raised by Coase.

[2] Cf. Coase, 'Business Organization and the Accountant', pp. 110-13. The loss in value of capital equipment due to the production of a particular item has been called the *user cost* of that item. John Maynard Keynes, *The General Theory of Employment, Interest and Money* (London: Macmillan & Co., 1936), p. 53.

period. The main items that are included in plant fixed costs are amortization allowances for this short period arising from the investment of finance for the plant; maintenance costs not related to plant utilization; insurance, property taxes, cost of licences, etc.; payments to managerial and supervisory personnel (if the firm is committed to employ them irrespective of the utilization of the plant in this short period); and a return for entrepreneurial effort and for the financial capital invested in the plant.

Amortization allowances are very important components of fixed costs, but their calculation involves subjective elements. The amortization allowance for a particular item of equipment should be set at such a level that when it is accumulated over the number of short periods in its expected economic life, the total should be sufficient to replace the item. The correct amount to allow for this purpose is very difficult to estimate, since it depends on future events, which cannot be accurately predicted. The economic life of an item generally differs from its physical life and is a function of the rate of technical progress that determines its rate of obsolescence. In cases where genuine uncertainty prevails, use is made of standard conventions in order to try to provide for an unknown future.[3] The economic life of items of capital equipment is taken to be shorter than the economic life of buildings, but the determination of their lengths of life must to some extent be arbitrary. When prices are increasing, it is not enough to set aside the original money cost in order to be able to replace an item when its economic life is at an end; an amount sufficient to replace it at the new prices should be accumulated. Here too the appropriate amortization allowances are determined by conventional standards that may not reflect the complexities of a changing world.

Accountants often use the term 'depreciation' to cover both obsolescence and wear and tear on machines from operation. They tend to ignore the effects of different rates of utilization on the lives of machines and base the depreciation charges for a short period on some standard formula, e.g. straight-line depreciation.

> The usual method is to include provision for obsolescence in depreciation, basing the annual charge for depreciation on an assumed working life which is much shorter than the potential working life—i.e. the physical life of the machine. Most conventional accounting, in fact, completely ignores the variable element in machine-cost; the annual depreciation charge is supposed to cover both obsolescence and wear-and-tear, but usually takes no account of variations in output. This is, in principle, quite wrong, since it distributes the charge for wear-and-tear arbitrarily and illogically between different

---

[3] Cf. *The Collected Writings of John Maynard Keynes* (London: Macmillan & Co., 1973), Vol. XIV, p. 114.

years of machine life. But where the main element in depreciation is a provision for obsolescence, the practical effect of this conceptual error is, of course, small.[4]

The wear and tear on plant due to its utilization is a variable cost (as was noted in the previous section).

Plant cost curves are used to illustrate the long-period equilibrium position of a firm (see Section 11.6), and it is therefore common practice to include in plant fixed costs an amount for 'normal profits'.[5] A businessman must expect to be able to earn at least normal profits before undertaking the necessary investment to enter a particular line of activity. *Normal profits* is an umbrella term that covers interest on the capital invested (whether borrowed or owned), the amount necessary to pay for the business ability and energy required to run the firm, as well as the organization required to bring together this business ability with capital.[6] The normal rate of profits may differ in different lines of activity if the risks involved differ.[7]

The concept of a normal rate of profits may be useful in considering investment decisions and in deciding whether to embark on a new venture or to expand an old one. The businessman's expectation of profits gives rise to the existence of plants, but once a plant is built, these investment expectations are irrelevant: the plant must be operated in the way that makes the best of the situation facing it.

8.4 The shapes of plant cost curves

The shapes of the plant cost curves depend on the nature of the production process within the plant. If the directly variable inputs are employed in fixed proportions and the rates of output and inputs increase in the same proportion until productive capacity is reached, then total variable costs can be represented by the straight line beginning at point G in Figure 8.1. (It is assumed in this diagram that productive capacity is an absolute physical limit to output.) The indirect variable costs are equal to $\$OG$ per week and the fixed costs per week are equal to $\$GH$. The total cost curve is obtained by adding $\$GH$ to the total variable costs for each rate of output.

---

[4] H. Speight, *Economics and Industrial Efficiency* (2nd ed.; London: Macmillan & Co., 1967), pp. 39-40.

[5] 'Thus the whole of the normal profits enter into true or long-period supply price.' Alfred Marshall, *Principles of Economics* (8th ed.; London: Macmillan & Co., 1920), p. 619.

[6] Marshall sometimes refers to normal profits as the 'supply price of business ability in command of capital' and notes that it is composed of three elements. 'The first is the supply price of capital; the second is the supply price of business ability and energy; and the third is the supply price of that organization by which the appropriate business ability and the requisite capital are brought together.' (*Ibid.*, p. 313.)

[7] *Ibid.*, pp. 612-14.

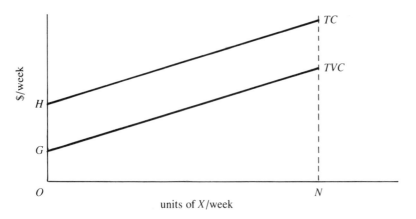

FIGURE 8.1 *Total cost curves when output increases in proportion to the employment of variable inputs*

Marginal cost (MC) is defined as the increase in total cost due to a small unit increase in output.[8] It is thus equal to the slope of the total variable cost curve (or total cost curve, since the slopes of these curves are the same by definition).[9] The marginal cost curve corresponding to the total cost curves in Figure 8.1 is drawn in Figure 8.2. Alternatively, this curve can be derived directly from the short-period marginal product of labour (defined in Section 7.9). Marginal cost is constant for constant values of the short-period marginal product of labour, given unchanged prices for the variable inputs.[10]

The average variable cost *(AVC)* for any rate of output is equal, by definition, to total variable costs divided by the rate of output. It is thus equal to the value of the slope of the line joining the point on the *TVC* curve

---

[8] The only costs that increase in this way are, by definition, the direct variable costs. If total cost (*C*) is represented by the function $C(x)$, where *x* is the rate of output, then the marginal cost (*MC*) is equal to the derivative of this function with respect to *x*. $MC = dC/dx$.

[9] If the function $C(x)$ is drawn in a figure with *x* on the abscissa (as in Figure 8.1), then its slope is equal to dC/dx.

[10] Let ΔQ be the increase in output resulting from increases in the employment of labour, ΔL, and the proportionate increase in co-operating inputs. The short-period marginal product of labour is represented by the ratio $\Delta Q/\Delta L$. The increase in total costs due to the production of ΔQ can be written as $w\Delta L + \Delta OC$, where *w* is the money-wage rate and ΔOC is the cost of complementary inputs required to increase output. Marginal cost—the increase in costs per unit increase in output—can thus be written as:

$$MC = (w\Delta L + \Delta OC)/\Delta Q = w/(\Delta Q/\Delta L) + \Delta OC/\Delta Q.$$

It is equal to the money-wage rate divided by the short-period marginal product of labour *plus* the increase in the non-labour variable costs per unit of output. Marginal cost is thus constant if the short-period marginal product of labour, the money-wage rate, and the non-labour variable costs per unit of output are constant.

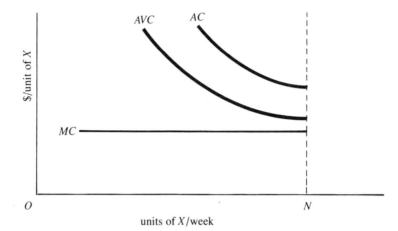

FIGURE 8.2 *Marginal and average cost curves corresponding to Figure 8.1*

(corresponding to that rate of output) to the origin. The average variable cost curve is drawn in Figure 8.2. It differs from the marginal cost curve, even though output and the employment of variable inputs increase in the same proportion because of the presence of indirect variable costs.[11] The plant average cost (*AC*) for any rate of output can be obtained by finding the value of the slope of the line joining the total cost curve to the origin. The two average cost curves are drawn in Figure 8.2. The *AVC* curve is a rectangular hyperbola, with the *MC* curve and the ordinate as its two axes. The vertical distance, at any rate of output, between *AVC* and *MC* curves, multiplied by this rate of output, must be equal to total indirect variable costs. Similarly the vertical distance between the *AC* and *AVC* curves, multiplied by the corresponding rate of output, must be equal to total fixed costs.

The cost curves drawn in Figure 8.2 end abruptly in a vertical segment because they were based on the assumption of a fixed technical limit to the possible rate of output with the given plant. This assumption can be relaxed without destroying the concept of the productive capacity of a plant, or the general approach underlying the cost curves in the figure. The concept of productive capacity contains a subjective element that has to do with the rate of output obtained when standard or normal operating procedures are followed. The term 'normal productive capacity' will thus be used to indicate the maximum rate of output that can be obtained when the plant is

---

[11] If indirect variable costs are ignored, then the *AVC* curve would coincide with the constant portion of the *MC* curve. It is drawn in this way, for example, in Tibor Scitovsky, *Welfare and Competition* (rev. ed.; Homewood, Ill.: Richard D. Irwin, 1971), p. 353.

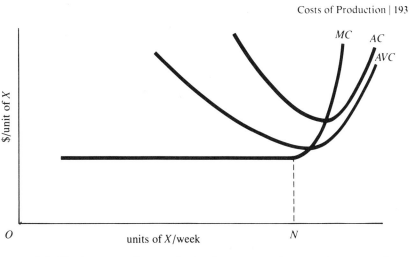

FIGURE 8.3 *Cost curves for a plant where normal operating procedures result in constant marginal costs*

operated normally (where the constant portion of the marginal cost curve terminates) rather than the maximum possible rate of output.[12] However, higher rates of output may be obtained by departing from normal operating procedures, but they would incur higher costs. These departures may take such forms as the use of older, and less efficient, standby equipment; or overtime operations where workers are paid at much higher rates.

Normal productive capacity for the plant whose cost curves are drawn in Figure 8.3 is equal to *ON* units per week. Marginal costs are assumed to increase sharply for output rates higher than *ON*. The average variable and average cost curves reach their minimum points to the right of *ON*, but not very far to the right, and they increase very sharply after that point because of the steep increase in marginal cost.

Plants that are normally worked for more than one shift may have constant portions for the marginal cost curve at more than one level. This would be the case, for example, when workers on the second and third shifts are paid at higher rates. The marginal cost curves would thus be at different levels for different shifts, as in Figure 8.4.

No distinction has been made in the diagrams drawn for this book between single- and multi-shift plants. In the case of the latter, the constant portion of the marginal cost curve will be for the most expensive shift. The marginal cost curves have not been drawn to touch the ordinate, and when there is a multi-shift operation the distance between the ordinate and the

---

[12] Cf. Jack Downie, *The Competitive Process* (London: Gerald Duckworth & Co., 1958), p. 65.

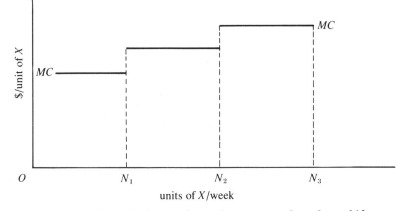

FIGURE 8.4 *Marginal costs for a plant operated on three shifts*

beginning of the curve may represent a high proportion of the total rate of output.

The assumption of constant marginal costs for manufacturing plants that can hire labour, materials, and energy at constant prices is a useful first approximation of actual plant cost curves as indicated by many empirical studies.[13] However, a complication involving the time available for adjustment to changes in output should be noted. Time is required before full adjustments can be made for changes in the utilization of plant; without these adjustments, marginal costs for both reductions and increases in output would be higher. Plant marginal cost curves, such as those in Figure 8.3, are drawn on the assumption that the firm has fully adjusted its variable inputs to each rate of output. A firm may postpone making an adjustment if changes in output appear to be temporary. For instance, it might try to avoid or minimize temporary layoffs in order to retain a trained work force that is attuned to the firm's method of operation—a valuable asset for a firm. Thus output per unit of labour might be observed to decline with falling output (marginal cost rising) and to increase with rising output (marginal cost falling).

Average variable costs decline in diagrams such as Figure 8.3 because of indirect variable costs. Declining marginal costs[14] provide an additional reason for falling average variable costs. The general effects of downward-sloping marginal cost curves on the firm's short-period decisions are conveyed by the downward-sloping average variable cost curve.

---

[13] See Section 8.14 for references.
[14] R.A. Lester argued that marginal costs would decline quite apart from problems of adjustment because plants are designed to achieve the least marginal costs at capacity. 'Equilibrium of the Firm', *American Economic Review*, Vol. 39 (March 1949), pp. 478-9.

8.5 Cost curves for neoclassical production functions: single variable input

In Section 7.13 the general features of the neoclassical production function were illustrated when there was only one variable input. The marginal and average products for this input were defined, and the corresponding product curves were derived. If payments for this variable input are the only variable costs, then the plant cost curves can be derived directly from the appropriate product curves and the price of the input. The marginal and average variable cost curves correspond to the marginal and average product curves.

Marginal cost has been defined here as the difference in total cost due to a unit difference in the rate of output. In order to achieve a higher rate of output, it is necessary to increase the rate of input of the variable element.[15] The increase in total cost associated with this change in the rate of output is equal to the cost of hiring the additional units of the variable element required to obtain the unit increase in the rate of output. These required additional units are equal to the reciprocal of the marginal product of this element—a conclusion that follows from the definition of marginal product. (Recall that for a neoclassical production function the marginal product is equal to the increase in the rate of output due to a unit increase in the rate of input of the variable element.) Marginal cost is thus equal to the product of the price of the variable element of production and the reciprocal of its marginal product.

Average variable cost is equal to total variable cost divided by the rate of output. When there is a single variable input, the total variable cost is equal to the payment for this input. Thus average variable cost must be equal to the ratio of the price of this input and its average product.

These relationships can be derived and shown using symbols. Let ΔTVC denote the increase in total variable costs for the period (TVC) resulting from a small increase in the rate of output denoted by Δx. The required increase in the rate of input of the variable productive element is denoted by Δv_1. We therefore have:

$$MC = \Delta TVC/\Delta x = p_{v_1}(\Delta v_1/\Delta x) = p_{v_1}/(\Delta x/\Delta v_1) = p_{v_1}/MP_{v_1}$$

where MP_{v_1} is the marginal product of V_1 at that point.[16]

---

[15] This differs from the situation in the preceding section where the rates of input of a group of complementary elements were increased in order to increase output, and the increase in cost covered the additional costs for *all* these inputs.

[16] This relationship can be derived by differentiating the total variable cost with respect to the rate of output:

$$MC = \frac{d\,(TVC)}{dx} = \frac{d\,(p_{v_1} \cdot v_1)}{dx} = p_{v_1} \cdot \frac{dv_1}{dx} = p_{v_1}/\frac{dx}{dv_1} = p_{v_1}/MP_{v_1}$$

Average variable cost (AVC) is equal to total variable cost (TVC) divided by the rate of output (x). Therefore,

$$AVC = TVC/x = p_{v_1} \cdot v_1/x = p_{v_1}/(x/v_1) = p_{v_1}/AP_{v_1}$$

With these results the marginal and average variable cost curves for a plant employing a single variable element of production may be derived from information on the price of that element and from the marginal and average product curves for that plant. Consider the neoclassical production function depicted in Figures 7.2 and 7.3. For the range of values in which the marginal product curve is rising, we know that the marginal cost curve must be falling, and vice versa. The marginal cost curve must have a (relative) minimum for the rate of output corresponding to the rate of input at which the marginal product curve is at its maximum. Similarly, the average variable cost curve and the average product curves are inversely related. The plant cost curves for this neoclassical production function are illustrated in Figure 8.5. (It is assumed that the price of the variable element of production is constant.)

The output rate OS, at which the marginal cost curve is at its minimum value, corresponds to the input rate OF in Figure 7.3. At this rate the marginal product curve is at its maximum value. Similarly, the output rate of OW in Figure 8.5, where the average variable cost curve is at its minimum value, is obtained when the input rate in Figure 7.3 is OJ. The *U-shaped* nature of the cost curves in Figure 8.5 is typical of cost curves derived from neoclassical production functions. This shape follows from

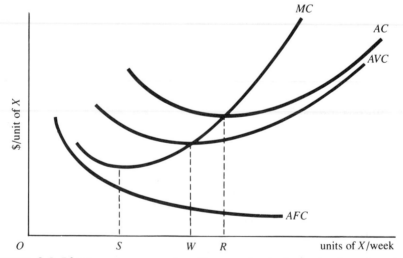

FIGURE 8.5 *Plant cost curves for the neoclassical production function depicted in Figure 7.3*

the assumption that the variable element first experiences increasing and then decreasing marginal products.

The fixed cost is required to complete the plant cost curve for this short period. In the neoclassical approach it is equal to the cost of the fixed inputs in this period. This cost is constant irrespective of the rate of output in this short period. Average fixed cost (AFC) for the period is equal to the total fixed cost (TFC) divided by the rate of output. The average fixed cost curve is thus a rectangular hyperbola, as in Figure 8.5. The products of the two co-ordinates (representing the average fixed cost and the rate of output) are constant for any plant by assumption (and equal to the total fixed cost). Average total cost (AC) can then be obtained by adding the average fixed cost to the average variable cost for any output rate. The vertical distance between the AC and AVC curves is thus smaller the larger the rate of output.

It should be noted that the marginal cost curve intersects both the average variable and average cost curves at their minimum values. This relationship follows from the definitions of marginal and average concepts (see Section 9.13). When the marginal values are below the corresponding average values, then the average curve must be falling; when they are above the corresponding average values, then the average curve must be rising. It therefore follows that when the marginal and average values are the same (with the marginal being lower for a lower rate of output and higher for a higher rate), the average curve has a (relative) minimum value.

The shape of the total variable cost curve can be inferred from the marginal cost curve. For an infinitesimally small increase in the rate of output (*lim* $\Delta x \rightarrow 0$), the marginal cost is equal to the slope of the total cost curve. Thus the value for the slope of the total variable cost curve increases when marginal cost increases, and it decreases when marginal cost decreases. This means that for the plant whose marginal cost curve is drawn in Figure 8.5, the total variable cost curve must be concave from below for input rates from zero to OS; for larger input rates it must be convex from below.[17] This total variable cost curve is drawn in Figure 8.6.[18]

The weekly rate of the total fixed cost is indicated in Figure 8.6 by a horizontal line drawn at a vertical distance from the abscissa equal to the

---

[17] If a curve is concave from below, its slope is *decreasing* in value for higher rates of output, and if it is convex from below its slope is *increasing* in value with higher rates of output.

[18] It can also be obtained in the present case directly from the total product curve in Figure 7.2. Total variable cost is equal to the rate of input of the single variable element V_1 multiplied by its price. The shape of the cost curve, with respect to the abscissa, must be the same as the shape of the total product curve with respect to the ordinate because of the inverse relationship between productivity and cost.

TABLE 8.1 *Derivation of plant cost curves from data on total, average, and marginal products (There is only one variable element of production)*

VARIABLE INPUT (units of V_1/week)	RATE OF OUTPUT (units of X/week)	AVERAGE PRODUCT (AP_{v_1}) (units of X/unit of V_1)	MARGINAL PRODUCT (MP_{v_1}) (units of X/unit of V_1)	TOTAL VARIABLE COST (TVC) (P_{v_1} = $20) ($/week)	AVERAGE VARIABLE COST (AVC) ($/unit of X)	MARGINAL COST (MC) ($/unit of X)	TOTAL FIXED COST (TFC) ($/week)	AVERAGE FIXED COST ($/unit of X)	TOTAL COST (TC) ($/week)	AVERAGE COST (AC) ($/unit of X)
1	2	3	4	5	6	7	8	9	10	11
		(2) ÷ (1)			(5) ÷ (2) = P_{v_1}/AP_{v_1}	$P_{v_1} \div MP_{v_1}$		(8) ÷ (2)	(5) + (8)	(10) ÷ (2) = (6) + (9)
1	10	10	—	20	2.00	—	100	10.00	120	12.00
2	30	15	20	40	1.33	1.00	100	3.33	140	4.66
3	51	17	21	60	1.18	0.96	100	1.96	160	3.14
4	70	17 1/2	19	80	1.14	1.06	100	1.43	180	2.57
5	80	16	10	100	1.25	2.00	100	1.25	200	2.50
6	84	14	4	120	1.43	5.00	100	1.19	220	2.62

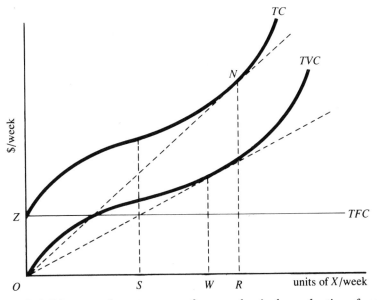

FIGURE 8.6 *Plant total cost curves for neoclassical production function depicted in Figure 7.3*

value for the fixed cost (*OZ* in the figure). Total cost is simply the sum of the variable and fixed costs. The shape of the total cost curve is precisely that of the total variable cost curve, and the initial point for the total cost curve is equal to the total fixed cost.

The average cost is equal to the total cost divided by the rate of output; it is therefore equal to the slope of the line joining a point on the total cost curve (corresponding to this rate of output) to the origin. For example, in Figure 8.6 the average cost, when the rate of output is equal to *OR*, is equal to the slope of the line *ON*. When the total cost curve has the shape drawn in Figure 8.6, then the average cost reaches its minimum value at a rate of output corresponding to the point at which the line joining the total cost curve to the origin is tangent to the curve. This occurs at an output rate of *OR* in Figure 8.6. It is greater than the output rate at which the average variable cost reaches its minimum value because of the presence of a fixed cost. The average fixed cost for a particular rate of output is equal to the slope of the line joining the total fixed cost curve to the origin.

8.6 A numerical example
A simple numerical example may serve as a useful illustration of the way in which costs can be derived from a neoclassical production function. The treatment of marginal products is always somewhat arbitrary in numerical examples, since they are defined for infinitesimally small differences, while

the differences shown in numerical examples are finite. In Table 8.1 the convention followed shows the marginal product corresponding to a rate of input as the difference in the rate of output when the rate of input has been increased by one unit. For example, the marginal product for a rate of input of 3 is shown to be the increase in the rate of output resulting from an increase in the rate of input from 2 to 3.

The numerical example in Table 8.1 is self-explanatory. Note that the minimum value for marginal cost is reached for a rate of output lower than that at which the minimum value of average variable cost occurs. Average cost has its minimum value at a higher rate of output than does average variable cost.

8.7 Neoclassical production functions: two variable inputs

Isocost curves can be used to illustrate the derivation of plant cost curves when there are two variable elements of production. An isocost curve shows the combinations of the quantities of the two inputs that cost the same amount. For example, in Figure 8.7 all points on the isocost labelled C_1 represent pairs of values for the inputs that cost $\$C_1$ per week to hire in the specified short period. Where the prices of the two elements are constant, as in the situation illustrated in Figure 8.7, then isocosts are linear. Isocosts are analogous to the budget lines introduced in the theory of consumer behaviour. The numerical values of the slopes of these curves are equal to the ratios of the prices of the two variable elements of production. This result can be obtained from the equation for an isocost line. This equation is equal to $C = p_{v_1} v_1 + p_{v_2} v_2$. C is total variable cost; v_1 and v_2 represent the rates of input of the elements V_1 and V_2 respectively. This equation can be re-written as $v_2 = (C/p_{v_2}) - (p_{v_1}/p_{v_2})v_1$. The numerical value of the slope of the isocost is thus equal to p_{v_1}/p_{v_2}.

The combination of the rates of input of the two variable elements that produces a specified rate of output at minimum cost is represented by the point of tangency between an isocost and the isoquant for that rate of output. For example, in Figure 8.7 the minimum cost for the production of the rate of output x_1, given the prices of the variable elements reflected in the isocost line C_1, is obtained when the input combination represented by point E_1 is employed. The appropriate rates of input are $O_{v_{11}}$ for V_1, and $O_{v_{21}}$ for V_2. All other combinations of these elements, which produce the output rate x_1, given the specified prices, lie on higher isocost curves. This does not mean they are technically inefficient. All the input combinations on the isoquant x_1 are technically efficient, by assumption, but *economic efficiency* depends on prices as well as technology.

An important property of least-cost combinations follows from the

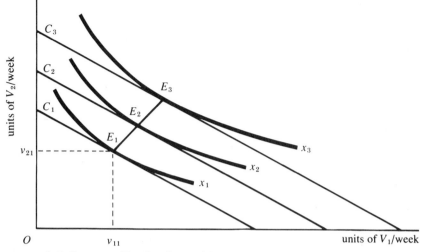

FIGURE 8.7 *Isocosts (C₁, C₂, C₃) and isoquants (x₁, x₂, x₃) for a neoclassical production function with two variable inputs*

tangency of isocosts and isoquants at points representing these combinations. The numerical value for the slope of an isoquant is equal, as we saw in Section 7.15, to the ratio of the marginal products of the variable elements of production. Since the slope of an isocost is equal to the ratio of the prices of the two variable elements of production, it follows that for a least-cost combination of the rates of input, the ratio of the marginal products of these two elements is equal to the ratio of their prices.

This result can be derived using the notation employed in previous sections: $MRTS_{v_1 v_2} = MP_{v_1}/MP_{v_2}$. At all these least-cost combinations, $MRTS_{v_1 v_2} = p_{v_1}/p_{v_2}$. Therefore for all combinations such as these, $MP_{v_1}/MP_{v_2} = p_{v_1}/p_{v_2}$. An alternative way of writing this, which will be useful when the number of variable elements is greater than two, is $MP_{v_1}/p_{v_1} = MP_{v_2}/p_{v_2}$.

The curve joining all points such as E_1 and E_2, representing the input combinations that produce the different rates of output least cost, is called the *expansion path*, which in Figure 8.7 is the curve $E_1 E_2 E_3$. It joins the points of tangency of the isocosts and isoquants. With given values for the fixed inputs and technology, and thus isoquants, the position of the expansion path depends on the ratio of the prices of the two variable elements of production when they are at least partially substitutable. Each point on the expansion path shows both a rate of output and the lowest cost for the variable elements required to produce that output rate in the given situation. The total variable cost of producing various rates of output is

TABLE 8.2 *Total variable cost derived from Figure 8.7*

OUTPUT (units of X/week)	TOTAL VARIABLE COST ($/week)
x_1	C_1
x_2	C_2
x_3	C_3

obtained from the expansion path. This derivation is illustrated in Table 8.2.[19]

The total fixed cost is added to the total variable cost in order to obtain the total cost. The different categories of average cost are then derived by dividing the appropriate total cost by the corresponding rate of output. The marginal cost is obtained by comparing the total costs (or total variable costs) of producing slightly different rates of output. The curves representing these costs for neoclassical production functions are usually drawn with the same shapes as the plant cost curves shown in Figures 8.5 and 8.6. Even though there are now two variable inputs rather than only one, there are still some fixed inputs. Diminishing returns are assumed to be encountered for rates of input of the two variable elements above some particular values. Figures 8.5 and 8.6 can thus be used to indicate the general pattern of short-period cost curves for all neoclassical production functions.

8.8 Neoclassical production functions: many variable inputs

When the number of variable inputs is greater than two, it is not possible to draw isocosts and isoquants, though the requirements for production at least cost would still be the same. A least-cost combination of the rates of input of the variable elements is one for which the ratios of their marginal products to their prices are equal. This condition can be written in symbols, when the number of variable productive elements is n, as:

$$\frac{MP_{v_1}}{p_{v_1}} = \frac{MP_{v_2}}{p_{v_2}} = \ldots = \frac{MP_{v_n}}{p_{v_n}}$$

The total variable cost of producing a particular output rate is equal to the cost of the least-cost combination of the direct variable elements, plus any other expenditure that depends on production in this period. The cost curves for this function follow the pattern of those drawn in Figures 8.5 and 8.6.

---

[19] If the production function is homogeneous (of any degree), then the expansion path will be a straight line. Why? (Recall Footnote 36 in Chapter 7.)

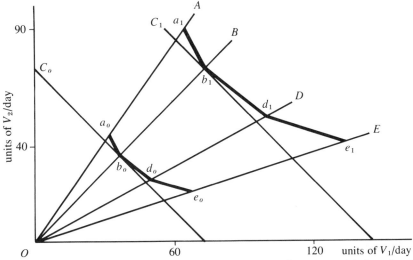

FIGURE 8.8 *Isocosts and isoquants for a production function with four basic linear production processes (*SOURCE: *Table 7.1)*

8.9 Derivation of cost curves: linear production processes

In our discussion of the theory of production we considered production functions that incorporate a finite (and possibly small) number of linear production processes. In each process the variable elements of production are combined in fixed proportions, and a process displays constant returns to equi-proportional variations in their rates of input. The four *basic linear production processes* used in Figure 7.7 appear again in Figure 8.8. All these processes are technically efficient. The choice of process to be used to produce a specified rate of output depends on the prices of the variable elements of production. The firm is assumed to produce each rate of output at the least cost. This means that it will choose, from all the possible technically efficient combinations for producing the specified rate of output, the combination that lies on the lowest isocost. Since the isoquants in Figure 8.8 are not smooth, the least-cost combination may not be characterized by tangency between an isocost and an isoquant.

$a_1 b_1 d_1 e_1$ is the isoquant for the unit rate of output. If the ratio of prices for the two variable elements is equal to the numerical value for the slopes of the isocosts C_0 and C_1, then process B produces the output at the least cost.

The expansion path—the curve showing the different least-cost combinations of the variable elements for different rates of output—will be linear in this case. It is the ray OB in Figure 8.8 when the isocosts are represented by C_0 and C_1. Knowing the isocosts and isoquants, we can read off from this expansion path the required expenditure on the variable elements for each rate of output. Because these production processes display constant returns, it can be shown that the required increase in expenditure on the variable elements is proportional to the increase in the rate of output. For example, the isoquant curve $a_0 b_0 d_0 e_0$ in Figure 8.8 represents a rate of output equal to one-half the unit rate. The rates of input of the two variable elements at point b_0 are one-half what they are at b_1. With prices for the inputs constant, total expenditures on these inputs at b_0 must also be one-half what they would be at point b_1. Thus the marginal cost curve for a plant with linear production processes must be horizontal (until the capacity rate of output is reached). A marginal cost curve of this type was drawn in Figure 8.2.[20]

The isoquants for a production function that incorporates more than one linear production process have 'corners' at points representing basic production processes. They differ in this respect from the 'smooth' isoquants derived from the standard neoclassical production functions where even a slight change in the relative prices of the variable elements will result in some substitution between these elements. With discrete production processes a substantial change in relative prices might be required for any substitution. In Figure 8.8, for example, a slightly higher price of V_2 relative to V_1, which decreases the numerical values of the slopes of the isocosts in Figure 8.8, will not lead to any change in the proportions in which these two elements are employed. Production process B would still be the one chosen. However, a more substantial shift in relative prices would change the process chosen and thus the ratio in which the two variable elements were employed.

When the price ratio of the two variable elements equals the numerical value of one of the slopes of the isoquants, both of the basic production processes that contribute to this segment, as well as all linear combinations of the two, are economically efficient. For example, if the price ratio for the variable elements is equal to the numerical value of the slope of segment

---

[20] Although the marginal cost curve in Figure 8.2, and that obtained for the production function in Figure 8.8, have the same shape, there is an important difference between the two. The short-period production function underlying Figure 8.2 contains only one production process, and a change to another process would require a change in the plant; that is, the types of machines installed would have to be different. Substitution between categories of elements can occur in this case only after sufficient time has passed so that the necessary changes in the plant can be made. In deciding whether to make these changes, the firm would consider expected future prices, not current prices. The production function shown in Figure 8.8, however, incorporates four basic production processes. It is assumed that the choice of production process can be altered within a short period. In this case it is the current prices for the elements of production, and plant technology, that determine the process chosen.

b_1d_1 in Figure 8.8, then both production processes B and D and all linear combinations of the two are the least-cost processes. Of course this condition does not change the nature of the cost curves derived from this production function: the marginal cost curve will be horizontal, given constant prices for the variable elements of production, because any combination of processes exhibits constant returns to these elements.

8.10 Plant and envelope cost curves

Plant cost curves are relevant for a firm's production decisions and financial accounts. There is another set of cost curves that may be useful for investment decisions. It shows the costs of producing different rates of output if the firm can choose the least-cost rate of input of *all* the elements of production. The term used for these cost curves in this book is *envelope cost curves* (in other textbooks they are usually referred to as long-run cost curves). They can be derived from a comparison of plant cost curves when special assumptions are made.

The levels and shapes of the cost curves for a plant, such as those drawn in Figure 8.3, depend on the technical characteristics and prices of the elements of production, technical knowledge, and the type and quantity of elements of production that make up the plant. If the plant were of a different size (that is, if the vector of quantities of the elements of production it contains, $\overline{K}$, had a different set of values), its costs for any specified rate of output would usually differ. This would be so even though the two plants were based on the same technology and the prices of all the elements of production were the same. Another way of indicating the size of the plant is in terms of its *scale*, i.e. the rate of output at which the plant would achieve minimum average costs. The larger the values for the elements of production in the fixed plant the greater, in general, is the output rate at which minimum average costs are achieved.

The expression 'based on the same technology', used when discussing different types or sizes of plants, is not an easy one to comprehend. It can be taken to mean that the technical information available and known to the builders and operators of any one of these plants was also available and known to the builders and operators of the other types of plants. However, the number of different-sized plants that may be built on the basis of a given technology may be very small. It may be that an advance in technical knowledge is specific to (and has been developed for and is embodied in) only one type of plant of a particular size. A comparison of the costs of producing different rates of output for this plant with the costs for other plants built earlier would reflect the differences in technical knowledge as well as the effects of the differences in the size of plants. If a plant much larger than any previously built is planned, then new technical problems would have to be faced and solved. This would also be the case for a plant much smaller than any previously built, as the many technical innovations in miniaturization that have come about as a result of the aerospace programs bear witness. Comparison of cost curves for different-sized plants based on the same technology thus leaves out important features of the investment process. However, as this comparison frequently appears in traditional neoclassical economic theory, it will be presented briefly here.

Some of the elements of production that comprise the plant (represented by the symbol $\overline{K}$ in the statement of the production function) may be available only in a few sizes. If this is the case, then the number of plants to be compared will be small. A situation in which the choice for investment is restricted to only three plants is illustrated in Figure 8.9. An important machine that dominates the production process here is available only in three sizes: small, medium, and large. It is further assumed in this example that employing two of these machines in a single plant is not feasible; there must be a separate plant for each machine.

A firm faced with a choice between these plants would, in effect, be choosing between alternative cost curves. If it is in a position to base its decisions only on considerations of the costs shown in Figure 8.9 (assuming that the prices of the elements of production are expected to be unchanged over the planning period), then the choice depends on the rate of output of commodity X that it requires from this plant. For example, if this rate is less than OF, the firm will choose the small plant. The medium plant will be chosen if it expects to produce in the interval FG; while the large plant will be chosen if it expects to produce more than OG. If the expected average weekly rate of output were much greater than OG, the firm might choose to build and operate more than one plant.

An *envelope average cost curve* can be constructed from portions of the individual plant average cost curves. This curve is labelled EAC in Figure 8.9, while the plant cost curves are labelled PAC. The envelope average cost curve shows the minimum plant average cost for producing any rate of output, given the state of technology and the levels of prices for all the elements of production. For output rates less than OF in Figure 8.9, the average costs for the small plant are the lowest, and the envelope average cost curve is, for these rates of output, the average cost curve for this plant. For output rates in the range FG, the envelope cost curve is obtained from the costs for the medium plant; and for outputs larger than OG it coincides with the average cost curve for the large plant.

When one of the important elements of production in the plant is available only in a finite number of sizes, as in the example illustrated in Figure

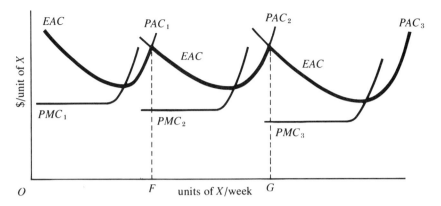

FIGURE 8.9 *Envelope average cost curve, and plant average cost curves for three plants based on the same technology in a specified short period*

8.9, the envelope average cost curve will not have unique values for its slope at all points. If the differences between the sizes of plants can be made as small as desired, the envelope average cost curve will be smooth. An example of such a curve is drawn in Figure 8.10. (In this example the cost curves are derived from neoclassical production functions and are U-shaped.) The marginal cost curve corresponding to the envelope average cost curve will be called the envelope marginal cost curve to distinguish it from plant marginal cost curves. The envelope marginal cost is equal to the marginal cost for the plant whose average costs for the rate of output are lowest.

The term 'envelope curve', without further identification, will always refer to the envelope average cost curve.

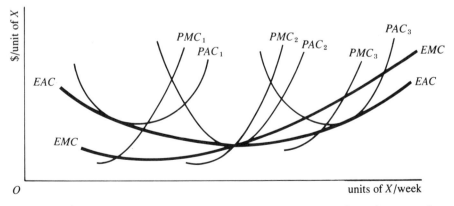

FIGURE 8.10 *Envelope average and marginal cost curves when plants can be of any size (neoclassical production functions)*

8.11 Envelope versus long-run cost curves

Plant cost curves are often referred to in the economics literature as *short-run* cost curves and envelope cost curves as *long-run* cost curves. These terms are not employed in this book because the adjective 'long-run' can be very misleading when applied to envelope curves.

Short run and long run refer to the passage of time. (Keynes's often-quoted statement, 'In the long run we are all dead', will be familiar to many.) Changes in the numbers and sizes of plants take time, and it is only 'in the long run', after a sequence of short periods, that these changes can be effected. However, an envelope cost curve has nothing to do with this lengthy passage of time. It shows the lowest average cost for producing any rate of output with plants that are based on the same technology. If the industry being analysed is dynamic and experiencing technical change, the new plants being constructed will be based on a technology that differs from that of the older ones. Over a long run of time the movement will not be from one point to another on the envelope curve but rather to *another* envelope curve. If the technology in the industry is unchanging over time, and prices of the elements of production are also constant, then firms may move from one point (plant) on the envelope curve to another point (plant) on the same curve. However, this would be a very special case and the designation 'long-run cost curves' should not be used because this would imply that it was the norm.

8.12 Returns to scale

The size of a plant will be indicated by an indirect measure that is the normal productive capacity for the plant.[21] For example, the capacity rate of output for the plant whose cost curves are shown in Figure 8.3 is ON units of X per week. Different-sized plants, even though they are 'based on the same technology', may have different values for their minimum average costs. The effects of size on minimum average costs are referred to by the term *returns to scale*.

If there are *constant returns to scale*, then the minimum average costs for different-sized plants will be the same. Plants of different sizes achieve minimum average costs at different rates of output, but these costs are the same for all. If this had been the case for the plants depicted in Figure 8.9, then the envelope curve would reach its minimum value at 3 rates of output. If the size of the plants can vary continuously, as in the case of Figure 8.10, then with constant returns to scale the envelope curve would be parallel to

---

[21] There is no unit for a direct measure of size. Plants may differ in the quantities and types of equipment.

the abscissa at a height equal to the minimum plant average costs. (The envelope marginal cost curve would coincide with the envelope curve.) With *increasing returns to scale* (or *economies of scale*), the minimum plant average cost would be lower the larger the size of plant within the range of plant sizes in which this tendency predominates. The envelope cost curve in Figure 8.9 exhibits increasing returns to scale for the range of rates of output shown. If there are *decreasing returns to scale* (or *diseconomies of scale*), then the minimum plant average costs for plants in the size range where this feature is to be found would be higher the larger the size of the plant.

A particular envelope curve may exhibit both increasing and decreasing returns to scale. The envelope curve in Figure 8.10, for example, exhibits increasing returns to scale for plants up to a certain size, then decreasing returns for larger plants. In some situations the appropriate envelope curve will exhibit increasing returns over the range of smaller-sized plants, then constant returns for a range of bigger plants, without any sign of diminishing returns. Envelope curves of this type are said to be 'L-shaped'.

8.13 Factors determining returns to scale

The importance of economies of scale in determining the growth possibilities of an economy has often been emphasized. (See the reference to Adam Smith in Section 2.2.) Various reasons have been advanced for the occurrence of these economies.

(i) *Indivisibilities*. There are some elements of production whose presence in the plant is independent, within some range of values, of its scale of output. Examples would be items of capital equipment that are available only in a limited number of sizes. (In other words they are indivisible.) The different items of capital equipment may have different capacity rates of operation. To make the most efficient use of them, the plant's scale of output should be equal to the lowest common multiple of these productive capacities. For example, consider two machines, one of which has a designed capacity of 1,000 units of output per week, while the other has a designed capacity of 1,500 units of output per week. The least common multiple of these capacities is 3,000 units per week, and a plant designed for this output rate would enjoy economies of scale when compared to plants with lower capacities. As these plants would not be able to utilize fully one or both of these machines, their costs would be spread over a smaller output. For example, a plant with a designed capacity of 2,000 units would still require two machines of each type, but the machines with a capacity of 1,500 units would be only partially utilized.

Some of the costs associated with making a plant available for production—such as initial development and design costs—might be independent, within some range of values, of the scale of output. The larger the scale of output of a plant within the appropriate range of values, the smaller the unit cost with respect to these costs.

(ii) *The economies of increased dimensions.* C.F. Pratten has written: 'For many types of capital equipment both initial and operating costs increase less rapidly than capacity. A typical example of such economies occurs in the construction of tanks, pressure vessels and road and sea tankers which are commonly used in the chemical and oil industries. If the thickness of the walls of a tank are not affected by its size, then the cost of increasing capacity increases approximately in proportion to the surface area, while the capacity of the tank rises in proportion to its cubic capacity. . . . Operating costs may also be affected by the size of units. In the processing industries the total direct labour costs of operating units of equipment are not much affected by their size, and maintenance costs are usually assumed to be proportional to the capital costs of equipment.'[22]

It has been estimated that the increase in cost due to increased dimensions is approximately 60 per cent of the increase in capacity.

(iii) *The economies of specialization.* Plants designed for larger rates of output provide more opportunity for the employment of labour with special skills and for the introduction of special-purpose capital equipment. For example, it may be possible to make use of more automated machinery.

(iv) *The economies of massed resources.* Pratten has also written: 'The operation of the law of large numbers may result in economies of scale of massed resources. For example, a firm using several identical machines will have to stock proportionately fewer spare parts than a firm with only one, because the firm with several machines can assume that its machines are unlikely to develop the same faults at the same time.'[23]

(v) *Pecuniary economies.* The amounts of the elements of production purchased by firms with large outputs are greater than those for firms with smaller plants. Large orders may enable firms to obtain some of these elements at lower prices because of greater bargaining power or because suppliers are able to fill these larger orders at lower unit costs. (In the discussion of envelope curves, we assumed that the prices of all the elements were unaffected by the scale of operations.)

Diseconomies of scale might occur for a variety of reasons. They may be due to:

(i) *Limitations on the availability of elements of production.* It may not

---

[22] *Economies of Scale in Manufacturing Industry* (Cambridge, Eng.: Cambridge University Press, 1971), p. 12.
[23] *Ibid.*, pp. 12-13.

be possible to increase the quantity of some essential element of production, or it may be increased only at substantially higher unit costs. For example, the labour supply in the area where the plant is to be located may be limited and more workers could be obtained only at higher costs. Similarly there may be limits to the supply at constant unit cost of a natural element such as water for the production process.

(ii) *Technical forces*. 'There are some technical forces which cause diseconomies of scale. As the capacity of individual units of plant is increased, increased stresses and strains and friction may result, and to combat these, wider gauge walls etc. must have to be used, different, and more expensive materials employed, cooling systems, or improved cooling systems be introduced, or more elaborate foundations may have to be built.'[24]

(iii) *Management*. The problems of supervising and co-ordinating the operations in large plants may become very difficult and costly to overcome.

Discussion of economies of scale within the context of given technology is very artificial. The scope for economies of scale is very much affected by changes in technology, which often result from decisions to change the scale of plant.

8.14 Empirical estimates of cost curves

The two types of theoretical cost curves discussed in this book have been based on different assumptions concerning the nature of the plant. The U-shaped neoclassical curves are based on the assumption that the given plant with its complement of equipment is very adaptable and that different proportions of the variable elements of production can be usefully employed in this plant. The marginal cost curves with large constant portions, such as the one drawn in Figure 8.3, are based on the assumption that the normal operation of the plant uses the variable inputs in constant proportions, and that variations in their rates of input result in equiproportional changes in the rate of output up to productive capacity.

Reliable empirical estimates of plant cost curves are difficult to obtain. Published data on costs and output are scarce, and much of the data available is not in a suitable form to permit a clear-cut test of the two sets of assumptions.[25] The limited evidence that is available tends to confirm the

---

[24] *Ibid.*, pp. 14-15.

[25] Many of these statistical studies are summarized in J. Johnston, *Statistical Cost Analysis* (New York: McGraw-Hill, 1960), Chapter 5. Johnston's impression from the studies he has examined 'is that the various short-run studies more often than not indicate constant marginal cost and declining average cost as the pattern that best seems to describe the data that had been analyzed.' (p. 168)

TABLE 8.3 *Relationship of relative unit costs to plant scale in seven manufacturing industries*

MINIMUM COST OUTPUT OF PLANT AS PER CENT OF TOTAL MARKET SALES	PLANT SCALE AS A PERCENTAGE OF TOTAL OUTPUT SOLD IN THE APPROPRIATE MARKET								
	5	4	3.5	3	2	1.5	1	0.5	0.25
	(lowest minimum average cost = 100)								
Cement	100	..	105	..	115	..	135	..	..
Rayon	..	100	..	..	108	..	125	..	..
Soap	..	100	..	..	103	..	105	..	..
Petroleum refining	..	100	100.5	101	102	103	105	108	115
Cigarettes	100	..	..	..	101	..	102	..	..
Tires and Tubes	..	..	..	..	100	101	..	104.5	105.5
Liquor	..	..	..	..	..	100	100.5	101	102

SOURCE: J.S. Bain, *Barriers to New Competition* (Cambridge, Mass.: Harvard University Press, 1956), p. 80.

view that operation of a manufacturing plant, at least within wide limits, exhibits constant returns to the variable direct elements of production. The marginal cost is thus constant over the corresponding range of output.

Economists have investigated the nature of the returns to different sizes of plant and their studies confirm the existence of economies of scale. Minimum average costs of production are lower for larger plants, at least until some minimum size of plant is reached. The pattern found in these studies is illustrated by the data in Table 8.3 collected by J.S. Bain.

Bain reports that his respondents (business executives) believed that a point will usually be reached where the minimum average costs will not be lower for larger plants. 'That is, the opportunities offered for cost reduction through specialization or through massive buying power are ultimately exhausted as the plant or firm increases in scale, until a point is reached in the range of possible scales beyond which further increases in scale will not bring about further reductions in cost. At some finite scale, therefore, there will be reached a point beyond which a larger plant or firm will not have lower unit costs.'[26] Economies of scale, therefore, are expected not to exist after a certain point.

'The evidence on diseconomies of scale is much less certain,' in the words of John Johnston, 'for, while there is in some studies a suggestion of an upturn at the top end of the size scale, it is usually small in magnitude and well within the range of variation displayed by the

[26] J.S. Bain, *Barriers to New Competition* (Cambridge, Mass.: Harvard University Press, 1956), p. 58.

data.'[27] This is also the general conclusion reached by Wiles after the examination of many sets of data.[28]

It would therefore seem reasonable that the analysis of the behaviour of firms in economic theory should not place any great emphasis on the rising portion of the envelope cost curve. The envelope curve does appear to follow an L-shaped pattern.

8.15 External pecuniary economies and diseconomies

In the discussion of the theory of production we introduced the terms 'external technical economies' and 'diseconomies'. The production possibilities facing a firm are affected by changes in the rates of output of other firms. These effects of the changes are reflected in the firm's costs owing to the consequent changes in the rates of input of the variable elements of production required to produce any specified rate of output. As a result of the activities of other firms, a firm's costs can also be affected when they cause changes in the prices the firm must pay for its inputs. If higher rates of output in other firms raise the prices of some of the elements of production it employs, then the firm is said to experience *external pecuniary diseconomies*. If these higher rates of output lower the prices of some of its inputs, then the firm is said to experience *external pecuniary economies*.

External pecuniary diseconomies could be created where firms hire labour from the same area. Increased production and employment on the part of some firms would tend to raise wage rates, and thus the costs of other firms. An example of external pecuniary economies would be where one of the byproducts of a production process was used as an element of production in some other process. Increased activity by plants of the first type would increase the supply of these elements and lower their prices for other plants. For example, sulphur could be a byproduct of some plants when pollution-control devices are installed. An increase in their rates of output would lower the price of sulphur for other plants that use it in their production processes.

8.16 Summary

This chapter distinguished between variable and fixed costs, and some of the possible shapes for plant cost curves were examined. These shapes depend on the assumptions made about the nature of the production function. Empirical estimates of plant cost curves give some support to

---

[27] J. Johnston, *Statistical Cost Analysis* (New York: McGraw Hill, 1960), p. 193.

[28] P.J.D. Wiles, *Price, Cost, and Output* (Oxford: Clarendon Press, 1956), pp. 227-51.

the assumption that the variable inputs and output increase in the same proportion. The resulting short-period marginal cost curve is constant for a large range of output up to normal productive capacity. Neoclassical production functions, which are based on the assumption of first increasing and then decreasing returns, give rise to U-shaped marginal cost curves. Both types of plant cost curves will be used in the analysis of the behaviour of firms in later chapters. The U-shaped curves will be employed when the neoclassical approach is being presented, and the reverse-L-shaped marginal cost curve when alternative approaches are being considered.

Envelope average cost curves show the lowest average cost of producing any rate of output, given technology, and the prices of all the inputs. These curves are built up from a comparison of the costs for different rates of output from alternative plants. They cannot be used to indicate the change in costs when output changes, unless the analysis is concerned with stationary states where technical knowledge is constant.

SUGGESTED READINGS

Chamberlin, E.H. 'The Cost Curve of the Individual Producer', Appendix B, *The Theory of Monopolistic Competition*. 6th ed. Cambridge, Mass.: Harvard University Press, 1950. Pages 230-259.

Johnston, J. *Statistical Cost Analysis*. New York: McGraw Hill, 1960. Chapters 5 and 6.

Pratten, C.F. *Economies of Scale in Manufacturing Industry*. Cambridge, Eng.: Cambridge University Press, 1971.

Scitovsky, T. *Welfare and Competition*. Rev. ed. Homewood, Ill.: Richard D. Irwin, 1971. Chapter 19.

Viner, J. 'Cost Curves and Supply Curves'. 1931 article reprinted in American Economic Association, *Readings in Price Theory*. Edited by G.J. Stigler and K. Boulding. Homewood, Ill.: Richard D. Irwin, 1952. Pages 198-232.

EXERCISES

1. Classify the following plant costs as either *fixed* or *variable*.

(a) Wages paid to a semi-skilled worker whose employment depends on the operation of the plant.

(b) Wages paid to a machinist who repairs machines that have suffered 'wear and tear' in production.

(c) Wages paid to a machinist who carries out routine maintenance on machines in the plant.

(d) Amortization allowances on plant and fixed equipment.

(e) The proportion of head-office expenses allocated to this plant.

(f) Municipal property taxes.

(g) Costs of raw materials.

(h) Payments to supervisors who are on annual contracts.

(i) Interest payments on working capital.

2. (a) Draw a complete set of short-period cost curves (marginal, average variable, and average cost curves) for a plant of the type described in Exercise 1 in Chapter 7 when the plant is operated on a single-shift basis.

(b) Draw the same curves as in (a) if the plant also has some older and less-efficient machines for use in periods of very high demand.

(c) Draw the plant cost curves under the same conditions as (a), with the plant being operated on three shifts. A shift premium is paid to workers on the middle shift and a double premium to those working the final shift.

3. What can we infer about the value for the slope of the average cost curve from the information that marginal costs are less than average costs? Why?

4. Assume that the cost of labour and all the machine services, fuel supplies, etc., that are included in the phrase 'with appropriate agricultural implements' in Exercise 2, Chapter 7, is $6,000 per man year. The farmer's fixed costs (the costs he is faced with in the particular year even if he does not use his land for production) are $10,000 per year.

(a) Derive the marginal, average variable, and average total costs for all the rates of output shown in the table in Exercise 2, Chapter 7.

(b) Draw these three types of cost curves and show their relationship.

(c) Why does the average cost curve have a positive slope when the marginal cost is greater than the average cost?

5. 'The envelope average cost curve joins up the minimum points on the plant average cost curves.' Do you agree? Why?

6. What do you understand by the term 'envelope average cost curve'? Why is it not a long-run average cost curve?

9
MARKET AND
INDUSTRIAL STRUCTURES

9.1 Introduction

Attempts to explain the factors determining the price and rate of output for a particular commodity must take into account the nature of its market. The examination of the determination of price in Chapters 2 and 3 was restricted to perfectly competitive markets, which are an idealized representation of markets for primary commodities in the absence of intervention by either the government or producer associations. The numbers of buyers and sellers in such markets are large, and individual buyers and sellers have no appreciable influence on the prices of the commodities. Also, the goods sold in each of these perfectly competitive markets are assumed to be homogeneous. They can be graded according to established criteria by independent authorities, and the outputs of individual producers are indistinguishable. For the products of manufacturing industries, however, the normal state of affairs is one in which the products of individual producers are distinguishable. The number of sellers (and even the number of buyers) is often not large. The determination of price and output for manufactured goods should thus be based on models that differ from those used for primary commodities.

There are many ways in which markets may be classified. It is customary to distinguish them according to the numbers of buyers and sellers, and the homogeneity (or lack of it) of the products sold. Further distinctions can be made according to the extent of the differentiation of their products. Some of the most commonly used categories will be defined here. We shall also examine the patterns of the demand curves facing individual sellers, and the supply curves facing buyers, in these types of markets.

Reality is difficult to channel into neat categories; it does not conform to the boundaries that analysts employ in order to arrive at precise conclusions. This is particularly true with respect to markets, where any actual market may be influenced by forces that economic theories attribute to markets of a different category. Market categories can be useful for purposes of economic analysis if they are considered only as rough-and-ready frameworks to be discarded when necessary, rather than as Procrustean beds within which all markets must be fitted.

9.2 Commodity and industrial classification

It is sometimes useful to make a distinction between commodity and industrial classification. Manufactured products are classified according to the market they supply, so that items that are close substitutes from the buyers' point of view are treated as though they are in the same commodity category. Two goods may be close substitutes for some uses but not for all (e.g. aluminum and copper), and this difference can influence the behaviour of the producers. Products from different manufacturers producing the same type of thing are never quite interchangeable. Each has its own style, and each manufacturer has his own reputation for reliability as well as his own particular geographical location. Not only does this competition exist in clearly defined markets, but any commodity competes in a certain sense with everything else as an object for expenditure. For example, a family's choice may be between a new automobile or a trip to Europe; between new furniture or a vacation, etc.

This separation of markets and the classification of commodities is thus a matter of degree. For some purposes the term 'market' can be given a broad meaning and for others a narrow meaning. To give an example, a study of the market for sources of domestic heating in Montreal would include the markets for fuel oils, natural gas, and electricity. At another time attention might be focused solely on the market for domestic fuel oils in Montreal, and of course the number of sellers would be less than in the former case. However, the general criterion for classification of commodities is the same in both cases. The commodities offered within a market are closer substitutes for each other than is any commodity classed as being outside the supply to that market. The decision about how narrowly to define a market in an empirical investigation may not be an easy one; the drawing of market boundaries is something of an art. Decisions in antitrust cases often hinge on what the courts judge to be the appropriate 'market'. (See Section 13.2.)

A particular commodity can be considered to be a 'distinct commodity' if it is reasonable to separate it off from other products for purposes of analysis. An example of a commodity that has been taken to be distinct is aluminum. It competes with other commodities in specific areas—in some markets with copper, in others with steel, in still others with plastics. But it is sufficiently different from these commodities in its range of possible uses to warrant separate treatment. However, the interdependence between it and the other commodities must be allowed for in analyses of the behaviour of firms producing aluminum.

In a similar rough-and-ready way, *plants* can be grouped into industries on the basis of their having in common a method of production, whether dictated by the object produced, the material used, or the type of technique employed. A plant was represented in the short-period production functions described in Chapter 7 by $\overline{K}$, a vector of values for a bundle of elements of production. This bundle forms a distinct entity (a factory) that is equipped to handle a certain range of production of particular commodities. A plant (and thus the industry to which it belongs) may serve several markets; its various products may not be substitutes from the point of view of purchasers (e.g. tennis balls and automobile tires may be produced in the same plant; this may also be the case for women's and children's clothing). The boundaries of an industry are drawn according to the criterion that productive capacity can be switched from one line of production to another within it more easily than across a boundary.

A firm[1] may control a number of plants and have a footing in several industries and markets. For the consideration of questions concerning production, a plant is a more convenient unit than a firm; while the firm is the appropriate unit for considering questions of policy and the earning and disposal of profits. In much of economic analysis, certainly at the level of this book, an implicit assumption is made that each firm controls a single plant with the total output being directed to a single market. This may be a legitimate simplification for many purposes, but it should be recognized as a special assumption. When this theory is applied, one should not forget that a plant's output could go to a variety of markets and that it may have to compete with plants in other industries located at home or abroad.

The cost curves developed in Chapter 8 were plant cost curves. For single-plant firms, they are also the firm's cost curves. The situation facing a firm in a particular short period is often summarized by its cost curves and by the demand curve for its output.

9.3 Definition of market structures
Four major categories of markets are usually distinguished in the economics literature: monopoly, oligopoly, monopolistic competition, and perfect (or pure) competition.

(i) *Monopoly* is a situation where there is a single seller in a particular market in the specific time period examined. This is not a very precise

---

[1] See Section 10.1 for a definition of a firm.

definition because a market may be defined, as we have seen, in a narrow or broad sense. This vagueness is a reflection of the fact that goods have substitutes. For some purposes two goods may be very close substitutes, while for other purposes they are not. A monopolist firm in a market that is narrowly defined—e.g. domestic fuel oils in Montreal—would have less scope for setting market prices that are very profitable to it than one whose market is more widely defined—e.g. sources of domestic heating in Montreal—assuming that both markets were not regulated.

If the term 'monopoly' is used without any further qualification, it is assumed that the number of buyers is large. If there is a single buyer as well as a single seller, then the term *bilateral monopoly* is appropriate. (Recall the brief discussion of exchange under bilateral monopoly in Section 6.9.)

(ii) *Oligopoly* is the term used for markets in which a relatively small number of sellers account for a substantial part of the total amount sold. It covers a wide range. For example, a market where two to perhaps a dozen firms control forty to ninety per cent of the supply is said to be oligopolistic. In this situation, any difference in the behaviour of one of these firms is likely to have a noticeable effect on the positions of the other firms. The analysis of markets of this type requires explicit recognition of this in-terdependence. Oligopolies are sometimes referred to as *pure* or *differentiated*, depending on whether the products of different sellers are differentiated or not.[2] These terms will not be used here, since there is always some differentiation between sellers of industrial products, even if only in terms of their reputations. There may, of course, be greater product differentiation in some industries than in others. For example, consumers' durable goods are generally more differentiated than producers' durable goods. The degree of product differentiation is one of the important elements in the analysis of market behaviour.

(iii) *Monopolistic competition* is the term often used to describe a situation in which there is a large number of sellers of differentiated varieties of a particular commodity (as well as a large number of buyers). Buyers may have attachments to particular sellers because they find appealing the manner in which their products are differentiated from others— even if it is only in the packaging or in the identification of the producer. Product differentiation distinguishes this type of market from the one characterized by pure competition. For manufactured products this market situation is the counterpart of perfectly competitive markets for primary commodities. The term *competitive* will usually be applied to it in this book, rather than the more cumbersome 'monopolistically competitive'.

---

[2] See, for example, Joe S. Bain, *Pricing, Distribution and Employment* (rev. ed.; New York: Henry Holt & Co., 1953), pp. 332-9.

(iv) *Perfect and pure competition* and *perfectly competitive markets* were defined in Sections 2.5 and 2.7.

The above are the four main types of market situations in terms of arrangements on the selling side of the market. Other special situations have also been recognized in the literature. For example, there is *duopoly*, a special case of oligopoly in which there are only two sellers. One should also take into account the buying side of the market, as noted above in the case of bilateral monopoly, in which the same general approach to classification and nomenclature is used. *Monopsony* is a situation in which there is a single buyer in the market; in *oligopsony* there are a few buyers who account for a significant proportion of total transactions; in *monopsonistic competition* there is a large number of buyers, but sellers are not indifferent about whom they sell to. They can, and do, distinguish between the potential buyers of their offerings, even if the price to be paid is the same.

There may be different combinations of participants on each side of the market. For example, a market may be characterized by both monopoly and oligopsony, and any description of a market must recognize its two-sided nature. If a market is characterized only by the number of participants on one side (for example, an oligopoly) there is usually an implicit assumption that the number of participants on the other side of the market is large. This is the convention that will be adopted here. The characteristics of some of these market structures are summarized in Table 9.1.

TABLE 9.1 *The characteristics of some market structures*

A
(There is a large number of buyers in all cases.)

	NATURE OF PRODUCT	
NUMBER OF SELLERS	HOMOGENEOUS	DIFFERENTIATED
Large	Pure or perfect competition (Perfectly competitive)	Monopolistic competition (Competitive)
Small (or a small number accounting for a substantial proportion of total sales)	Oligopoly	Oligopoly
One	Monopoly	Monopoly

B
(There is a large number of sellers in all cases.)

If 'sellers' is substituted for 'buyers', and vice-versa, in section A of this table, then the appropriate classifications can be obtained from section A by substituting the suffix *psony* for *poly*. Instead of oligopoly, we would have oligopsony; instead of monopolistic competition, we would have monopsonistic competition; and instead of monopoly we would have monopsony.

9.4 Definition of industry structures

The terms used to describe industry structures are the same as those used for market structures. If there is a single producer, the industry is a monopoly; if there are a few producers controlling a significant proportion of total output, then it is an oligopoly; and if there is a large number of producers, none of whom produces a significant proportion of total output, then the industry is competitive.

An industry's structure, and the structure of the markets in which its plants sell their outputs, may be very different. For example, an industry in a particular economy may, in terms of the number of firms in the national economy, appear fairly competitive. However, the nature of the product, its costs of transportation, etc., may be such that there are many relatively separate regional markets, and some of these markets may be almost completely supplied by only a very small number of firms. For example, the cement industry is one where the cost of transporting its products over long distances is high relative to price, and concentration figures for the industry in the country as a whole might seriously overstate the extent of competition in the relevant regional markets. Alternatively, all the plants in an industry may be controlled by a single firm, but there may be other sellers in many of its markets. An example of such a situation would be the position of the Aluminum Company of Canada, the sole producer of aluminum in Canada until very recently, whose products were in close competition with copper and steel in many markets. When moving from information on industrial structures to inferences about market structures, it is necessary to define the markets for an industry's products and to investigate the sources of competition in these markets.

A *concentration ratio* is the percentage of total industry sales (or employment, or value added, or assets) that is accounted for by a small number—say three to eight—of the largest firms in the industry. Concentration ratios are often calculated for industries in particular countries, and they serve as an indication of the degree of competition. Table 9.2 contains data on concentration ratios for some industries in the United States, the United Kingdom, and Canada. They may be useful as the starting point for the analysis of particular industries in the economy, but great care must be taken in using them to infer the degree of competition in domestic markets. The ratios depend, all other things given, on the industrial breakdown. They are lower the larger the industry grouping; for example, they are lower for the rubber products industry than for the rubber footwear industry. Even industries that are rather narrowly defined produce many commodities, and commodities from different industries may be substitutes. For example, substitutes for rubber footwear are

TABLE 9.2 *Concentration ratios for selected industries: United States,
United Kingdom and Canada, 1948, 1951 and 1954*

| | PERCENTAGES OF SHIPMENTS OR VALUE ADDED OR EMPLOYMENT | | |
	United States 1954 *Value of shipments* Four largest firms	*United Kingdom* 1951 *Value Added* Three largest firms	*Canada* 1948 *Employment* Three largest firms
Primary aluminum	100	43	100
Passenger automobiles	98	74	100
Locomotives	91	53	—
Cigarettes	82	74	85
Steel ingots	64	32	81
Railway cars	64	25	79
Aircraft	47	47	78
Shipbuilding and repairing	43	23	32
Petroleum refining	32	93	79
Cement	31	89	100
Beer and ale	27	11	49
Pharmaceutical products	25	24	20
Hosiery mills	22	12	39
Wool yarn	20	12	39
Cotton textile	18	4	60
Sawmills and planing mills	7	5	—

SOURCE: J.S. Bain, *International Differences in Industrial Structure*. New Haven and London: Yale University Press, 1966. Pages 78 and 104.

produced by industries that do not belong to the rubber products group.

This possible substitution is often fostered by technical changes that open up new uses for existing products. Aluminum, copper, steel, and plastics can now compete in many markets, and an existing market for any one of these products may be invaded by one or more of the others as a result of technical change. Man-made fibres have successfully invaded and taken over many of the markets for natural fibres, and there is also competition among different man-made fibres. For example, cotton was used in the manufacture of tire-cord fabric before it was replaced by rayon. Then nylon entered this market and shared it with rayon; but later still, both of these fabrics were being replaced by polyester.

Another limitation of concentration ratios from the point of view of inferring market behaviour arises from the fact that they are calculated for the industry in a particular country. Competition from foreign producers may be actually, or potentially, very important in its effects on the behaviour of domestic firms. For example, the Canadian primary iron and steel industry has a much higher concentration ratio than has the United States steel industry, as shown in Table 9.2. But the Canadian industry, although benefiting from some tariff protection, has developed in an environment in which foreign competition has been pervasive. In the pre-war and early post-war period, competition came mainly from the United States and in the 1950s and 1960s from European and Japanese firms as well. This actual and potential competition from foreign firms has influenced the behaviour, and price and production policies of the Canadian firms. On the whole the Canadian industry in the post-war period seems to have shown more price restraint and a greater awareness and exploitation of technological developments in iron and steel production than the American industry. The behaviour of firms in the American steel industry appears to have become more competitive in recent years, in the face of a significant increase in the proportion of their markets that have gone to imports (and possibly as a result of more threatening gestures by the government on antitrust measures).

9.5 Short-period and long-period competition

Concentration ratios and the number of sellers in a particular market are all measured in a specific period of time—usually a particular year, as in Table 9.2. However, the planning horizon of a firm often extends well beyond this time period. The possibility of entry over time of other producers into these markets—either firms established in the same industry in other countries or those new to this type of activity—has some influence on its current actions. The greater the possibility of entry, the greater the competitive pressures currently felt by firms in an industry, and this will be reflected in their behaviour. All the classifications based on concentration ratios are thus short-period classifications. But long-period considerations must also be taken into account before assessing the competitiveness of particular markets and industries.

Industries will be said to be *competitive in the short-period sense* if there is a large number of firms in that industry and they act independently, with none of them producing a significant proportion of the total output. Even though an industry does not qualify for the adjective 'competitive' in this sense, it may be described as *competitive in the long-period sense* as a result of pressures felt by firms because of the possibility of entry. The extent of these pressures depends on the barriers to entry that protect firms in the industry. (These barriers will be discussed in some detail in Chapters 13 and 14.) They depend on such things as the problems of acquiring the technical knowledge necessary for production, the amount of funds required to become securely established in the industry, the accessibility of necessary raw materials, etc. The rates of profits obtained in industries that are competitive in the long-period sense would, on the average, over fairly long periods, be close to those obtained in comparable industries with lower concentration ratios. Firms in industries that are competitive in the long-period sense would be just as conscious of the need to keep costs under constant check as those in industries that have lower concentration ratios. Furthermore, they would have to be active in the development and implementation of new techniques of production, and in product-innovation, in order to ensure their survival over time.

9.6 Individual seller in a perfectly competitive market

The number of sellers in a perfectly competitive market is by definition very large, and the goods they have for sale are identical. Individual sellers in these markets have a negligible effect on market price, which is not affected by changes in the quantities offered for sale by any one of them. The demand curve facing an individual seller in such a market can thus be represented by a horizontal line drawn at a level corresponding to the market price. This reflects the individual seller's inability to affect price by varying the quantities he is able to place on the market. If the individual supplies Oq_1 units as shown in Figure 9.1, his total receipts, or total revenue (TR), for the particular period would be given by the area of the rectangle OP_1Bq_1. The *average revenue* (denoted by AR) he obtains from this exchange (the total revenue divided by the quantity sold) is equal to the price. The demand curve facing an individual seller in any specified period of time, when all his sales are made at the same price, is often called his average revenue curve. This curve is horizontal in Figure 9.1 and one of its identifying labels is thus AR.

For many purposes it is useful to introduce the concept of marginal revenue (MR), which is the increase in total revenue (TR) resulting from a small unit increase in the quantity sold.[3] In this case, since the price is not affected by differences in the individual seller's supply of this commodity, the marginal revenue is equal to the price.[4] The marginal revenue and average revenue curves are thus identical for firms selling in perfectly competitive markets. The seller's demand curve in Figure 9.1 also has the identification MR.

---

[3] Marginal revenue can thus be written as $\lim\limits_{\Delta q \to 0} \dfrac{\Delta TR}{\Delta q} = \dfrac{dTR}{dq}$.

[4] Total revenue is equal to the product of price and quantity (pq). Using calculus, we find $MR = \dfrac{d}{dq}(pq) = p$ (when p is constant).

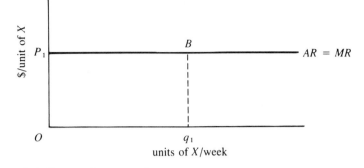

FIGURE 9.1 *Demand curve facing an individual seller in a perfectly competitive market*

9.7 Demand curve facing a monopolist

A single seller of a distinct commodity in a particular market has some latitude in the setting of the price of his product. His demand curve is similar to the total market demand curves drawn in Chapters 2 and 3 for commodities with perfectly competitive markets. The quantities he can sell, given the nature of his product, his sales expenditures, prices of other commodities, consumers' incomes, etc., depend on the prices he charges. At a higher price he can sell a smaller quantity than he can at a lower price. This is reflected in drawing the demand curve facing him with a downward slope. It is assumed that, in each case considered here, all his sales in the specified period of time are made at a single price.

The monopolist's demand curve is also called his average revenue curve. The area of the rectangles under this AR curve in Figure 9.2 shows the total

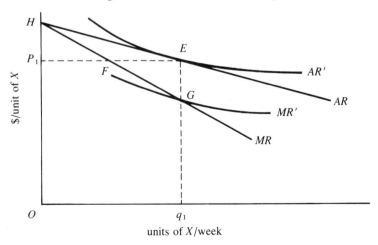

FIGURE 9.2 *Monopolist's demand curve*

revenue he can obtain under the conditions prevailing in the particular time period. For example, total revenue is OP_1Eq_1 if the rate of sales in the period is equal to Oq_1. Average revenue (total revenue divided by the quantity sold) is equal to price when all the monopolist's output is sold at a single price. Since a larger quantity can be sold only at a lower price, the addition to total revenue is less than the price at which the additional unit is sold. Marginal revenue is thus not equal to average revenue when the average revenue curve is downward sloping. In order to illustrate the relationship between these two concepts, consider the numerical example in Table 9.3.

TABLE 9.3 *Relationship between price charged and quantity sold of commodity X by a monopolist*

PRICE ($/unit of X)	QUANTITY OF X SOLD (units of X / week)	TOTAL REVENUE ($/week)	MARGINAL REVENUE ($/unit of X)
10.00	100	1000.00	—
9.98	101	1007.98	7.98
9.95	102	1014.90	6.92
9.90	103	1019.70	4.80
9.84	104	1023.36	3.66

In this numerical example the firm must have a lower price on all units sold in order to sell a larger quantity. The arithmetic makes clear that in such a situation marginal revenue, at any positive rate of sales, must be less than average revenue. This relationship is reflected in diagrams such as Figure 9.2 by marginal revenue curves that lie below average revenue curves. The monopolist's marginal revenue curve can be derived geometrically from the corresponding average revenue curve.

Assume that the individual demand curve is linear and given by the curve labelled AR in Figure 9.2. If the rate of sales is Oq_1, price (average revenue) is equal to OP_1, and total revenue is equal to the area of the rectangle OP_1Eq_1. Total revenue when Oq_1 is sold can alternatively be represented by the area under the marginal revenue curve $OHGq_1$. It follows from the definition of marginal revenue that the area under the marginal revenue curve must be equal to total revenue from this rate of sales. Triangles P_1HF and EGF are similar and equal in area; therefore they are congruent. P_1F is thus equal to FE and P_1H is equal to GE. When output is Oq_1, marginal revenue is therefore equal to the average revenue at that output *minus P_1H*. Since the marginal revenue curve is linear when the average revenue curve is linear, the full marginal revenue curve can be derived in this special case by finding one other point on the curve. Such a point could be F, the point that bisects the line joining the average revenue curve to the ordinate at the price corresponding to the rate of sales Oq_1.

If the monopolist's average revenue curve is non-linear, then each point on the corresponding marginal revenue curve must be derived separately. For example, if the firm's demand curve is represented by the curve AR', the marginal revenue corresponding to a sales rate of Oq_1 will be found by first drawing a tangent to the curve AR' at point E. This tangent is then treated as though it were a linear demand curve. The marginal revenue corresponding to the rate of sales Oq_1 can then be found using the formula for linear demand curves. This value must also be the marginal revenue at Oq_1 for the non-linear demand curve AR', since it can be shown that the rate of change of total revenue is the same for both at that point. Total revenue at the sales rate Oq_1 is the same for both, and their slopes—which show the rate at which prices, and thus total revenues, change for small changes in the quantities sold—have the same value. To find the marginal revenue corresponding to another point on the AR' curve, another tangent would have to be drawn to the curve at that point and the whole process repeated. Since the slope of AR' to the right of point E is numerically smaller than the slope of AR, the marginal revenue curve corresponding to it, MR', must be declining at a slower rate than the marginal revenue curve corresponding to AR. The curve MR' thus lies above MR for rates of sales greater than Oq_1. Conversely, MR' lies below MR for rates of sales below Oq_1.

This examination of the formal properties of a given demand curve facing a monopolist seller should not be allowed to obscure his role in determining the nature and slope of this curve. The monopolist will try to improve his position by altering this curve through selling expenditures, e.g. advertising, packaging, etc. He will consider altering the nature of his product, possibly offering different varieties to appeal to different tastes, interests, or income groups. He may find it both possible and profitable to split his market into two or more segments and to charge different prices in each. These aspects of a monopolist's behaviour will be examined in more detail in Chapter 13.

9.8 General relationships between marginal and average revenues

There is a convenient way of expressing the relationship between average and marginal revenues that involves the elasticity of the average revenue curve (or the price elasticity of demand). It can be derived geometrically, or with calculus, and both methods will be used here. This single relationship can appear in two forms, depending on whether the independent variable is assumed to be the rate of sales, measured on the abscissa, or the price that is measured on the ordinate. As we saw in Section 2.10, in calculating the elasticity of demand, price is assumed to be the independent variable even though it is measured on the ordinate (contrary to standard mathematical procedure). For marginal revenue, however, the independent variable is assumed to be the rate of sales and it is measured on the abscissa. The elasticity of the average revenue curve (denoted by η_{AR}) is thus equal to the relative difference in average revenue divided by the relative difference in the rate of sales. It is equal to the reciprocal of the elasticity of demand (η_D).[5]

When the price is OP_1, the price elasticity of the demand curves, AR and AR', in Figure 9.2 can be represented (as in Section 2.14) by the ratio $-OP_1/P_1H$. We also know from the discussions of the derivation of the marginal revenue curve from the average revenue curve that $P_1H = GE = q_1E - q_1G$. Furthermore, $q_1E = OP_1 = AR$, and $q_1G = MR$, when the rate of sales is equal to Oq_1. When these terms are substituted in the expression for the elasticity of demand at point E, it can be written as $\eta_D = -AR/AR - MR$. This expression can be rearranged to display the relationship between marginal and average revenues. It becomes $MR = AR(1 + 1/\eta_D)$.[6]

The equivalent expression, using the elasticity of the average revenue curve, follows readily. Since $\eta_{AR} = 1/\eta_D$, then $MR = AR(1 + \eta_{AR})$.

The appropriate expression to use in a particular application is determined by finding the independent variable. For example, if the firm is assumed to set the price and then sell all it can at that price, the expression with η_D is the appropriate one.

When we make use of the elasticity of demand to describe the relationship between marginal and average revenues, the following statements can be readily deduced. Marginal revenue is positive for all points on the demand curve with a numerical value of elasticity of demand greater than one. It is equal to zero when the elasticity of demand is numerically equal to one, and negative when the demand curve has an elasticity value numerically less than one. When demand is perfectly elastic—that is, when it has an elasticity value of minus infinity—marginal revenue is equal to average revenue. This is the situation for a seller in a perfectly competitive market. Some of these statements are summarized and illustrated in Tables 9.4 and 9.5 and Figure 9.3.

---

[5] $\eta_{AR} = \dfrac{dAR}{dq} \cdot \dfrac{q}{AR}$, and $\eta_D = \dfrac{dq}{dp} \cdot \dfrac{p}{q}$. $\eta_{AR} = \dfrac{1}{\eta_D}$, since $p = AR$ in the situations considered in this chapter.

[6] The relationship between marginal and average revenue can be derived very easily with calculus: $MR = \dfrac{d}{dq}(pq) = p + q\dfrac{dp}{dq} = p(1 + \dfrac{q}{p}\dfrac{dp}{dq}) = AR(1 + \dfrac{1}{\eta_D})$

TABLE 9.4 *Relationship between price elasticity of demand and marginal revenue*

VALUE FOR ELASTICITY	VALUE FOR MARGINAL REVENUE
$\eta_D = -1$; unitary elasticity	zero
$\eta_D > -1$; inelastic demand	negative
$\eta_D < -1$; elastic demand	positive

TABLE 9.5 *Numerical examples of relationship between price elasticity of demand, average revenue, and marginal revenue*

ELASTICITY (pure number)	AVERAGE REVENUE $/unit of commodity	MARGINAL REVENUE $/unit of commodity
-0.5	10.00	-10.00
-1.0	10.00	0
-1.5	10.00	3.33
-2.0	10.00	5.00

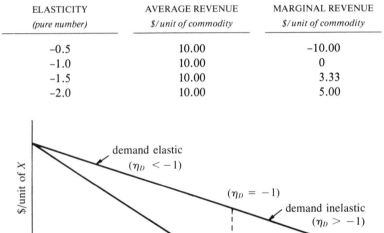

FIGURE 9.3 *Relationship between average and marginal revenue curves and the elasticity of demand*

9.9 The demand situation for an oligopolist

The recognized interdependence of the behaviour of oligopolists contrasts with the situations facing both a monopolist and a seller in a perfectly competitive market. This interdependence makes it impossible to draw a demand curve for such sellers, except for special situations where the form of this interdependence is specified. To illustrate: consider the position of an oligopolist for whom some possible demand curves are drawn in Figure 9.4.

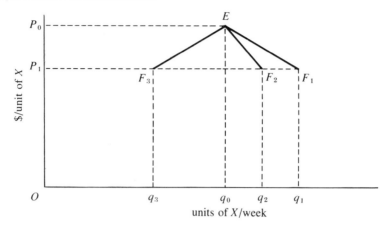

FIGURE 9.4 *Quantities that an individual oligopolist may sell in different circumstances at two different prices.*

Assume that at a price of OP_o, the oligopolistic firm has been able to sell its product at the weekly rate of Oq_o in the preceding time period and that the fundamental market conditions in the current period are unchanged. On the basis of this information, such a firm would expect to be able to continue to sell its product at the same rate if the price remains unchanged. This price and this rate of sales make up one point on the demand curve facing this firm. To find the other points on this curve, it would be necessary to know the firm's expected rate of sales when it sets prices other than Op_1. What an oligopolistic firm can expect to be able to sell at a different price depends, in part, on what it considers the response of the other sellers will be to a difference in its price. Three of the many possibilities are indicated in Figure 9.4. (i) If the firm expects that, when it offers its product for sale at the lower price OP_1, other sellers will maintain the prices they had before, then the oligopolistic firm would expect to be able to sell at a substantially higher rate than Oq_o—for example, at the rate of Oq_1. The demand curve facing this firm under this assumption would be EF_1. (ii) If the firm expects that the other sellers will lower their prices by an equivalent amount, then it would still expect some increase in sales reflecting the market's elasticity of demand for this commodity (e.g. to Oq_2). The increase here would be much smaller than in case (i), because the firm would not be in a position to increase its proportion of the total sales of this commodity as a result of a change in its price relative to that of others selling in this market. (iii) If the firm expects that the other sellers will lower their prices by an amount significantly larger than the decrease in its price, then its proportion of total market sales may decrease sufficiently to lower its rate of sales, e.g. to Oq_3 in Figure 9.4. This inherent uncertainty concerning the responses of other firms to changes in their prices is one factor leading oligopolists to concentrate on features other than the prices of their offerings in order to protect and improve their market positions.

Elaborate mathematical methods have been developed to analyse the behaviour of firms when their demand curves are given, but they are not generally applicable to oligopolistic markets because of the difficulty of specifying the demand curve for individual oligopolists.

9.10 The demand curve facing a firm in monopolistic competition

In monopolistic competition the items offered for sale by the large number of sellers are differentiated from the point of view of the buyers; each seller is assumed to supply only a small part of the total market. The demand curves for these sellers can be drawn if they are assumed to be *equidistant* from each other, so that their actions are independent. This means that any change in the policy of one seller will affect all sellers to the same extent. Since one seller supplies only a very small part of the total market, any difference in his behaviour, even if it leads to quite a substantial difference in his situation, will have only a negligible effect on each of the other sellers in the market. The restrictive nature of this assumption can be seen by considering the competition between retail outlets for a particular range of products (e.g. grocery stores). There may be a large number of such outlets in a metropolitan area, but any one seller is not at an equal distance from all others. The effects of changes in the prices charged by one seller on firms in the same neighbourhood is greater than its effects on those in more distant areas.

The general shape of the demand curve for individual sellers in monopolistic competition can be readily deduced. Since there is a large number of very close substitutes, the individual firm's demand curve will be relatively flat when viewed from the abscissa. It differs from the demand curve facing a seller in a perfectly competitive market in not being perfectly elastic because of the presence of product differentiation, which provides the seller with some control over his sales. Some buyers who have a preference for this firm's differentiated product will continue to purchase it, even though its price is higher relative to similar products produced by other firms. This curve is more elastic than the typical demand curve for a monopolist owing to the large number of very close substitutes for the product.

We have seen that a firm's marginal revenue curve is related to its average revenue curve through the elasticity of demand. The demand curve in Figure 9.5 is based on the assumption, underlying all the demand curves we

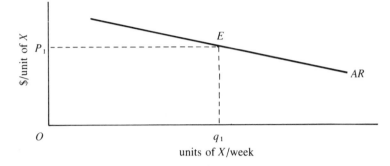

FIGURE 9.5 *Demand curve facing a seller in monopolistic competition*

have drawn (with the exception of the conjectural demand curves for the oligopolistic firm in Figure 9.4), that prices for the other goods are constant. In this case these other goods include in particular the prices of other brands of the same product. Also kept constant are the characteristics of all the products, their degree of differentiation, and the sales expenditures incurred by their producers.

Caution should be exercised in order not to read too much into the less than perfect elasticity of the demand curve for the seller of a differentiated product in a competitive market. It is much easier for an economic theorist to draw such a curve than it is for a seller to determine the slope of the curve facing him. Sellers' estimates of the effects on their sales of changes in prices are subject to very large margins of error.

9.11 The supply curve facing an individual buyer in a perfectly competitive market

An individual buyer in a perfectly competitive market cannot affect the price at which he purchases the commodity by changing his demand. He accounts for only a very small part of total sales, and none of the sellers would prefer to trade with him rather than with other buyers. Thus the supply curve for this commodity that faces him is horizontal to the abscissa, at a height equal to the market price.

If the individual purchases a quantity Oq_1, the total cost to him is equal to the rectangle OP_1Eq_1. The average cost is equal to the price OP_1. When all purchases of a particular commodity by an individual are made at a single price, the average cost of his purchases is equal to the price. The supply curve facing the individual in such cases can thus be labelled the buyer's average cost of purchases, or AC_B, as in Figure 9.6. In this case his marginal cost of purchases (MC_B)—the addition to his total cost of purchasing one more unit of X—is equal to AC_B.

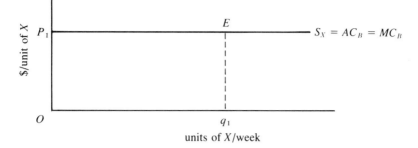

FIGURE 9.6 *Supply curve facing a buyer in a perfectly competitive market in a specific period*

9.12 The supply curve facing a monopsonist

A *monopsonist* is defined as the sole purchaser in a particular market. If there is a large number of suppliers selling a homogeneous commodity, the supply curve facing the monopsonist will be the same as the market supply curves in perfectly competitive markets. An upward-sloping curve of this type, labelled S_x, is drawn in Figure 9.7.

The supply curve facing the monopsonist indicates his average costs (denoted by AC_B) for different rates of purchases if all his transactions are made at a single price. In this case, since the supply curve is upward sloping, the buyer's marginal cost of purchases (denoted by MC_B) will be greater than the price or average cost. If more is to be purchased, a higher price is paid not only for the additional unit but also for the other units purchased. The marginal cost curve will thus lie above the average cost curve as shown in Figure 9.7.

The marginal cost curve can be derived from a linear, upward-sloping average cost curve in the following way. The total cost of purchasing Oq_1

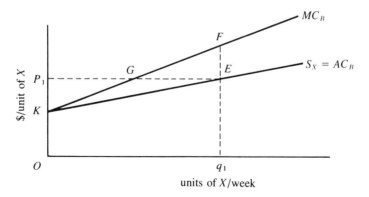

FIGURE 9.7 *Supply curve facing a monopsonist*

units per week is shown in Figure 9.7 by both the rectangle OP_1Eq_1 and by the area under the marginal cost curve, $OKFq_1$. Therefore the areas of triangles KP_1G and FEG are the same. These triangles are also similar, and thus they are congruent. This means that $P_1G = GE$ and $KP_1 = EF$. With these relationships, it is possible to derive the marginal cost curve. A line is drawn from any point on the linear average cost curve (such as point E in Figure 9.7) to cut the ordinate, and the mid-point of this line (point G in Figure 9.7) is then found. A line is then drawn joining this mid-point and the point at which the average cost curve cuts the ordinate (point K in Figure 9.7). This line is the appropriate marginal cost curve.

When the average cost curve is non-linear, as in Figure 9.8, the corresponding marginal cost curve can be derived by drawing tangents to the average cost curve and by using the relation between linear average and marginal cost curves. The tangent to the average cost curve can be assumed to be a linear average cost curve. At a point of tangency (e.g. point E in Figure 9.8), the rate of change in total cost—the marginal cost—must be the same for both the average cost curve and its tangent, since their slopes are equal. We know from the relationship derived above for a linear cost curve that the marginal cost for the line KE, when Oq_1 is purchased, can be obtained by adding $EF(=KP_1)$ to q_1E. Point F must also be on the marginal cost curve that corresponds to AC'_B. Other points on this curve can be obtained by repetitions of this procedure: for example, by drawing the

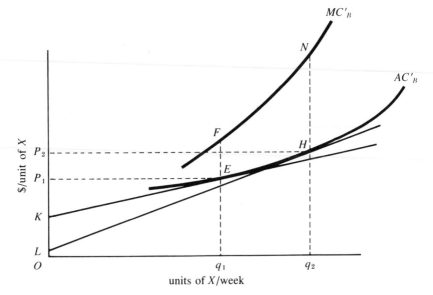

FIGURE 9.8 *Illustration of the method of deriving geometrically the marginal cost curve for a non-linear average cost curve*

tangent to point H and then adding LP_2 to q_2H to obtain the marginal cost q_2N. The marginal cost curve MC'_B can be filled out by proceeding in this manner.

The supply curve facing a buyer in a market characterized by monopsonistic competition would have the same general relationship to the supply curve facing a monopsonist that the demand curve of a seller in monopolistic competition has to the demand curve of a monopolist. An oligopsonist's supply curve is subject to the same sources of indeterminacy that beset the demand curve for an oligopolist.

9.13 General relationship between average and marginal curves

Marginal and average costs are related in a manner identical to that for marginal and average revenues. If, in Figures 9.7 and 9.8, the rate of purchases is Oq_1, then the elasticity of the supply curve at that point is equal to OP_1/KP_1 (according to the formula derived in Section 2.19). From the construction of the marginal cost curve, we know that $KP_1 = EF = q_1F - q_1E$. This means that, for the rate of purchase Oq_1, $MC_B - AC_B = KP_1$. Therefore, $\eta_S = OP_1/KP_1 = AC_B/MC_B - AC_B$ (all terms evaluated for output Oq_1) and thus $MC_B = AC_B (1 + 1/\eta_S)$. *This is a general relationship between an average curve and its corresponding marginal curve.* The expression has the form shown when the independent variable is on the ordinate. If standard mathematical convention is followed and the independent variable is placed on the abscissa, this general relationship will be $M = A(1 + \eta_A)$. For example, average and marginal cost curves for the production of a particular commodity are drawn with the rate of output on the abscissa. Output is generally taken as the independent variable, with cost as the dependent variable. The elasticity of the average cost curve is thus equal to the relative difference in average cost divided by the relative difference in quantity produced, and the formula connecting marginal and average curves is more conveniently written as $MC = AC(1 + \eta_{AC})$.

The following *convention* will be observed in this book. When the terms elasticity of demand (η_D) or elasticity of supply (η_S) are employed, the independent variable (price) is assumed to be on the ordinate, in keeping with the Marshallian tradition. The relation between marginal and average concepts is written as $MR = AR (1 + 1/\eta_D)$ and $MC = AC (1 + 1/\eta_S)$. When the term elasticity of the average curve is used, the independent variable (quantity) is assumed to be on the abscissa, in keeping with conventional mathematical usage. The general relationship between the marginal and average curves (revenue or cost) can be written as:

$$MR = AR(1 + \eta_{AR}) \quad \text{or} \quad MC = AC(1 + \eta_{AC}).$$

9.14 Summary
This chapter clears the way for consideration of the behaviour of firms in manufacturing industries. The principles of market and industrial classification were examined and the major categories were defined. The general shapes of the demand curves facing firms in three of these market categories were deduced, but the demand curve facing an oligopolist was indeterminate without information on the responses of all other firms selling to that market. The general relationship between average and marginal curves was derived for both demand and supply curves.

SUGGESTED READINGS

Caves, Richard. *American Industry: Structure, Conduct, Performance*. 3rd ed. Englewood Cliffs, N.J.: Prentice-Hall, Inc., 1972. Chapter 1.

Chamberlin, E.H. *The Theory of Monopolistic Competition*. 6th ed. Cambridge, Mass.: Harvard University Press, 1950. Chapter IV.

Robinson, E.A.G. *The Structure of Competitive Industry*. Cambridge, Eng.: Cambridge University Press, 1953.

Robinson, Joan. *The Economics of Imperfect Competition*. London: Macmillan & Co., 1933. Chapters 1 and 2.

Robinson, Joan. *Exercises in Economic Analysis*. London: Macmillan & Co., 1960. Pages 167-72.

10

THE THEORY OF THE FIRM: INTRODUCTION

10.1 Introduction

A *firm* is an independent organization that is in the business of producing goods and services for sale. It allocates and directs the elements of production (resources) within its organization and controls, through ownership and borrowing, the financial resources required to carry on production; it can survive over time only if it can augment, or at least maintain, these resources by its activities. Its legal structure may take a variety of forms. A firm may be owned and managed by one man, or it may be a partnership, or it may be incorporated, with management and legal ownership vested in only partially overlapping groups of people. The sizes of firms, the capital assets they control, their scales of operation and rates of sales vary tremendously, but together they account for a large proportion of the goods and services produced in capitalist economies.[1]

The activities of a firm are organized according to the interests of those controlling it. A great deal of individual variation is possible in these interests, and in the extent and tenacity with which they are pursued. In this book the pursuit of profits will be given a key role in our examination of the behaviour of firms, but other motives will also be considered. Differences in the types of markets faced by firms affect the opportunities available to those in charge of firms and may influence their choice of behaviour.

10.2 Why firms?

Economic theory has traditionally placed great stress on the allocative role of markets that co-ordinate the diverse activities of large numbers of individuals who perform varied tasks. But there are also to be found '. . . islands of conscious power in this ocean of unconscious co-operation, like

---

[1] Goods and services are also produced in these economies by governmental and charitable institutions.

lumps of butter coagulating in a pail of buttermilk. The factory system itself, while it involves endless specialization of the work of ordinary men, involves also deliberate co-ordination of their diverse activities by the capitalist employer.'[2] Various explanations have been advanced for the emergence of firms. Frank H. Knight gives an important role to the uncertainty surrounding the results of undertaking productive activity. This led to the concentration of uncertainty-bearing in the hands of entrepreneurs who are identified with firms. 'With uncertainty present, doing things, the actual execution of activity, becomes in a real sense a secondary part of life; the primary problem or function is deciding what to do or how to do it. . . . In the first place, goods are produced for a market, on the basis of an entirely impersonal prediction of wants, not for the satisfaction of the wants of the producers themselves. The producer takes the responsibility of forecasting the consumers' wants. In the second place, the work of forecasting and at the same time a large part of the technological direction and control of production are still further concentrated upon a very narrow class of the producers, and we meet with a new economic functionary, the entrepreneur.'[3]

R.H. Coase argues that the presence of uncertainty was not a sufficient reason for the existence of firms. Specialized services could still be performed without direction on the basis of market contracts, and those prepared to bear uncertainty would contract for services and products from others for eventual resale. The reason given by Coase for the existence of firms is that the operation of a market costs something and the formation of an organization with an entrepreneur directing resources saves marketing costs.[4] The size of firms depends on the relative costs of organizing transactions within a firm and through markets.[5]

Armen A. Alchian and Harold Demsetz have pointed to the possibilities for increasing output through team-oriented production and estimating marginal productivities by observing input behaviour as the two necessary conditions for the emergence of firms.[6] A firm centralizes decision-making, and input behaviour is co-ordinated and specified by a 'central monitor'

[2] Sir Dennis Robertson and Stanley Dennison, *The Control of Industry* (Cambridge, Eng.: Cambridge University Press, 1960), p. 73.

[3] Frank H. Knight, *Risk, Uncertainty and Profit* (London: London School of Economics and Political Science Reprints, 1948), p. 268.

[4] R.H. Coase, 'The Nature of the Firm', reprinted in American Economic Association, *Readings in Price Theory*, ed. by G.J. Stigler and K.E. Boulding (Homewood, Ill.: Richard D. Irwin, 1952), p. 338.

[5] *Ibid.*, pp. 340-4. See also John C. McManus, 'The Costs of Alternative Economic Organizations', *Canadian Journal of Economics*, Vol. 8 (August 1975), pp. 334-50.

[6] Armen A. Alchian and Harold Demsetz, 'Production, Information Costs, and Economic Organization', *American Economic Review*, Vol. 62 (December 1972), p. 783.

whose efforts are concentrated on making the most effective use of these inputs because the monitor's payment is directly related to the difference between the values produced and the payments that must be made to the other inputs. Alchian and Demsetz hypothesize that 'If we look within a firm to see who monitors—hires, fires, changes, promotes, and negotiates—we should find him being a residual claimant or, at least, one whose pay or reward is more than any others correlated with fluctuations in the residual value of the firm. They more likely will have options or rights or bonuses than will inputs with other tasks.'[7]

These explanations of the emergence of firms are deductive, rather than historical, and they tend to treat all resource owners as potentially equal participants in the formation of firms. It is true that participation in a firm is voluntary, but not all participants are on an equal footing, since the alternatives open to them differ. The ability to obtain capital is a necessary requirement for becoming an entrepreneur. Knight observed that 'In actual society freedom of choice between employer and employee status depends normally on the possession of a minimum amount of capital.'[8] Alchian and Demsetz approach this question indirectly when considering the kinds of inputs to be owned by the firm. They state that the residual-claimant can demonstrate his ability to pay the other hired inputs the promised amount even if the venture fails by committing wealth sufficient to cover losses. This commitment will take the form of machines, land, buildings, or raw materials.[9]

Karl Marx and Marxist writers have considered the ownership of capital to be a necessary prerequisite for the control of production. Capitalism has been defined by them as a mode of production in which the ownership of the means of production is concentrated 'in the hands of a class, consisting of only a minor section of society, and the consequential emergence of a propertyless class for whom the sale of their labour-power was their only source of livelihood.'[10] Ownership of capital has also been seen as a factor determining the size of firms. 'The limitation of the size of the firm by the availability of entrepreneurial capital goes to the very heart of the capitalist system. Many economists assume, at least in their abstract theories, a state of business democracy where anybody endowed with entrepreneurial ability can obtain capital for starting a business venture. This picture of the ac-

---

[7] *Ibid.*, p. 786.

[8] Knight, *Risk, Uncertainty and Profit,* p. 274, n. 1. Knight did not consider this an important obstacle. 'The degree of abstraction involved in assuming such freedom is not serious, however, since demonstrated ability can always get funds for business operations.' (*Ibid.*)

[9] Alchian and Demsetz, 'Production, Information Costs, and Economic Organization', p. 791.

[10] Maurice Dobb, *Studies in the Development of Capitalism* (rev. ed.; London: Routledge & Kegan Paul, 1963), p. 7.

tivities of the "pure" entrepreneur is, to put it mildly, unrealistic. The most important prerequisite for becoming an entrepreneur is the *ownership* of capital.'[11] Developments in technology that favour large-scale 'team production' make the ownership and control of substantial amounts of capital prerequisites for the organization of production.

10.3 The motivation of firms

The economic analysis of the behaviour of firms is based on the assumption that the entrepreneur acts in a rational way to make the best of the situations facing him. In traditional economic theory rational action for the entrepreneur-owner was taken to be the maximization of profit (or residual), since he was the residual claimant.[12] A firm's profit in any period is equal to the difference between its revenues (receipts plus credits to its account) and costs (payments plus charges against its account), plus the net change in the value of its assets in that period.[13] The value of the assets may appreciate as a result of investment or owing to an improvement in a firm's future prospects. It will tend to depreciate if the assets are used up in the period without adequate replacements or if the firm's future earnings prospects appear to have decreased. According to this definition changes in future prospects are thus reflected in current profit.

If the net value of a firm's assets is unchanged in the current period, its profit is equal to the difference between its revenues and its costs for the period. This assumption is implicitly made in standard textbook analyses of the behaviour of firms so that the profit-maximizing rate of output can be determined on the basis of the firm's revenue and cost functions for the current period.[14] This is not the general case, however, even though the assumption has figured prominently in the presentations of economic theory because of the simplifications it makes possible.[15]

A distinction should be made between short-period and long-period

[11] Michal Kalecki, *Selected Essays on the Dynamics of the Capitalist Economy, 1933-1970* (Cambridge, Eng.: Cambridge University Press, 1971), p. 109. (Italics in the original.)

[12] The possible differences between maximization of an entrepreneur's satisfaction and maximization of profit were examined by T. Scitovsky, 'A Note on Profit Maximisation and Its Implications', reprinted in American Economic Association, *Readings in Price Theory*, pp. 352-8.

[13] Cf. Knight, *Risk, Uncertainty, and Profit*, p. xxxvii.

[14] See, for example, Edwin Mansfield, *Microeconomics: Theory and Applications* (2nd ed.; New York: W.W. Norton & Co., 1975), p. 202.

[15] Both graphical and mathematical presentations of the theory are greatly simplified by this assumption. Its lack of generality is not always made clear. For example, in James M. Henderson and Richard E. Quandt, *Microeconomic Theory, A Mathematical Approach* (2nd ed.; New York: McGraw-Hill, 1971), p. 95, profit maximization is introduced with the definition of profit as 'the difference between total revenue from the sale of all outputs and the expenditure upon all inputs'.

profit maximization. Short-period profit maximization refers to the difference between current revenues and costs in a short period, while long-period profit maximization refers to the difference between current revenues *plus* changes in the value of a firm's assets and its costs in a short period. Attainment of a position of short-period profit maximization can be inconsistent with long-period maximization, since some action other than the maximization of the difference between current revenues and costs might increase the firm's future earnings. For example, a higher price might increase the difference between current revenues and costs while at the same time attracting new firms to this industry and decreasing the firm's expected future profits. This lower value for expected future profits would be reflected in a lower current value for the firm's assets.[16] In this case a firm following a policy of short-period profit maximization would raise price, while a firm with a policy of long-period profit maximization might not raise price because of its adverse effect on the value of the firm's assets.

10.4 Full-cost pricing
Some economists have challenged the assumption that the maximization of profit holds the key to the explanation of entrepreneurial behaviour. On the basis of interviews and questionnaires, a group of Oxford economists in the late 1930s satisfied themselves that businessmen do not maximize their profits by weighing up increments of revenues and costs at the margin of production. They suggested that prices are established by calculating average direct costs per unit of output and then adding an appropriate percentage for overhead costs and profits: firms then try to sell all they can at the prices set in this way. This procedure, known as 'full-cost' pricing, is not necessarily the same thing as maximizing profits in a given short-period situation.[17]

It is difficult to evaluate the significance of empirical studies of businessmen's behaviour with respect to the light they shed on the role of profit maximization.[18] The results are subject to different interpretations, especially with regard to the effects of any specific rule of behaviour (such

[16] See Section 16.10 for a discussion of the relation between the present values of assets and expected future earnings.
[17] This study was reported in R.L. Hall and C.J. Hitch, 'Price Theory and Business Behaviour', *Oxford Economic Papers* (May 1939), reprinted in *Oxford Studies in the Price Mechanism,* ed. by T. Wilson and P.W.S. Andrews (Oxford: Clarendon Press, 1951), pp. 107-38.
[18] For a discussion of some of the issues raised by empirical studies, see Fritz Machlup, 'Marginal Analysis and Empirical Research', *American Economic Review*, Vol. 36 (September 1946), pp. 519-54; R.A. Gordon, 'Short-Period Price Determination in Theory and Practise', *American Economic Review,* Vol. 38 (June 1948), pp. 263-88; R.A. Lester, 'Equilibrium of the Firm', *American Economic Review*, Vol. 39 (March 1949), pp. 478-84.

as the pricing rule just given) on profits over a period of time. Full-cost pricing, by providing for relatively stable prices, even though demand fluctuates, helps firms to co-ordinate their policies; it might also have a place in a policy of long-period profit maximization.

10.5 Profit satisficing

H.A. Simon has argued that the motivation of firms can be more accurately expressed by the term 'profit satisficing' than by 'profit maximizing'. In his view, firms aim for satisfactory rather than maximum profits. They operate in a world of uncertainty and their 'search' for a reasonable line of action ends when their profit aspirations (expressed, for example, as a target rate of return) are satisfied, rather than when profits are maximized. The level (or rate) of profits that is 'satisfactory' is not assumed to be given once and for all for a particular firm, but to vary with its experience and circumstances.[19]

The differences between actions based on profit 'satisficing' and those based on profit maximizing could be significant when the fundamental conditions affecting the firms are changing. A firm that is satisficing may implement policies that result in profits that are much lower than those it could have earned in these circumstances if it had continued searching for, and had found, the more profitable alternatives that were available. According to this view, the difficulties involved in finding the most profitable options in a changing and uncertain world result in behaviour that cannot be characterized as profit maximization. In a stationary state, however, the differences between the satisficing and maximizing approaches would tend to disappear with increasing knowledge, as the profits that satisfy the firm's goals adjust over time to its maximum profit opportunities. Simon's contribution lies in emphasizing the effects of uncertainty and the lack of full knowledge on a firm's behaviour, which may make the firm aim for satisfactory outcomes because it is not in a position to determine the best outcome.

10.6 Maximization of sales, managerial utility, and growth

The separation of management from ownership in large firms provides some room for managers to pursue policies that might be more in their interests than in those of the shareholders. W.J. Baumol has suggested that

---

[19] H.A. Simon, 'Theories of Decision-Making in Economics', *American Economic Review*, Vol. 49 (June 1959), pp. 262-3. Simon's approach has been elaborated by R.M. Cyert and J.G. March, *A Behavioral Theory of the Firm* (Englewood Cliffs, N.J.: Prentice-Hall, Inc., 1963).

where this separation exists managers maximize the value of their firm's sales, subject to a profit constraint, rather than profits. He argues that managers have an interest in increasing the size of the organization even if it means moving away from the most profitable size, as long as expected profit is equal to some minimum level in the period that is sufficient to generate internal, and to attract external, funds for the implementation of the firm's investment program and to protect the position of the management from shareholder dissatisfaction.[20]

O.E. Williamson has assumed that the managers' conduct of the affairs of the firm is guided by their own utility functions rather than by profit maximization.[21] They are interested in their own incomes, and in lavish offices, expense accounts, etc., which are not strictly required for the operation of the business. Managers can obtain these extra emoluments only if their firm can earn more than the minimum profit required to pay sufficient dividends to prevent a takeover by another group. The possible significance of Williamson's approach, as with Baumol's, depends on the firm's being sheltered from effective competition so that it can earn more than this minimum profit.

R.L. Marris has placed special emphasis on the managerial group's interest in the expansion of its firm. He argues that its rewards are a reflection of success in achieving this growth.[22] For a firm to grow, profits are necesssary both to provide internal funds for investment and to attract outside funds. Marris argues, however, that there is some trade-off between the firm's rate of profit and its rate of growth; and that the firm's managers will choose a rate of growth that is higher than the one consistent with the maximization of profits. According to this approach, as well as with the approaches of Baumol and Williamson, a firm's output in situations where it has discretion is expected to be greater than its short-period profit-maximizing rate of output. The firm would tend not to increase price to take advantage of more favourable demand conditions; rather it would respond by increasing its rate of output to meet the higher demand.

10.7 Large firms and profits

The separation of management from ownership in large firms is not a sufficient condition for a significant deviation of managerial goals from profit maximization. Firms must also be sheltered from competition in their

---

[20] W.J. Baumol, *Business Behavior, Value and Growth* (New York: Macmillan Co., 1959).

[21] Oliver E. Williamson, *The Economics of Discretionary Behavior: Managerial Objectives in a Theory of the Firm* (Englewood Cliffs, N.J., Prentice-Hall, Inc., 1964), pp. 59-60.

[22] R.L. Marris, *The Economic Theory of Managerial Capitalism* (London: Macmillan & Co., 1964).

markets, and the managerial group must be secure from take-over bids.[23] The management of a firm (which is taken here to consist of the board of directors plus the chief executive officers) tends to be a self-perpetuating group, with shareholders signing over proxies to be voted by the board of directors. It can maintain its relative autonomy by generating through the firm's operations a major part of the funds needed for expansion. The earning of profits, and the retention of a substantial portion of them, are necessary for the maintenance of a firm's financial independence. This internal generation of funds—the growth of stockholders' equity—makes it possible for the firm to borrow to supplement its own resources for investment at terms that do not threaten the control exercised by the current managerial group. Thus profits, and the pursuit of profits, must be given a key role in any attempt to explain the behaviour of firms.[24] Management's dedication to profit maximization is further strengthened by a system of stock options and bonuses that ties the remuneration of the firm's chief executives to the firm's profits.[25]

Any significant deviation of the policies pursued by a firm's management from those that maximize profits makes the firm a likely prospect for a take-over bid. Lower profits due to this deviation are reflected in lower prices for the firm's shares, which make it possible for a group contemplating a take-over to offer attractive terms to a firm's shareholders for their shares. However, there would still be room for the new group to earn significant capital gains. The improvement in a firm's prospects of future earnings as a result of the take-over of a poorly managed firm will increase the market's valuation of the firm's shares because of the capitalization of expected future earnings.[26] Thus aggressive managerial groups have an

---

[23] These requirements are recognized by the proponents of the alternative goals presented in the preceding section. Williamson notes that his model gives the results obtained from profit maximization under conditions of pure competition (Williamson, *The Economics of Discretionary Behavior*, p. 60). Baumol's minimum profit constraint is designed to prevent take-overs. Sales maximization supersedes profit maximization in his approach only when the maximum profit is greater than the minimum profit constraint. Baumol and Williamson, however, tend to concentrate on short-period competition and do not give sufficient emphasis to the long-period competitive pressures that may limit the discretion of management in oligopolies.

[24] Cf. Paul A. Baran and Paul M. Sweezy, *Monopoly Capital* (New York: Monthly Review Press, 1966), Chapter 2, and James S. Earley, 'Developments in Economic Theory—Discussion', *American Economic Review*, Vol. 47 (May 1957), pp. 330-5.

[25] For example, it was reported in the *New York Times* of March 19, 1977, that John J. Riccardo, board chairman of the Chrysler Corporation, received $700,066 in salary and bonuses in 1976, when Chrysler earned $423 million. In 1975, when Chrysler lost $260 million, Mr. Riccardo's earnings were $214,625. His bonus in 1976 was $445,900, but no bonus was paid in 1975.

[26] The capitalization of future incomes will be discussed in Section 16.10.

incentive to search for attractive take-over situations, and the threat of take-overs is an important disciplinary force on management.

Even though the pursuit of profit must be given an important role in the explanation of the behaviour of firms, it is not clear how this motive should be expressed in theoretical models. The price a firm sets in the *present* may affect its profit possibilities in the *future* in various ways. For example, it might induce other firms to undertake the risks and expenditures required to enter its market in the future, thus lowering future profitability; or the government might lower tariffs on imports of the product and thus diminish the protection the firm enjoys. Of course there is no way in which a firm can be certain of the effects of its present actions on its future prospects; there may even be some doubt about their effects on profit in the present. This *important element of uncertainty*, which is an inevitable accompaniment of the changes in the fundamental conditions affecting a firm's position, is not reflected in the diagrams of textbooks (this book included) that are drawn up to represent the situation faced by the firm. One should not ignore the ever-present uncertainty that clouds all the decisions of a firm, even though it is much easier to deal with the more quantifiable technical aspects of the very abstract situations depicted in the diagrams. Economic analysis is much less precise than it appears to be because of the qualifications that must be introduced when the simple assumptions on which it is based are relaxed.

10.8 Multi-product firms and plants

The standard analyses of the price and output behaviour of a firm are carried out under the simplifying assumptions that it owns only one plant and produces a single product. These assumptions will be made in the analyses to be presented in the following chapters. However, some features must be added to these analyses so that they can handle multi-product and multi-plant firms.

A firm's product and sales policies may extend beyond the search for better varieties of its existing product. The firm may be prepared to enter new fields as well as to maintain, or even to extend, its activities in established areas. A large firm will control substantial resources and can engage in extensive research and development efforts in order to develop new products as well as different varieties of its product.

In a certain sense what a firm has to sell is not a product, or even a particular line of products, but rather its capacity to produce and sell within a certain area of specialization. Its activity within that area, in any one period, is a reflection of the firm's history and market opportunities. A firm's area of specialization is subject to change over time as the firm grows and develops new expertise both from internal sources and recruitment, and through mergers with other firms.[27] Any market reasonably accessible to the firm in which the expected product price is greater than the expected costs of production and sales constitutes an invitation to invade. If some of the firm's existing productive capacity is likely to be idle (and is expected to remain so for some time) and it can be used to supply a new market, then the relevant costs to compare with expected product price are the plant marginal costs of producing the commodity (*plus* the necessary selling costs per unit). If new productive capacity is required, then the relevant marginal costs should include amortization allowances for the new plant, or an extension to plant, as well as the minimum return required on this investment.

A multi-product firm may have more scope for an independent price policy for some products than for others. It may be a monopolist in some markets while following the prices of other firms in its remaining markets. Some of the markets in which it sells may be oligopolistic, while others may even be competitive. Even if it has some discretion with respect to price for all its products, and it uses a full-cost approach for pricing, there is still scope for taking into account particular demand situations. Various methods are used to allocate fixed and indirect variable costs to different commodities produced in the same plant. They may be allocated on the basis of labour costs, total direct costs, weight of product, etc.[28] But once this allocation, and thus the total costs attributed to each product, is determined, there is still room for judgement in deciding on the value of the firm's mark-up over cost. For different products, therefore, the ratios of price to marginal cost might be very different, reflecting the different conditions in their markets. As Joan Robinson has put it, 'Presumably the most successful firms are those who do not take the conventions of cost accounting too seriously.'[29]

It is the search for new markets by firms that affects the competitive prospects of other firms. A market situation that in a particular interval of time is not competitive in the short-period sense may be competitive in the long-period sense (see Section 9.5) because of entry, or the threat of entry, by other firms. The analysis of monopolistic or oligopolistic markets is not complete without making allowance for the possible effects of entry on the policies of established firms in these markets: a simple count of the number

---

[27] Cf. Edith Tilton Penrose, *The Theory of the Growth of the Firm* (Oxford: Blackwell, 1959).
[28] A table listing the different principles used to allocate overhead production costs in his sample of firms is found in B. Fog, *Industrial Pricing Policies* (Amsterdam: North-Holland Publishing, 1960).
[29] Joan Robinson, *Exercises in Economic Analysis* (London: Macmillan & Co., 1960), p. 198.

of sellers in a market is not a sufficient indicator of the competitive pressures in that market.

10.9 Summary

Firms are very important organizations in modern capitalist economies. They control many resources and allocate the activities of large numbers of individuals. Some of the reasons for the existence of firms include the presence of uncertainty about future events, the costs of using markets to co-ordinate activity, and the advantages of team production. The ownership and control of capital is a prerequisite for the establishment and growth of a firm. Economic theory has traditionally concentrated on the behaviour of entrepreneur-owners, and has assumed that firms try to maximize their profits. The growth of large corporations whose management is almost completely divorced from ownership has led to suggestions that these firms' managements pursue other goals. Some of these alternative goals were briefly examined, but it was concluded that the pursuit of profits must be given a key role in theories of the behaviour of firms. A distinction was made between long-period profit maximization and short-period profit maximization, and it is the former that is the firm's goal. The discretionary powers of management are limited by the possibility of take-over bids and the competitive pressures in their markets due to the threat of entry. The remuneration of management is related to the profits earned by a firm.

SUGGESTED READINGS

Alchian, Armen A., and Harold Demsetz. 'Production, Information Costs, and Economic Organization'. *American Economic Review*, Vol. 62 (December 1972), pp. 777-95.

Baran, Paul A., and Paul M. Sweezy. *Monopoly Capital*. New York: Monthly Review Press, 1966. Chapter 2.

Coase, R.H. 'The Nature of the Firm'. Reprinted in American Economic Association, *Readings in Price Theory*. Edited by G.J. Stigler and K.E. Boulding. Homewood, Ill.: Richard D. Irwin, 1952. Pages 331-51.

Dobb, Maurice. *Studies in the Development of Capitalism*. Rev. ed. London: Routledge & Kegan Paul, 1963. Chapter 1.

Knight, Frank H. *Risk, Uncertainty and Profit*. London: London School of Economics and Political Science Reprints, 1948. Chapters IX and X.

Penrose, Edith Tilton. *The Theory of the Growth of the Firm*. Oxford: Basil Blackwell, 1959.

11

THEORY OF THE FIRM IN A PERFECTLY COMPETITIVE INDUSTRY

11.1 Introduction

It has been emphasized in earlier chapters that perfectly competitive markets are idealized representations of markets for primary commodities. Nevertheless, in neoclassical economics an important place is accorded to the analysis of firms in manufacturing industries with perfectly competitive markets. The theory of the firm in perfectly competitive industries is a basic element in the analysis of the general equilibrium of production and exchange. If the individual preference functions and the state of technical knowledge are given, along with the resources available for production, then the long-period equilibrium position in a perfectly competitive economy displays certain optimal characteristics. It has been used as an 'ideal' position, with which equilibrium positions for firms in other types of market structures are compared.

The long-period equilibrium position of a perfectly competitive economy (*if there are no externalities*) satisfies the conditions of Pareto optimality. A position of *Pareto optimality* is one from which it is not possible to make one person better off without making at least one other person worse off. Even with given preference functions, a given state of technical knowledge and productive resources, there are very large numbers (an 'infinity') of combinations of prices and outputs that are Pareto-optimal. Each of these combinations corresponds to a different initial distribution of ownership of productive resources among individuals.[1]

---

[1] This, as well as other features of Pareto optimality, will be considered in some detail in Chapter 18.

The theory of perfect (or pure) competition proceeds at a very high level of abstraction. When applied to manufacturing industries it ignores the differentiation of products, which is a standard characteristic in these industries, and when it is applied to primary industries it ignores the uncertainties surrounding the results of productive efforts due to the vagaries of the weather. The neoclassical treatment of perfectly competitive firms and industries also lacks a satisfactory explanation of *how* these industries will achieve the ideal position of long-period equilibrium. However, the analysis of perfectly competitive markets and industries does contain important lessons for governments that try to change market prices, as was indicated in Chapter 3. Successful interference with perfectly competitive markets in order to favour buyers or sellers requires methods for nullifying excess demands or supplies.

11.2 Profit maximization by perfectly competitive firms

Profit maximization is generally accepted as the key to the behaviour of perfectly competitive firms. They are subject to constant competitive pressure and do not have sheltered markets that allow them to follow other goals for any length of time. There is also no distinction between short- and long-period profit maximization for such firms. A firm cannot, by the definition of perfectly competitive markets (Section 2.5), affect by its current actions the conditions in the markets facing it either in the present or in the future. In order to maximize profits over time, a firm should try to maximize profit in each short period.

A firm's profit (π), in a short period, is the difference between the total value of output, which is assumed to be equal to its total revenues (R),[2] and total costs (C) for that period $(\pi = R - C)$. The firm tries to produce and sell the rate of output that maximizes this difference. It is clear that, starting from some output rate, an increase in output is profitable if the increment in revenue that would result is greater than the increment in costs, and vice versa. These conceptual adjustments would continue to be profitable as long as the increase in revenue was greater than the corresponding increase in costs. An output rate would be one of maximum profit if, for increases in the rate of output from this point, costs increased by more than revenues; while for decreases in output, the decrease in revenue would be greater than the decrease in costs.[3] If the cost and revenue functions are continuous, then

---

[2] This analysis assumes that there is no change in a firm's inventories.

[3] These conditions define a local maximum. This rate of output provides a higher level of profit than all other rates of output in its vicinity. But there may be other rates of output that are also local maxima. If there are, information on total revenues and total costs is needed in order to determine the rate of output that maximizes profit.

for an infinitesimally small increment in output at the profit-maximizing rate of output, the increment in revenue is equal to the increment in costs. That is, at this rate of output marginal revenue is equal to marginal costs.[4] Thus in trying to maximize its profits a perfectly competitive firm would attempt to produce and sell, in the specified short period, that rate of output at which its marginal revenue was equal to its marginal cost.

11.3 Short- and long-period aspects of behaviour

There are two aspects of a firm's behaviour: the short-period and long-period aspects. Short-period decisions deal with the operation of existing productive capacity, while long-period decisions are concerned with investment; that is, with changes in productive capacity. Although it is important to distinguish between these two aspects, this distinction should not obscure the fact that everything that happens in an economy happens in a particular short period; that is, in a situation with given productive capacity. There is no such thing as 'being in the long-run'. Joan Robinson has stressed this point:

> Everything that happens in an economy happens in a short-period situation, and every decision that is taken is taken in a short-period situation, for an event occurs or a decision is taken at a particular time, and at any moment the physical stock of capital is what it is; but what happens has a long-period as well as a short-period aspect. Long-period changes are going on in short-period situations. Changes in output, employment and prices, taking place with a given stock of capital, are short-period changes; while changes in the stock of capital, the labour force and the techniques of production are long-period changes.[5]

Firms in any specified short period have plants with particular characteristics embodying various states of technology they have inherited as a result of past investment. The nature of these plants, their operating knowledge, and the prices of the elements of production determine the costs they face for different rates of output. Firms may be making decisions about investment—that is, about the provision of new plants and facilities for the future—but the impact of these decisions on their operations will be felt only in future periods.

---

[4] The above can be briefly stated with calculus. A firm's revenue and costs are assumed to be functions of its rate of output (x). The necessary and sufficient conditions for (local) profit maximization are:

$$\frac{\partial \pi}{\partial x} = \frac{\partial R}{\partial x} - \frac{\partial C}{\partial x} = 0 \quad \text{or} \quad \frac{\partial R}{\partial x} = \frac{\partial C}{\partial x}$$

$$\text{and} \quad \frac{\partial^2 \pi}{\partial x^2} = \frac{\partial^2 R}{\partial x^2} - \frac{\partial^2 C}{\partial x^2} < 0 \quad \text{or} \quad \frac{\partial^2 R}{\partial x^2} < \frac{\partial^2 C}{\partial x^2}$$

[5] Joan Robinson, *The Accumulation of Capital* (London: Macmillan & Co., 1956), p. 180.

11.4 Short-period equilibrium

A firm will produce in the short period only if the revenue it expects to obtain for this output is greater than the costs arising from its production. These production decisions are based on what John Maynard Keynes called *short-term expectations*. He wrote: 'the behaviour of each individual firm in deciding its daily output will be determined by its *short-term expectations*—expectations as to the sale-proceeds of this output.'[6]

Short-term expectations, which affect the degree of utilization of existing plants, are contrasted with *long-term expectations*, which are important for investment decisions (e.g. the construction of new plants). Short-term expectations about revenues from current production can often be checked against actual revenues almost immediately, and adjustments in these expectations can be made, if necessary, to bring them in line with actual market conditions. However, this is not the case with long-term expectations, which are concerned with events over a sequence of *future* short periods. Action must be taken on the basis of these expectations quite some time before they can be checked against events. There is no way they can be revised in the light of the actual conditions in the periods they cover, and these expectations can differ substantially from the actual conditions they are predicting. It is often assumed that short-term expectations accurately reflect current conditions because they relate to events in the very near future and can be checked and revised as these events unfold.[7] This assumption will be made in this book, unless otherwise noted.

A decision-making unit (such as a firm) is said to be in equilibrium when its choices are the most appropriate ones in the circumstances (see Section 2.23). These circumstances, in the short period, include the firm's plant and cost curves, as well as the market price for its product. The firm's best choice for its rate of output, given its goal of profit maximization, is the rate at which marginal revenue is equal to marginal cost. A perfectly competitive firm that is producing a profit-maximizing rate of output is said to be in *short-period equilibrium*.

---

[6] J.M. Keynes, *The General Theory of Employment, Interest, and Money*, (London: Macmillan & Co., 1936), p. 47. (Italics in the original.) Keynes appended the following footnote to the word 'daily' in this quotation. '*Daily* here stands for the shortest interval after which the firm is free to revise its decision as to how much employment to offer. It is, so to speak, the minimum effective unit of economic time.'

[7] This assumption may not be satisfied. For agricultural commodities the decision on how much to produce must be taken several months before the produce is available for sale. Market conditions might change substantially during this interval, and revisions in short-term expectations cannot be reflected in output. The existence of futures markets allows producers to contract for their expected output at the time they decide on their production. Forward selling by producers, however, covers only part of their expected output, and their short-term expectations are frequently disappointed.

Even though it is producing a profit-maximizing rate of output, the firm may be showing a loss in its financial statements for this period. Only part of the firm's total costs, the plant variable costs, are relevant to production decisions, since these are the only costs that can be avoided by *not* producing in this short period. The rate of production thus depends on the relationship between expected revenue and variable cost in the current period.

11.5 Short-period supply curves

The *short-period supply curve* for a perfectly competitive firm shows the rate of output the firm would choose to supply, in the specified short period, at alternative product prices. All the points on a firm's short-period supply curve represent possible positions of short-period equilibrium. If the price considered is so low that the variable cost could not be recovered, no matter what rate of output is produced, then the firm's profit-maximizing decision would be to produce nothing in that short period. A positive amount would be produced (and supplied) only if the price of the product was greater than the average variable cost for at least one rate of output. If this condition is satisfied, then the rate of output (supply) will depend on the values for the plant marginal cost curve and the market price. It was shown above that the firm's profit-maximizing rate of output is that rate at which its marginal revenue (for perfectly competitive firms this is identical to the price of the product) is equal to its marginal cost. Therefore, *the firm's short-period supply curve is that portion of its marginal cost curve that lies above the minimum point of the average variable cost curve.*

The derivation of the short-period supply curves for a firm, and for an industry, with perfectly competitive markets is illustrated in Figure 11.1.[8] (The firm's short-period supply curve is called the short-run supply curve by neoclassical economists.) The firm would not produce at prices less than OP_1, since the variable cost would not be covered. At a price of OP_2 it would produce and supply the rate of output Oq_2, and at a price of OP_3 the short-period equilibrium rate of output is Oq_3. The firm is covering all its costs, including the amount required to provide a normal rate of return on its investment, when the price is equal to OP_2.

The short-period (or short-run) supply curve for the industry is obtained through horizontal summation of the short-period supply curves for all the firms in that industry. For each of the alternative prices, the rates of output for all the firms in the industry are added together, since each firm decides

---

[8] In this chapter a firm's plant cost curves will be based on neoclassical production functions as discussed in Chapter 7 and illustrated in Figure 8.4.

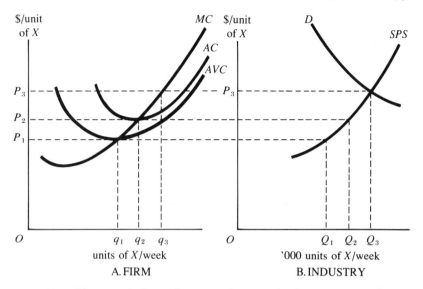

FIGURE 11.1 *Short-period supply curves for a perfectly competitive firm and a perfectly competitive industry*

on production independently of the others. It can be deduced that the industry depicted in panel B of Figure 11.1 contains some firms (plants) whose minimum average variable costs are lower than the minimum average variable cost for the firm shown in panel A of the same figure. A positive quantity would be supplied at prices lower than OP_1 because some firms can cover their average variable cost at these prices.

A situation of short-period equilibrium for the industry is illustrated in panel B of the figure when the price is equal to OP_3. At this price the rate at which the good is supplied is equal to the rate at which it is demanded. Each firm is supplying that rate of output, given the values for the parameters— the size of its plant, its technology, the prices of the variable elements of production, the price of product—that it judges to be best. This quantity may be zero, as in the case of firms whose minimum average variable costs exceed the price in this short period. It will be positive for all plants in which the price exceeds the minimum average variable costs, whether or not all plant fixed costs are covered. These positive rates of output are determined by the intersection of the price (marginal revenue) line and the marginal cost curve. Short-period equilibrium values for the industry thus depend on the market demand curve, the plants available for production in that industry in the specified short period, and on the prices of the variable elements of production.

The derivation of the short-period supply curves and the investigation of the likelihood of reaching a position of short-period equilibrium complete the analysis of the short-period aspects of a perfectly competitive firm's behaviour.

If a firm is not covering all its fixed costs (including a normal rate of return on its investment) over a sequence of short periods, then it is likely to leave the industry eventually. Plant maintenance costs will be kept to a minimum, and whatever amortization costs are recovered will not be invested in a new plant if the firm does not expect to be able to earn a normal rate of return on its funds. Conversely, if the firm is currently earning more than the normal rate of return, and the buoyant conditions that give rise to these profits are expected to continue, it will plan to remain in the industry and possibly even to expand the size of its plant. Also, new firms will be attracted by the possibilities of making profits in this industry. (An important feature of a perfectly competitive industry is the ease with which new firms can enter this line of activity if they so choose.) However, it should be stressed that the state of long-term expectations determines whether productive capacity in the industry should be expanded or contracted. Even if normal profits are being earned in the short period, investment decisions will be made on the basis of expectations about future conditions.

11.6 Long-period equilibrium

Neoclassical equilibrium analysis examines these *long-period* (or *long-run*) aspects within the context of a stationary state and concentrates on the factors determining equilibrium values in such a state.[9] Technical knowledge, supply conditions for the elements of production, and all factors underlying demand curves (tastes, population, money incomes, prices of other commodities) are assumed to have constant values over an indefinite run of time. *Long-period equilibrium* for perfectly competitive industries can be formally defined as follows: *a perfectly competitive industry is in a position of long-period equilibrium when the rates of input of all the elements of production are those that firms would choose if there were no constraints on their choices other than those imposed by the state of technology.* A perfectly competitive industry is thus in long-period equilibrium if (i) all the firms in the industry are in long-period equilibrium and (ii) there is no inducement for new firms to enter.

---

[9] Alfred Marshall explained the meaning of the phrase 'in the long run' with reference to 'the normal or "natural", value of a commodity . . . which economic forces tend to bring about *in the long run*. It is the average value which economic forces would bring about if the general conditions of life were stationary for a run of time long enough to enable them all to work out their full effect.' *Principles of Economics* (8th ed.; London: Macmillan & Co., 1920), p. 347. (Italics in the original.)

Long-period equilibrium must be defined with respect to conditions in a particular short period. If we assume different values for the parameters in the short period, then the long-period equilibrium values would also differ.[10] The method of comparative statics (outlined in Section 4.2) can be applied to either short-period or long-period equilibrium values. In comparative statics involving short-period equilibrium the comparisons are between equilibrium positions with the same productive capacity, but they differ with respect to market conditions. When long-period equilibrium positions are compared, their productive capacities will also differ, and in each case these capacities will be appropriate for the conditions of demand.

A firm in long-period equilibrium would be making the best of the situation facing it in the short period examined—subject to the constraints of technology, market conditions, its potential command over resources, and managerial ability. This means that it would be maximizing profits in the current short period. The necessary condition for this is that it produce a rate of output at which marginal revenue is equal to marginal cost. Marginal cost, where long-period equilibrium is concerned, refers to envelope marginal cost—the marginal cost for the plant that has the lowest average cost, given the state of technology and the prices of the elements of production at this particular rate of output (see Section 8.10). Therefore, in a manner analogous to the derivation of the short-period supply curve for a firm, it can readily be deduced that the long-period (long-run) supply curve for a firm is that portion of its envelope marginal cost curve that touches or lies above its envelope average cost curve. The firm would not be producing in long-period equilibrium unless it could at least cover its total cost.

Both the long-period equilibrium price and the rate of output for a perfectly competitive industry are determined by the intersection of the market demand curve and the long-period supply curve for the industry in a specified short period. This supply curve can be derived by observing the requirements for long-period equilibrium. All points on this supply curve represent, by definition, positions in which the fixed costs (including a normal rate of return on investment) for all plants in the industry are at least covered. The equilibrium number of plants in the industry in the specified short period would be larger, other things given, the greater the demand for the product. In long-period equilibrium for the industry all firms that choose to produce at the equilibrium price are producing their chosen rates of output. The general shapes of the industry long-period

---

[10] Marshall noted this dependence: 'For indeed demand and supply schedules do not in practice remain unchanged for a long time together, but are constantly being changed; and every change in them alters the equilibrium amount and the equilibrium price . . . ' (*Ibid.*, pp. 346-7.)

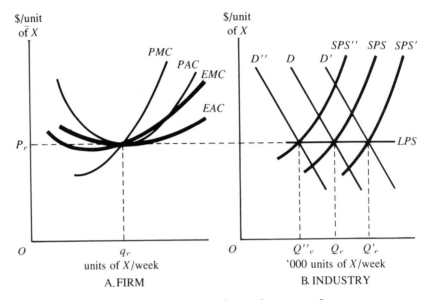

FIGURE 11.2 *Derivation of long-period supply curves for a constant-cost industry*

supply curves for three special cases will be determined in the next four sections.

11.7 Long-period supply curve for a constant-cost industry

In Figure 11.2 the long-period supply curves for a typical firm and for a perfectly competitive *constant-cost industry* are illustrated. All firms in the industry, and those that may choose to enter, are assumed to be identical in terms of their potential situation with respect to costs; that is, they have the same envelope cost curves. Further, the number of firms in the industry (and the resulting industry rate of output) does not, on balance, affect the level of costs of these firms. This means that economies or diseconomies that are external to the firm but internal to the industry either do not exist or else fortuitously offset one another. The economies of scale for a particular firm must be limited in order to allow room for the large number of firms that are necessary for a perfectly competitive industry.

Given the market demand curve D in panel B, and the envelope cost curves in panel A, the long-period equilibrium price must be OP_e and the rate of output OQ_e. A higher price would not be consistent with long-period equilibrium, since firms in the industry would then be making excess profits. A lower price than OP_e would also not be consistent with long-period equilibrium, since this is the minimum price on the firms' long-period supply curves. The long-period equilibrium rate of output, given the equilibrium price OP_e, is then determined by market demand. If the market demand curve is D in Figure 11.2, then this rate of output is OQ_e. The long-period equilibrium number of firms in the industry can be obtained by dividing the rate of output of a firm (Oq_e) into this industry rate of output (OQ_e).

If the market demand curve in the specified short period were to the right of its position in panel B of Figure 11.2 (e.g. the curve D'), but with the state of technology and prices of the elements of production remaining unchanged, then the long-period equilibrium output for the industry would be greater than OQ_e. Since the envelope cost curves in panel A would be unchanged, the long-period equilibrium price and output of a typical firm would also be unchanged. The greater equilibrium rate of output (OQ'_e) is produced by a larger number of firms (equal to OQ'_e/Oq_e). This argument can be reversed for a market demand curve (D'') lying to the left of the demand curve D. There would be a smaller number of firms in the corresponding long-period equilibrium position. The long-period supply curve can thus be traced out by assigning different positions to the demand curve.

For a constant-cost industry, therefore, the long-period equilibrium price is determined solely by the state of technology and the prices of the elements of production. The industry's rate of output (and thus the equilibrium number of firms) is determined by demand. Each point on the industry's long-period supply curve represents a potential long-period equilibrium position; and the relevant one for the specified short period is determined by the market demand curve. Only one of the points on a firm's long-period supply curve contributes to the industry's supply curve, and that is the point at which the envelope average cost is at a minimum.

The short-period supply curve, corresponding to any long-period equilibrium position, can be obtained from the relevant portions of the plant marginal cost curves. The curve labelled SPS in Figure 11.2 is derived by a horizontal summation of the plant marginal cost curves (for prices above minimum average variable costs), when the number of plants is determined by the demand curve D. Similarly, the short-period supply curves SPS' and SPS'' correspond to the long-period equilibrium number of plants for the demand curves D' and D'' respectively. The greater the demand, the larger the long-period equilibrium number of plants, and the further to the right is the corresponding short-period supply curve, which determines the effects of changes in demand on price and output until productive capacity can be changed. Even though the long-period supply curve in a constant-cost industry is horizontal, an increase in demand would, at least for some time, result in a higher price for the product.

11.8 Long-period supply curve for an increasing-cost industry

Demand conditions have a role in the determination of the long-period equilibrium price if the industry is subject to increasing or decreasing costs. Differences in long-period equilibrium costs could be encountered even if all firms in the industry (and potential entrants) were equally efficient. An industry is said to be subject to *increasing costs* (or, alternatively, *decreasing returns*) if, the larger the long-period equilibrium rate of output in the industry, the higher the minimum envelope cost for a typical firm. This positive relationship could occur if the prices of some of the elements of production were affected by this industry's demand for them. For example, if a higher demand led to higher prices for the elements it employs, then a greater demand for the industry's product would raise the long-period equilibrium price as well as the rate of output.

An industry may be subject to increasing costs if there are differences, from its point of view, in the qualities of different units of a particular element of production. The units of an element of production may differ in efficiency when used in one industry but be indistinguishable when used in others. For example, the productive process in an industry might require workers with particularly supple wrists to carry out an operation that involves wrist-twisting. Workers with this quality, who are in limited supply, might be indistinguishable from other workers for all other operations in this or other industries. With higher rates of output in the industry, demand for expert wrist-twisters would be higher, and since their supply was limited, the prices (wage rates) paid to them would be higher, thus raising the cost curves of the firms. Somewhat less efficient wrist-twisters would also be able to find employment; but even though they could be recruited at lower wage rates, the effective costs of the firms hiring them would be no lower than those of firms hiring (and paying higher wages to) the more expert wrist-twisters. Another example of increasing costs would be that of mining companies with differing access to raw materials. In this case the differences in costs would be geologically determined. Higher demand and prices would allow even more costly operations to be profitable.

The neoclassical discussion of the equilibrium of the firm and industry is usually conducted within the confines of partial equilibrium analysis (see Section 3.3). The prices of all other commodities are assumed to be the same at the different long-period equilibrium positions examined. For this approach to be an appropriate one, when an industry is subject to increasing costs, the elements of production whose prices are higher with higher rates of output must, strictly speaking, be used only by this industry. If they are not, these higher prices will affect the costs and equilibrium prices in other industries. The basis for partial equilibrium analysis is that the prices of

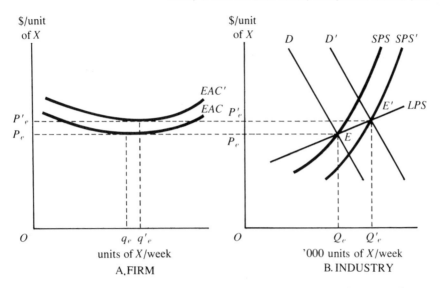

FIGURE 11.3 *Derivation of a long-period equilibrium supply curve for an increasing-cost industry*

other commodities can be taken to be constant, and this would not be even approximately true if these elements of production played an important role in the production of related commodities. It would then be unreasonable to consider the determination of the equilibrium prices for each of these commodities separately: they would have to be considered together in a more general analysis.[11]

In panel B of Figure 11.3 the long-period supply curve for the industry (labelled *LPS*) reflects a situation of increasing costs, even though all firms are of equal efficiency. The only relevant point on the firm's long-period supply curve is still the point of minimum envelope average costs, but its height (and possibly the rate of output at which this minimum is achieved) would vary with industry output. The shape of the industry's long-period supply curve in the increasing-cost case can be deduced from the changing positions of the minimum point on the envelope cost curve. The long-period equilibrium price is OP_e, given the envelope cost curve EAC in panel A of Figure 11.3. The corresponding market demand curve is indicated by D in panel B, and thus the long-period equilibrium rate of output is OQ_e. If the demand were greater, as illustrated by D', then the quantity demanded at the price OP_e would be larger than OQ_e. However, a larger rate of output in

---

[11] Cf. Piero Sraffa, 'The Laws of Returns Under Competitive Conditions', *Economic Journal* (1926). Reprinted in American Economic Association, *Readings in Price Theory*, ed. by G.J. Stigler and K.E. Boulding (Homewood, Ill.: Richard D. Irwin, 1952), pp. 180-97.

the industry, and thus greater demands for the elements of production, means in this case that their prices would be higher. This would be reflected in higher envelope cost curves in panel A, such as EAC'. Thus the long-period equilibrium price, when the demand curve is to the right of the curve D in panel B, must be greater than OP_e.

For demand curves that lie to the left of the curve D, the above argument would be reversed and the corresponding long-period equilibrium price would be less than OP_e. Thus the long-period supply curve for an increasing-cost industry (the curve joining all points representing possible long-period equilibrium positions) must be upward sloping. The number of firms in the industry, in each of the possible long-period equilibrium positions, can be determined by dividing the long-period equilibrium rate of output for the industry by the rate of output at which minimum envelope costs are achieved.

Two short-period supply curves for the industry are also shown in panel B of Figure 11.3. The curve labelled SPS is obtained from the marginal cost curves of the plants that contribute the minimum point to the envelope curve EAC. The number of such plants, in a position of long-period equilibrium, is equal to OQ_e/Oq_e. The label SPS' is attached to the short-period supply curve, corresponding to the long-period equilibrium position when market demand is represented by D'. The plant cost curves in this case have minimum costs at the minimum point of the envelope cost curve EAC'. The number of these plants is equal to OQ'_e/Oq'_e.

11.9 An increasing-cost industry where firms are not of equal efficiency

An industry might belong to the increasing-cost category even though there are no external diseconomies. Higher long-period equilibrium prices accompanying greater demand could also occur if the firms did not have the same cost curves. This would be the case if some owner-managers were better at this line of activity than others, even though they would be no better if they employed their talents in another industry. The envelope cost curves of the firms controlled by the more efficient managers would be lower even if the prices for the elements of production were the same for all. These envelope cost curves include the opportunity costs to the industry of the managers as well as a normal rate of return on investment in the plants. The opportunity costs for a manager to a particular industry in a specified short period are the highest earnings he could obtain if he were employed in some *other industry*.

All firms in this industry in a position of long-period equilibrium would be earning, by definition, at least a normal rate of return on their investment. But the more efficient owner-managers would obtain an ad-

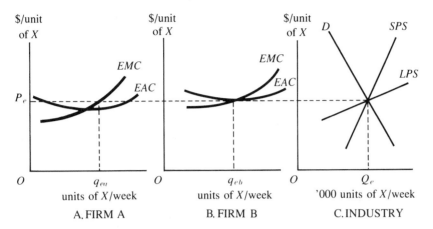

FIGURE 11.4 *Derivation of the industry long-period supply curve when firms are of unequal efficiency*

ditional amount, which can be called *economic rent* (this term is explained in Section 16.12). The difference between the earnings of the more efficient owner-managers and what they could earn in the highest-paying alternative industry (i.e. their opportunity costs) is 'rent' from the point of view of the industry being studied. The greater the demand for the industry's output, other things equal, the greater this 'rent'. A situation in which firms are of unequal efficiency is illustrated in Figure 11.4. For the more efficient firms, such as firm A, the price is greater than the minimum envelope average cost: these firms are earning more than the minimum required to keep them in this line of activity. They contribute to the industry's long-period supply curve those portions of their envelope marginal cost curves that lie above their envelope average cost curves.

The category of *marginal* firms—those earning only the amount required to justify their position in the industry in long-period equilibrium—is represented in Figure 11.4 by firm B. In the long-period equilibrium with a lower price, other things given, they would not be part of this industry. If, however, the long-period equilibrium price were higher than that shown in Figure 11.4, they would become intra-marginal firms, earning something more than a normal rate of return on their investment. The upward-sloping long-period supply curve in panel C of Figure 11.4 shows that the long-period equilibrium price would be higher if the demand for this industry's product were greater than that shown by the demand curve D. In the corresponding long-period equilibrium position, there would be more firms in the industry. They would include a new group of marginal firms that are less efficient than firms of type B, but their higher costs would be covered by the higher price for the product.

If the market demand were lower than is indicated by the curve D in panel C, it could be met by a smaller number of more efficient firms. The costs that have to be covered in long-period equilibrium would then be lower, and so would the price.

When managerial rent is included in envelope cost curves, as it often is in textbooks,[12] the long-period equilibrium price, by definition, must be equal to the minimum average costs for all firms. The costs of marginal and intra-marginal firms then appear identical, but the latter also include rent from the point of view of the industry. Managerial rent is not included in cost curves in this book because it is influenced by demand factors: it is *not* price-determining. Before this rent can be calculated, the long-period equilibrium price must first be deduced.

Panel C of Figure 11.4 also shows a short-period curve for the number and type of plants in the long-period equilibrium position when the demand curve is D. This curve is obtained by a horizontal summation of the relevant portions of the plant marginal cost curves from the plants in that long-period equilibrium position. A short-period supply curve can be derived for each point on the long-period supply curve.

11.10 Long-period supply curve for a decreasing-cost industry
The long-period supply curve for a perfectly competitive industry may be downward sloping, even though the long-period supply curves for all the firms are upward sloping. A curve of this type would be found if there were important economies that are external to the firm and internal to the industry. These economies would result in lower costs for the elements of production the larger the industry. Lower costs might arise, for example, from the lower training costs per worker when the fixed costs of specialized technical schools are spread over a larger number of trainees.

The derivation of a long-period supply curve for a decreasing-cost industry with identical firms is illustrated in Figure 11.5. With the market demand curve D, and the supply conditions for the elements of production, the envelope cost curve is that labelled EAC in panel A of the figure. The long-period equilibrium price is thus OP_e, and the industry rate of output is OQ_e. If the demand were higher—e.g. the curve D' in panel B—then the long-period equilibrium price would be lower because the envelope cost curve would be lower. These lower costs, indicated by EAC', arise because of the economies of scale made possible by the higher rate of output in the industry. In order to permit a partial equilibrium analysis of a perfectly competitive industry, these economies must be external to the firms

[12] See, for example, Edwin Mansfield, *Microeconmics: Theory and Applications* (2nd ed.; New York: W.W. Norton & Co., 1975), p. 245.

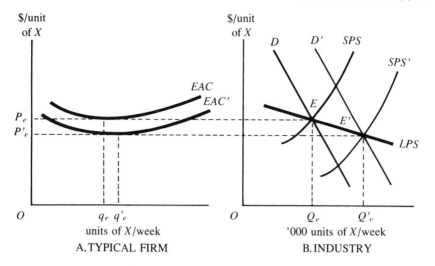

FIGURE 11.5 *Derivation of a long-period supply curve for a decreasing-cost industry*

(otherwise there would not be room for a large number of firms) and internal to the industry (otherwise a general equilibrium analysis would be required). These requirements are very restrictive. Decreasing-cost industries cannot be easily fitted into the framework of partial equilibrium analysis of perfectly competitive industries.[13]

Panel B shows two short-period supply curves: the one labelled *SPS* is obtained from the marginal cost curves for the plants with the lowest average cost on *EAC*. Similarly the *SPS'* curve is obtained from the (larger number of) plants that have the lowest average cost on *EAC'*. Even though this is a decreasing-cost industry, an increase in demand will increase price in the short period.

11.11 Long-run equilibrium analysis and change

In Section 11.7 the long-period equilibrium values for a perfectly competitive industry were deduced, given the values of the parameters influencing the demand curve, the state of technology, and the supply conditions for the elements of production. The presentation was very formal, and deliberately so. There was no reference to a 'movement' from one position to another. It is important to remember that in all the cases being considered here, alternative market conditions in a short period are being examined. Additional assumptions are required before intervals of time

[13] This point was made with considerable force by Sraffa in 'The Laws of Returns Under Competitive Conditions'.

greater than the short period can be brought into the analysis, and before any judgements concerning the movement of prices to long-period values can be made. This special quality of long-period equilibrium is emphasized in the following quotation from Joan Robinson: 'Long-period equilibrium is not at some date in the future; it is an imaginary state of affairs in which there are no incompatibilities in the existing situation, here and now.'[14]

Neoclassical theorists introduce time into the analysis of long-period equilibrium with the assumption (often implicit) that a stationary state is being examined. Long-period equilibrium to them is not 'an imaginary state of affairs' but something that serves to attract the actual values for the variables. This can be illustrated by a statement made by the late Sir Dennis Robertson. He wrote (and taught for many years, as holder of the Chair in Economics at Cambridge University that had been occupied by Alfred Marshall) that 'The value of a thing produced under conditions of free competition tends in the long run to equal its average cost of production per unit.'[15] Robertson was very careful in his discussion of this statement to emphasize that it says 'tends in the long run to equal', and not 'equals'. He went on:

> We must not think of the 'long-run value' of a thing as something which will be attained after so many months or years and then stay put. It is more nearly legitimate to think of it as a norm around which actual value oscillates, as a pendulum does about a vertical line, or a 'sine curve' about a horizontal one, so that even though the moments when value actually equals cost of production are few, yet whenever it diverges from it a force, which will ultimately be victorious, is at work tending to bring it back again. Yet even that conception, though helpful, may be too clear-cut for application to a changing world. It may be that in such a world long-run equilibrium is *never* attained. It is the state of affairs which *would* be attained if all forces at work had time to work themselves out; but it may be that in any particular case they never *will* have time to work themselves out, since other events, altering the whole set up, will have occurred before they do.[16]

The words of caution in the latter part of the above quotation are very important and should not be ignored. They make clear that the neoclassical long-run equilibrium tools of analysis are appropriate to stationary conditions where firms are able over time to figure out, with reasonable accuracy, the nature of their environment and the proper investment as well as output responses, so as to 'tend' to long-run equilibrium. However, this

---

[14] Joan Robinson, *Collected Economic Papers* (Oxford: Basil Blackwell, 1965), Vol. III, p. 101.
[15] Sir Dennis Robertson, *Lectures on Economic Principles* (London: Staples Press, 1957), Vol. I, p. 94.
[16] *Ibid.*, pp. 94-5.

analysis is often used to try to explain the workings of capitalist economies that are anything but stationary. For this type of world, actual values in any short period might differ substantially from long-period equilibrium values, and it might not even be reasonable to treat the latter 'as a norm around which actual value oscillates'. Long-period equilibrium values are themselves changing with changes in fundamental conditions such as technology and supply conditions for productive resources.[17]

11.12 Investment decisions and long-period equilibrium values

Consider a particular short-period situation in which actual values differ from the appropriate long-period equilibrium values. Conditions in this period are one of the factors that affect investment decisions. If the price is high enough relative to costs to permit most firms to earn profits in excess of the normal rate, and *this relationship is expected to continue for some time into the future*, then this will act as a spur to new investment in the industry. Existing firms will try to modernize and expand their plant capacity, or even to build new plants. Firms not in the industry at present might try to enter it. Conversely, if the price is low relative to the costs of many plants, a substantial portion of the productive capacity in the industry may be idle because variable costs cannot be covered. The plants that are being operated may not be covering their fixed costs, let alone earning a normal rate of return on investment. If present conditions are *expected* to continue, this will discourage investment; and the productive capacity available in the industry might be reduced over time. It is these *expectations* concerning future conditions and *not* the differences between short- and long-period equilibrium positions as such that are the important factors in the investment decisions affecting the industry. Movements over time in prices and rates of output cannot be explained without reference to expectations.

The importance given to present conditions, and the change from the previous period in the formation of expectations, depend on the history of the industry and the extent to which firms might or might not feel that present conditions were exceptional. Firms will invest in new productive capacity if they expect to be able at least to cover all their costs over the effective working life of the plant. A firm might decide to invest in a new plant, even if many of the existing plants are not covering fixed costs, when it believes that conditions in the industry will be favourable for it in the future. Projected profits might be explained, for example, by an expected

---

[17] See G.B. Richardson, *Economic Theory* (London: Hutchinson, 1964), Chapters 6 and 7. Richardson argues that firms in perfectly competitive industries do not have the information required to achieve long-period equilibrium.

increase in demand, or by the nature of the plant it proposes to instal, which will enable it to produce at costs substantially lower than those of existing plants. Conversely, a firm might decide not to invest, even if existing firms are more than covering all their costs in this period, because it considers that this is an exceptional situation and that in the near future prices will be much lower relative to costs.

A comparison of short- and long-period equilibrium values might not even indicate the direction of change in short-period values over time, because in a changing world the long-period values in a particular period might not be a good guide to such values in the future. Not only might the industry (and the economy) never 'be in the long-run', but its prices and rates of output might never tend toward 'long-run' values unless conditions are relatively stable over time.

11.13 An application: the pricing of natural gas

The theory of the firm in perfectly competitive industries can produce useful insights into the problems involved in trying to change market values when markets are competitive. The regulation of the price of natural gas by the United States Federal Power Commission is a case in point.

The Federal Power Commission (FPC) was given a mandate by the Supreme Court in 1954 to regulate the field price of natural gas, and regulation became effective in the 1960s. The justification given was the prevention of monopoly pricing. However, a careful examination of the structure of markets for field reserves of natural gas in the late 1950s had concluded that these markets were competitive rather than monopolistic.[18] Even the monopsonistic power of pipeline transmission companies had been largely eroded in many of the producing areas. The FPC can thus be viewed as regulating a perfectly competitive industry.[19]

The short-period supply curve for natural gas reserves becomes steeply upward sloping because of the sharp rise in marginal development costs as the percentage of reserves recovered increases. A curve of this type, labelled *SPS*, is drawn in Figure 11.6. The long-period supply curve (*LPS*) is drawn upward sloping because of the increasing costs of finding and developing new reserves. The market price corresponding to the short-period supply

---

[18] Paul W. MacAvoy, *Price Formation in Natural Gas Fields* (New Haven: Yale University Press, 1962). See also Paul W. MacAvoy 'The Regulation-Induced Shortage of Natural Gas', *Journal of Law and Economics*, Vol. 14 (April 1971), pp. 167-200, and P.W. MacAvoy and R.S. Pindyck, *The Economics of the Natural Gas Shortage (1960-1980)* (Amsterdam: North-Holland Publishing, 1975). MacAvoy's writings are the main source for this section.

[19] The natural gas produced is not of uniform quality, but allowance can be readily made in price for the cost of compressing gas to a standard pressure. Price differences can also compensate for differences in accessibility to the main transmission lines.

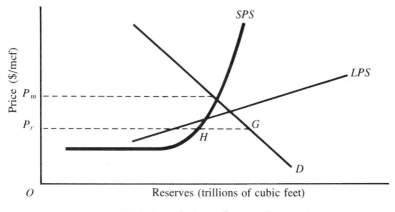

FIGURE 11.6 *Regulation of natural gas prices*

curve (which determines the currently available supply) and the demand curve would be OP_m. If the regulated price is set below this competitive market price (as it is in the United States), then excess demand will develop. The regulated price in Figure 11.6 is OP_r, and the excess demand is equal to HG. Regulation increases excess demand in two ways. The lower price lowers the quantity supplied and increases the quantity demanded. An additional complication existed in the United States because only natural gas sold for interstate distribution was subject to regulation. Prices for intrastate sales were substantially higher;[20] and when producers committed their production to these markets, this further increased excess demand in interstate markets.

The regulation of natural gas prices has affected the distribution of income. It has favoured consumers with assured supplies but harmed producers and potential customers who have been frozen out of the market. There are large groups with a vested interest in regulation who are opposed to a return to market-determined prices. The serious shortages during the winter of 1976-7 have resulted in many suggestions for changes in regulation, but the price of natural gas has become a major political issue.

---

[20] For example, Texas buyers were paying about $2 per thousand cubic feet for natural gas produced in Texas, while the maximum price that could be charged to out-of-state buyers was $1.42 per thousand cubic feet. 'Texas Keeping Much of its Gas for Top Prices', *New York Times*, January 31, 1977.

11.14 Summary

The theory of the firm in a perfectly competitive industry has an important role in economic analysis.[21] It proceeds at a very high level of abstraction and concentrates on the effects of impersonal market forces. Its main area of application is for primary commodities. It is less useful for the analysis of manufacturing industries because it leaves out essential features such as product differentiation and the effects of individual firms on prices.

Short- and long-period supply curves for perfectly competitive firms and industries were derived for constant-cost, decreasing-cost, and increasing-cost industries, and the special nature of long-period equilibrium was emphasized. A comparison of short- and long-period equilibrium prices does not necessarily indicate the direction of change in prices over time. Long-term expectations and the ways in which these expectations are formed must be introduced into the analysis before any statements can be made about the movement of prices and output over time. Industries that have some of the characteristics of perfectly competitive industries—such as the natural gas industry in the United States—may be regulated because of political concern over the distributional implications of high prices for their products.

SUGGESTED READINGS

Chamberlin, E.H. *The Theory of Monopolistic Competition*. 6th ed. Cambridge, Mass.: Harvard University Press, 1948. Chapter 2.

Marshall, Alfred. *Principles of Economics*. 8th ed. London: Macmillan & Co., 1920. Book V, Chapters 3, 4, 5, 12, and 13.

Richardson, G.B. *Economic Theory*. London: Hutchinson, 1964. Chapters 6 and 7.

Robertson, Sir Dennis. *Lectures on Economic Principles*. Vol. I. London: Staples Press, 1957. Chapters 7, 8, and 9.

Sraffa, Piero. 'The Laws of Return Under Competitive Conditions'. *Economic Journal* (1926). Reprinted in American Economic Association, *Readings in Price Theory*. Edited by G.J. Stigler and K.E. Boulding, Homewood, Ill.: Richard D. Irwin, 1952. Pages 180-97.

---

[21] An indication of the position accorded to this theory by many economists is indicated by the following statement written by an eminent theorist: ' . . . it has to be recognized that a general abandonment of the assumption of perfect competition, a universal adoption of the assumption of monopoly, must have very destructive consequences for economic theory.' J.R. Hicks, *Value and Capital*, (2nd ed.; Oxford: Clarendon Press, 1946), p. 83.

EXERCISES

1. Should a firm that owns a plant in a perfectly competitive industry produce a positive rate of output in each of the following short-period situations?

	PRICE ($/unit of X)	MINIMUM AVC ($/unit of X)	MINIMUM AC ($/unit of X)
(i)	5	4	6
(ii)	8	6	7
(iii)	10	11	—
(iv)	15	—	20

2. You are given the following information on the demand and supply conditions for a perfectly competitive industry in a particular short period.

(i) For weekly output rates in the range 100 to 250, the plant marginal cost curves of all firms are given by the equation $MC = 10 + 0.1q$, where q is the weekly rate of output for one of the identical firms.

(ii) The average variable cost curve in the same output range is given by the equation $AVC = 10 + 0.05q + 980/q$. (The constant term in this equation indicates that there are indirect as well as direct variable costs for these plants.) Average variable costs are at a minimum when the weekly output rate is 140.

(iii) The weekly fixed costs for each of the identical plants total $1,500.

(iv) There are 1,000 identical firms (and plants) in the industry.

(v) The total market demand for the industry's product in the short period is given by the equation $Q_D = 350,000 - 5,000\,p$.
On the basis of this information you are asked to:

(a) Derive the short-period supply curve for a typical firm and draw it. What is the minimum price required to bring forth a positive rate of output?

(b) Derive the short-period supply curve for the industry and draw it.

(c) Solve for the short-period equilibrium price and quantity.

(d) What is the value for the price elasticity of the market demand curve at the point corresponding to the short-period equilibrium position?

(e) Are the short-period equilibrium values derived in (d) also long-period equilibrium values? Why?

(f) If they are not long-period equilibrium values, would you expect this industry to move to a position of long-period equilibrium? Why?

3. The government imposes a specific tax of $5 per unit of output on the perfectly competitive industry described in Question 2. If all other conditions facing that industry are unchanged: (a) Derive the new short-period supply curves for a typical firm and for the industry. (b) What are the values for the new short-period equilibrium price and quantity? (c) Is it reasonable to assume in this type of analysis that all other conditions are unchanged when a tax is imposed as in this case? Why?

12

THEORY OF THE FIRM IN A COMPETITIVE INDUSTRY (MONOPOLISTIC COMPETITION)

12.1 Introduction

The adjective *competitive* will be used to designate the market structure for manufactured goods that corresponds to perfectly competitive markets for primary goods. (It was stated in Chapter 9 that a large number of firms sell in this type of market, with only a small proportion of total market sales accounted for by any one firm.) There is some product differentiation in all manufacturing industries, with brand names or other means being used to identify the producers. For example, clothing manufacturers in Canada sell in competitive markets, and their brand names and reputation for quality are known to those in charge of retail clothing outlets and to many consumers.

This type of market structure was first analysed explicitly by E.H. Chamberlin in *The Theory of Monopolistic Competition*.[1] He coined the

---

[1] The first edition of Chamberlin's book was published in 1933, but the basis for the book was submitted as a doctoral dissertation at Harvard University in 1927. Joan Robinson's *The Economics of Imperfect Competition* (London: Macmillan & Co.,) was also published in 1933 and the similarity in subject matter and in some of the techniques led to judgements that the analyses in the two books were the same. But there are important differences between these two theories, as Chamberlin repeatedly pointed out. (See, for example, Chapter IX, 'The Difference Between Monopolistic and "Imperfect" Competition' in the sixth edition of *The Theory of Monopolistic Competition* [Cambridge, Mass.: Harvard University Press, 1950].) Robinson takes the firm's demand curve as given (and known to the firm) in *The Economics of Imperfect Competition* (p. 21), and then analyses the implications of downward-sloping demand curves for individual firms. Chamberlin's analysis, on the other hand, recognizes the complexities facing firms in trying to determine their demand curves, as well as their role in influencing their sales through advertising and product policies. In the preface to the second edition of *The Economics of Imperfect Competition* (1969), as well as in earlier writings (e.g. 'Imperfect Competition Revisited', *Economic Journal*, Vol. 63 [September 1953], reprinted in *Collected Economic Papers* [Oxford: Basil Blackwell, 1964], Vol. II, pp. 222-38), Robinson repudiated the features of her analysis that were dependent on the demand curve for the individual firm. This preface contains useful suggestions for the analysis of the behaviour of manufacturing firms.

term 'monopolistic competition' to cover all market situations lying between perfectly competitive markets (which he called pure competition) and monopoly. Within this wide range, he further distinguished between markets where there are large numbers of sellers of a differentiated product (the 'Large Group') and small numbers (the 'Small Group'). The term 'monopolistic competition'—now generally used to refer to Chamberlin's 'Large Group', with the 'Small Group' being referred to as an oligopoly—was designed to emphasize the monopolistic aspect of the firm's sole control of its own differentiated product and the competition it faces from producers of similar products. This market situation can be described simply as 'competitive' once it is recognized that some product differentiation is an almost automatic consequence of production in manufacturing industries in modern capitalist economies.

Chamberlin's analysis directed attention to important features of the industrial world that had not previously been incorporated into economic theory: product variation, selling costs, the nature of the firm's demand curve, and ways in which the firm might influence this curve. These aspects of reality were all accorded roles in Chamberlin's analysis, which made an important contribution to economic theory and inspired many empirical industry studies that have made useful contributions to economic knowledge. Though his theoretical analysis of the large group was unnecessarily confined by the equilibrium framework he used, it is this analysis that is given in the textbook presentations on monopolistic competition.[2] This chapter will also outline a *causal* analysis of the behaviour of firms in competitive industries.

12.2 Product differentiation

Products of individual firms in manufacturing industries are generally identifiable, even though they may be very similar to the products of other firms. A firm's name or brand and its reputation for quality and reliability tend to be associated with its products. The nature of product differentiation was clearly set out by Chamberlin:

> A general class of product is differentiated if any significant basis exists for distinguishing the goods (or services) of one seller from those of another. Such a basis may be real or fancied, so long as it is of any importance whatever to buyers, and leads to a preference for one variety of the product over another. Where such differentiation exists, even though it be slight, buyers will be paired with sellers, not by chance and at random (as under pure competition), but according to their preferences.

---

[2] See, for example, Edwin Mansfield, *Microeconomics: Theory and Applications* (2nd ed.; New York: W.W. Norton & Co., 1975), Chapter 10.

Differentiation may be based upon certain characteristics of the product itself, such as exclusive patented features; trade-marks; trade names; peculiarities of the package or container, if any; or singularity in quality, design, color, or style. It may also exist with respect to the conditions surrounding its sale.[3]

This differentiation of product—particularly the association of a firm with its product—means that a firm sets the price of its product (it is a *price maker*) in a formal sense. In setting the price a competitive firm may feel that it is doing no more than 'following the market', but it is setting the price at which the product is sold rather than sending its output to market to fetch the best price that can be obtained. For example, a clothing manufacturer sets his price and then sells all he can under the conditions prevailing in the market. This behaviour is in contrast to that of producers, such as wheat farmers, selling in perfectly competitive markets: they are *price takers*. They base their production decisions on expectations of price and send the resulting output to market. It is the market, through the interplay of demand and supply, that then determines the price for their products.

12.3 Individual equilibrium analysis of monopolistic competition

The standard approach to the behaviour of firms in competitive industries is concerned, in Chamberlin's words, with 'the problems of individual equilibrium, and of equilibrium within a group large enough to render each member of it a negligible influence upon the others . . .'.[4] Figure 12.1 can be used to illustrate the short-period equilibrium of an individual firm in this type of industry.

The firm's average and marginal cost curves, drawn in Figure 12.1, depend on the way in which its product is differentiated, as well as on the factors affecting costs discussed in Chapter 8 (the prices of the elements of production, the firm's plant, and the state of technical knowledge). The variety of the product being produced also affects the position and slope of the firm's demand curve. Chamberlin recognized sales expenditure as a necessary part of a firm's business activity: selling costs are included in the average and marginal cost curves and they too affect the demand for the firm's output.

The firm's demand curve (represented by AR in Figure 12.1) shows the weekly amounts the firm could sell at alternative prices, given the conditions for which the curve is appropriate. They include, as usual, consumers' tastes, money incomes, prices of goods produced in other in-

---

[3] Chamberlin, *The Theory of Monopolistic Competition*, p. 56.
[4] *Ibid.*, p. 100.

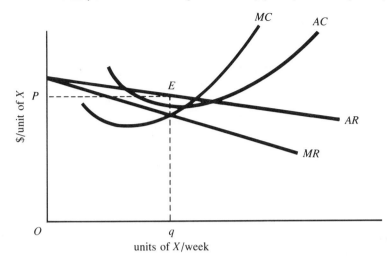

FIGURE 12.1 *Short-period equilibrium position of a firm in monopolistic competition*

dustries, and expectations about future prices. They also cover the prices charged by firms producing other versions of this product, the nature or degree of differentiation of their products, and their selling (including advertising) expenditures. It is assumed that the competitive firms are related symmetrically. The effects of a difference in the price set by one firm have a negligible influence on the policies of any other firm because they are evenly spread over a large number of firms. It is therefore considered reasonable to draw a demand curve for a firm in a large group that assumes that all other prices are constant, although the situation would differ if the industry were oligopolistic, or if the effects of a change in one firm's price were concentrated on only some of the other competitive firms. (No claim is being made in this book that this assumption is in any way realistic.) The standard assumption underlying the analysis of price behaviour of firms in monopolistic competition is that other firms in the group will not reconsider their pricing decisions because this firm charges a different price.

Profits are maximized for the firm in the short period when (as we have seen) it produces and sells the rate of output at which marginal revenue and marginal costs are equal. For the conditions depicted in Figure 12.1 this short-period profit-maximizing output rate is equal to Oq, and the corresponding price is equal to OP.

When the short-period output decisions of firms in perfectly competitive markets were considered in Chapter 11, it was concluded that the firms would not produce unless the price at least covered average variable costs. This conclusion might have to be slightly modified for firms in competitive

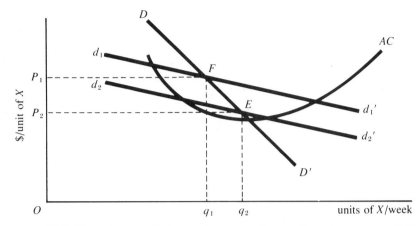

FIGURE 12.2 *Two types of demand curves for a firm in monopolistic competition*

markets because a firm's action in one period affects the situation facing it in a future period. It might be in a firm's interest to produce in a short period in order to retain its customers, even though revenues cannot cover variable costs, if it expects that demand will increase in the near future. However, even a single-plant firm is unlikely to keep a plant operating for any length of time when revenues do not cover total variable costs. In continuing with Chamberlin's analysis in the next few sections, we shall employ the usual assumptions of short-period profit maximization.

12.4 Short-period equilibrium for the group (monopolistic competition)

An additional demand curve concept is introduced to illustrate the analysis of group equilibrium. This curve is labelled DD' in Figure 12.2. The firm can sell the weekly rate of output Oq_1, at a price OP_1, given the values for all the factors affecting a firm's demand curve (including the prices of the differentiated products of the other firms in the group). This initial price-sales combination is represented by point F. The demand curve labelled d_1d_1' drawn from this point is of the same type as the demand curve labelled AR in Figure 12.1. It shows the quantities the firm can sell at alternative prices assuming that *all* prices, including the prices of its closest competitors, are unchanged from the values that result in a weekly sales rate of Oq_1 when price is OP_1. The second type of demand curve, labelled DD', differs in that the prices charged by the firm's closest competitors, the other members of the group, are not constant at different points on the curve. For example, consider point E on DD'. The corresponding price for the firm being examined is lower here than it was at point F (it is OP_2 instead of OP_1), but prices are also lower by the same proportion for all the other firms in the group. The firm's dd' curves are more elastic than the DD' curve since the firm's product-price is assumed to change relative to its competitors' prices.

Firms will base their pricing decisions on their expectations of the dd' curve facing them because in the theory of monopolistic competition it is assumed that a firm's actions do not affect the prices of any of its competitors. However, this does not mean that when a firm decides that its profits would be higher if it charged a lower price, its competitors might not also charge lower prices. The reasons that lead a firm to decide to charge a lower price might lead other firms, quite independently, to decide to set prices at a lower level. For example, consider the situation facing the firm at point F in Figure 12.2. The marginal cost curve intersects the marginal revenue curve for $d_1 d_1'$ at some rate of output greater than Oq_1. (These marginal curves are omitted from the diagram in order not to complicate it.) Thus price OP_1 is not the short-period profit-maximizing price for the firm. It would set a lower price when trying to maximize short-period profits. If this situation is facing all other firms in the group, then they too will independently set lower prices. When a firm lowers its price, it will not be moving along $d_1 d_1'$ but along DD'.[5]

The firms in monopolistic competition will all be in short-period equilibrium if they are each producing that rate of output at which their marginal revenue is equal to their marginal costs. Point E in Figure 12.2, with price OP_2 and the rate of output Oq_2, represents a position of short-period equilibrium for all members of the group when they are identical. Marginal revenue and marginal costs (not shown) are equal when the weekly rate of output is equal to Oq_2. This is not a position of long-period equilibrium, since the firms are making excess profits; if this situation is expected to continue, then new firms will be attracted into the industry. There are no significant barriers to entry in a competitive industry. The managerial and technical knowledge required is within the grasp of many not in the industry at any particular time; the amount of capital needed to set up in business can be readily obtained; and there is no control of essential raw materials by a small group of producers.

12.5 Long-period equilibrium for the group

Differences in the number of firms in the industry or group are reflected by a different position for the DD' curve. Two curves of this type, labelled $D_1 D_1'$ and $D_2 D_2'$, are drawn in Figure 12.3. The two curves differ in that

---

[5] Recall the warnings about the phrase 'movement along a curve' in Section 2.16. This analysis is concerned with the comparison of alternative positions and not with a change through time.

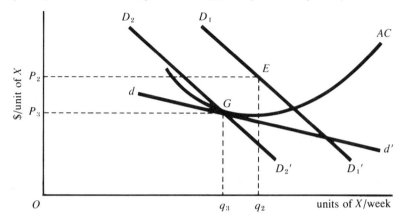

FIGURE 12.3 *A position of long-period equilibrium in monopolistic competition*

there are *more* firms in the group for D_2D_2' than is the case for D_1D_1'. When there are more firms, all other things given (in particular, total market demand), the amount an individual firm can sell at each price will be less. Similarly, a situation with fewer firms in the industry would be reflected by a curve lying to the right of D_1D_1'. The amount an individual firm could sell at each price under these conditions would be greater.

The short-period equilibrium position represented by point E in Figure 12.3 is not a position of long-period equilibrium, since profits are being earned in excess of a normal rate of return and they will serve to attract entry into the group. When firms are identical, a position of long-period equilibrium would be represented by point G, the point of tangency between the average cost curve and a '*dd*' curve. Of course this position is also one of short-period equilibrium. Even though the marginal revenue and marginal cost curves are not shown in Figure 12.3, we can infer that they intersect at the weekly output rate of Oq_3. From the relation between marginal and average curves derived in Section 9.14, we know that marginal revenue and marginal cost must be equal for the rate of output corresponding to the point of tangency of the average revenue and average cost curves.

All that analyses of this type do is illustrate the conditions that are consistent with long-period equilibrium; they do not provide information on how such a position is achieved. It is important to note that this analysis has *not* shown how, starting from a position such as point E, a position of long-period equilibrium is reached by the entry of firms. In order to discuss this question, the values over many short periods for the parameters affecting the industry, and the information available to the firms in the group and to potential entrants, must be introduced into the analysis. This aspect of the analysis of competitive industries will be considered briefly below.

12.6 Product variation and selling costs

The attempt of manufacturing firms to try to increase profits by successful differentiation of their products usually leads to increased selling costs. In a theoretical treatment of the behaviour of firms in manufacturing industries there is very little to be said about the details of sales and product policies. They are more important, however, than the lack of attention given to them in economic theory suggests. A firm's survival and growth are very closely bound up with its ability to formulate and carry out successful sales and product policies over time.

A firm reassesses its position and policies at regular intervals. It might consider, for instance, possible changes in its selling costs, such as the advantages in terms of higher revenue to be gained from more advertising, say, or fancier packaging as compared to their costs. It might try to weigh up the expected costs of an expansion in selling activities against the expected returns from such a policy over the period it considers relevant for this purpose. Higher selling costs raise cost curves, and if these costs are not foolishly incurred, or if their effects are not cancelled by unexpected events, they lead to higher sales than were possible in their absence, all other things being given. If these higher selling costs eventually lead to lower unit-production costs, when there are possible economies of scale, then some of these selling expenditures can be justified by the greater efficiency of the larger-scale production they help to promote. Some selling costs vary directly with output and sales (e.g. salesmen's commissions), while others are fixed as far as the rate of output in a particular short period is concerned (e.g. general advertising costs or the costs for the design of new packages, etc.).

Some of these statements about selling costs can be illustrated by Figure 12.4.[6] The curve labelled AC_P shows the plant average costs of producing alternative rates of output of a differentiated product. The curve labelled AC_T shows the average costs of producing *and* selling different rates of output of this product when its price is equal to OP_1. The vertical distance between the AC_T and AC_P curves is the selling cost per unit of output required to sell the corresponding quantity of output. For example, GF is the average selling cost per unit required to sell a weekly rate of output of Oq_1 units when the price is OP_1. The curve labelled MC_T is the curve that is 'marginal' to the AC_T curve, and the firm's most profitable output in the

---

[6] For a discussion of selling costs and further diagrammatic analyses, see Chamberlin, *The Theory of Monopolistic Competition*, Chapter 6.

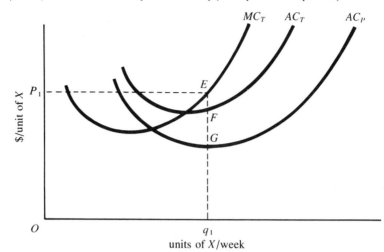

FIGURE 12.4 *Variations in selling costs required to sell different quantities of a differentiated product at a set price*

given circumstances is Oq_1. It could sell more by increasing its selling expenditures, but it would not be profitable to do so.

In the two-dimensional drawings used in economic theory, product differences are indicated by differences in production costs, with a higher demand curve (other things being given) associated with a higher-cost and 'improved' product. The dividing line between production costs and selling costs can be vague. (Is a more expensive wrapping part of an improved product or does it represent higher selling costs for a given product?) But this distinction does not affect the discussion here. A more expensive product will be more profitable if the higher demand will enable the firm to obtain revenues that are higher by more than the increase in costs over some relevant time period. A cheaper product will be more profitable if it lowers revenues by less than it decreases costs. A firm that is interested in surviving and growing must keep alert to the possibilities for improving its position by altering its product or by bringing out new varieties in line with marketing opportunities.

These general statements about product variations can be illustrated by the two alternative situations depicted in Figure 12.5. When the firm's production and selling costs are represented by the average cost curve AC_1, then its demand curve is d_1d_1'. Under these circumstances the firm will not be able to cover all its costs in this short period no matter what price it sets. A more expensive variety, with higher costs as represented by the cost curve labelled AC_2, would result in the demand curve d_2d_2'. This would permit the firm to earn profits.

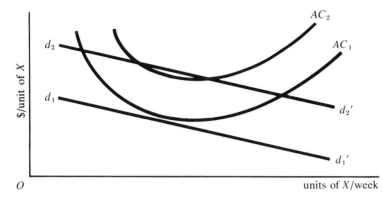

FIGURE 12.5 *Demand and cost curves for two alternative varieties of a firm's product*

A firm in monopolistic competition is in long-period equilibrium if it is earning at least a normal rate of return on investment and if no change in price, selling costs, product variety, or plant would increase its earnings. The industry is in long-period equilibrium if all its firms are in such a position, and also if no potential entrant can expect to be able to earn more than a normal rate of return on its investment if it were in the industry. As in a perfectly competitive industry, the firms here may be of unequal efficiency. In long-period equilibrium, the incomes of the more efficient managers are greater than the incomes they could earn in other industries; that is, they obtain economic rent from the point of view of the industry.[7] There is more scope with monopolistic competition than in a perfectly competitive industry for differences in managerial efficiency because price, product variety, and selling costs are all subject to individual control.

12.7 Firms in competitive markets: a causal approach
An alternative approach to Chamberlin's equilibrium analysis of firms in competitive industries makes use of Joan Robinson's suggestions concerning the nature of a causal model: 'To build up a causal model, we must start not from equilibrium relations but from the rules and motives governing human behaviour. . . . The independent elements in the model must correspond with the features of reality which are given independently of each other, either by the brute facts of nature or by the freedom of individuals within the economy to decide how they will behave.'[8] The technical conditions to be found in the industry and the behaviour reactions of firms and individuals, as well as the initial values of the variables, which

---

[7] Economic rent is defined and discussed in Section 16.12.
[8] Joan Robinson, *Essays in the Theory of Economic Growth* (London: Macmillan & Co., 1962), p. 34.

are unlikely to be equilibrium ones, are taken as given. The model then tries to work out what will happen next.

The industry examined in this model is assumed to be part of an economy in which changes have occurred over time in population, incomes, tastes, and technology; some of these changes have affected this industry. The industry's barriers to entry are low. The technical and managerial expertise and financial resources required are widely available in the economy, and all the elements of production can be purchased on fairly equal terms in open markets. Industries that are described as competitive are those for which the concentration ratio is low. Many textile and clothing industries and some metal fabricating industries fall into this category.

Although none of these firms is assumed to account for a significant proportion of total output (e.g. over 20 per cent), a change in policy of any one might have a noticeable effect on the situations facing a few firms that have some similarities—in their physical locations, for instance, or in the variety of products produced—while having negligible effects on all other firms in the industry. (For this reason a firm might not have an individual demand curve of the type dd', which was assumed in Chamberlin's analysis of monopolistic competition.) The interdependence among groups of firms in competitive industries has some similarity to the situation faced by firms in oligopolistic markets. The extremes of competitive and oligopolistic markets can be readily distinguished, but the dividing line between them cannot be drawn precisely. The major difference between them is the greater control exercised by oligopolies over price.[9]

12.8 Normal price

Firms in manufacturing industries are price makers, or as Joan Robinson observed, 'the prices of manufactures in the nature of the case are administered prices'.[10] Prices in competitive industries can be viewed as being

---

[9] An example of the empirical support for this hypothesis is contained in the study by the Council on Wage and Price Stability of the price behaviour of the United States aluminum industry in the recession of 1974-5. Among its major conclusions were the findings that 'the prices of those mill products for which four-firm levels of concentration were relatively high remained quite firm throughout the recession . . . The prices of extrusions and secondary aluminum products, produced by a large number of firms, were more flexible during the recession, declining substantially as demand declined.' Council on Wage and Price Stability, Staff Report, *Aluminum Prices 1974-75* (Washington, D.C.: September 1976), p. ii.

[10] Joan Robinson, *The Economics of Imperfect Competition*, Preface to the Second Edition, pp. vii-viii. This was also the view of Michal Kalecki, who incorporated this approach into his macroeconomic models. (See, for example, 'Costs and Prices', *Selected Essays on the Dynamics of the Capitalist Economy 1933-1970* [Cambridge, Eng.: Cambridge University Press, 1971], pp. 43-61.) He distinguished between the sources of short-term price changes for primary and manufactured goods. Primary-good prices are very susceptible to changes in demand, while changes in the prices of manufactured goods are cost-determined. Kalecki's insight has been reflected in the approach taken in this book.

set in order to recover costs and earn a 'fair' or 'normal' rate of profit. This is the minimum rate of return on the value of their investment that firms in this line of activity must expect to be able to earn in order to continue investing. The setting of a 'normal' price requires estimates of the firm's costs and its average rate of sales over the expected economic life of its plant. A firm's plant cost curves (drawn in Figure 12.6) will be assumed to follow those indicated by empirical studies (see Section 8.4).

The sizes of the plants built by firms in a particular industry depend on the potential economies of scale and the financial resources of the firms. A large number of firms coexist in competitive industries because these economies are achieved with plants whose capacity rates of output are small in relation to total industry output. The price that will allow a firm to earn a normal rate of return on its investment over the expected life of a plant, given the plant fixed and variable costs, depends on the average rate of output it can sell at that price. The rate of output that enters into a firm's calculations cannot exceed normal productive capacity, but it could be less. If the industry is one where firms have experienced fluctuations in rates of sales and output, they would base their investment plans on an average rate of output that is less than the maximum rate. This difference could vary somewhat between firms, depending on their history and traditions, but in competitive industries it must be rather small because of the competitive pressures from other firms and potential entrants. In comparing two normal prices that differ only because of the rates of plant utilization used in their calculation, it will be found that the price based on a lower rate of utilization would be higher because unit fixed costs would be higher.

In Figure 12.6 the output rate ON' is taken as the basis for the calculation

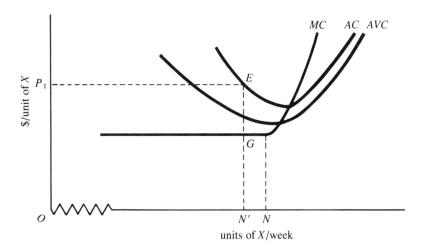

FIGURE 12.6 *Plant cost curves and normal price*

of the normal price. The AC curve includes all costs as well as the amounts required in each short period, over the plant's expected life, to provide the normal rate of return on its cost. The normal price corresponding to the output rate ON' is OP_1. At that rate of output, unit fixed costs (including a normal profit for the period) plus indirect variable costs are equal to GE, and the normal price can be shown as being determined by 'marking-up' unit prime or marginal costs. The mark-up in this case is $GE/N'G$. We can write:

$$OP_1 = \left(1 + \frac{GE}{N'G}\right)MC$$

Since MC is equal to $N'G$, we see that this equation reduces to $OP_1 = N'G + GE = N'E$. This, of course, is the price at which a normal rate of return on investment would be earned if the rate of sales were equal to ON'.

No demand curve is drawn in Figure 12.6, but the influence of demand conditions in the particular short period are felt in the sales made at the normal price. These sales will often differ from the output rate (ON') used to calculate the normal price. Sales may exceed the current rate of output if the difference can be supplied by drawing down the level of inventories of finished goods. Similarly, if the current rate of sales is less than the rate of output, then the level of inventories is increasing. It is more convenient here to treat sales and output rates as though they were the same. Thus we shall assume that firms immediately adjust output rates to sales rates and that inventory levels are kept constant.

If the sales rate at the price OP_1 is equal to ON', then normal profits for the period are being earned by this firm. If the sales rate is higher than ON', then more than the normal profits are being earned. If it is lower than ON', total revenue is insufficient to cover costs plus normal profits.

12.9 Deviations from normal conditions

Competitive pressures might lead to lower prices when firms find that their rates of sales at normal prices are smaller than the 'normal' rates of output used to calculate these prices. Lower prices would not be in the interests of the industry as a whole, since the market demand is usually inelastic, but any single firm could increase its profits by cutting price if the others maintain normal prices. The possible gains from individual price cuts will tempt some firms to lower prices, especially since the number of sellers in competitive markets is too large for the group to maintain effective pricing discipline. In order to try to avoid general price reductions, a firm might attempt to disguise its price cuts in various ways—such as special (secret) discounts to certain customers or the provision of additional services at no extra charge. However, once such concessions begin, they become widespread, as those who initially try to maintain normal prices find that their market shares are declining. Industry associations in the retail trades have in the past tried to protect the mark-ups built into normal prices by means of fair-trade laws, which require resale price maintenance (the reselling of products at prices established by manufacturers). In North America most of these laws have been repealed, but some still protect margins in drug stores.[11]

When demand conditions are very buoyant the net price can increase (over and above any cost increases). The increase could be a hidden one, realized by the elimination of some of the conventional discounts or regular services, especially when sales are made to new customers who might not return in the future. (Ostensibly the normal price would be charged.) In these circumstances increases in average prices could also be due to the above-average prices of high-cost ('marginal') producers for whom only the increased demand—which enables them to sell at higher prices—makes it worth their while to utilize their equipment.

The plants available for production in a competitive industry in any given period are of many ages and sizes, and this is reflected in their cost curves. Some might be fully amortized but have relatively high operating costs, while others might be charged with sizeable amortization allowances but have low operating costs. Market conditions that permit some to operate, and even to make profits, might be too unfavourable to permit others to cover variable costs. Even with this diversity, a general statement can be made about market conditions. If demand for the product of an industry is such that plants that were expected to be operated in the current period (when investment decisions concerning them were made) can cover all their costs, with at least some making more than normal profits in this period, then the situation can be called a *sellers' market*. If, on the whole, demand is too low for these plants to cover all costs, it can be called a *buyers' market*.[12]

Assume that initial conditions for a typical firm in the industry are represented by point *H* in Figure 12.7, in which a sellers' market exists: many firms are earning more than normal profits and even high-cost producers can profitably utilize their equipment. Sellers' markets in competitive industries tend to be rather short-lived in modern industrial countries because of the entry of new productive capacity in search of the higher-than-normal profits that appear to be available. The barriers to entry

[11] Leonard W. Weiss, *Economics and American Industry* (New York: John Wiley & Sons, Inc., 1961), pp. 418-27.

[12] Cf. Joan Robinson, *Exercises in Economic Analysis* (London: Macmillan & Co., 1960), pp. 117-19.

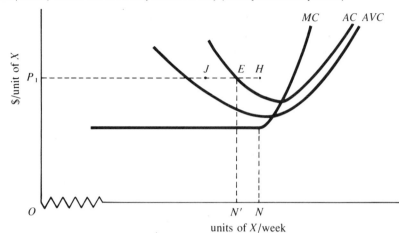

FIGURE 12.7 *Plant cost curves and sales at normal prices in buyers' and sellers' markets*

are not great. The capital, technical, and raw-material requirements are not out of the reach of many potential entrants, whose decisions to enter depend on their estimates of the prospects of obtaining a sufficient return on their investment over time. There is never any reason to expect that competitive industries will adjust to some equilibrium position in the future as a result of current investment, since future conditions cannot be known when this investment is planned. Miscalculations can occur in a changing world: over-investment might take place, making a profitable situation short-lived and ushering in a long interval of below-normal profits and even losses (both of which are features of buyers' markets).

Sales are below normal in buyers' markets, as shown by point *J* in Figure 12.7, and firms find it difficult to maintain normal prices because of the attractions of having a lower price than one's competitor—a situation that cannot be effectively policed because of the size of the competitive industry. When the conditions that give rise to a buyers' market persist, price cuts become general, leading to some shutdowns in plants and to lower investment.

The analysis of sellers' and buyers' markets for competitive industries indicates that prices relative to unit prime costs tend to move in the same direction as changes in demand, with boom conditions leading to higher prices and depressed conditions to lower prices. In oligopolistic industries this cyclical movement in prices is much less pronounced[13] and may not exist at all, as we shall see in Chapter 14.

---

[13] Recall the reference to aluminum pricing during the recession of 1974-5 in Footnote 9 of this chapter.

12.10 Summary

This chapter has presented Chamberlin's equilibrium analysis of monopolistic competition (the 'large group') and has outlined a causal approach to the examination of the behaviour of firms in competitive industries. It has been stressed that there are large numbers of firms in these industries, none of which accounts for a significant proportion of total output. The products of firms in manufacturing industries are differentiated, and firms try to improve their positions by adjusting their product variety and sales policies as well as their prices whenever such changes appear advantageous.

The large number of producers selling very close substitutes in competitive industries means that these markets are competitive in the short-period sense and that fluctuations in demand tend to result in fluctuations in price. These industries are also competitive in the long-period sense because of the low barriers to entry. The problems of entry facing new firms are not insurmountable for many in the economy. Technology and raw materials are easily accessible to new entrants, and the capital costs are not high in relation to available sources of capital. As a result of this ease of entry, and because of the lack of accurate information on total investment intentions to potential entrants, competitive industries are rather unstable. Favourable changes in conditions affecting a competitive industry that lead to a sellers' market are often followed by excessive entry and a long interval of buyers' markets and disappointed expectations.

SUGGESTED READINGS

Chamberlin, E.H. *The Theory of Monopolistic Competition*. 6th ed. Cambridge, Mass.: Harvard University Press, 1950. Chapters 5, 6, 7, and 9.

Dewey, Donald. *The Theory of Imperfect Competition: A Radical Reconstruction*. New York: Columbia University Press, 1969.

Robinson, Joan. *The Economics of Imperfect Competition*. 2nd ed. London: Macmillan & Co., 1969. Preface to the Second Edition.

EXERCISES

1. What are the two demand curves that appear in Chamberlin's analysis of the determination of prices in monopolistic competition? What are the assumptions on which these curves are based?

2. (a) Draw demand and cost curves to illustrate a short-period equilibrium situation for a firm in monopolistic competition.

(b) Draw curves to illustrate a long-period equilibrium position for a firm in monopolistic competition.

(c) Can a firm in monopolistic competition be earning more than normal profits in a situation of long-period equilibrium? Explain.

3. (a) Derive a competitive firm's 'normal' or 'fair' price from the following information:

(i) The normal rate of return on investment in this particular industry is 15 per cent. (ii) The *annual* amortization allowance required to replace the plant at the end of its expected economic life is $25,000. (iii) All other overhead costs amount to $65,000 per year. (iv) Marginal (or direct) costs are constant at $10 per unit of X, up to normal productive capacity. (v) The normal rate of utilization of capacity used by the firm in its planning is 90 per cent of the plant's capacity rate of output of 20,000 units per year.

(b) What would you expect to happen to price in a buyers' market where the firm can sell only at an annual rate of 14,000 units at its normal price? Why?

(c) Would your answer to the first question in (b) be different if the firm were a monopolist? Why?

13

MONOPOLY

13.1 Introduction

A monopolist is a single seller in a particular market. There are important elements of judgement in drawing the boundaries of a market, and the designation of a seller as a monopolist is thus also a matter of judgement. We shall examine here the behaviour of monopoly firms that are the sole sellers in a particular interval of time. The maintenance of this position depends on their success in discouraging entrants into their markets. A monopoly position can be destroyed by changes in technology, the discovery of new sources of raw materials, and governmental intervention to protect consumers. A firm with a *natural monopoly*, where entry is impractical because the nature of the product and technology are such that the market cannot be large enough to allow more than one firm to enjoy the economies of scale, is usually regulated by public authorities, who must approve the prices to be charged. Examples of natural monopolies are the distribution of electricity or telephone services to a particular area. The regulation of monopolies will not be considered in this book.

Many of the issues considered in this chapter—such as the effect of barriers to entry on the firm's pricing policy, the use of pricing formulas, and the resort to price discrimination—can also be found in oligopolistic markets. The distribution of topics between this and the following chapter is therefore arbitrary, and the two chapters should be read together as an investigation into the behaviour of large firms with protected markets.

13.2 Monopoly: one seller, one market. But what is a market?

While a firm is a monopolist in a particular market at a certain time if it is
the sole seller in that market, it is not so easy to determine whether a firm is
a monopolist in a given situation because the extent of the market might be
in dispute. A particular market is defined with respect to both the commodity sold and its geographical extent. (Are close substitutes to be considered as being sold in this market? Recall the example of the Montreal
market for sources of domestic heating in Section 9.2. Is the relevant
geographical boundary Montreal or the province of Quebec?) A firm may
be a monopolist if the market boundaries are drawn in one way, and not a
monopolist if they are drawn in another way. The problem of defining the
appropriate geographical boundary is well illustrated by the Canadian
Western Sugar Case.

In 1957 the Canadian Restrictive Trade Practices Commission issued a
report expressing the view that the British Columbia Sugar Refinery
Company had an almost complete monopoly of the sale of sugar in British
Columbia,[1] Alberta, and Saskatchewan, and that its proposed acquisition
of the Manitoba Sugar Company, the only other producer in Western
Canada, would not be in the public interest because it would tend to
eliminate competition in Manitoba. However, the British Columbia Sugar
Company proceeded with its acquisition of Manitoba Sugar and the
government brought suit in court under the Combines Act. Ruling against
the government, the trial judge held that the sugar refiners in Eastern
Canada could provide competition in the province of Manitoba, and that
the merger would not result in a monopoly in Western Canada. He stated: 'I
am satisfied that there has always been and still is competition, even in the
limited area, from the eastern refiners or some of them.'[2] Without
discussing the merits of this decision, it is clear the judge felt that Manitoba
was part of a national, rather than a regional, market. In his view even a
small degree of actual competition (i.e. some sales by others in this market)
or potential competition (i.e. the possibility of sales in this market by
others) was sufficient to rule out the charge of monopoly.

Two cases in the United States, where the courts arrived at different
conclusions, will be used to illustrate some of the problems that are encountered when defining the commodity dimensions of a market. They
involved the Aluminum Company of America (Alcoa) and du Pont.

Alcoa was the sole American producer of primary, or ingot, aluminum in

---

[1] Restrictive Trade Practices Commission, *Report Concerning the Sugar Industry in Western
Canada and a Proposed Merger of Sugar Companies* (Ottawa: Department of Justice, 1957.)
[2] *Regina v. British Columbia Sugar Refinery Company Limited and B.C. Sugar Refinery
Limited* (1960) 32 W.W.R. (N.S.) 577, 129 C.C.C.7.

1937, when it was charged under Section 2 of the Sherman Antitrust Act. It also fabricated a substantial amount of its own ingot production. Aluminum fabricators made use of secondary (or scrap) aluminum as well as primary aluminum. The judgement in this case revolved around two questions: (i) whether the market for aluminum included both secondary and primary aluminum; (ii) whether Alcoa's total production of ingot, or only the part that it sold to others, should be used to determine its market share. Three measures of Alcoa's market share were obtained for the years 1929-38 inclusive. With the market defined as comprising secondary as well as primary aluminum production, and with Alcoa's production of aluminum for fabrication on its own account excluded from the market, its market share was 33 per cent. With the same definition of the market, but with Alcoa's total ingot production being counted, a market share in the neighbourhood of 60 to 64 per cent would be obtained. Finally, if the market was defined to include only primary aluminum, and Alcoa's total production of ingot was taken, its market share would be over 90 per cent. (The remaining sales were accounted for by imports.) Judge Learned Hand, of the Court of Appeals, said that 90 per cent is enough to constitute a monopoly. He considered it doubtful whether 60 or 64 per cent would be enough, and certainly 33 per cent would not. Reversing the judgement of the District Court judge, he then ruled that the appropriate market included only primary aluminum, and that all of Alcoa's ingot production should be counted. He thus arrived at the 90-per-cent market share and found Alcoa to be a monopoly.[3]

The E.I. du Pont de Nemours company (du Pont) was for several years the sole producer of cellophane in the United States. When another firm began production of cellophane as a result of patent-licensing arrangements, du Pont continued to dominate this market with a stable share of about 75 per cent. In 1947 du Pont was charged by the U.S. government, under Section 2 of the Sherman Antitrust Act, with having monopolized the manufacture and sale of cellophane. The final judgement, handed down by the Supreme Court in 1956, revolved around the question of whether cellophane was a distinct product with its own market. A majority of the Court ruled in 1956 that it had many close substitutes in items such as waxed paper, glassine, and aluminum foil, and that the appropriate market for computing market shares was one that included all flexible wrapping materials. This majority thus found that du Pont's control of cellophane did not give it monopoly power. Chief Justice Warren, in a dissenting

---

[3] For a summary of this case, see Irwin M. Stelzer, *Selected Antitrust Cases: Landmark Decisions* (4th ed.; Homewood, Ill.: Richard D. Irwin, 1972), pp. 25-30.

opinion joined by two other justices, contended that cellophane was the relevant market, and that the cross-elasticities of demand between cellophane and the other flexible wrapping materials were not high enough to indicate close competition.[4]

Our examination of these three monopoly cases in this section makes clear the difficulties involved in defining the appropriate market in any practical application. They illustrate the need for judgement and intimate knowledge of the facts of any actual situation before economic analysis can be applied. However, it is still possible to define a market along the lines indicated by our discussion of markets in Section 2.3: a market comprises all buyers and sellers of a distinct commodity who are in at least potential communication with each other for the purpose of conducting transactions. Buyers and sellers of a commodity who are separated by distances, which would result in transportation and other related charges (including tariffs) that are high in relation to the normal price of the product, are generally not in the same market. Included in a distinct commodity are all the differentiated versions of a product that are close substitutes as shown by the values for their cross-elasticities of demand. In the models examined here, the demand curves shown are for markets with unequivocal geographical and product spaces between them and other markets.

13.3 Birth and growth of a monopoly—Alcoa

The demand curve facing a monopolist firm, insofar as it remains the sole seller, is the total market demand curve for its product. Before considering a theoretical approach to a monopolist's behaviour in developing and exploiting its market opportunities, it might be useful to examine a particular case of monopoly, to see how it arose and how it was maintained.

The original restriction working in Alcoa's favour was a patent. In the late 1880s a new process for producing aluminum was patented in the United States by Charles M. Hall (a similar process was also patented in France by Paul L.T. Heroult). This and other patents gave the company (its name at the time was the Pittsburgh Reduction Company) a legal monopoly in the United States until 1909. By the early 1900s the firm had developed a mass of unpatentable technical knowledge that newcomers would have had to learn the hard way. *Even without patents, an established firm has an edge that competitors can wear away only after considerable expense and hardship. Its average costs would be lower because of the extensive operating knowledge developed by this firm.* This is one reason why entry into an industry by firms established in the same industry *in other countries* may be

---

[4] See *ibid.*, pp. 41-54, and George W. Stocking and Willard F. Mueller, 'The Cellophane Case and the New Competition', *American Economic Review*, Vol. 45 (March 1955), pp. 29-63.

an important source of potential competition. On the basis of the Heroult process and patents, efficient producers established themselves in Europe, but the United States company was partly protected from the foreign producers by a substantial import duty. There still were imports, but they were severely limited by tariff and other arrangements. The major international firms entered into cartel agreements establishing output quotas and limiting competition.

The absence of a successful domestic rival until after 1940 was due in part to Alcoa's control of convenient sources for some of the elements of production—in particular, bauxite properties and hydro-power sites. But there were several more-or-less serious attempts to enter the American industry. In 1912 a French company started to build a plant in North Carolina and planned to use French bauxite. But the First World War intervened, its foreign finance disappeared, and in the absence of alternative American support it sold out to Alcoa in 1915. In 1924 J.B. Duke (of the American Tobacco Company) developed power rights on the Saguenay River in Quebec and made plans for aluminum production, but in 1925 the power company merged with Alcoa.

Alcoa's operating knowledge meant that its costs would be lower than those of most potential competitors. Alcoa followed a price policy that was designed to maximize profit over a long period; it did not try to maximize profit in any short-period situation. Its 'promotive price policy', along with engineering developments, were designed to increase demand and to open up new markets for aluminum. Another way in which entry was discouraged was by the building of productive capacity in excess of current demand. Judge Learned Hand, in the decision mentioned previously, stated:

> Alcoa effectively anticipated and forestalled all competition, and succeeded in holding the field alone. True, it stimulated demand and opened new uses for the metal, but not without making sure that it could supply what it had evoked . . . It was not inevitable that it should always anticipate increases in the demand for ingot and be prepared to supply them. Nothing compelled it to keep doubling and redoubling its capacity before others entered the field. It insists that it never excluded competitors; but we can think of no more effective exclusion than progressively to embrace each new opportunity as it opened, and to face every newcomer with new capacity already geared into a great organization, having the advantage of experience, trade connections and the elite of personnel.[5]

Alcoa's example makes clear some of the factors that allow for the emergence and maintenance of monopoly: (i) patents; (ii) unpatentable technical knowledge developed through operating experience; (iii) control

---

[5] Quoted in Stelzer, *op. cit.*, p. 30.

over low-cost sources of productive elements; (iv) protection from foreign imports; (v) a price policy designed to limit the attractiveness of entry, combined with the building of productive capacity in advance of market demands; and (vi) the requirement of large amounts of capital for entry by a competitor and the high probability of losses in at least the early years of the venture, because of the monopolist's excess capacity and price policy.

13.4 Short-period profit maximization

The price a monopolist firm will charge in the short period for its product will depend on the goals of the firm, its knowledge of costs and demand conditions in the present, and the ways in which its present policies will affect sales in the future. The standard textbook analysis of monopoly pricing[6]—which implicitly assumes full knowledge of costs and demand, stationary conditions, and short-period profit maximization as the firm's goal—will be presented first.

The situation facing a monopolist in a short period is summarized by its cost and revenue curves for that period, as illustrated in Figure 13.1. (The U-shaped cost curves obtained from neoclassical production functions are drawn to illustrate the standard textbook approach to monopoly pricing.) As we have seen in Section 10.3, short-period profit maximization requires the production of the rate of output at which marginal revenue is equal to marginal cost. Translated into a short-period profit-maximizing price policy, this would read: set the price corresponding to sales equal to the rate of output at which marginal revenue is equal to marginal cost. For the firm whose situation is described by the demand curve AR in Figure 13.1, this price is OP and its weekly rate of sales and production would be Oq. (This firm would have product and sales policies as well, but there is nothing more to be added here to the brief comments made about these policies in Section 12.7. The cost and revenue curves in this book are drawn on the assumption that the firms are implementing the sales and product policies they consider to be most advantageous.)

A testable hypothesis can be derived from this short-period profit-maximizing approach. It states that changes in demand, with given cost curves, will result in price changes in the same direction as the changes in demand. For example, a second demand curve AR', with lower demand at each price, is drawn in Figure 13.1. The corresponding profit-maximizing price would be OP'. Conversely, higher demand with given cost curves would result in higher prices. Available evidence is not consistent with this

---

[6] See, for example, Edwin Mansfield, *Microeconomics: Theory and Applications* (2nd ed.; New York: W.W. Norton & Co., 1975), Chapter 9.

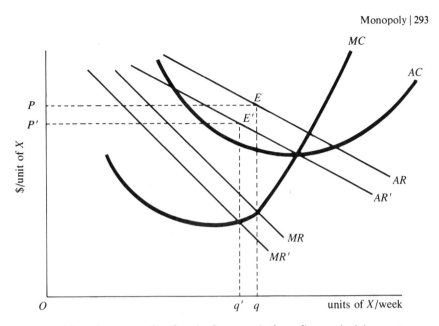

FIGURE 13.1 *A monopolist firm's short-period profit-maximizing output*

hypothesis. Firms enjoying monopolistic positions tend to keep prices stable relative to costs in the face of fluctuating demand.[7] (As we noted in Section 10.3, there is an important difference between short-period profit maximization and profit maximization when current actions affect future prospects.)

The standard textbook analysis then proceeds to consider the 'long-run equilibrium' position of a monopolist. It is illustrated in Figure 13.2. The firm's envelope average and marginal costs and two of its plant cost curves are drawn. If the firm has a plant whose cost curve is PAC, then the firm is in short-period equilibrium, producing Oq and charging a price OP, but the plant is inappropriate for long-period equilibrium. The plant that is consistent with long-period equilibrium, given the firm's demand curve AR, has the average cost curve PAC'. The long-period equilibrium price for this firm is OP'. Profits that exceed some normal rate of return, such as those shown at point E' in Figure 13.2, are compatible with long-period equilibrium in a monopolist's market if the monopolist is protected from the entry of competitors.

This standard textbook approach contains many unsatisfactory features. Even those who feel that profit maximization is still the most useful single

[7] For a summary of some of the evidence, see John M. Blair, *Economic Concentration, Structure, Behavior and Public Policy* (New York: Harcourt Brace Jovanovitch, 1972), pp. 424-37, and Chapter 17.

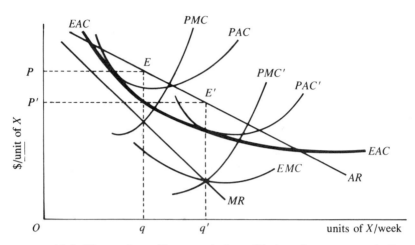

FIGURE 13.2 *Illustration of long-period equilibrium for a monopoly firm*

motive to attribute to a firm when its behaviour is analysed do not assume that firms maximize short-period profits. The analysis of 'long-run equilibrium' is appropriate only to stationary states: it is too mechanical to capture important aspects of a changing world. Firms deciding on plant size in their investment programs will choose the scale that is appropriate to their expected rate of sales. However, this insight does not imply any movement through time over 'long-run' cost curves that are based on the assumption of unchanging technology.

13.5 Pricing with the aid of a cost-plus formula

The prices of manufactured goods are set in relation to costs; variations in demand (other things given) tend to be reflected in changes in output rather than in prices.[8] This stability of prices in relation to costs is most evident in markets dominated by one or a few sellers where competitive forces can be restrained—an observation that need not be inconsistent with profit maximization over time in an uncertain world where alternative points on a demand curve cannot be readily determined. A monopolist's price policy would incorporate a target rate of return on investment to provide a profit when a standard rate of output is sold at the marked-up cost. Target rates of return can differ for different firms, and for any one firm at various periods

[8] Cf. Michal Kalecki, *Selected Essays on the Dynamics of the Capitalist Economy 1933-1970* (Cambridge, Eng.: Cambridge University Press, 1971), p. 43.

in its history.[9] These differences reflect the cumulative experiences of the firms and their views of their long-term opportunities. (It is important to keep in mind that they know they may be disappointed in their expectations.) These target rates are given in any short period by the firm's past history and view of the future; changes in demand, over relatively short periods of time, will not lead to changes in price unless costs are also changing. This hypothesis differs from that derived from the assumption of short-period profit maximization. A monopolist can maintain prices that are calculated with the aid of a cost-plus formula because of his market control. Prices for manufactured goods sold in competitive markets will be more sensitive to cyclical variations in demand than prices of goods sold in markets with high concentration ratios.[10]

When interviewed by economists, business executives often explain the price policies of their firms in terms of their being designed to secure some target rate of return on their investment.[11] These policies are said to be carried out with the aid of pricing formulas that bring costs directly into pricing. With prices set in this way, the firms sell what their markets will take and of course they do their best, through advertising and other forms of sales promotion, to increase the quantities sold.

To illustrate the use of a cost-plus formula[12] it will be assumed that a firm has only one plant and sells only in one market (but the analysis can be readily generalized). The price is obtained by marking up plant marginal costs, which are assumed to be constant for a considerable range of output (as reported in many empirical studies). The mark-up is designed to result in a gross-profit margin, when sales are at some standard rate,[13] sufficient to cover fixed costs and to provide a target rate of return on investment.

The cost-plus pricing formula can be written as

$$p = (1 + k) MC_s$$

---

[9] See Section 14.13 for a list of target rates of return for some United States firms.

[10] Blair compared price changes for sixteen pairs of products that are subject to reasonably comparable shifts in demand. He found greater variability in the prices of the products in markets with the lower concentration ratios. (*Economic Concentration, Structure, Behavior and Public Policy*.)

[11] See, for example, R.F. Lanzillotti, 'Pricing Objectives in Large Companies', *American Economic Review*, Vol. 48 (December 1958), pp. 921-40, and *Report of the Committee on Turnover Taxation* (United Kingdom, Command Paper No. 2300, March 1964).

[12] For examples of pricing formulas, see Joel Dean, *Managerial Economics* (Englewood Cliffs, N.J.: Prentice Hall, Inc., 1951), pp. 444-57.

[13] The United States Steel Company is reported as using, in its pricing formulas, standard costs computed 'on the basis of 80 per cent of capacity' in A.D.H. Kaplan, Joel B. Dirlam, and Robert F. Lanzillotti, *Pricing in Big Business: A Case Approach* (Washington, D.C.: The Brookings Institution, 1958), p. 15.

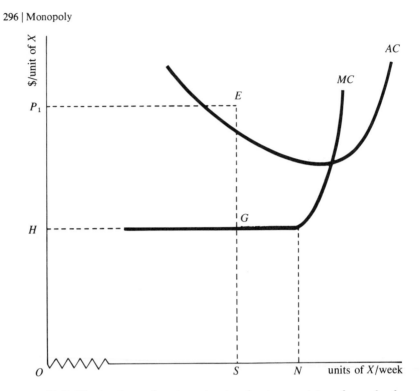

FIGURE 13.3 *Illustration of a target-rate-of-return pricing formula for a monopoly*

where MC_s is the constant value for marginal cost and k is a pure number derived with reference to the standard rate of output. The product of k and MC_s is equal to average fixed costs plus the target amount of profit per unit of output. The value for k can be obtained from this equation, since all the other values are assumed to be known or determined by the firm.

The operation of this pricing formula is illustrated in Figure 13.3. ON is the normal productive capacity of the plant and OS is the standard rate of output. The value for marginal costs along the horizontal portion of the curve is equal to OH ($=SG$) and the weekly amount required to cover plant fixed (and indirect variable) costs,[14] plus the targeted amount of profit when the standard rate of output is sold, is equal to the area $HP_1 EG$. The mark-up is equal to GE divided by SG. (Alternatively, the mark-up can be written as the ratio HP_1/OH, and the price OP_1 can be derived using the formula $OP_1 = (1 + HP_1/OH)OH$.)

The relative stability of monopolistic prices in the face of fluctuating

---

[14] The plant cost curve AC in Figure 13.3 does not include any provision for normal profit.

demand provides empirical support for cost-plus pricing; but *this does not mean that demand conditions are of no consequence in the determination of price*. Multi-product firms use different mark-ups for products facing different degrees of competition. There can also be considerable variation in the mark-up used by a firm over the life of a new product, with falling prices over time reflecting both falling costs and mark-ups as cost economies are achieved and competitive brands appear.[15] Demand conditions can also affect the timing of cost-indicated changes in prices, with firms delaying an increase in price or moderating the increase during a recessionary period.[16]

A pricing-formula approach leaves many factors unresolved. The target rate of return appearing in the formula depends on a firm's history and experience, but how these targets are formed and under what circumstances they may be changed are not explained by the formula.[17] This approach is presented here as a better starting-point for the analysis of monopolistic prices than the standard textbook short-period profit-maximization approach depicted in Figures 13.1 and 13.2, since it is consistent with both pricing data and statements by executives of monopolistic firms about their pricing practices. The use of a pricing formula for analysis is not to deny that the interrelation of prices and costs is complex and that firms are often forced by competitive pressures to keep a continuing check on costs. However, it makes clear the price-making role of monopolists and the importance of both costs and long-term profit goals in determining prices.[18]

---

[15] For a discussion of 'life-cycle pricing', and a pictorial history of prices of six new drugs, see Dean, *Managerial Economics*, pp. 410-27.

[16] Automobile pricing in the United States for 1976 model-year cars can be given as an example. (The U.S. automobile industry is an oligopoly with a dominant firm, General Motors, and a monopoly-type explanation of behaviour is appropriate even though the industry is not a monopoly.) The automobile producers experienced a sharp drop in sales for 1975 model-year cars, and in setting prices for the 1976 model-year cars they passed on only 57 per cent of the expected increase in production costs (the average increase in announced prices was $222). Their experience of depressed conditions in the previous year, plus uncertainty over the extent of the economic recovery, apparently led to a reduction of the mark-up for that year. See 'Government Report Cites Lower Rises on the 1976 Autos', an article on a report from the Council on Wage and Price Stability, in the *New York Times*, November 11, 1975, p. 59.

[17] Cf. J. Fred Weston, 'Pricing Behavior of Large Firms', *Western Economic Journal*, Vol. 10 (March 1972), pp. 1-18.

[18] The identification of a firm with its product and its terms of sale precludes frequent changes in price and the resulting loss of goodwill. Thus variations in sales around target levels do not, other things given, result in changes in a monopoly firm's price for its product. Some examples of the hesitation of firms to change prices, based on an investigation of pricing policies of Danish manufacturers, are given in B. Fog, *Industrial Pricing Policies* (Amsterdam: North-Holland Publishing, 1960).

13.6 Sales, output, and inventories

Production can differ from sales in a short period. The differences may be expected—for example when demand is seasonal—or unexpected. In the latter case, firms face the difficult problem of judging whether the unexpected change in demand is temporary or not; that is, whether they should alter their rates of output to keep them in line with the rates of sales. If production is greater than sales, the firm adds to its inventories of finished goods; if it is smaller, the inventories of these goods are reduced. Where changes in the rate of production are costly, and variations in sales from some steady production level are expected to be temporary, a firm's best policy may be to allow inventories to increase when demand is low and to draw on them when demand is high in order to limit fluctuations in production. In general the cost of producing a particular amount of the good over, say, a time interval of five months at a steady production rate in each month will be less than if this same amount is produced with substantially different production rates in each month.

Of course a firm cannot maintain production rates that differ substantially from sales over any fairly long interval of time. Unless otherwise noted, it will generally be assumed that production is equal to sales in each short period. Product orders in any short period may differ from both sales and production for goods that take a long time to produce. Variations in the 'length' of the firm's 'order-book' may be explained by the way in which production is kept fairly steady in these cases, with delivery dates increasing when orders are high and decreasing under slack conditions. Order backlogs play an important role in determining the rate of production for investment goods that are tailored to the purchasers' specifications and not produced for inventories, as in the case of ships, large items of capital equipment, etc.

13.7 Barriers to entry: 'entry-excluding' and 'entry-inducing' prices

A monopoly firm's market position will be protected by various barriers to entry, some of which were mentioned in our brief look at the history of Alcoa. They include patents, technical knowledge and operating experience, control of low-cost sources of productive elements, and high capital costs of entry. Some protection may also be obtained from product differentiation, i.e. consumer recognition and acceptance of brand names. In order to get the same product acceptance, an entrant would have to bear substantial costs. But given these barriers, the higher the current price relative to costs the more other firms are likely to take a chance and enter the market.[19] A

---

[19] Joe S. Bain, *Barriers to New Competition* (Cambridge, Mass.: Harvard University Press, 1956), Chapter 1. Paolo Sylos-Labini, *Oligopoly and Technical Progress* (Cambridge, Mass.: Harvard University Press, 1962).

monopoly firm's pricing behaviour is one of the factors affecting entry.

Let us assume that fundamental conditions are constant over time. This means that demand, the prices of the elements of production, and technology are unchanging. In deciding whether to enter an industry, a potential entrant must consider what policy the established firm will follow if entry occurs. This problem did not arise when we discussed entry in a competitive industry, in which any one firm produces only a small proportion of total output and it is not unreasonable for a new competitor to assume that price will be unaffected by its entry. Its expectations concerning market price after its entry are thus independent of its own actions. But this will not generally be true of a firm entering a monopolist's (or an oligopolistic) market. Its entry will appreciably change the market share of the existing firm, and this firm's expected response to entry will be an important factor in the potential entrant's decision to engage in the new market.

It will be assumed that the potential entrant expects that the existing firm will be inhospitable only to the extent of maintaining its current rate of output. This means that it will accept whatever consequences this policy might have on the price for its product. Thus the demand curve the potential entrant expects to face is the segment of the market demand curve for this commodity lying to the right of the point corresponding to the current rate of output of the monopolist. (For the purposes of this analysis, product differentiation is ignored.) In Figure 13.4 the monopoly firm's current price is assumed to be OP_1; its weekly rate of sales is OF; the expected demand curve facing the potential entrant is that portion of the demand curve to the right of point G. Point F is the origin from which the potential entrant's output is to be measured. If the current price were higher than OP_1, this origin would be to the left of point F; if the price were lower, it would be to the right. Given cost factors, the position of this origin determines the placing of the potential entrant's envelope cost curve. It is clear that the further to the left is the position of this origin (i.e. the higher the monopolist's price), the likelier it is that the potential entrant's cost curve will cut its expected demand curve at some point, making entry appear to be a profitable course of action.

In Figure 13.4 the minimum entry-inducing (or limit) price is OP_1. If a price OP_1 is charged by the monopolist, the potential entrant will expect, under the assumed conditions, to be able to find a rate of output (FH), and an appropriate size of plant, at which it can cover all its costs (including the minimum required rate of return on its investment) at the expected price for its output (OP_2). If the monopolist charged a price lower than OP_1, then the potential entrant's envelope cost curve would be everywhere above its

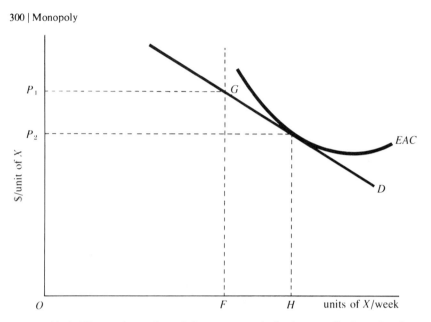

FIGURE 13.4 *Illustration of a minimum entry-inducing (or limit) price for a monopoly*

expected demand curve; it could not expect to cover all its costs and would thus be deterred from entering this line of activity, given these assumptions concerning expectations. A price lower than OP_1 would thus be an *entry-excluding price*. Conversely, a price higher than OP_1 would be clearly an *entry-inducing price*. (It is important not to forget that OP_1 is the limit price only if the potential entrant believes that the established firm will just maintain its rate of output. If it expected this firm to lower its rate of output, the limit price would be lower; if it expected the firm to raise its output, the limit price would be higher.) If a lower price discourages entry, a profit-maximizing firm might judge it to be in its best interests to charge a price less than that corresponding to the output at which short-period marginal revenue and marginal costs are equal.

The extent to which the monopoly firm is ready to sacrifice current profits for future profits depends in part on the relative weight it gives to a given amount of income in the present as compared with the same amount in some future time period. The higher this relative weight, the higher the price the established firm is likely to set. One should remember that an established firm can be mistaken in its view of entry possibilities; what it considers an entry-excluding price might in fact induce entry.

Changes in fundamental conditions have an important role in the decisions of firms to enter markets and industries. (For this reason the concept of a limit price is not a precise one, particularly when changes are occurring.) Entry might be made feasible because of changes in the technical opportunities facing firms, either through their own efforts or due to the expiry of patents or some combination of these factors. Expectations of substantial market growth or the discovery of new sources of supply may also play a vital role. For example, the British Petroleum Company was able to gain entry into the retail distribution of gasoline in the United States market by partial exchange of its rights to newly discovered oil deposits in Alaska's North Slope.

A potential entrant would probably expect a less inhospitable reception in a growing market than in a stationary one, since in a growth situation the effect of its entry on price would be less for any given output response of the established firms. Growth in the market dampens down the observed effect of entry on the existing firm and serves to absorb some of the new firm's output.

13.8 Price discrimination

A firm may be in a position to practice price discrimination—to charge more than one price for its output—even if this output is basically homogeneous. There are three categories of price discrimination. First-degree discrimination is said to occur if a consumer pays a different price for each unit of the good he buys. (Theoretically the charging of a different price for each unit purchased could deprive a consumer of all consumer's surplus with respect to this commodity; see Section 6.12.) Second-degree discrimination is said to occur if consumers are charged different prices for blocks of units of the product. The pricing of public utilities offers examples of this practice. Consumers pay at a lower rate for additional units of electricity after some initial level is purchased; the rates charged decrease with amounts consumed according to some step function. Third-degree price discrimination is said to occur if different consumers are charged different prices (when there are no fully compensating differences in the costs of providing the product to the consumers). Second- and third-degree discrimination may be combined. The electricity rates for domestic and industrial users differ, and there is also second-degree price discrimination within each category of users. Attention will be focused here on third-degree price discrimination; henceforth the term 'price discrimination' will refer to this category.

Two conditions are necessary for price discrimination: (i) differences in the elasticities of demand for different groups of customers so that a firm's revenues would be higher if different prices were charged; and (ii) the inability (due to the nature of the product or the firm's effort) of those who

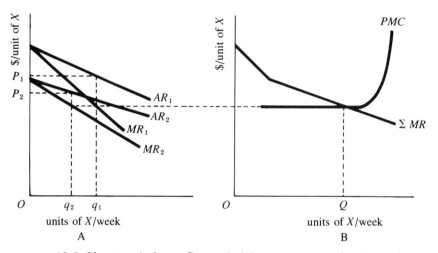

FIGURE 13.5 *Short-period profit-maximizing output and prices for a monopoly firm practising price discrimination*

buy at a low price to re-sell to those who have to pay a higher price. Assume that the firm can effectively separate its customers into two groups and, if it so chooses, set a different price for each. Both groups are supplied from the same plant and the costs are the same. Since this illustration is presented only to show that a firm may be in a position to increase its profit by practising price discrimination, it is convenient and not misleading in this special context to assume that the firm is trying to maximize short-period profit.

Since the cost of providing the product to the two groups is the same, the firm will maximize the revenue (and thus the short-period profit) it can obtain from a given rate of output for sale if the output is distributed between these two markets in such a way that the marginal revenues are the same in both. The appropriate marginal revenue curve to use in conjunction with the plant marginal cost curve in determining the short-period profit-maximizing output is obtained through a horizontal summation of the marginal revenue curves for each market. For the firm whose position is illustrated in Figure 13.5, the aggregate marginal revenue curve ΣMR is drawn in Panel B along with the plant marginal cost curve. The profit-maximizing rate of output and sales in the specified short period is thus seen to be OQ. Of this total, Oq_1 is sold in the market where the demand curve is AR_1, as shown in Panel A, and the remainder, Oq_2, is sold in the market where the demand curve is AR_2.

The relation between prices in the two markets depends on the values for their elasticities of demand at the equilibrium positions. In equilibrium, the marginal revenues in both markets must be the same (since marginal costs are assumed to be the same). Therefore we know that the following equality holds:

$$P_1\left(1 + \frac{1}{\eta_{D_1}}\right) = P_2\left(1 + \frac{1}{\eta_{D_2}}\right) \qquad (1)$$

where P_1 and P_2 are the prices in the respective markets and η_{D_1} and η_{D_2} are their price elasticities of demand.

Rearranging equation 1, we find:

$$\frac{P_1}{P_2} = \frac{1 + \dfrac{1}{\eta_{D_2}}}{1 + \dfrac{1}{\eta_{D_1}}} \qquad (2)$$

From equation 2 we can deduce that the price is higher in the market with the lower (numerical) value for the elasticity of demand. For example, if $\eta_{D_1} = -3/2$ and $\eta_{D_2} = -2$, demand in the first market is less elastic at the position of equilibrium than demand in the second, and $P_1/P_2 = 3/2$. In Figure 13.5, OP_1 is greater than OP_2 because at equilibrium the demand in the first market is less elastic than the demand in the second. If the market elasticities of demand were the same at equilibrium, then it can be seen from equation 2 that prices would be the same. Even though the firm could charge different prices, it would not be in its interest to do so in this case.

Even though the costs of providing a particular product to different groups differ, the term 'price discrimination' might still be appropriate. A difference in costs could be due to transportation costs, or because the versions of the product sold to different groups are physically differentiated (as in first- and economy-class air travel). In this case, differences in price for these varieties would not be sufficient to reveal discrimination, since they may only be compensating for differences in costs. Price discrimination would then be said to exist if the ratios of price to the marginal costs of producing and delivering the goods differed; that is, if $P_1/MC_1 \neq P_2/MC_2$. Firms are unlikely to have the type of information assumed in the above example, especially with regard to marginal revenue, but it is not uncommon for a firm to charge different prices in different markets in line with what it assumes a market can bear. Price discrimination appears in pricing formulas in the guise of different mark-ups for different varieties, or for outputs destined for different markets.

13.9 Examples of price discrimination

Price discrimination often occurs in personal and health services (doctor's fees are often tailored to the patient's purse), where the nature of the 'product' is such that resale is inherently impossible[20]: different groups can therefore be effectively separated for pricing purposes. It is also found in transportation services, both for people and commodities, since again groups can be separated. Also, transportation rates may vary geographically, when the degree of competition (the existence of alternative forms of transportation), and thus the nature of the demand curve facing the transportation firm, varies geographically. Price discrimination is practised by oligopolists as well as monopolists. An example of price discrimination, brought to public notice by a report of the Canadian Royal Commission on Farm Machinery, concerns the pricing of tractors in Canada and the United Kingdom. Two multinational firms (Ford and Massey-Ferguson) produced in the United Kingdom the tractors they sold in Canada. The price they charged in Canada, even after allowance is made for extra equipment and transportation costs, was much higher than the price they set for customers in the United Kingdom. In order to separate these two markets, they went to great lengths to prevent distributors of their products in the United Kingdom from selling to Canadian buyers.[21]

13.10 Taxation of a monopolist

The effects of differences in the assumptions concerning the goals of a monopoly firm can be illustrated by examining the effects of different types of taxation on its price. The three types of tax examined are (i) a specific tax of a given amount per unit of output; (ii) a tax on profits; (iii) a lump-sum tax (a fixed amount of tax irrespective of output). It will be assumed first that the firm tries to maximize its short-period profits, and the effects of each of these taxes on its behaviour will be examined.[22] The effects of a profits tax when a monopoly firm tries to maximize profits over some long period of time, and when it tries to maximize sales subject to a profit constraint, will also be considered.

In all these examinations of the effects of taxes on a monopoly firm, it will be assumed that *neither the tax itself, nor the use the government makes of the tax revenue, affects the firm's demand curve or the prices of the*

---

[20] Reuben A. Kessel, 'Price Discrimination in Medicine', *Journal of Law and Economics*, Vol. 11 (October 1968), pp. 20-53.

[21] Royal Commission on Farm Machinery, *Special Report on Prices of Tractors and Combines in Canada and Other Countries* (Ottawa: Queen's Printer, December 1969).

[22] This is the standard textbook assumption when monopoly taxation is considered. See, for example, Donald S. Watson and Mary A. Holman, *Price Theory and Its Uses* (4th ed.; Boston: Houghton Mifflin, 1977), pp. 296-7. It is surprising to find that Alfred Marshall made this same assumption when examining the effects of taxes on a monopolist's price and output, since he noted that a monopolist sets price with a view to future developments (*Principles of Economics* [8th ed.; London: Macmillan & Co., 1920], p. 486).

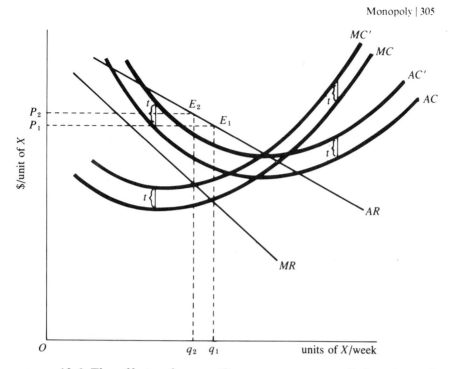

FIGURE 13.6 *The effects of a specific tax on a monopolist's price and output, assuming short-period profit maximization*

elements of production it employs. This is a very restrictive assumption and could not be maintained if the industry were large or if the tax were also imposed on other industries. Thus the following is an example of partial equilibrium analysis. To deal fully with the effects of changes in tax rates, a more general analysis is required, one that recognizes the interdependence of different industries and the macroeconomic as well as microeconomic effects of tax changes.[23]

13.10a Short-period profit maximization

A specific tax of t per unit is assumed to be imposed on the firm whose cost and revenue curves are drawn in Figure 13.6. As a result of this tax, its marginal and average cost curves are shifted upward by t, since this is the increase in the firm's unit cost of operation. In Figure 13.6 these tax-inclusive curves are labelled MC' and AC'. Before the imposition of the tax, the short-period profit-maximizing price was OP_1, and the corresponding rate of output was Oq_1. After a specific tax of t per unit is imposed, the

[23] A. Asimakopulos and J.B. Burbidge, 'The Short-Period Incidence of Taxation', *Economic Journal*, Vol. 84 (June 1974), pp. 267-88.

short-period equilibrium price becomes OP_2, and the corresponding output rate is Oq_2. Part of the tax is shifted to consumers and part is absorbed by the firm. The difference in price, P_1P_2, is less than the specific tax rate t, since the monopolist's demand curve in the short period is not perfectly inelastic.

If a lump-sum tax instead of a specific tax were imposed on such a firm, it would have no effect on the short-period equilibrium price and output (as long as it was not so large as to drive the firm out of business). This can be deduced by examining Figure 13.6. A lump-sum tax does not affect the marginal cost curve, and since the MR curve is assumed to be unchanged, Oq_1 is still the short-period profit-maximizing output and OP_1 the appropriate price. A similar conclusion can be drawn for a tax on profit. For any rate of tax on profit, a firm's profit (net of tax) is at a maximum when its pre-tax profit is at a maximum. A lump-sum tax appears to be a way of extracting the monopolist's excess profit without any cost to consumers, but this conclusion is no more convincing than the behavioural assumption that gives rise to it. (One should keep in mind the warning given previously about the partial nature of this examination of the effects of taxes on a monopoly firm.)

13.10b Profit maximization over time

When the firm's governing motive is the maximization of profit over some fairly long time span, lump-sum or profits taxes are likely to increase the price of the monopolist's product. In the initial short-period situation before the imposition of the tax, the monopoly firm will not necessarily be charging the short-period profit-maximizing price. It may be deterred from doing so by fear of entry, or by the desire to foster demand in future periods, or by fear of adverse government action. The imposition of a tax may make the short-period profit-maximizing position more attractive to the firm. The tax on profits makes the industry less profitable and tends to discourage potential entrants, thus raising the entry-inducing price; the reduced after-tax profitability in the present makes it more difficult for the firm to take a long view of profits. The firm has much less scope for delaying the earning of profits: after-tax profits are necessary in the present for the survival and growth of the firm. The more they are reduced by taxes, the more difficult it is for the firm to forego present profits in the expectation of greater profits in the future. Also, the imposition of the tax may provide an excuse for raising the price—it would tend to deflect and moderate public criticism of the firm. For any one or a combination of the above reasons, the price might be higher as a result of a lump-sum or profits tax, even though the firm is profit-maximizing over time.

It was argued in Section 13.5 that one method for maximizing profit over time in an uncertain world is based on a price policy that uses a target rate of return (net of taxes) on investment. A change in the tax rate on profits would change the mark-up required to achieve a given rate of return on investment. For example, assume that the target rate of return (net of profits tax) is 20 per cent, the value (at cost) of the investment is $1,000,000, the marginal cost is $10 per unit of output, and the standard rate of output is 100,000 units per year. The target net profit (after taxes and after depreciation and amortization allowances) is equal to $200,000 per year. If there is no profits tax, the value of that part of the mark-up required to produce this target return per year is equal to 0.20. ($200,000 = .20 × 100,000 × $10.) If a profits tax of, say, 20 per cent is imposed with no change in the firm's profit objectives, its mark-up will be increased. In order to provide a net profit of $200,000 when the target rate of output is sold, the rate of return element in the mark-up must be equal to 0.250. (Profits before tax must be $250,000 in order to provide an after-tax profit of $200,000: $250,000 = .25 × 100,000 × $10.) Even if there were some downward revision in a firm's target rate of return after the change in tax, there would still be considerable scope for some increase in price.[24]

The conclusion deduced for the price effect of a specific tax differs from that obtained for short-period profit maximization. In this case the monopolist would likely increase the price by the full extent of the tax. Such an increase would not induce entry or alter the relationship between the firm's expectations of current and future profitability; furthermore, the imposition of the tax would provide a public justification for a price increase.

13.10c Maximization of value of sales

If a firm's management is following policies that maximize the value of sales subject to a profit constraint, a lump-sum or profits tax will affect price. Assume that the firm can earn more than the minimum profit per unit of time that management feels is needed to preserve its position. It will therefore be producing a rate of output greater than that at which short-period profit is maximized. A situation of this type is illustrated in Figure

---

[24] A comment on the results of an interview of business executives in the United Kingdom, *Report of the Committee on Turnover Taxation* (Cmnd. 2300), March 1964, may be of interest in this connection: 'Three witnesses implied a more immediate connexion between prices and direct taxation on profits. They thought that pricing policy aimed to produce a certain margin (which would vary according to the nature of the business) of net profit after tax in relation to capital employed and that in this way the level of profits taxation had an overall influence on prices at the planning stage' (p. 74).

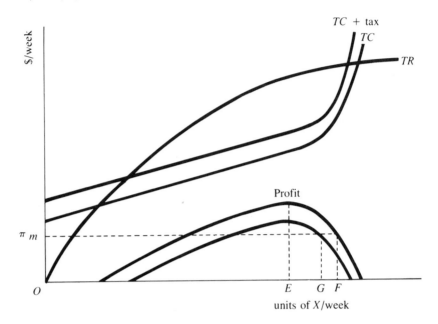

FIGURE 13.7 *Effect of a lump-sum tax on a monopoly firm maximizing sales subject to a profit constraint*

13.7. The firm's total revenue curve is concave from below, indicating that larger amounts (given the selling expenditures included in the cost curve) can be sold only at lower prices. The shape of the total cost curves indicates constant marginal costs until the region of normal plant capacity is reached, when they increase sharply. The short-period profit-maximizing output is where the slopes of the cost and revenue curves are the same. Since the maximum possible profit, under the conditions specified in Figure 13.7, is greater than the profit constraint, the firm produces and sells more (*OF*) than the profit-maximizing output (*OE*). The imposition of a lump-sum tax raises the total cost curve by the same amount at all rates of output, and lowers profit by this amount. It is clear from the figure that the profit constraint can now be met only when the rate of output (and sales) is lower. The lower rate of output would be *OG* in Figure 13.7 and the firm would set the higher price at which this rate could be sold.

A tax on profit would also lead to lower after-tax profits at each rate of output, and a higher price would be required to satisfy the profit constraint.

In Figure 13.7 a specific tax on the firm's output increases the slope of its total cost curve (the resulting cost curve is not drawn in the figure), and thus it would shift the point of maximum profit (after tax) to the left. The price would be higher and the output lower.

13.11 Summary

The mechanics of the standard textbook analysis of the behaviour of a monopolist, with revenue and cost curves fully known, have been explained. The severe limitations of this analysis and its dependence on the assumptions of short-period profit maximization as the firm's goal have been emphasized. Predictions made on the basis of this model could be very misleading. The world in which monopolies operate cannot be conveyed effectively in such a simple manner. Recognition of the interdependence of present and future profits, along with the ever-prevailing uncertainty about the future, introduces difficulties into the analysis of monopoly-firm behaviour even if profit maximization is assumed to be the primary goal of the firm.

A firm can discourage entry into its market by constructing productive capacity in advance of demand and by following a conservative price policy that sacrifices profit in the present for greater returns in the future. A model that assumes that monopoly firms act in this way leads to the prediction (contrary to that obtained from the short-period profit-maximizing model) that short-term variations in demand would result in changes in the rates of output, with price relative to costs remaining approximately unchanged. The height of the barriers to entry into its markets affects the competitive pressures felt by the firm and the rate of return it can earn on its investment over time. The firm's long-term profit goals are reflected in the mark-ups it applies to costs in setting prices.

The effects of differences in the assumptions concerning the goals of monopoly firms were illustrated by examining the conclusions on the price responses of a monopolist firm to various taxes.

SUGGESTED READINGS

Clemens, Eli W. 'Price Discrimination and the Multiple-Product Firm'. *Review of Economic Studies*, Vol. 19 (1950-1), pp. 1-11. Reprinted in American Economic Association, *Readings in Industrial Organization and Public Policy*. Edited by Richard B. Heflebower and George W. Stocking. Homewood, Ill.: Richard D. Irwin, 1958. Pages 262-76.

Marshall, Alfred. *Principles of Economics*. 8th ed. London: Macmillan & Co., 1920. Book V, Chapter XIV.

Modigliani, Franco. 'New Developments on the Oligopoly Front'. *Journal of Political Economy*, Vol. 66 (June 1958), pp. 215-32.

Robinson, Joan. *The Economics of Imperfect Competition*. 2nd ed., London: Macmillan & Co., 1969. Chapters 15 and 16.

Weiss, Leonard W. *Economics and American Industry*. New York: John Wiley & Sons, 1961. Chapter 5.

EXERCISES

1. Assume that a monopoly firm can separate the demand for its product into two markets and that if it so chooses it could set a different price in each. Assume that the two demand curves are given by:

$$q = 20 - p/8 \text{ and } q = 160 - 2p$$

Plot these two demand curves and the marginal cost curve, $MC = 4 + q$. Assume that the firm is maximizing profits in the short period, then determine the prices it sets in the two markets and the total profit. What would its profit be? What price would it charge if it could *not* separate demand into these two markets and could set only one price? What would its profit be in this case?

2. Illustrate the effects of the following three types of taxes on a monopolist's price, output, and profit:

    (a) Profits tax—i.e. the tax payment is a constant percentage of profit;

    (b) Specific tax—i.e. he pays t per unit of output;

    (c) Ad valorem tax—i.e. he pays a tax of t per cent of the price per unit sold for three kinds of price policy: (i) short-period profit maximization; (ii) sales maximization subject to a profit constraint; (iii) target-rate-of-return or full-cost pricing.

14
OLIGOPOLY

14.1 Introduction

Oligopolistic market structures (a few sellers accounting for a substantial part of total sales) are very common in modern capitalist economies, and industries that are oligopolistic produce a significant proportion of the total value of output in the manufacturing sector. The difficulties that make a simple analysis of the behaviour of monopoly firms potentially very misleading are also found here. Profit maximization cannot be collapsed into short-period profit maximization; and the uncertainty about the future consequences of present actions affects pricing decisions as well as investment decisions. When they set prices for their products, oligopoly firms must consider the possibility of attracting entry or of inducing government intervention as well as future demand for their products. For a theorist who tries to develop a simple model for the analysis of the behaviour of firms in oligopolistic industries, there are additional problems that are a consequence of the nature of oligopoly situations. Each industry (or market) is dominated by a relatively small number of firms that cannot fail to recognize the interdependence of their actions. They sell products that are close substitutes, and changes in their actions have noticeable effects on the market positions of others in the industry. When an oligopolistic firm is contemplating a change in policy, it must take into account the expected responses of rival firms.

Some of the traditional approaches to the behaviour of oligopoly firms will be examined and their limitations noted. In the absence of any acceptable general theory, it is necessary to try to analyse oligopoly situations in an almost case-by-case approach. The history of the particular industry and the nature of its product and its technology play an important role in the determination of its current policies. It will be argued that here, as in the case of monopoly firms, the appropriate starting point for the analysis of the determination of prices is with a pricing formula based on costs.

14.2 Reasons for oligopolistic markets and industries

There are various factors that alone, or in some combination, lead to oligopolistic markets and industries. They will be discussed under five headings.

(i) *Economies of large-scale production.* In many industries a relatively small number of firms may be able to supply the entire market at a lower cost than could be attained if this total output were divided among a larger number of firms. (The output of one optimal-size firm would represent a substantial fraction of total industry output.) The importance of scale-economies depends not only on technological factors that influence the firm's costs but also on the size of the market. The smaller the market, other things given, the larger the proportion of total industry output accounted for by a plant that achieves all the economies of scale. If these economies are significant, it would not be surprising to find that a few large firms are dominant. In some cases a few firms may have produced a substantial proportion of the total output from the early days of the industry; while in others the small number may be the result of competitive pressures, following changes in technology, that drove out (or led to the absorption through mergers of) all but a few firms that survived by attaining the lower costs of large scale.

(ii) *Profit possibilities of mergers and restricted competition.* The firms in an industry may find it to their advantage to merge in order to eliminate competition among themselves. This would bring about a structure within the industry sufficiently concentrated that competition among the remaining sellers would be easily suppressed. The profits expected from the limitation of intra-industry competition would thus encourage the promotion of an oligopoly through mergers. The development of 'trusts' in the late nineteenth and early twentieth centuries was clearly based on these expectations of profits,[1] and there is no reason to believe that this motive is not present in some more recent mergers. For mergers to succeed in producing profits over time, there must be high barriers to entry; otherwise the establishment of new firms in the industry would tend to restore the competitive situation the mergers were designed to overcome. (However, short-term profit opportunities might be sufficiently enticing to lead to mergers irrespective of the barriers to entry.)

---

[1] See the reference to the formation of the United States Steel Company in Section 16.13.

(iii) *Product differentiation*. In some cases a few firms may obtain an important advantage from product differentiation. Buyers prefer their products to other varieties of the same good, and this enables these firms to secure a major share of the market. In a detailed study of barriers to entry in twenty industries in the United States (listed in Table 14.1), Joe S. Bain examined, among other factors, the importance of product differentiation as a barrier to entry.[2] His rating varied from 'Negligible' for some producer-good industries (copper, rayon, and cement) to 'Great' for some consumer-oriented industries (liquor, cigarettes, typewriters, and automobiles). In the latter case he found the primary bases of product differentiation to be some combinations of factors such as advertising, differences in design, control of retail-dealer and customer-service systems, and quality maintenance. Where the nature of the product and the expertise of the buyers did not leave much scope for differentiation—for example, in steel—some slight basis was found in 'customer service; personal sales representation'. For metal containers, Bain's ranking was 'slight or moderate', since the leasing of equipment to customers and design differences in some products, based on patents, were added to customer service as a means of increasing buyer-seller attachment. In consumer-goods industries there is more scope for product differentiation, even with homogeneous products. For example, in petroleum refining (classified primarily on the basis of gasoline) product differentiation was raised to a moderate degree of importance as a result of maintaining retail-dealer outlets and of advertising.

(iv) *Absolute cost advantages of existing firms*. A relatively small number of firms may have absolute advantages in cost over all others that permit them to operate profitably at a price that is too low to allow others to recover all their costs. Absolute advantages of this sort may be obtained by securing patents on the most economical techniques of production; through operating experience, even though the knowledge acquired and 'tricks of the trade' are not patentable; and through acquiring control of low-cost sources of important raw materials. Bain found that in three industries, potential entrants were at an absolute cost disadvantage. With gypsum products the basis for this disadvantage was that 'know-how is extremely important in wallboard production, and that established firms generally have various gadgets and technical improvements protected primarily by secrecy. A new firm might be at an appreciable disadvantage for several years before acquiring or developing sufficient know-how, and in the

[2] Joe S. Bain, *Barriers to New Competition* (Cambridge, Mass.: Harvard University Press, 1956), pp. 114-43.

TABLE 14.1 *Summary of relative heights of specific entry barriers in 20 United States industries. (Higher numbers denote higher entry barriers.)*

INDUSTRY	SCALE-ECONOMY BARRIER	PRODUCT-DIFFERENTIATION BARRIER	ABSOLUTE-COST BARRIER	CAPITAL-REQUIREMENT BARRIER
Automobiles	III	III	I	III
Canned goods	I	I to II	I	I
Cement	II	I	I	II
Cigarettes	I	III	I	III
Copper	n.a.	i	III	n.a.
Farm machinery	II	I to III	I	n.a.
Flour	I	I to II	I	Φ
Fountain pens	n.a.	I to III	I	I
Gypsum products	n.a.	I	III	I
Liquor	I	III	I	II
Meat packing	I	I	I	Φ or I
Metal containers	n.a.	II	I	I
Petroleum refining	II	II	I	III
Rayon	II	I	I	II
Shoes	II	I to II	I	Φ
Soap	II	II	I	II
Steel	II	I	III	III
Tires and tubes	I	II	I	II
Tractors	III	III	I	III
Typewriters	II	II	I	n.a.

SOURCE: Joe S. Bain, *Barriers to New Competition* (Cambridge, Mass.: Harvard University Press, 1956), p. 169.

meantime would have difficulty in establishing and controlling the quality of its wall-board.'[3] With steel and copper, the control of adequate supplies was felt to provide advantages to established firms.

(v) *Financial capital requirements.* The sums of money that have to be invested in order to enter an industry on a scale that may permit eventual success can be substantial in some cases. Not only may the costs of building the necessary production facilities be high, but substantial sums may be required for advertising and for establishing dealer systems, as well as to cover expected losses during the first few years of operation.

Bain's findings on barriers to entry, summarized in Table 14.1, give some indication of the way the importance of barriers may vary between industries and of how, for any one industry, the relative importance of different barriers may differ. The higher the number given to a barrier, the

---

[3] *Ibid.*, pp. 152-3.

higher the rating of importance for the barrier. Four rankings are given for the importance of capital requirements, with the smallest being designated by Φ. *It is important to remember that these ratings are based on United States data at a particular period of time (the early 1950s). The importance of barriers in an industry may of course change over time owing to changes in technology and new discoveries of raw materials, etc.* The rating for the scale-economy barrier is very much affected by the size of the markets for the particular industry's products. The larger the market, the less important this barrier, other things being given (technology especially). The scale-economy barriers in many of these industries would be relatively more important for, say, Canadian industries than is indicated by Bain's data.

14.3 The demand curve and oligopoly
Oligopoly poses many problems to economic theorists analysing individual firms in this market because the standard techniques available to them are centred on the firm's demand curve and its derivatives. As we discussed in Section 9.9 a firm's demand curve in an oligopolistic market is more than usually conjectural because it is largely dependent on the reactions of other firms to differences in the prices the firm sets. In spite of this serious difficulty, theorists have tried to employ demand curves by making specific assumptions about the behaviour of the oligopolists. Some of these attempts will be examined in the following sections.

14.4 Cournot and reaction curves
The first theoretical treatment of oligopoly markets was published by a Frenchman, Augustin Cournot, in 1838.[4] He was aware of the problem of the conjectural nature of a firm's demand curve in oligopoly and in order to arrive at a mathematical solution he made the special assumption that each firm believes the rates of output produced and put on the market by its rivals to be independent of its own rate of output and sales. The demand curve on which a firm bases its price and output decisions is thus the total market demand curve (which is assumed to be known) *minus* the quantities being currently sold by all other firms (also assumed to be known). This is illustrated in Figure 14.1. The total market demand curve is labelled *DD*, with weekly quantities measured from the origin *O*. The sum of the current weekly rates of sales of all the other firms in this market is equal to *OA*. Thus the demand curve that Cournot's firm assumed it was facing would be *DD*, but with its sales measured from point *A* as its origin. (Recall that in

---

[4] Augustin Cournot, *Researches into the Mathematical Principles of the Theory of Wealth* (1838), trans. by N.T. Bacon (New York: Macmillan Co., 1929).

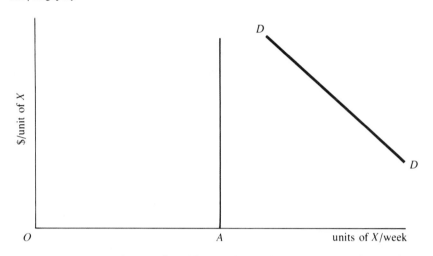

FIGURE 14.1 *Demand curve faced by an oligopolist when sales of other firms are assumed to be determined independently*

order to illustrate the concept of 'limit pricing' in Section 13.8, the demand curve the potential entrant assumed he would be facing on entry was arrived at in this way.)

Cournot's analysis will be demonstrated by a market where there are only two sellers (a duopoly) whose products are perfect substitutes. All fundamental conditions will be assumed constant over time: the firms are in a stationary state and the market demand curve for the good is therefore the same in each time period. It is assumed that the firms are trying to maximize their profits in each short period.

The larger the rate of output (and sales) of one firm, the lower the market price for any given rate of output that is placed on the market by the other firm. Point *A*, the origin for the firm's demand curve in Figure 14.1, is further to the right the larger the rate of output (and sales) of the other firm, while the position of the market demand curve is unchanged. Thus this firm's profit-maximizing rate of output will generally be lower, given its costs, the greater the output of its rival. If the latter's rate of output is large enough, the firm's profit-maximizing rate of output will be zero. The curve joining the points representing the short-period profit-maximizing rates of output for one firm that correspond to different rates of output for the other is called a *reaction curve*. Reaction curves for the duopolists are drawn in Figure 14.2.

If firm 2's sales were at the rate *OB* in the specified short period, the market price would be so low that it would not pay firm 1 to produce anything; its profit-maximizing output would be zero. Point *B* thus lies on

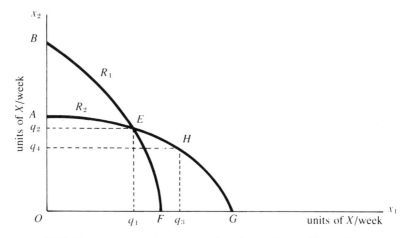

FIGURE 14.2 *Cournot reaction curves for duopolists selling a homogeneous product in a stationary state*

firm 1's reaction curve and the output OB was called the 'competitive' rate of output by Cournot. If firm 2's sales were less than OB, firm 1 would produce and place on the market the positive quantities shown by its reaction curve BF. If firm 2's sales were zero, firm 1 would produce and sell at the rate OF. Cournot called this the 'monopoly' output. Firm 2's reaction curve, AG, is interpreted in a similar manner. If the cost curves are the same for both firms, OG would be equal to OB and OA would be equal to OF.

The duopoly equilibrium position for the situation depicted in Figure 14.2 is at point E, with firm 1 producing and selling a weekly rate of Oq_1 units and firm 2, Oq_2 units. The output rates of the two firms at this point are consistent with the assumptions they are making about their environment (in particular, the behaviour of the other firm) and each would judge that it had made the best choice. If the actual position of the firms were represented by some other point, at least one of the firms would want to change its rate of output in the given circumstances. (For example, the rates of output, Oq_3 and Oq_4, corresponding to point H, are not consistent. If firm 2 maintains its output rate of Oq_4, we can see from firm 1's reaction curve that it would want to produce an output rate lower than Oq_3.)

Not only is point E an equilibrium position for the duopolists, it is also a position of *stable* equilibrium if the assumptions on which the reaction curves are based correctly describe the responses of the firms. If there is some temporary disturbance that moves the firms off the equilibrium position, forces will be set in motion to return them to the equilibrium position—as long as each firm continues to believe that its output decision does not affect the rate of output of the other firm. For example, if they both happened to be at point H, firm 1 would lower its rate of output below Oq_3; we see from firm 2's reaction curve AG that it would respond by raising its output rate. This process—one firm lowering and the other raising its rate of output—would continue as long as each firm acted as though its output decisions had no effects on its rival's actions until the firms reached point E. The assumption that the firms would continue to act in this way makes clear the weaknesses of this approach: it requires that firms do not learn, from their experience of non-equilibrium positions, that in fact *their output decisions are interdependent*.

Many variations on the Cournot approach can be found in the literature of economics. One of these variants assumes that firms adjust price rather than quantity. Another assumes that one of the firms knows the reaction curve of the other and chooses its optimal output on this basis.[5] Cournot solutions to different situations continue to appear in economics journals—they provide scope for mathematical games—but the possibilities inherent in oligopoly situations are too varied to be adequately handled in this manner.

14.5 Chamberlin and the small group

In his *Theory of Monopolistic Competition*, E.H. Chamberlin contrasted the behaviour of firms in a 'Small Group' (oligopoly) with that of firms in a 'Large Group' (monopolistic competition). For a firm in a given short-period situation two demand curves can be defined, each drawn through the point representing the firm's price and rate of sales. (See Section 12.4 where these curves were discussed.) These are drawn in Figure 14.3.

Point G in Figure 14.3 represents the firm's price and weekly rate of sales (and output), given particular values for the prices of the products of other firms selling in this market. The standard firm demand curve, based on the assumption of constant values for all prices, including those for close substitutes, is represented in this figure by the curve dd. The curve DD indicates the rates of output the firm could sell if it set different prices when the prices for the products of the other firms in the group differ in the same proportion. (The product and selling policies of all firms, and all other parameter values, are assumed to be constant.)

Chamberlin argued that a firm in a large group would base its pricing decisions on the dd curve. If a firm is in a small group, however, it is no

---

[5] See E.H. Chamberlin, *The Theory of Monopolistic Competition* (6th ed.; Cambridge, Mass.: Harvard University Press, 1950), Chapter III and William Fellner, *Competition Among the Few* (New York: Augustus M. Kelley, 1960), Chapter 2, for a review of these writings.

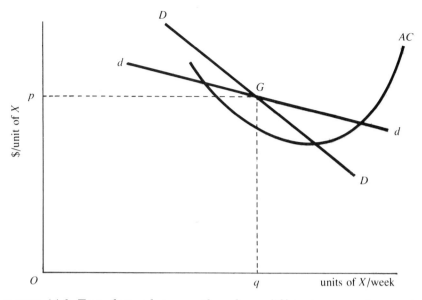

FIGURE 14.3 *Two demand curves (based on different assumptions concerning prices of other firms) facing a firm in an oligopoly market*

longer appropriate to assume that its actions have negligible effects on the positions of other sellers in the group. Chamberlin emphasized that firms in such a situation would recognize their interdependence and that price might be determined on the basis of the *DD* curve. Given costs, a short-period profit-maximizing firm would set a higher price if it assumed that the demand curve *DD*, rather than the curve *dd*, were facing it. The marginal revenue for the *DD* curve, corresponding to point *G*, lies below the marginal revenue for the *dd* curve at the same point, and the intersection of its marginal revenue curve with the marginal cost curve would lie further to the left. A monopoly-type price might thus tend to emerge through the *independent* action of these firms when they recognize their *mutual interdependence*.

Profits may not exceed 'normal' levels over time, however, even though higher prices corresponding to the *DD* curves are charged by the firms. If the barriers to entry are not very high, the entry of new firms (reflected by a leftward shift of the *DD* curves for established firms) would tend to eliminate excess profits over time under stationary conditions. This point can be illustrated by comparing the two equilibrium positions for a short-period profit-maximizing oligopolist in Figure 14.4.

Point E_1 represents the equilibrium position corresponding to the firm's demand curve *DD* and its cost curve *AC*. If the number of firms in the

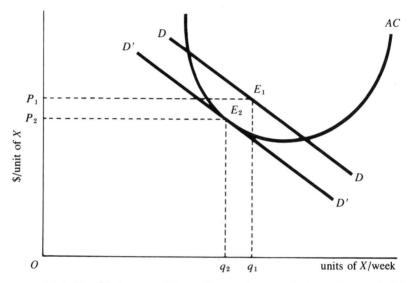

FIGURE 14.4 *Equilibrium positions for a short-period profit-maximizing oligopoly firm when all price changes are matched by other firms*

industry (group) were larger because the above-normal profits attracted new firms, and the total market demand did not increase proportionately, then the demand curve facing the firm would lie further to the left—for example, at $D'D'$. This curve shows that, owing to the larger number of sellers in the group, the amount that this firm can sell, at any price, is less than it would be if there were fewer firms. Marginal revenue and marginal cost curves are not drawn in Figure 14.4, but we can infer from the tangency of the $D'D'$ and AC curves at point E_2 that the marginal revenue curve corresponding to the demand curve $D'D'$ and the marginal cost curve intersect at the output rate Oq_2.[6]

Pricing on the basis of a firm demand curve such as DD or $D'D'$, which assumes that the prices of other firms in the group change proportionately, has been characterized as 'monopoly-type' pricing. These curves are miniature industry demand curves; if all firms in the group were identical, they would be exact small-scale replicas of the total market demand curve. Monopoly profits over time do not necessarily follow from monopoly-type pricing because of the possible effects of entry into the group. The price

---

[6] Recall the relationship derived in Section 9.13 between marginal and average values and the elasticity, $M = A(1 + \eta_A)$, when the independent variable is on the abscissa. At E_2 the $D'D'$ and AC curves have the same value and their elasticities are the same; therefore the marginal values must be the same.

OP_2 in Figure 14.4 is a monopoly-type price, but profits are at a normal level because of the number of firms in the industry. This analysis points up the importance of barriers to entry in determining profitability over long intervals of time. An industry would be competitive in the long-period sense, in the terminology explained in Section 9.5, if the pressure of new entrants kept firms close to positions such as E_2.

Chamberlin's approach to oligopoly pricing is more reasonable than that given by variations of the Cournot approach because it is built around the recognition by firms of their mutual dependence. This does not mean that a monopoly-type outcome, with firms maximizing their joint profits, will result. Achievement of such an outcome requires tacit mutual understanding of each firm's position and some at least implicit agreement on market shares or on ways in which these shares can be adjusted. Uncertainty over the effects of their actions and unsuppressed rivalry could produce an outcome that does not maximize joint profits.

Differences in costs and market opportunities are two of the obstacles in the way of the achievement of a monopoly-type outcome by the independent actions of firms in oligopolies. Even if they wanted to practise collusion on the basis of their DD-type curves, they could not do so by setting prices independently. For example, assume that in Figure 14.4 DD is the demand curve facing a duopolist firm that has a product differentiation advantage and $D'D'$ is the demand curve facing the other firm (the costs of both firms being the same). They cannot price independently on the basis of the DD-type curve drawn in that figure since their actions would be inconsistent. On that basis each firm would want to set a different price. Whatever price is finally set in such a situation must be arrived at by some sort of implicit agreement that may be very fragile in the face of changing circumstances. It should be remembered that curves such as those drawn in Figure 14.4 depict alternatives in a specified short period, and that even if the firms have the same cost and demand curves, they may differ in other respects. They may not have the same views of future prospects or of the effects of present policies on future profit possibilities, or one of the firms may place a higher priority on growth, etc. All these differences make it difficult to analyse oligopoly pricing on the basis of a short-period demand curve that assumes that all firms in the group vary price to the same extent.[7]

---

[7] This brief sketch of Chamberlin's analysis of the small group cannot do justice to all the insights contained in his work. He was well aware that in many situations oligopoly pricing would be based on costs: '. . . businessmen may set their prices with reference to costs rather than to demand, aiming at ordinary rather than at maximum profits.' *The Theory of Monopolistic Competition*, p. 105. See also E.H. Chamberlin, '"Full Cost" and Monopolistic Competition', *Economic Journal*, Vol. 62 (June 1952), pp. 318-25.

14.6 Stationary conditions and the maximization of joint profits

William Fellner suggests that in oligopoly markets there is a tendency toward the maximization of the joint profits of the group.[8] In oligopoly situations there is 'implicit bargaining' among the firms involved, leading normally to implicit agreements. In terms of the analyses examined here, these implicit agreements are based on demand curves of the type *DD* in Figure 14.4. Differences between the positions and relative strengths of different firms must be somehow resolved to permit implicit bargaining to arrive at joint-profit maximization. These agreements, or quasi-agreements, cannot be reached for all relevant variables; e.g. advertising and product developments are areas where firms remain competitive. In the preface to the 1960 printing of his book, Fellner writes:

> I continue to believe that it is fruitful to regard oligopolistic relations as bargaining relations, in a somewhat extended sense of the term, and to suggest that the implicit bargaining of oligopolists tends to lead to implicit agreements. Furthermore I continue to believe that the 'content' of implicit agreements deviates from joint-profit maximization because of the existence of uncertainty which precludes dependable forecasts of the available joint profits and of the relative strength of the rival parties. . . . The uncertainty which I have in mind here is in part uncertainty about future developments in the joint markets in which the participants do business, and it is in part uncertainty about the relative skills of participants.[9]

He emphasizes that the implicit agreements and joint-profit maximization characterizing oligopolist behaviour in a stationary state do not normally hold in a dynamic context, where uncertainty and changing values for the fundamental conditions tend both to make new agreements more difficult to reach and to disrupt existing agreements.[10] Of course firms in actual economies do operate in such dynamic contexts.

14.7 The kinked-demand curve and rigid prices

An ingenious, if rather artificial, device to obtain a demand curve for the analysis of oligopoly pricing is to assume that the responses of rival firms to changes in the price set by the firm being studied are asymmetrical. When the firm raises its price, rival firms are assumed to maintain constant prices, thus increasing their market shares, and to follow any price decreases so as

---

[8] William Fellner, *Competition Among the Few*, originally published in 1949 and reprinted in 1960 with a New Preface.

[9] *Ibid.*, pp. v-vi. (Emphasis in the original.)

[10] George J. Stigler in 'A Theory of Oligopoly', *Journal of Political Economy*, Vol. 72 (February 1964), pp. 44-61, accepts the hypothesis that oligopolies wish to practise collusion to maximize joint profits. He argues that collusion is often ineffective because of the problem of policing these agreements. He views this as a problem in the theory of information.

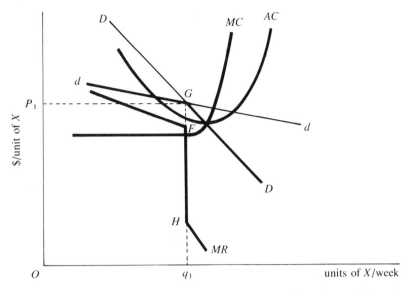

FIGURE 14.5 *A kinked-demand curve and short-period profit maximization*

to prevent erosions in their market shares.[11] Under this assumption, the oligopoly firm's demand curve would be composed of a portion from each of the two types of demand curves that were developed in Chamberlin's analysis. These are joined together at the point corresponding to the ruling price and rate of sales. For example, in Figure 14.5 the ruling price is OP_1, the weekly rate of sales is Oq_1, and the portions from the two demand curves are joined at point G. For prices greater than OP_1, the demand curve *dd* is the appropriate one for this firm, since other firms are assumed to maintain their prices unchanged; while for prices lower than OP_1, the demand curve *DD* provides the firm's sales rate, since rival firms are assumed to lower their prices to the same extent. Thus the firm's demand curve is represented in the diagram by the darkened (angled) curve, *dGD*. The reason for the name 'kinked-demand curve' is obvious. It must form an angle at the prevailing price (point G) because the assumed responses of rivals to price increases and decreases differ. (A 'reverse kink'—that is, a demand curve given by *DGd*—could also be obtained if the responses of rivals to price changes were assumed to be reversed.)

---

[11] R.L. Hall and C.J. Hitch, 'Price Theory and Business Behaviour', *Oxford Economic Papers*, Vol. 4 (May 1939), pp. 12-45; and Paul M. Sweezy, 'Demand Under Conditions of Oligopoly', *Journal of Political Economy*, Vol. 47 (August 1939), pp. 568-73. For a critical appraisal of this approach to oligopoly pricing, see George J. Stigler, 'The Kinky Oligopoly Demand Curve and Rigid Prices', *Journal of Political Economy*, Vol. 55 (October 1947), pp. 432-49.

The kink in the demand curve in Figure 14.5 is reflected in a discontinuity in the marginal revenue curve. For output rates less than Oq_1, the firm's marginal revenue curve is derived from the dd-demand curve, and for output rates greater than Oq_1 it is derived from the DD-demand curve. The difference in the slopes of these curves (and thus their elasticities at point G) accounts for the substantial difference (HF) in the values for their marginal revenues at this point. As a result of this discontinuous segment in the marginal revenue curve, it is possible for different marginal cost curves to intersect the marginal revenue curve at the output Oq_1. For a short-period profit-maximizing firm, quite substantial differences in the values for marginal costs at output Oq_1 may not result in any difference in price as long as the assumptions underlying the demand curve are unchanged. A kinked-demand curve can thus be used to explain the observed rigidity of the prices of oligopolists.

The ability to predict the relative stability of oligopoly prices with a kinked-demand curve is not a particularly strong argument in favour of this approach. The case it makes for rigid prices is too strong. If the increase in a firm's marginal costs is due to general changes in the industry, which also change the costs of other firms, then it would be surprising if these higher costs were not reflected in higher prices. A firm might reasonably expect that, contrary to the kinked-demand curve assumption, other firms would follow its price rise. The kink would then appear to have moved. Such a possibility indicates a major weakness of this approach: *it purports to show why an established price might be rigid but it does not provide an explanation for the factors determining this price, or the conditions under which it will change.*

14.8 The theory of games and oligopoly

The term 'uncertainty' has kept reappearing in our examination of attempts to provide a theoretical analysis of pricing policies under oligopolistic conditions. It has a role in analyses of all market structures because of the fundamental uncertainty concerning the precise state of the world in the future. In oligopoly there is also uncertainty over the present responses of rival firms to changes in a firm's policies. It has been suggested that the mathematical theory of games can provide some insight into the behaviour of oligopolists in situations where implicit agreements, or conventional rules and traditional modes of behaviour, do not substantially reduce uncertainty concerning the behaviour of rivals. This possible application was noted[12] in the title of the first book devoted to the development of the

---

[12] John von Neumann and Oskar Morgenstern, *Theory of Games and Economic Behavior* (Princeton, N.J.: Princeton University Press, 1944).

games theory. For certain types of games—two-person, zero-sum games—it can be shown that there exists a *minimax strategy* (or set of strategies) that promises each participant higher average payoffs than any alternative set of strategies, assuming that each rival intelligently tries to improve his position. A zero-sum game is one where the sum of the payoffs to both players is constant, so that what one gains the other loses. Therefore only the possible payoffs for one player need to be shown; the payoffs for the other must be the exact opposite (e.g. a payoff of three for one player is a payoff of minus three for the other). For example, consider the following zero-sum game:

B

	b_1	b_2	b_3	*Row min*
a_1	3	1	2	1*
a_2	-4	-1	3	-4
a_3	2	-2	-1	-2
Col-max	3	1*	3	

A

The payoff matrix shown is that for player A. Each player has three strategies. The row minimum shows that if A chooses strategy a_1 he will be at least assured of a payoff of 1, no matter what B does. The column maximum shows that player B, by choosing b_2, can ensure that he does no worse than pay 1 to player A. The best choice in these circumstances for A is a_1, and for B it is b_2. These choices are consistent; the maximum of the row minimas is equal to the minimum of the column maximas (or *minimax* equals *maximin* equals 1), and there is a minimax solution involving pure strategies for each player. If minimax does not equal maximin when pure strategies are employed, then the minimax solution will involve mixed strategies. At least one of the players may then choose more than one strategy. Each strategy in the solution will have some probability value attached to it that shows the likelihood of its being chosen in any play of the game.[13] Unfortunately, from the point of view of applying this theory to oligopolistic markets, economic situations do not lend themselves to presentation in forms suitable for two-person, zero-sum games. The kinds of rivalry encountered in oligopoly can seldom be put in this form because the payoffs to firms can be improved if they practise collusion. Consider the following game representation of a duopoly situation. Each firm must decide, in ignorance of the other's decision, the price to charge for its

---

[13] For a simple and amusing introduction to the theory of games, see J.D. Williams, *The Compleat Strategyst* (New York: McGraw-Hill, 1954).

product. Assume that they have a choice between two prices and that they will be committed to the price they choose for the specified short period. The possible weekly profits for both (the payoffs are in thousands of dollars) are as follows:

		B *price*		A *minimum*
		$10	$15	
A *price*	$10	20,20	28,8	20
	$15	8,28	24,24	8
B *minimum*		20	8	

The minimax strategy for both firms is a price of $10, but it is clear from the payoff values that if they could communicate and reach an effective agreement to charge $15, they would obtain higher profits. This type of situation is known as the *Prisoner's Dilemma*. If the events that give rise to a situation whose payoff matrix takes the above form are singular, and the participants have not experienced it together before, the minimax solution may result. However, if this situation keeps being repeated over time for the same firms in oligopolistic markets, they may learn how to communicate and to reach the collusive solution. (Prices would then be set at $15 in the above example.) Whether this will actually be the result depends on entry conditions, and the institutional and legal arrangements in the particular economy. This collusive solution with the maximization of joint profits is what Fellner predicted would occur under stationary conditions where situations were being continually repeated (see Section 14.6).

The theory of games has not provided solutions to many oligopoly problems, but it has given some useful insights into the strategic aspects of the behaviour of firms.[14]

14.9 Theory, history, and institutional factors in the analysis of oligopoly

The brief survey of oligopoly theories in the preceding sections has not turned up a model that can be used as a general method of analysis for this market structure. The search for a general theory may in fact turn out to be fruitless, given the nature of oligopoly markets and the many possible courses of action inherent in them. The role of economic analysis in this area may be the more modest if still important one of providing a theoretical framework within which specific arrangements can be analysed. The specific arrangements that would be likely to arise in any situation would depend on historical and institutional factors, and on the nature of technology in the industry and its potential for change. This means that a

[14] Martin Shubik, *Strategy and Market Structure* (New York: John Wiley & Sons, 1959).

purely theoretical analysis of oligopoly would be severely limited, and very likely misleading, since it would abstract from features that are important determinants of behaviour in any particular case.

Firms in oligopolistic situations have common as well as conflicting interests. They all have a common interest in the profitability of their industry since, with given market shares, their own profits depend on it. There is of course a natural basis for conflict in terms of the proper market shares for each, and this conflict is very difficult to suppress for long periods as conditions, opportunities, and even the participants change. Some agreement, explicit or implicit, on approved ways of trying to change market shares would help produce an environment in which firms could pursue their common interests in making their markets generally profitable. Price competition tends to be most disruptive to common interests. The consequences of a firm's decrease in price in an attempt to increase market share would be open to immediate retaliation in kind, with adverse effects on industry profits. This feature of price competition makes it unattractive to firms in most situations, and it is usual to find them competing in terms of product varieties, services, sales promotions, etc., but avoiding price competition. The way this would be done depends on the nature and history of the industry and its firms, the type of products produced, legal and institutional arrangements, and the general state of the economy.

In the following sections, some of the possible arrangements within which oligopolists operate will be examined, and references will be made to particular cases. These arrangements will be analysed within a framework provided by economic theory, and particular emphasis will be placed on barriers to entry, seller concentration, and the goals of firms. It should be remembered that particular arrangements may be operational only for a certain period of time and that they may be eventually superseded as a result of changes in the industry.

14.10 Cartels

If the existing firms have reached an agreement on their profit (or market) shares, then their common interest in profitable markets would dominate their pricing decisions. They may pursue this interest by forming a *cartel*—a central organization that tries to co-ordinate prices and determine quotas. Highly centralized cartels would also include a central sales bureau to receive orders from customers and distribute them to the various firms in line with the agreement on market shares. The cartel organization might also be empowered to undertake a rationalization of the industry that could lead to closing down the less efficient plants and to the distribution of orders between the remaining plants in a manner that minimizes the cost of production. With a highly centralized cartel, industry prices, costs, and profits more closely approximate monopoly profits; and profits are distributed among the member firms according to an agreed formula.

A Canadian example of a cartel involves firms in the Shipping Container Industry in the period 1931-7.[15] They belonged to Container Materials Ltd., a cartel through which prices were set and quotas for each firm were determined. Orders were received directly and filled by individual firms, but firms whose sales exceeded their quotas paid fines into a fund that was used to compensate those that did not fill their quotas. This cartel was apparently successful. The industry was profitable, even though some plants often operated substantially below normal capacity. The attraction of high profits led to entry in spite of this excess capacity in the industry and the strenuous efforts by cartel members to discourage it. These firms tried to make it difficult for new firms to obtain raw-material (containerboard) supplies, and they were active in bidding for plants that might provide productive capacity for new entrants. Once entry occurred, however, the new firms were brought into the cartel.

There are different degrees of cartel arrangements. The retention by individual firms of their identities and of control over orders is an important feature in some cartels but not in others. Firms may not agree to a cartel rationalization scheme if they believe that their plants might be shut down, since this would weaken their bargaining power if disagreements over shares arose. Cartel arrangements may break down over time, quite apart from governmental action, if the unsuppressed rivalry over shares becomes a serious issue. This could happen if there were differential changes in efficiency or market opportunities for firms or if the cartel's success in raising profits attracted new entrants. They would have to be brought into the agreement in order to avoid price competition, and the question of the appropriate shares would then have to be reviewed.

Product orders are sometimes obtained through the placing of bids. In this case some of the sharing effects of a central sales bureau can be obtained by prearranging the way in which firms will decide on their 'competitive' bids. For example, the Water-Tube Boilermaker's Association in the United Kingdom operated a bidding-cartel that kept price competition in check. When requests for tenders were made, member firms submitted quotations to the association director. The director then nominated one of the firms to undertake the job in order to maintain the agreed-upon shares

---

[15] Combines Investigation Commission, *Investigation into an Alleged Combine in the Manufacture and Sale of Paperboard Shipping Containers and Related Products* (Ottawa: Queen's Printer, 1939).

of the market and disclosed to it the lowest quotation. The nominated firm could then send a revised bid to the buyer that enabled it to obtain the order. Since there was no particular advantage in submitting the lowest bid initially, firms were not tempted to cut prices, which were determined by standard cost arrangements.[16]

Some of the problems facing cartels in deciding on prices, even when they have governmental sanctions, are illustrated by the continuing difficulties experienced by members of the International Air Transport Association (IATA) in reaching agreement on air fares on the North Atlantic routes. High prices set in earlier periods have provided firms outside the cartel—the non-scheduled airlines operating charter flights—with market opportunities that they have seized, and their share of total passenger-miles has grown over the years. There has been disagreement within IATA as to how best to meet this competition. Some of the larger airlines have argued in favour of fare structures that would include much lower fares to meet this competition, while others have preferred higher fares even at the cost of a declining market share. The resolution of these different approaches has been made more difficult by the uncertainty of the results if either policy is adopted, since they depend on future factors about which only rough estimates can be made.

Such differences in views of members of a cartel agreement are stressed by Bjarke Fog in his investigation of negotiations on cartel prices with regard to six (legal) cartels in Denmark. He found that unsuppressed rivalry frequently prevented these cartels from agreeing on policies that would maximize joint profits.[17]

14.11 Collusive agreements

The arrangements made by firms to suppress at least some aspects of competition between them may be less formal than those found in cartels, but such collusive agreements often produce similar results and face the same difficulties. When product lines are very complex, firms must practise collusion on specific product details and the handling of 'extras' if the price agreement is to be effective. For example, the cartel in the Shipping Container Industry in Canada was replaced in the post-war period by collusive arrangements that were made easier by an elaborate common price manual (originally developed in the pre-war cartel period and maintained during wartime by price-control authorities). Shipping containers are often

---

[16] See the discussion of these arrangements in F.M. Scherer, *Industrial Market Structure and Economic Performance* (Chicago: Rand McNally, 1970), p. 163.

[17] Bjarke Fog, 'How are Cartel Prices Determined', *Journal of Industrial Economics*, Vol. 5 (November 1966), pp. 16-23.

made up to meet the special requirements of particular customers, but the adherence to the price manual made possible identical quotations for any kind of container by all manufacturers. Monopoly-type prices appear to have been set at the highest import-excluding level: that is, the United States price for these containers plus the Canadian tariff plus differences in transportation costs.

This policy proved to be very profitable for the firms in this industry. Profits (before tax) in a sample of ten firms for the years 1948 to 1954 were estimated to vary from 34.4 to 55.4 per cent of capital. These rates of return were among the highest in Canadian manufacturing industries.[18]

Collusive behaviour has also been documented (and the firms were brought to trial and found guilty) in the Containerboard Industry in Canada.[19] Many of the firms in this industry also owned plants in the Shipping Container Industry, and their control over the supply of containerboard helped make collusion effective in that industry. Collusion in the Containerboard Industry was fostered by an active association of manufacturers. Agreements were reached on specifications for different types of containerboard, and there was an exchange of information on each producer's share of the market. Recognition of common interests appears to have been strong, and weaker firms were protected. Producers of the newer types of containerboard sold some of their output at cost to producers of obsolete types so as to enable the latter to maintain their share of the market. The effects of the collusion were not only limited to prices: the incentive to introduce new varieties was also affected, since the consequent disturbance of market shares was considered undesirable. There was a noticeable time-lag in the introduction of new qualities of containerboard in Canada as opposed to the United States. This kind of technical change was thus retarded by the collusive arrangements.

Even though Canada has a comparative advantage in international trade in the production of wood and paper products, Canadian prices, as a result of successful collusion, were set at the highest import-excluding level. In the post-war period the most-favoured-nation tariff rate on imports of containerboard products was twenty-two-and-a-half per cent. The Canadian price was generally the U.S. price plus freight plus duty, a pricing practice that allowed regional discrimination against buyers who were far from the low-cost sources of supply in the United States (e.g. buyers in the Prairie

---

[18] H.C. Eastman and S. Stykolt, *The Tariff and Competition in Canada* (Toronto: Macmillan Company of Canada Ltd., 1967), p. 203.
[19] Restrictive Trade Practices Commission, *Report Concerning the Manufacture, Distribution and Sale of Paperboard Shipping Containers and Related Products* (Ottawa: Queen's Printer, 1962).

Provinces). Collusion was not disturbed and prices were still set at import-excluding levels, even though in 1956 an important entry occurred: Canadian International Paper, a subsidiary of a large American company, which followed the prices of other firms. However, this entry substantially increased productive capacity in the industry and resulted in pressure on all firms to find new markets. In the 1960s Canadian exports to the United Kingdom and West Germany increased substantially as producers gained entry to these markets, in part by buying firms making shipping containers in those countries. As foreign markets were more competitive, the prices at which they sold their containerboard in these markets were lower than the prices they charged in Canada!

Another example of collusion, which combines many of the features of such arrangements, is to be found in the United States Electrical Equipment Industry in the 1950s. Excess productive capacity led to intermittent price warfare and there was a felt pressure to make arrangements that would restore profitability. Several collusive systems were created to handle the requirements of different product lines. Agreements were reached on prices for standardized products; but for products that were produced to meet the special requirements of individual buyers, a large pricing-formula book was devised. By using the listed prices for each component and feature, all firms could arrive at the same price for an individual order, though one firm was designated as low bidder. They would then co-ordinate their bidding, with the designated firm subtracting a small percentage from the formula price and the other firms adding random percentages to it. In the high-voltage switch-gear field the designation of low bidder was made by a 'phases of the moon' system: it changed every two weeks.

This collusive behaviour helped produce substantial profits, even though agreements were difficult to enforce. When entry occurred during the period of collusion, a recalculation of market shares was required, and in order to maintain the agreement the larger firms accepted lower shares. However, if an order were large enough a firm might submit an unauthorized bid to capture it, even though it endangered the collusive arrangements in doing so.[20] It was possible for a firm to 'cheat'—that is, put in a lower bid to capture an order that was not assigned to it—if the agreed procedures were followed, since the bids of others were known to all. This could be very profitable, at least temporarily, because of the high level of collusive prices.

---

[20] See Scherer, *Industrial Market Structure and Economic Performance*, pp. 159-60; and John Herling, *The Great Price Conspiracy* (Westport, Conn.: Greenwood Press, 1962), Chapter IX.

14.12 Price leadership

When legislation and government enforcement agencies make cartels and collusive agreements very difficult to operate, firms might resort to less formal ways of communicating and co-ordinating their actions. One common method is price leadership, in which changes in list price are announced by a specific firm accepted as a price leader by other firms that follow its initiatives. This method of making adjustments minimizes the risk that price changes will be interpreted as action designed to change market shares. For price leadership to be successful there must be at least implicit agreement among firms that price competition is not in their common interest and that no firm can expect to gain individually from such competition.

The price leaders are typically the largest firms in the industry but not necessarily the lowest-cost firms. Some firms have been price leaders in their industries for fairly long periods. In the United States this list would include U.S. Steel, General Motors (in automobiles), and Alcoa. A similar list for Canada would include Stelco for most steel products, Imperial Oil, and Imperial Tobacco. If a price leader is to succeed in its aim of setting a profitable price structure that other firms will accept, *it must set prices with a view to the position of others as well as to its own position*. It must be prepared to forego a price change that might be in its own interests if all other firms followed it but that could create serious difficulties for others. The compromises that are reached with great difficulty in cartels and collusive agreements, because of differences in the positions of firms and their profit horizons, must be arrived at here much more circumspectly. As a consequence the deviations of actual prices from monopoly-type prices may be greater.

Even in industries with rather well-developed forms of price leadership (e.g. gasoline in Canada, aluminum in the United States), price changes will occasionally be initiated by other firms. If the price leader agrees with these changes—its lack of initiative being due, perhaps, to slight differences in timing or hesitation caused by some uncertainty over the positions of the other firms—it would then validate the changes by moving its prices in line. If it disagrees, it would take counter action to try to restore the initial position. When prices have been increased, this might require that it do no more than maintain its initial prices. For price decreases, it might have to undertake some form of price warfare to reassert its price leadership.

The bases for the quotations of prices by price leaders are often the pricing formulas that were discussed in Section 13.5. They use standard costs when plant is operated at some standard rate of utilization and they provide for a target rate of return on investment. Special features of the markets for particular products, or at particular time periods, are recognized by adjustments in these formula prices. One example of this has been described as follows: 'United States Steel states that it employs a "stable margin" price policy, that is, in general it aims at maintaining margins despite variations in sales volume. In so doing it uses standard costs, computed on the basis of 80 per cent of capacity as normal, and including an assignment of overhead burden to every product.'[21] However, competitive factors do have a role in prices over and above their influence on the 'stable margin'. ' . . . the company has sought to apply a uniform, universally applicable pricing policy . . . Nonetheless even such a company has difficulty in following a formula in pricing steel products—partly because of the differences in costs among plants and the heavy overhead factor, and partly from the desire to hold customers.'[22]

Another example, that of General Motors, belongs in this category: 'The formula given by the company for arriving at unit cost requires the calculation of standard costs at "normal" sales volume (generally 80 per cent of capacity). Profit per car based on a target rate of return, is added to obtain the provisional manufacturer's price. . . . This formula for pricing is subject to modifications arising from the nature of the production process and from the peculiarities of the market for automobiles.'[23]

There is no scope for price followers to use target-rate-of-return pricing. They may have in mind what they consider would be an appropriate rate of return on their investment, which they use in deciding on new investment projects, but they cannot use this rate in setting prices. The mark-ups they obtain are derived mark-ups. They are given by the ratio of the price (basically set by the price leader) to the firm's marginal costs. The following exchange between United States Senator O'Mahoney and Mr Theodore Yntema, vice-president of the Ford Motor Company, illustrates the situation in which price followers can find themselves:

MR. YNTEMA: . . . in our own particular company, we do not have a simple cost-plus formula. We do not have any simple way in which you go just from cost to price.

We have to look at our competitive situation. Ordinarily, what we find is this: We have very little leeway.

SENATOR O'MAHONEY: Do you have a goal of a certain profit on invested capital or net worth?

MR. YNTEMA: We are not in the fortunate position—we would like to do better

---

[21] A.D.H. Kaplan, Joel B. Dirlam, and Robert F. Lanzillotti, *Pricing in Big Business* (Washington, D.C.: The Brookings Institution, 1958), pp. 14-15.

[22] *Ibid.*, pp. 23-4.

[23] *Ibid.*, pp. 50-1.

than we are doing . . . Sometimes we get more than 15 per cent. It just depends upon the competitive situation. I mean we do not just have costs and add a profit margin and arrive at a price. We are in this tough, rough business of trying to get business from General Motors and Chrysler and they are trying to get it from us.[24]

Chrysler's position was similar to Ford's. Senator Kefauver inquired whether Chrysler, like General Motors, had a 'definite profit figure' in mind in arriving at prices. Chrysler president, L.L. Golbert, replied: 'We do not have a definite profit figure. All we know is our profits in recent years have been far too low and we are trying to improve them.'[25]

It should be noted that co-ordination of price policies is made particularly difficult by product differentiation, which can be due to real differences— as between light and heavy fuel oil—or imagined differences—for example, branded and unbranded gasolines (with some accepted 'stable' price differences between varieties). Any change in price level requires attention to price differentials and to the possibility that low-priced brands might start price-wars. In cases where style and fashion are important, product qualities can change from year to year, possibly leading to substantial changes in market shares and to a revival of price competition.

Price leadership does not necessarily arise because of some form of collusion among firms. It might be an inevitable result of the industry structure, or it might be due to the continued astuteness of a particular firm in sensing changes in market conditions that call for price responses. If the industry is dominated by one large firm—e.g. one that produces at least half the total industry output, with the remainder being spread over several much smaller firms—then the large firm would automatically be the price leader. This has been called 'dominant firm' price leadership.[26]

The pricing policy of a dominant firm would be similar to that of the monopoly firm discussed in Chapter 13. However, it must allow for the effects of its pricing policies on the other firms in the industry, as well as on potential entrants. To a large extent these other firms would be in the position of competitive firms, and the indirect influences of changes in their actions would be negligible as long as they remained small. They would accept the price set by the dominant firm as the market price (plus or minus

---

[24] U.S. Senate Subcommittee on Antitrust and Monopoly, *Hearings on Administered Prices*, Pt. 6 (1958), p. 2683, as quoted in John M. Blair, *Economic Concentration, Structure, Behavior and Public Policy* (New York: Harcourt Brace Jovanovich, 1972), pp. 498-9.
[25] *Ibid.*, p. 499.
[26] See Stigler, 'The Kinky Oligopoly Demand Curve and Rigid Prices'; and Jesse W. Markham, 'The Nature and Significance of Price Leadership', *American Economic Review*, Vol. 41 (December 1951), pp. 891-905.

a recognized margin for effective product differentiation) and sell what they could at that price. Their response to substantial positive differences between normal productive capacity and sales would probably be to engage in some form of price discounting, among other things[27] (including close attention to costs as firms try to restore profitability).[28]

In industries without a dominant firm and in which price leadership does not act in lieu of a collusive agreement, *'barometric' price leadership* is said to occur.[29] The 'barometric' firm might, but need not, be the largest firm in the industry. Its success in initiating price changes that are followed is simply due to its proven ability to read changes in market conditions correctly. Stigler has argued that a barometric firm 'commands adherence of rivals to his price only because, and to the extent that, his price reflects market conditions with tolerable promptness.'[30] The barometric firm's task of judging when a price change that would be followed can be made is facilitated by the use of a mark-up formula when changes in costs are general throughout the industry and market shares are relatively stable.

14.13 Target and realized rates of return
Empirical studies[31] of the pricing behaviour of large firms show frequent use of target-rate-of-return price formulas by dominant firms. Of course the aim and the achievement of this target often differ even for large firms that can control prices, because the state of the economy is an important determinant of their profit possibilities. Table 14.2 gives a comparison of realized and target rates of return for two slightly overlapping periods: 1947-1955 and 1953-1968. The latter period was less profitable for all firms for which data are available, though it was one in which realized returns were close to the target rates.

The firms in Table 14.2 are all very large, but their profit opportunities

---

[27] An example is found in the response of two of the smallest firms in the United States Aluminum Industry during the recession of 1974-5. Capacity utilization for the aluminum industry in May 1975 was approximately 75 per cent, but two of the firms accounting for approximately 5 per cent of total industry capacity were operating at 100-per-cent utilization rates. The explanation given for this disparity was the use by these firms of small discounts, while the larger ('dominant') firms held to list prices. Council on Wage and Price Stability, *Aluminum Prices 1974-75*, pp. 121-3.

[28] R.B. Heflebower has noted that 'The present writer has frequently found the reponse to the question "What do you do when sales volume falls off?" to be "We get busy on our costs"'. National Bureau Committee for Economic Research, *Business Concentration and Price Policy*, A Conference of the Universities (Princeton, N.J.: Princeton University Press, 1955), p. 371.

[29] Markham, 'The Nature and Significance of Price Leadership', p. 892.

[30] Stigler, 'The Kinky Oligopoly Demand Curve and Rigid Prices', p. 446.

[31] For example, Kaplan, Dirlam, and Lanzillotti, *Pricing in Big Business*.

TABLE 14.2 *Comparison of target with actual rates of return: 1947-1955 and 1953-1968*

FIRM	TARGET RATE OF RETURN (AFTER TAXES) %	ACTUAL RATE OF RETURN AFTER TAXES (AVERAGE)	
		1947-1955 %	*1953-1968* %
Alcoa	10.0	13.8	9.5
du Pont	20.0	25.9	22.2
Esso (Standard Oil of N.J.)	12.0	16.0	12.6
General Electric	20.0	21.4	—
General Motors	20.0	26.0	20.2
International Harvester	10.0	8.9	—
Johns-Manville	15.0	14.9	—
U.S. Steel	8.0	10.3	8.4

SOURCE: R.F. Lanzillotti, 'Pricing Objectives in Large Companies', *American Economic Review*, Vol. 48 (December 1958), pp. 921-40; John M. Blair, *Economic Concentration, Structure, Behavior and Public Policy* (New York: Harcourt Brace Jovanovich, 1972), p. 483. Excerpts from *Economic Concentration: Structure, Behavior and Public Policy* by John M. Blair, copyright © 1972 by Harcourt Brace Jovanovich, Inc. and reprinted with their permission. The rates of return for 1947-55 are from Lanzillotti and those for 1953-68 from Blair. Both give the (same) target rates for Alcoa, General Motors, and U.S. Steel. In addition, Lanzillotti provides the target rates for General Electric, International Harvester, and Johns-Manville, while Blair provides them for du Pont and Esso (now Exxon). The actual rates of return are obtained when actual profits are divided by stockholders' equity plus long-term debt.

differ because their operations are concentrated in different areas. Their target rates of return reflect both their experiences over long periods and their expectations.

The relative consistency of average returns with target rates over long periods of time (in this case over twenty years) is in line with the predictions made by the cost-plus-formula approach to pricing favoured in this book. The formula provides a target rate of return on investment if plant is operated at standard rates; and the firm's investment activity tries to keep its productive capacity growing in such a way that on the average, over time, standard operating rates are experienced. In the face of short-term fluctuations in demand, the mark-ups would be relatively stable.

Although this cost-plus formula approach emphasizes the relative stability of mark-ups, it should never be forgotten that a stable mark-up is not an end in itself. For the analysis of the pricing behaviour of large firms this approach is put forth here as *a much better starting-point than the traditional marginal-revenue-equals-marginal cost approach.* However, *it is not a substitute for the detailed examination of the industry and its environment that is required if price changes are to be explained.* Mark-ups will be stable only if firms—which are constantly striving to survive, prosper, and grow—decide that it is in their best interests to keep them stable. However, changes in a stable mark-up policy can be brought about by special circumstances. In the severe recession of 1974-5 the behaviour of firms showed both the relative stability of many mark-ups in the face of sharp declines in rates of sales and the adjustments brought about by mistaken short-term expectations.[32]

Some econometric studies of price determination offer a tentative confirmation of mark-up pricing in oligopolistic industries. James Tobin, in commenting on a series of such studies, wrote:

> In noncompetitive industries prices appear to be a percentage mark-up over variable cost at normal operating rates. Indeed, prices are set primarily on this basis no matter how far or in which direction actual operating rates deviate from normal . . . . The behaviour evidently reflects monopolistic and oligopolistic calculations that long-run profits are not served by demand-related price adjustments . . . . The tacit collusion against price warfare on which oligopoly is based is a fragile structure. It can withstand price changes that are easily seen to be cost-related, but it may be destroyed by other price movements. Moreover, both monopoly and oligopoly covet long-term customer relationships that may be undermined by frequent demand-related price adjustments.[33]

Tobin also noted that the estimated equations do indicate that when demand and utilization are greater or smaller than 'normal', there are some price adjustments up or down.

14.14 Administered prices and price stability
Gardiner Means has distinguished between administered prices and 'market' prices.[34] It is not clear what he meant by the latter term. It seems to represent either pricing in competitive markets or prices that would be

---

[32] For example, firms in the aluminum and steel industries increased prices in 1975 because of cost increases even though demand was slack. The United States automobile industry provides an example of mistaken short-term expectations and temporary price cuts. The short-term expectations on which car manufacturers had based their production of 1975 model-year cars were too optimistic and they found themselves holding large inventories. Chrysler was the first company to announce a price-rebate program in early January 1975. By that time it had accumulated a huge inventory that was equivalent to sales for 120 days. Its rebates, which were subsequently introduced by other firms, were aimed at reducing inventories and were offered initially for periods of about six weeks. The auto manufacturers did not adjust basic prices; they apparently hoped to be able to return to them after the reduction in inventories.

[33] James Tobin, 'The Wage-Price Mechanism: Overview of the Conference', *The Econometrics of Price Determination Conference* (Washington, D.C.: Board of Governors of the Federal Reserve System and Social Science Research Council, June 1972), p. 9.

[34] Gardiner C. Means, *Industrial Prices and their Relative Inflexibility*, U.S. Senate Document 13, 74th Congress, 1st session, Washington, 1935.

observed in all markets if they were arrived at by equating marginal revenues and marginal costs. However, he defined an administered price as 'a price set for a period of time and a series of transactions'. His thesis holds that 'in business recessions administered prices showed a tendency not to fall as much as market prices while the recession fall in demand worked itself out primarily through a fall in sales, production, and employment. Similarly, since administered prices tended not to fall as much in a recession, they tended not to rise as much in recovery while rising demand worked itself out primarily in a rising volume of sales, production, and employment.'[35] To support his thesis Means made use of the Bureau of Labour Statistics wholesale prices of a few well-defined products collected from a few sellers of each representative commodity. Critics of his approach have claimed that his data, based on *quoted* prices, overstate the degree of rigidity in actual *transactions* prices. Data obtained from buyers of industrial commodities[36] made possible a recent test of these claims that tended to confirm Means' thesis. It showed that the prices of products of concentrated industries are relatively more inflexible than prices in competitive industries and even move contra-cyclically in response to cost changes.[37]

14.15 Basing-point pricing

Spatial differentiation of products is important when their costs of transportation are high relative to their values. If price agreements for such products are to be effective they must specify how transportation costs are to be handled. To illustrate, assume that only two firms produce a standardized product with this characteristic in Eastern Canada. One of them has a plant in Montreal and the other in Toronto. When both firms quote identical F.O.B. plant or mill prices, the Toronto firm sells to all points west of Toronto and east up to, say, Kingston, while the Montreal firm makes all the sales from that point east. However, if a large order became available in Ottawa, the Toronto firm might be tempted to absorb some of the freight charges. (Its mill net price on this transaction would be less than its F.O.B. price and this would be an example of price discrimination.) In this way it would meet (or even shade) the price of the Montreal firm and obtain the

---

[35] Gardiner C. Means, 'The Administered-Price Thesis Reconfirmed', *American Economic Review*, Vol. 62 (June 1972), pp. 292-3.

[36] These prices are in G.J. Stigler and J.K. Kindahl, *The Behavior of Industrial Prices* (New York: National Bureau of Economic Research, 1970).

[37] See Means, 'The Administered-Price Thesis Reconfirmed'; Milton Moore, 'Stigler on Inflexible Prices', *Canadian Journal of Economics*, Vol. 5 (November 1972), pp. 486-93; and Blair, *Economic Concentration, Structure, Behavior and Public Policy*, pp. 461-6.

order. If the sales involved were substantial, such an action would be unlikely to go without retaliation from the Montreal firm. The effect of its response, if it took the form of freight absorption, would be a general erosion of the price structure, *even though F.O.B. mill prices were unchanged.*

In such a case as this, agreement on F.O.B. prices is obviously not enough to make collusion effective. One way in which a collusive agreement can be buttressed is through the adoption of *basing-point pricing*, a system that offers identical delivered prices to customers in a specific place, even though the supplying plants might be located in different areas, and results in a well-defined price structure. A delivered price would be calculated by adding to the base price the cost of shipping the good to the customer from a 'basing point'. A famous example of the basing-point system was that of the United States Steel Industry's use of Pittsburgh as the base for calculating delivered prices (abandoned in 1924). The price of steel in Chicago included the freight charge from Pittsburgh even though it might have been produced and shipped from Gary, Indiana.

There can be more than one basing point, and in the limit each plant could be a basing point. For example, in the illustration given above, Montreal and Toronto might both be basing points. The delivered price of the product at some other location would then equal the F.O.B. price plus the cost of transportation from the closest mill, irrespective of which firm made the sale. To arrive at identical prices, transportation costs would be estimated by both firms using a common freight book—for example, a rail freight book—and to make these delivered prices effective, customers would not be allowed to pick up the goods at the plants and use their own (possibly cheaper) means of transportation. In such a situation there is always a significant amount of market interpenetration, when a mill absorbs some freight costs because it sells to a customer that is closer to another mill that also serves as a basing point. (The difference in mill net prices for customers in different locations is a form of price discrimination, as noted above. In this case changes in the degree of price discrimination would be evidence of price competition.)[38]

There is a two-way relationship between basing-point systems and collusive agreements.[39] Not only is some basing-point arrangement

[38] Carl Kaysen, 'Basing Point Pricing and Public Policy', *Quarterly Journal of Economics*, Vol. 63 (August 1949), pp. 289-314, reprinted in American Economic Association, *Readings in Industrial Organization and Public Policy*, ed. by Richard B. Heflebower and George W. Stocking (Homewood, Ill.; Richard D. Irwin, 1958), pp. 153-75.
[39] Samuel M. Loescher, *Imperfect Collusion in the Cement Industry* (Cambridge, Mass.: Harvard University Press, 1959), Chapter 1.

necessary to supplement price agreements when plants are dispersed and costs of transporting the product are high, but the existence of a basing-point system facilitates collusive-type pricing policies. If it is effective, it removes an element of potential competition among firms that might extend to prices. Markham has argued that 'a sufficient explanation for similar price movements among producers abiding by a basing point system is the presence of the basing point system itself. The best evidence that this is so is the undisciplined pricing which occurs when the basing point system temporarily breaks down.'[40]

14.16 Barriers to entry, and profitability

The discussion of pricing policies of oligopolies in the preceding sections implies that where common interests are recognized and firms can communicate, profits will be higher. Communication, and agreement on common interests, might be easier the greater the degree of concentration. Some confirmation that this is so was found by Bain in his study of twenty United States industries.[41] In the two periods examined, 1936-40 and 1947-51, very high barriers to entry appear to result in higher profits. However, there did not seem to be any difference in average profit rates in industries with 'substantial' entry barriers as opposed to those with 'moderate to low' ones. The latter result might be explained by the fact that in the United States there are many potential entrants with the financial resources and technical and managerial expertise required to overcome even substantial barriers to entry. Thus firms in industries with these barriers are not left alone to exploit fully the profit opportunities they might otherwise have without the pressure of entrants. These industries seem to be competitive in the long-period sense.

A study by H.M. Mann for a later period generally confirms Bain's tentative conclusions.[42] Both barriers to entry and seller concentration were found to have some positive influence on rates of return on investment. Thus there seems to be some statistical support for the hypothesis that concentration and barriers to entry lead to higher profit rates.[43]

---

[40] Markham, 'The Nature and Significance of Price Leadership', p. 899.

[41] Bain, *Barriers to New Competition*, pp. 190-201.

[42] H.M. Mann, 'Seller Concentration, Barriers to Entry and Rates of Return in Thirty Industries, 1950-60', *Review of Economics and Statistics*, Vol. 48 (August 1966), pp. 296-307.

[43] For a review of studies on the effects of concentration and barriers to entry on profit rates, see John M. Vernon, *Market Structure and Industrial Performance, a Review of Statistical Findings* (Boston: Allyn & Bacon Inc., 1972), Chapters 3 and 4; and Leonard Weiss, 'Quantitative Studies of Industrial Organization', in *Frontiers of Quantitative Economics*, ed. by Michael D. Intriligator (Amsterdam: North-Holland Publishing, 1971), pp. 362-403.

14.17 Investment decisions of firms

Firms *in all market structures* are subject to uncertainty about conditions in future time periods, and their investment decisions are sometimes based on optimistic forecasts that turn out to be mistaken. This inability to know how fundamental conditions affecting their markets are going to change, and the actions of other firms that affect their prospects, has been reflected in our criticisms of analyses that place great emphasis on 'movements to long-run equilibrium'. A firm's investment decisions are made in the light of its commercial connections, the technical knowledge and experience of its staff, and the product and market opportunities they make possible. A firm might see market opportunities in products whose markets are competitive if existing plants are operating at capacity and prices are high relative to costs, or if it believes that demand will increase substantially in the not-too-distant future. Its decision to invest would depend on estimates of the likelihood of its being able to recover its capital costs over the expected life of the plant and of obtaining a risk-compensating return. For an affirmative decision, this expected return should be at least as large as the return that would be expected from other alternatives open to it, with similar risks. A firm does not have much pricing discretion in a competitive market, and the prices that enter its investment calculations are expected market prices. It will enter only if it believes that it can produce at costs that make these prices profitable.

Market opportunities can arise if a firm has developed some special features that effectively differentiate its product from that of its competitors. It would then be in a position to decide on the margins between its price and the prices other firms charge: ' . . . a price must look reasonable in relation to other commodities in the same field—not so high as to put it at a competitive disadvantage and not so low as to waste potential revenue. No doubt "business instinct" has more to do with the matter than nice calculations, though in some cases market research is brought into play to help provide data for the decision.'[44] On the basis of this best price and expected sales, the firm desiring to enter a market would make estimates on the feasibility of embarking on a new line of production.

The size of plant chosen, if entry takes place, would depend on the technical conditions of production, the possible economies of scale, the financing available to the firm, and the expected levels of sales at prevailing prices. A firm might first enter a particular line of activity with a sub-optimal size of plant (one for which minimum average costs are higher than

---

[44] Joan Robinson, *Exercises in Economic Analysis* (London: Macmillan & Co., 1960), pp. 176-7.

the minimum envelope average cost), and increase it to optimal size later as its finances and demand conditions permit.

When a firm has the possibility of producing a new product—say a substitute for an established commodity, but one that is superior in many respects or cheaper to produce—it has more scope for pricing discretion. The price chosen for marketing the product depends on the firm's estimate of the potential demand for it, the costs at different rates of production, and the expected costs over time as its experience with the production of this product increases. In making this choice the firm should be concerned about possible entry. High prices and profits serve as an irresistible lure for competitors. An example of an initial price that was too high and invited entry was the policy of Goodrich with respect to polyvinyl chloride (PVC), a basic building block in plastics.

> One of the first companies to market this material, Goodrich priced PVC so that profit margins were extremely high . . . . As new applications were found for the plastic, the market grew rapidly and Goodrich spent heavily to expand production. But more chemical companies, attracted by the high profits and strong growth, began making PVC and prices tumbled sharply. In 1954 general-purpose PVC sold for 38 cents a pound; last year the average price was 10 cents. Goodrich is still the world's largest producer of PVC and has the lowest-cost manufacturing process, but there is a widespread belief that its pricing policies of the fifties . . . may have invited competitors into the field too soon.[45]

In making its investment decision a firm can have no more than a general impression of future possibilities no matter how detailed the forecasts made by its experts. It would know that prices over time are much affected by product developments, technological changes, and factor price changes. To protect and possibly increase its market share a firm must, as part of a long-term policy, invest in product improvements, engage in a search for new uses for its product, and develop new techniques of production. It must be prepared to expand its plant facilities to avoid intensive and high-cost utilization of capacity in periods of buoyant demand, which also serve to attract entry, and to introduce new equipment as it becomes available. Expenditures on product developments and the introduction of product improvements increase the cost at any given rate of utilization of plant, but they can also add to a firm's profit if they lead to increased sales and output. And these expenditures could be more than offset by the lower average cost of production due to a larger rate of output if the firm was initially producing substantially below capacity output. The expansion of capacity would also lower costs if there were unexploited economies of scale

---

[45] Editors of Fortune, *The Conglomerate Commotion* (New York: Viking Press, 1970), p. 161.

that were due either to the development of new techniques of production or to the initial installation of a sub-optimal plant because of the limited size of the market.

The net effects of these changes on 'normal' prices (prices that bring the firm a 'normal' rate of return on investment when plant is utilized at standard rates) cannot be determined on an *a priori* basis. Increases in money-wage rates over time will act to offset the pressures to lower prices that result from increases in productivity, which tend to lower costs by more than product improvements tend to raise them. A firm's ability to survive and grow in a particular market depends on the extent to which it is making adequate technological and product responses to its changing environment.

These general observations about investment decisions and the use of pricing discretion with new products can be illustrated by a brief examination of the three new products introduced by du Pont: cellophane, nylon, and corfam.

Du Pont began the production of cellophane after receiving a licence in 1923 from a French company that had exclusive rights to the secret process for its manufacture. Du Pont also made many technical improvements in the product and in operating procedures over the years; its patented process for moisture-proofing cellophane was particularly important. Its pricing policy seemed to reflect the view that price reductions would substantially expand the uses of cellophane and that increasing production would lower costs. 'Volume increased rapidly and the profit rate was unchanged while prices were continuously reduced from $2.508 [per pound] in 1924 to $0.38 in 1940.'[46]

Du Pont research developed nylon and commercial production began in 1939. It could compete with other fibres, even though their prices were considerably lower, because of its desirable qualities, and this factor was reflected in the increasing volume of sales over time as new uses were developed. A direct comparison with the price history of cellophane is not meaningful because of differences in general economic conditions during the early years for each of these products. But ' . . . in the view of the company . . . the price history of nylon has been one of continuous decline in *real price*. Presumably, if the first ten years of nylon production had occurred in the 1920's and 1930's, as was the case with cellophane, similar price declines would have been shown for nylon; whereas a steady price with improvement in quality during a period of rising costs of equipment, materials, and wages, was the way in which the real price reductions in nylon were expressed.'[47]

---

[46] Kaplan, Dirlam, and Lanzillotti, *Pricing in Big Business*, p. 97.
[47] *Ibid.*, p. 107.

Both cellophane and nylon are examples of very successful investment decisions, but the risks inherent in this type of undertaking should not be ignored. Du Pont's experience with corfam can serve as an illustration of an unsuccessful investment decision. A poromeric material, corfam was developed by du Pont, which produced it commercially in the 1960s. It had many of the characteristics of leather and the expectation was that it could repeat the success achieved by the synthetic fibres in competition with natural fibres. However, it failed to do so and du Pont decided in 1971 to cease production after incurring substantial losses. Corfam's problems were two-fold: it was not a suitable substitute for leather in some uses (even though it was superior in others, e.g. golf shoes), and it was priced out of other markets by lower-cost man-made products that were similar to it. The company clearly erred in its estimates of market opportunities for this product.

The expansion of capacity for products produced by a firm are affected by the rates of plant utilization it has experienced. A firm is likely to invest in new capacity when sales are restricted by physical capacity or are expected to be thus affected in the near future. Failure to do so would mean that other firms that have increased capacity could expand *their* market shares. Unsatisfied demand also provides an opportunity for other firms to enter the market. (Price increases by established firms to restrain demand to capacity limits will also attract entry.) The behaviour of the Canada Cement Company provides an example where a low-price policy did not deter entry because it was not combined with sufficient investment to increase capacity. This firm's experience of excess capacity prior to the Second World War led to an extremely cautious policy of plant expansion. It seriously underestimated the growth of demand for cement in the post-war period and this provided market opportunities for new firms (mainly foreign-owned). In 1946 Canada Cement owned more than four-fifths of the cement-producing capacity of Canada, but by 1957 its share had dropped to slightly more than one-half.[48]

Investment plans are based on calculations, but in the nature of things, the future is uncertain and final decisions also include other elements. Joan Robinson has written: 'Tension between fear of excess capacity and fear of losing markets is what governs investment plans, rather than any exact calculation of costs, prices and prospective profits.'[49] It is also well to remember the role played by Keynes's 'animal spirits':

Most, probably, of our decisions to do something positive, the full con-

---

[48] Eastman and Stykolt, *The Tariff and Competition in Canada*, p. 158.
[49] Robinson, *Exercises in Economic Analysis*, p. 199.

sequence of which will be drawn out over many days to come, can only be taken as a result of animal spirits—of a spontaneous urge to action rather than inaction, and not as the outcome of a weighted average of quantitative benefits multiplied by quantitative probabilities. Enterprise only pretends to itself to be mainly actuated by the statements in its own prospectus, however candid and sincere. Only a little more than an expedition to the South Pole, is it based on an exact calculation of benefits to come. Thus if the animal spirits are dimmed and the spontaneous optimism falters, leaving us to depend on nothing but a mathematical expectation, enterprise will fade and die;— though fears of loss may have a basis no more reasonable than hopes of profit had before.[50]

14.18 Summary

The discussion in the last three chapters of the behaviour of firms in competitive, monopolistic, and oligopolistic markets has revealed some of the factors influencing prices in these markets. This type of market classification can be useful in indicating that different factors are important influences on pricing in different circumstances, but the dividing line between these categories might not be very clear in reality. Whether a particular firm is taken to be a monopolist or an oligopolist is often a question of who is making the judgement. The distinction between oligopolistic and competitive markets also involves problems of interpretation because of the role of competing products in limiting the scope for independent pricing policies even though the firms comprise a small group. For example, the existence of close substitutes for rayon (such as silk, cotton, wool, nylon, and terylene) means that the oligopolists producing rayon might have very little control over their prices. Another industry that might be in a similar position is the copper industry, where prices are very dependent on the prices of competing metals, such as tin and aluminum. Jesse Markham, in his discussion of price leadership, has characterized the copper and rayon industries as 'oligopolies within monopolistically competitive markets'.[51]

The leading oligopoly firms are typically very large. Problems of managerial-shareholder relations and questions about goals are as relevant for them as for monopolists. Short-period profit maximization is not a good indicator of their behaviour in specific circumstances, and the possible effects of present actions on entry into the group can influence oligopolists' behaviour as well as that of monopolists. In oligopolies there are additional problems arising from the existence of rival firms. The ways in which

---

[50] J.M. Keynes, *The General Theory of Employment, Interest and Money* (London: Macmillan & Co., 1936), pp. 161-2.

[51] Markham, 'The Nature and Significance of Price Leadership', p. 899.

oligopolies compete among themselves, and the devices they use to allow for their mutual dependence, are affected by the nature of their technology and markets and by their particular histories. These arrangements may, and do, change over time in the dynamic worlds characteristic of capitalism. There is some evidence that leading firms in oligopolies practise the same type of pricing policies we attributed to monopolies.[52] Prices that are relatively stable in relation to costs, in the face of short-term fluctuations in demand, are found in oligopolistic as well as monopolistic markets.

There is no general theoretical model that can be applied to the analysis of oligopolistic markets. Economists have provided models for special cases, and some of them have been described in this chapter, but the useful application of these models requires a fairly detailed knowledge of the industry being studied. What economic theory can provide in this area is a theoretical framework within which to examine actual situations. This framework—whose usefulness should not be underestimated—provides a set of questions to serve as a guide in studying events in these markets as well as the basis for making predictions about the effects of policy changes.

SUGGESTED READINGS

Bain, Joe S. *Barriers to New Competition*. Cambridge, Mass.: Harvard University Press, 1956.

Blair, John M. *Economic Concentration, Structure, Behavior and Public Policy*. New York: Harcourt Brace Jovanovich, 1972.

Fellner, William. *Competition Among the Few*. New York: Reprints of Economic Classics, Augustus M. Kelley, 1960.

Kaplan, A.D.H., Joel B. Dirlam, and Robert F. Lanzillotti, *Pricing in Big Business*. Washington, D.C.: The Brookings Institution, 1958.

Lanzillotti, Robert F. 'Pricing Objectives in Large Companies', *American Economic Review*, Vol. 48 (December 1958), pp. 921-40.

Scherer, F.M. *Industrial Market Structure and Economic Performance*. Chicago: Rand McNally, 1970.

Shubik, Martin. *Strategy and Market Structure*. New York: John Wiley & Sons, 1959.

Stigler, George J. 'A Theory of Oligopoly', *Journal of Political Economy*, Vol. 72 (February 1964), pp. 44-61.

---

[52] See Robert F. Lanzillotti, 'Pricing Objectives in Large Companies', *American Economic Review*, Vol. 48 (December 1958), pp. 921-40.

EXERCISES

1. (a) Why does Chamberlin expect that firms in a small group would price on the basis of the demand curve labelled *DD* in Figure 12.2, while firms in a large group would price on the basis of the demand curve labelled *dd*?

(b) What obstacles might prevent firms in an oligopoly from maximizing joint profits?

2. It has been argued that the relative stability of prices in oligopolistic markets can be explained by 'kinked-demand' curves.

(a) What do you understand by the term 'kinked-demand curve'? Is the 'kink' a reflection of consumers' tastes?

(b) In what way does a kinked-demand curve support the view that prices in oligopolistic markets would be relatively stable?

(c) Would you expect prices to be stable in such markets in the face of rising money-wage rates?

3. What explanation (or explanations) do you prefer for pricing in oligopolistic markets? What are the factors that this approach (or these approaches) point to as being important in determining the movement of prices in oligopolistic markets over time?

4. (a) What do you understand by the terms 'competitive in the short-period sense' and 'competitive in the long-period sense'?

(b) What do Bain's findings on average rates of return in his sample of twenty industries indicate about the nature of competition in these industries?

15

THEORIES OF THE DISTRIBUTION OF INCOME

15.1 Introduction

The preceding chapters have been concerned with the determination of prices and the rates of output of goods in different types of markets. The prices of the inputs (elements of production), or at least their conditions of supply, were taken as given. To complete this analysis, it is necessary to consider the determination of input prices, which are affected by many factors including the demand for goods, technical conditions of production, market structures, and the overall level of output and employment. An adequate treatment of this very large subject is beyond the scope of this book, but in the next two chapters we will present some important features of it, along with the ways in which it has been approached in the development of economic theory.

In examining the theory of distribution, attention can be focused on the determination of the prices of the specific elements of production that appear in the production functions examined in Chapter 7. (An approach along these lines will be sketched in the next chapter.) Alternatively one can focus on the determination of the returns to the three factors of production (land, labour, and capital) of the classical economists.[1] They identify a social class with each of these factors: landowners, who own land; the working class, who sell their labour power; and capitalists, who own the non-human means of production and organize and control production. In

---

[1] This classification was made by Adam Smith in *The Wealth of Nations*, first published in 1776.

the Preface to his famous work, *The Principles of Political Economy and Taxation* (first published in 1817), David Ricardo wrote:

> The produce of the earth—all that is derived from its surface by the united application of labour, machinery, and capital, is divided among three classes of the community; namely, the proprietor of the land, the owner of the stock or capital necessary for its cultivation, and the labourers by whose industry it is cultivated.
>
> But in different stages of society, the proportions of the whole produce of the earth which will be allotted to each of these classes, under the names of rent, profit and wages, will be essentially different; depending mainly on the actual fertility of the soil, on the accumulation of capital and population, and on the skill, ingenuity, and instruments employed in agriculture.[2]

The well-defined social classes that appear in the writings of the classical economists have become somewhat blurred in modern capitalist economies, even though a very small proportion of the population owns a relatively large proportion of the total property in such an economy. For example, it was estimated that in Great Britain in 1968, 31 per cent of total personal wealth was owned by the top 1 per cent of the population, and 56 per cent was owned by the top 5 per cent.[3] Similarly in the United States it was estimated that in 1969, the richest 1 per cent of persons held approximately 25 per cent of national wealth.[4] In so far as people derive income from more than one source (for example, they can obtain income from interest on their ownership of bonds issued by firms as well as from their labour), none of the three factor payments—rent, profit, and wages—can be identified with the income of a single social class.

This chapter examines theories of the determination of these factor payments. It will not be concerned with the distribution of incomes by persons, an analysis of which would require an investigation of government redistribution measures, such as taxes and transfers of all kinds, that is beyond the scope of this book.

It should be noted that the theories to be examined are concerned with the distribution of income rather than wealth. As stated in Section 2.8, income is a *flow* concept, while wealth is a *stock* concept. The total wealth in a particular country in a particular year is the value of the assets *minus* the value of liabilities of all individuals in that country in that period. The corresponding income is the total of wages, salaries, profits, rents, and

---

[2] Piero Sraffa, ed., *The Works and Correspondence of David Ricardo* (Cambridge, Eng.: Cambridge University Press, 1951), Vol. I. p. 5.

[3] A.B. Atkinson, *The Economics of Inequality* (Oxford: Clarendon Press, 1975), p. 134.

[4] James D. Smith and Stephen D. Franklin, 'The Concentration of Personal Wealth, 1922-1969', *American Economic Review*, Vol. 64 (May 1974), pp. 162-7.

interest in the period. Because of the incomes accruing to those owning assets, the personal distribution of income is affected by the distribution of wealth—which in turn could be affected by the distribution of income, over a series of time periods, as a result of personal saving and dissaving.

15.2 Social and technical arrangements in the economy and the categories of income

The categories of income recognized in any analysis depend on the social arrangements in the economy being examined and the way in which they are reflected in the organization of production. Each category reflects a particular type of activity or attribute. For example, there would be three categories of income in an agricultural economy where land is owned by individuals who lease it to others ('farmers'), who then hire labourers, supervise their activities, and provide equipment and working capital (for seed and payments to labourers in advance of the harvest). These categories are the incomes of landowners ('rent'), the incomes of labourers ('wages'), and the incomes of farmers ('profits'). If we introduce another activity, the lending of funds to farmers to make up deficiencies in their working capital, there is a sub-category of profits: 'interest' (the payment for the loan of funds). In an artisan economy, on the other hand, where each artisan owns his place of work, equipment, and working capital, there would be only one category of income: the income of artisans. 'Wages', 'profits', and 'rent' have no meaning in this economy, since there are no hired labourers or rented premises.

The distribution of income is an area in which rival theories jostle for pride of place. Various models will be examined to illustrate some of the approaches taken by economists and to emphasize the importance of social arrangements as well as technical relations in determining the distribution of income.

15.3 Distribution in models of an agricultural economy

The following models, derived from Joan Robinson's writings,[5] are intended to show how *in principle* the theory of distribution could be influenced by social and technical relations. The technical relationship between inputs and output is the same in all cases, and so are the resource endowments and the quantities and varieties of land, labour, and agricultural implements. While the distribution of income is affected by

---

[5] Joan Robinson, *Exercises in Economic Analysis* (London: Macmillan & Co., 1960), pp. 57-69. A similar treatment is to be found in Joan Robinson and John Eatwell, *An Introduction to Modern Economics* (London: McGraw-Hill, 1973), pp. 61-87.

these technical relations, the categories of income and the share of each in total income are also affected by the social arrangements in the economy.

There is only one product, corn, which is produced by someone organizing production and combining land, seed, and labour. Production takes time, in this case a year. Labour and land are required throughout this period and the product is available only at the end of it. Each worker provides the agricultural implements he needs to work the land effectively. In these models it is assumed that the amount of seed required per unit of land is technically determined. Thus there are two joint inputs—land *plus* seed; and labour *plus* agricultural implements—and the technical relations of production allow for substitution between them. The employment of these inputs is under the control and supervision of the organizers of production. Though organization is the result of the physical and mental activities of individuals, in these models such activities differ from labour in that they are inextricably tied up with control of the enterprise. Unlike land and labour, there are no units with which to measure the organizational input, but its importance in the production process should not be ignored. The length of the working periods of labour, and the intensity of work, are assumed to be the same in all the exercises. One of the tasks of the organizers is to ensure that labour is employed effectively.

15.4 Model in which only labour may be hired
In this model, land is privately owned and a large number of individuals (or families) own land. Some own a lot relative to the amount of labour they are able to provide, while others own little or none. Assume that social conventions permit labour to be hired, but that *land cannot be rented or sold*. If the land is to be farmed, production must be organized by the landowner, who may hire labour for this purpose in addition to the labour that he and members of his family can provide. All workers are assumed to be equally efficient, they own the necessary agricultural implements, and they receive the same wage rate. They have the means to support themselves while the final output is being produced and they are paid at the end of the production period. The problem of distribution in this simple model can be reduced to the question: how is the payment to labour determined?[6] After labour is paid, the part of total output remaining—that is, the residual—is the income of the landowner-organizers of production.

---

[6] The wage is paid in corn and not, as in the industrial model examined in a later section, in terms of money. If the wage bargain is made in terms of money, the real-wage rate also depends on the price of the wage-goods and is not determined in the labour market. Cf. J.M. Keynes, *The General Theory of Employment, Interest and Money* (London: Macmillan & Co., 1936), Chapter 2.

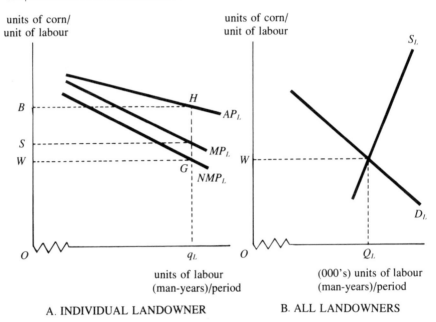

units of corn/
unit of labour

units of corn/
unit of labour

S_L

B

H

AP_L

S

W

MP_L

W

G

NMP_L

D_L

O

q_L

O

Q_L

units of labour
(man-years)/period

(000's) units of labour
(man-years)/period

A. INDIVIDUAL LANDOWNER

B. ALL LANDOWNERS

FIGURE 15.1 *Equilibrium position when landowners hire equipped labour*

It can easily be shown that in this case the equilibrium payment to labour is determined by the marginal productivity of labour and the cost of supervising it. An equilibrium position in this economy is defined as one where both landowners and workers are satisfied that, given the parameters of the situation, they cannot improve their positions (see Section 2.23).

The marginal product of labour (supervised labour, properly equipped) is determined by the technical conditions of production and is subject to the law of diminishing returns (see Section 7.11). The marginal product of labour curve (MP_L) facing an individual landowner is drawn in panel A of Figure 15.1. If there is a cost to the organizer of production for the supervision of an additional worker, the payment to labour must be less than this marginal product, since he must retain from the product of this worker an amount sufficient to compensate him for the cost of supervision. This cost is assumed to be WS units of corn per worker in the model depicted in Figure 15.1.[7]

It would be in the individual landowner's economic interest to employ

---

[7] This amount of corn may vary with the size of the work force he is supervising. For example, the amount required to compensate for supervising an additional labourer when he is already supervising five workers may differ from the amount required when he is supervising ten. Any such difference would be reflected in Figure 15.1 in the vertical distance between the MP_L and NMP_L curves at different values for the input of labour.

labour on his land up to the point where the marginal product of labour was equal to the wage rate plus his cost of supervising the additional labour. If this marginal product were greater than the sum of these two costs, he could clearly increase the return he obtained from his land and his efforts in organizing cultivation by hiring additional units of labour: these additional workers would add more to the landowner's total product than they would to his total costs. Conversely, if the marginal product of labour were smaller than the cost of hiring and supervising the last unit of labour employed, the landowner's return could be increased by hiring fewer workers: his total costs would be lower by an amount greater than the decrease in the total product.

In Figure 15.1 the individual landowner's demand curve for labour, which shows the amount of labour he is prepared to hire at alternative wage rates, is labelled NMP_L (for net marginal product of labour). It is obtained by subtracting the cost of supervising additional units of labour from the marginal product of labour curve (MP_L). The total demand curve for labour in the community is obtained by horizontal summation over all landowners of these individual demand curves. This aggregate demand curve is represented by D_L in panel B of Figure 15.1. The total supply curve of labour, showing the units of labour supplied at different wage rates, is indicated by the curve labelled S_L. The equilibrium wage rate and quantity of labour employed in the specified period is then determined by the intersection of these total demand and supply curves. The equilibrium wage rate in Figure 15.1, OW, is equal to the net marginal product of labour.

Figure 15.1 can also be used to illustrate other possible equilibrium positions. For example, given technology, the quantity of land, and the physical characteristics of land and labour, a supply curve of labour to the left of that shown in panel B (that is, one where there are fewer labourers, or where labourers are more reluctant to work) would result in a higher equilibrium wage rate. Under the same conditions a supply curve of labour to the right of S_L would result in a lower equilibrium wage rate. Given the technical relations of production and the physical characteristics of land and labour as well as the supply curve of labour, a larger quantity of land would mean that D_L would be further to the right, and the corresponding equilibrium wage rate would be higher.

The return to an individual landowner from ownership of the land *and* organization of production on it is equal to the total output on his land minus the total amount of labour employed multiplied by the wage rate. For the landowner whose position is illustrated in panel A of Figure 15.1, this return is equal to the area of the rectangle *WBHG*. It would be affected by differences in the supply of the factors of production. For example, with a larger amount of labour assumed to be available at each wage rate, employment and total output would be higher; the net marginal product of labour (and the equilibrium wage rate) would be lower; and the return from the ownership of land *and* organization of production would be greater.

15.5 A model in which both labour and land may be hired

In this model the society's traditions and organization are different. All landowners are assumed to have extensive landholdings, and the social conventions are such that they do not take part in production. Production is organized by farmers who hire both labour and land and also provide seed. Workers own the necessary agricultural implements and are paid in kind at the end of the production period.

At an equilibrium position the wage rate is equal to the net marginal product of labour, as in Section 15.4. With land now being hired on the same basis as labour, the return or payment for a unit of land cultivated must equal the net marginal product of land (for the same reason that the payment to labour in equilibrium must equal its net marginal product).

Figure 15.2 illustrates an equilibrium position for given supply conditions for homogeneous land and labour. There is no incentive for the farmers to hire more labourers or to rent more land. The demand for labour curve (D_L) in panel A of the figure is obtained by the horizontal summation of the net marginal product of labour curves over all farms. It is below the marginal product of labour curve (MP_L) because of the cost of supervising workers. The average product of labour curve (AP_L) is equal to the total output corresponding to each value for the labour input (when land is equal to OR units) divided by the amount of labour. In this equilibrium position the quantity of labour is distributed over all farms in such a way that its net marginal product is everywhere the same. Given the quantity of labour OL, technical knowledge, and the supervisory activity of farmers, it is possible to determine the marginal product of land. This is the difference in total output due to a small unit difference in the amount of land employed by a farmer (along with the necessary difference in seed and organizational efforts required because of the additional unit of land). The net marginal product curve of land (NMP_{LAND}), when labour input is equal to OL, is shown in panel B of Figure 15.2. It is obtained from the marginal product of land curve by subtracting the seed and organizational costs of farming additional units of land. The average product curve of land (AP_{LAND}) is obtained by dividing the total output obtained by the total input of land.

The total output in this model is divided into three types of payments: rent for the landowners, wages for the labourers, and the incomes of farmers. It is shown in Figure 15.2 as equal to the areas of either of the rec-

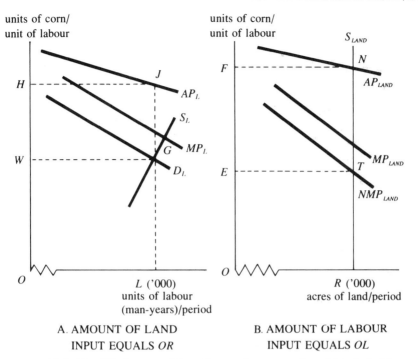

FIGURE 15.2 *Equilibrium position for a given supply of land (of homogeneous quality) and labour when both may be hired*

tangles *OHJL* in panel A or *OFNR* in panel B. The technical relations of production and the supplies of land and labour determine the marginal products of land and labour, but this is not sufficient to determine the three types of payments in this model. The payment for a unit of land will be less than the marginal product of land because of the cost of organizing production on that land (and providing seed).[8] This cost is not technically determined and is affected by the social conventions in the economy, which influence the productive activity of different groups, and the availability of farmers and their eagerness to expand the areas they cultivate. Similarly, the wage rate would be less than the marginal product of labour; the difference would depend on the interrelations within and between social groups.

---

[8] Joan Robinson arrives at the conclusion 'that rent absorbs the whole marginal product of land', because of the assumption that a landowner 'will not accept any deduction from rent on account of being spared the bother of organizing its use himself'. *Exercises in Economic Analysis*, p. 68. Presumably this would be so if there are no costs of organizing production and providing seed.

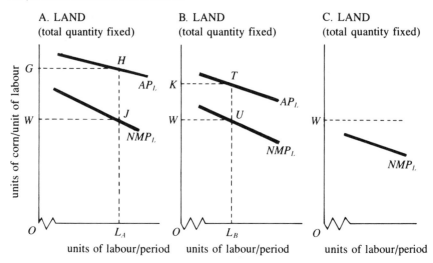

FIGURE 15.3 *Equilibrium position for a situation in which there are fixed quantities of three qualities of land:* A, B, *and* C

15.6 Heterogeneous land

If land is not homogeneous, equilibrium requires that the net marginal product of labour on all land cultivated be equal to the wage rate, and that the net marginal product of labour on land not cultivated be less than the wage rate. A situation of this type is illustrated in Figure 15.3. The supply curve of labour is not shown, but the total quantity supplied when the wage rate is OW is equal to $(L_A + L_B)$ units. L_A units of labour are employed on land of quality A and L_B units on land of quality B. No labour is employed on the poorest quality of land, C, because the net marginal product of labour is lower than the equilibrium wage rate at all positive values for the labour input, even if the land-to-labour ratio is very high. If the supply of labour were greater, all other things the same, the equilibrium wage rate would be lower and land of quality C might also be cultivated. In this case the qualities of land cultivated under the initial conditions (A and B) would be more intensively cultivated and more units of labour would be employed on each unit. When the differences in the qualities of land are very fine (a continuous gradation), and there is a very large number of different grades of land, the equilibrium position is one at which the effect of adding additional labour at the intensive or extensive margins of cultivation is the same; that is, the net marginal product of labour is the same for labour employed on land already cultivated as on the most fertile land not cultivated.

The payment for a particular unit of land of a certain quality would equal the total output on that land minus wage payments and the gross income of the farmer. The payment would be greater the more fertile this particular type of land is relative to the other types available. In Figure 15.3 the total return to A-type land, *plus* the incomes of the farmers cultivating it, is equal to the area *WGHJ*. The return for the ownership of this land (the area *WGHJ* minus the gross income of farmers) is called *rent*. The more fertile the land the higher the rent, other things being equal. Rent on A-land is greater than rent on B-land, since the area *WGHJ* is greater than the area *WKTU*. Of course there is no rent on C-type land under the conditions prevailing in Figure 15.3.

15.7 The wage fund

In this model, workers are still assumed to own the agricultural implements they need for production, but they now have no way of maintaining themselves and their families during the period of production, and the means of subsistence (in the form of corn) must be advanced to them. Thus farmers must have at their disposal stocks of corn that can be used for advance payments to workers.

The ability to dispose of stocks of corn is a prerequisite for being an employer (farmer). Those who own these stocks can obtain a premium by transferring control over them to farmers during the period of production. This premium is called *interest*. In this model there may be a class of rentiers, individuals 'whose income is derived from owning debts',[9] who provide a major portion of these stocks of corn or wage funds. Even if a farmer owns the wage fund he uses, he should act as though he were paying interest for it, since there is an opportunity cost to his using it. It is in the self-interest of the farmer to hire labour up to the point where what an additional worker (with his agricultural implements) adds to the product is equal to what is added to the cost of employing him. In equilibrium the addition to product is the marginal product of labour, and the addition to cost is the amount paid to the worker (the wage rate) plus the interest cost on the worker's wage and the cost of supervision. *Thus the marginal product of labour differs from the wage rate in equilibrium because of the interest cost on the wage fund, even when the cost of supervision is ignored.* This interest cost is not explained by marginal productivity; it depends on the demand and supply conditions for the financing of the wage fund.

Figure 15.4 illustrates the four categories of payments arising from productive activity when there is a wage fund. Landowners receive rent,

---

[9] Joan Robinson, *The Accumulation of Capital* (London: Macmillan & Co., 1956), p. 8.

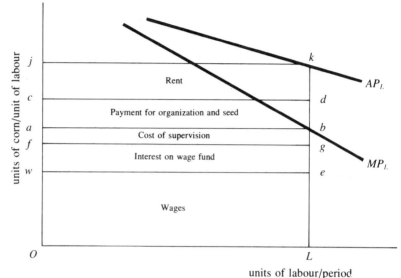

FIGURE 15.4 *Four categories of payment arising with a wage fund, given amount of labour to be employed* [10]

workers obtain wages, rentiers (and farmers who own corn) obtain interest, and farmers receive an amount given by the area *fcdg* to cover the costs of undertaking and supervising productive activity on land. Marginal productivity can explain the determination of the payments for 'organization and seed plus rent', and the joint payments for labour, the supervision of labour, and interest on the wage fund, but it cannot explain the breakdown of these payments into their components. [11]

15.8 Distribution in a capitalist industrial economy
The next model to be examined is that of an industrial economy with a *capitalist mode production*. This term is used to denote a system in which the ownership of the means of production is concentrated in the hands of a group or class ('capitalist') that forms only a relatively small proportion of

---

[10] The amount of land (of each particular quality) cultivated must be specified in order to allow these curves to be drawn.

[11] The dividing line between the costs of organizing production on land and of supervising labour is arbitrary. Nothing in the analyses in this or the preceding sections depends on the particular way in which this division is made. They are based on the recognition that there are costs to undertaking production and to supervising workers and that these costs will be reflected in the differences between the marginal product of land and rent and the marginal product of labour and the wage rate.

the population.[12] Capitalists can be divided into two groups: those actively engaged in the organization of production through their control and operation of firms; and rentiers who are not directly involved in these activities. Rentiers place part of their command over resources at the disposal of entrepreneurs in return for an expected payment. There is also a much larger group ('workers') in the economy whose members' only means of livelihood is the sale of their labour power. In this model two major categories of income appear: *wages* are the payments to workers for their labour power; and *profits* is the term used to describe the income of capitalists. Profits include interest,[13] the payment to rentiers, and the returns obtained by entrepreneurs for organizing and controlling production.[14]

Markets in this economy are assumed to be oligopolistic. Prices are set by price leaders who apply mark-ups to marginal costs that are designed to provide target rates of return on investment when these plants are operated at standard rates. The plant marginal costs are assumed to be constant until normal productive capacity is reached, and then to increase sharply.[15] Indirect as well as direct variable costs are incurred in operating plants. If we further assume that all plants are fully integrated, producing their own raw materials, then the gross value of the output from each plant in any short period is divided into gross profits and wages. We shall further ignore user costs, the wear and tear on the plant of increased operations: all marginal costs are therefore wage costs. The wage rate in this model, unlike the agricultural models in the preceding sections, is set in terms of money and not of the good consumed by workers. The real-wage rate depends on the price of this good as well as on the money-wage rate. Thus the mark-up on the wage-good that firms are able to establish has an important role in the distribution of income in this model. If all the labour hired is of the

---

[12] Cf. Maurice Dobb, *Studies in the Development of Capitalism* (rev. ed.; London: Routledge & Kegan Paul, 1963), Chapter 1.

[13] For a more extended treatment of interest payments, see Section 16.9. In this model, interest includes the opportunity cost to the entrepreneurs of investing their funds in the firms they control.

[14] In this model, therefore, all the payments to members of boards of directors and to the senior management of firms are included in profits. In actual economies, of course, this is true only of part of the payments to senior executives, since they also receive salaries. However, the profit element is a very important part of their total remuneration, as we pointed out in Section 10.7. For example, it was found in an American study of 950 senior executives, covering the period 1940 to 1953, that the 'over-all picture is one of a man who enjoys a $600,000 aggregate annual income, $500,000 of which originates from equity or equity-like sources.' Wilbur G. Lewellen, 'Managerial Incomes and Stockholder Returns', *New Challenges for Economic Research*, National Bureau of Economic Research, 49th Annual Report (1969), pp. 98-9.

[15] Cost curves of this type were drawn in Section 8.4.

same quality (or if relative wage rates are used to express all labour quantities in man-hours of unskilled labour[16]), we can express the gross value of the output of a typical plant as:

$$(1 + \mu)wl_1$$

where μ is the mark-up, w is the money-wage rate, and l_1 is the employment of direct labour in the plant.[17] The total weekly wage bill of the plant is equal to $w(l_o + l_1)$, where l_o is the employment of overhead (or indirect) labour. Gross profits per week, when the weekly rate of output is sold at the predetermined marked-up price, is thus equal to $(1 + \mu)wl_1 - w(l_o + l_1)$; that is, $\mu wl_1 - wl_0$. Therefore the ratio of gross profits to the total wage-bill (P/W) for the plant can be written as:

$$\frac{P}{W} = \frac{\mu l_1 - l_0}{l_0 + l_1} \qquad (1)$$

If l_0 is given by the nature of the plant available to the firm in the particular short period, the distribution of output depends on the mark-up and the level of direct employment.[18] The higher the mark-up, other things given, the greater the profit share; and the higher the level of direct employment, other things given, the greater the profit share. Each firm tries to sell as much as it can, subject to capacity constraints on its output, at the prices it sets for its products. The amounts it can sell in any short period, and thus its rate of output and the direct employment it offers in that period, depend on demand conditions. We are not concerned here with the individual peculiarities of a firm's situation that might affect the demand for its product, but rather with the factors that influence the demands facing all firms. The rate of output that a typical firm can sell depends on

[16] This device was used by Keynes (in *The General Theory of Employment, Interest and Money*, p. 41) to obtain a measure of the total quantity of employment.

[17] The derivation of this expression for total output follows from the pricing formula and the assumption of constant marginal costs. Let a be the output per unit of *direct* labour for the constant portion of marginal costs; marginal cost is then equal to w/a (recall that labour cost is assumed to account for all of marginal cost). According to the mark-up formula the price is equal to $(1 + \mu)w/a$ and the total output is equal to al_1. The gross value of total output is thus equal to the product of these two terms; that is to $(1 + \mu)wl_1$.

[18] Note that the money-wage rate does not appear in equation 1. Collective bargaining between unions representing workers and the firms that arrive at money-wage rate settlements would affect only the distribution of income if these settlements resulted in changes in either the mark-up or direct employment. M. Kalecki argued that the mark-up might be lowered when money-wage rates are increased sharply, owing to the improved bargaining power of unions, if the firms in one industry feel constrained by the competitive pressures from firms in other industries and do not pass on all the higher costs. 'Class Struggle and Distribution of National Income', *Selected Essays on the Dynamics of the Capitalist Economy 1933-1970*, pp. 156-64.

effective demand in the economy.[19] This is a *macroeconomic* concept and will not be examined in any detail here, but its introduction makes clear that the analysis of distribution in this model cannot be completed without reference to macroeconomic conditions. The level of effective demand in a particular short period in a model of a capitalist economy (when governmental activity and international trade are left out of the model) depends on the amount of investment firms are carrying out in that short period and on the propensities to save in the economy. The higher the level of investment, other things given, the higher the level of effective demand, the higher the level of employment of direct labour in typical firms, and the higher the profit share in total income. The higher the propensity to save in the economy, other things given, the lower the level of effective demand, the lower the level of employment of direct labour in typical firms, and the lower the profit share in total income.[20]

In this simple model of a capitalist economy we see that distribution, although conditioned by the technical relations of production that determine output per man and its variation with the level of employment, is very much affected by other factors. The competitive structure of markets, the organization of workers, and the factors determining effective demand all have a role to play in arriving at the profit and wage shares. A theory of distribution that concentrates solely on the activity of individual units and does not deal with the determination of the level of employment in the economy would not be a satisfactory theory for this model.

The rate of profits can be introduced into the analysis if the short period being examined is one of a series of short periods that are characterized by long-period as well as short-period equilibrium. Long-period equilibrium means that the firms' investment expectations have been borne out by events and that plants are being utilized at standard rates, with target rates of return being earned. The rate of profits in the economy would be equal to the level of profits for the period divided by the value of the firms' plants. In this special case the values set on existing plants are the same whether reference is made to their costs or to expected future revenues.[21] The values obtained by using historical costs less expected depreciation would be equal

---

[19] The principle of effective demand was developed by Keynes in *The General Theory of Employment, Interest and Money*, Chapter 3. It was also developed independently, and first published in 1933 (although the term 'effective demand' was not used), by M. Kalecki, 'Outline of a Theory of the Business Cycle', *Selected Essays on the Dynamics of the Capitalist Economy 1933-1970* (Cambridge, Eng.: Cambridge University Press, 1971), pp. 1-14.

[20] In periods of increasing activity, when an economy is recovering from a recession, we would expect, on the basis of this theory, that profit shares would be increasing. This pattern is reflected in data on changes in profit shares over business cycles.

[21] The capitalization of expected future income is discussed in Section 16.10.

to the present values of the plants obtained by capitalizing expected future profits on the basis of the target rate of return.[21] The rate of interest would be less than the rate of profit: the difference provides the compensation for the business ability of entrepreneurs and the risks involved in organizing production in a world of uncertainty. (Even though expectations held in the past have been borne out by events, the future is unknown.) The rate of profit would depend on the same general factors that determine the share of profits in each short period—the rate of accumulation and the propensities to save. The real-wage rate in the model, when a time path characterized by long-period equilibrium is being followed, is a residual. It is equal to the difference between the output per man and the profit share in output per man, which provides the equilibrium rate of profit on the value of capital per man.[22]

Some of the features of our simple models are to be found in prominent theories of distribution. Four theories will be sketched briefly. Three of them are identified with particular economists, while the fourth, the marginal productivity theory of distribution, was developed in the late nineteenth century by economists who were associated with the development of the theory of marginal utility.[23]

15.9 David Ricardo

Ricardo's theory of distribution can be discussed in terms of our agricultural model. Ricardo assumes that landowners typically do not engage in production; their land is rented by farmers who hire labourers and organize production. The social arrangements are similar to those outlined in Section 15.7. Farmers require wage funds, which they obtain either from their own savings or by borrowing, in order to hire labour that is paid in advance (rent is paid after the crop is harvested).

Figure 15.4 can be used to illustrate an initial position of equilibrium for this model. It will be assumed that organizational costs vary both with the amount of land cultivated and with the quantity of labour hired. (These costs are usually ignored in presentations of Ricardo's theory.) The marginal product of labour is determined, given technical knowledge and the fertility of the land, by the fixed amount of labour, which is deployed in

---

[22] If the equilibrium rate of profit is represented by r, and the corresponding value of capital in a typical plant by K, then the equilibrium wage bill can be written as: $w(l_o + l_i) = pal_i - rK$, therefore $w/p = al_i/(l_o + l_i) - rK/p(l_o + l_i)$. Thus the wage in terms of the product (the real-wage rate) is equal to output per man (indirect as well as direct labour) minus the output per man that goes to profit.

[23] See George J. Stigler, *Production and Distribution Theories* (New York: Macmillan Co., 1948).

equilibrium (by the individual self-interest of farmers) to produce the largest output. This marginal product is equal to *Oa* in Figure 15.4. Although Ricardo was the first to introduce marginal analysis into the theory of distribution, he did not believe that distribution was fully explained by marginal productivity. The wage rate was obtained by taking both the amount of labour employed and the total wage fund as fixed. Profit, the compensation for organizing production and interest on the wage fund, is equal to the sum of the areas of the rectangles *wfge*, *fabg*, and *acdb* in Figure 15.4. The rate of profit can be readily calculated because there is only one product, corn, and production requires one year. It is equal to profit divided by the value of capital, which is equal here to the wage fund, *OweL*.

Ricardo accepted the Malthusian theory of population. This states that wages become adjusted over time to the 'natural price' of labour—'that price which is necessary to enable the labourers, one with another, to subsist and to perpetuate their race, without either increase or diminution.'[24] It should be noted that Ricardo did not give a crudely physical interpretation to the concept of a subsistence wage. He saw it as being socially determined, with habits and customs playing a role in setting its value, which could change over time as the result of experience and changing standards of life. If the wage rate *Ow* in Figure 15.4 were greater than the subsistence wage for that economy, the population and number of labourers available would increase over time. Given unchanged availability of land and agricultural technology, this would result in a lower marginal product of labour and higher rent. If situations with the same subsistence wage rate, land, and technology, but different amounts of labour, were compared, the rate of profit as well as the marginal product of labour would be lower. The difference between the marginal product of labour and the unchanged subsistence wage, accounting for interest and payment for the supervision of labour, would be smaller when the labour employed was greater.

The dynamic element in Ricardo's model, the item that produces growth, is profit. Saving and accumulation are assumed to occur only out of profit. Increases in the wage fund due to the saving of farmers (capitalists) may lead initially only to higher wages, but with growth in the labour force they are translated into higher employment. Over time, however, profit (the source of growth) would be squeezed between the fixed subsistence wage and the declining marginal product of labour. When the rate of profit reaches some minimum positive rate, accumulation will cease and a stationary state will be attained.

---

[24] Sraffa, *The Works and Correspondence of David Ricardo*, p. 93.

The above outline is the basis of Ricardo's theory of distribution, which holds even when an industrial sector is added to the model. The industrial sector in Ricardian models is assumed to be characterized by constant costs, and to make the analysis precise the assumption that wage payments are made only in corn is maintained. Capitalists and capital funds are assumed to be able to move freely between agricultural and industrial activity in search of higher returns, and this ensures that, in a situation of long-period equilibrium, the rate of profit will be the same in both sectors. This rate of profit must be determined in agriculture by the mechanism discussed above, and the rate of profit in industrial activity must conform to it. The equilibrium price ratio of agricultural and industrial output would be such as to allow the same rate of profit to be earned in both sectors. Increasing population and the lower marginal productivity of labour in agriculture would tend to lower the rate of profit in manufacturing, as well as in agriculture, and to bring accumulation to an end.[25]

15.10 Karl Marx

Marx's theory of distribution is concerned with the division of the output of industrial production—the pre-eminent form of capitalist activity—into wages and profits. Marx emphasized the importance of the social relations of production. To subsist, workers must sell their labour power to capitalists, who own the means of production. Profits are possible in this system because workers are required to work longer than the amount of time required to produce the wage goods, and they are 'realized' because capitalists' expenditures for investment and consumption provide a market for the products of surplus labour. The rate of exploitation (or rate of surplus value) is equal to the ratio of the amount of *surplus labour* (the amount of labour performed in excess of that required to produce the wage-goods received by the workers) to the amount of labour performed.

The rate of exploitation in any one period of time depends on the balance of the class struggle—the relative bargaining power of capitalists and workers.[26] Increasing demand for labour, given the size of the labour force,

---

[25] If the subsistence wage consists of manufacturing goods as well as corn, the rate of profit cannot be determined as the ratio of two items measured in the same physical units. The wage fund—the denominator—would consist of manufactured goods as well as corn. Prices must be introduced to obtain a value for this wage fund. These prices are not independent of the rate of profit in equilibrium, since they must provide for this rate of profit, and the simplicity of the analysis based on a subsistence wage specified in physical terms is lost.

[26] This struggle was often fought over the length of the working-day because, with given technical knowledge and equipment, this determined the rate of exploitation. Karl Marx, *Capital* (New York: Modern Library Edition), Vol. I, Chapter X.

would tend to improve the bargaining position of workers and drive up wage rates in real terms. The fall in profits and investment that result from these pressures would bring the increasing demand for labour to an end, and even produce a movement in the opposite direction, as depressed conditions followed the boom.[27] Marx did not accept the Malthusian theory of population; he termed it a 'libel on the human race'. What played the same role in his model and tended to keep the wage rate down to some historically conditioned 'subsistence' level was 'the industrial reserve army of labour' that is created by the capitalist process. This reserve army comes into being as a result of the capitalist invasion of pre-capitalist areas of production. Factory-produced goods take away the markets for goods produced by artisans. Artisans and their families, deprived of their traditional means of livelihood, are forced to seek work as wage-labour in order to survive. Factors leading to the maintenance or re-creation of the industrial reserve army are the regular capitalist crises (the depressions that follow booms) and the implementation of labour-saving technical progress.[28]

Despite his prediction that business would become concentrated in fewer hands, Marx assumed a system that was competitive at least in the long-period sense. No producer could stand still in his routine; others would innovate and undercut his price and drive him out of business. A firm must increase its investment in order to maintain its position; it must invest because costs fall with scale of output and it can take advantage of the latest inventions and machines only by investing. Marx summed it up in a credo for capitalists: 'Accumulate, Accumulate! That is Moses and the Prophets!'[29]

Technological change is one of the crucial determining factors in Marx's analysis. He argued that the introduction of labour-saving (and capital-using) techniques, often adopted in response to rising wage rates, would place a time-bomb under the system and would lead to a long-run tendency for the rate of profits to fall. To illustrate how this could come about, the

---

[27] 'If the quantity of unpaid labour supplied by the working-class, and accumulated by the capitalist class, increases so rapidly that its conversion into capital requires an extraordinary addition of paid labour, then wages rise, and, all other circumstances remaining equal, the unpaid labour diminishes in proportion. But as soon as this diminution touches the point at which the surplus-labour that nourishes capital is no longer supplied in normal quantity, a reaction sets in: a smaller part of revenue is capitalised, accumulation lags, and the movement of rise in wages receives a check.' *Ibid.*, p. 680.

[28] 'Capitalist production can by no means content itself with the quantity of disposable labour-power which the natural increase of population yields. It requires for its free play an industrial reserve army independent of these natural limits.' *Ibid.*, p. 696.

[29] *Ibid.*, p. 652.

firm's expenditures in a year can be divided into two categories: v, 'variable' capital, which is used to pay for labour, and c, 'constant' capital, the cost of materials and all capital equipment. The 'organic composition of capital' is defined as c/v and is assumed to be rising over time as a result of technical progress. If we let s denote the surplus value—the difference between the value produced by labour and the value of the wage received—the rate of surplus value is s/v. The rate of profit can be written as $r = s/(c + v)$, where *all* capital is assumed to be turned over in a year. This expression can be written as $r = (s/v)/(c/v) + 1$. It can be seen immediately that if s/v is constant while c/v is rising, then r will fall. However, there is no reason why higher values for c/v will not be accompanied by higher values for s/v, and so there may be no tendency for the rate of profit to fall even when the organic composition of capital is higher. Marx's analysis does not contain a proof for his proposition that the rate of profit in a capitalist system will fall over a long run of time.[30]

Marx's theory of distribution emphasized that the division of the total product between labour and capital depended on the 'class struggle', and that distribution itself would be influenced by changes in technology (e.g. labour-saving inventions), population growth, the organization of workers, and the extension of capitalist production to new areas.

15.11 Alfred Marshall

Marshall's theory of distribution resembles that of Ricardo in being based on a subsistence payment for one factor of production, with the payment for the other a residual. But the roles are reversed; in long-period equilibrium the rate of interest is equal to the reward for 'waiting' (this can be viewed as a 'subsistence' payment for the maintenance of capital), and the wage rate is a residual. Marshall makes clear the distinction between entrepreneurs and rentiers. Thus there are four major categories of income to be explained in his analysis: land rent, profits, interest, and wages. Marshall accepted Ricardo's theory of land rent. He also noted that in the short period, plant and equipment have the same characteristics as land; they are available for production even though there is no payment for them. Thus he coined the term *quasi-rent* for the excess of revenues over operating costs.

Interest is the payment made by a borrower for a loan of money, while profits are defined as the total net gains from business. The difference between profits and interest represents the earnings of undertaking or

---

[30] Cf. Joan Robinson, *An Essay on Marxian Economics* (London: Macmillan & Co., 1949), Chapter V.

management.[31] The latter is the return for business ability and energy, and the organizing activity 'by which the appropriate business ability and the requisite capital are brought together'.[32]

Marginal conditions appear in Marshall's treatment of distribution when he considers the decisions made by entrepreneurs—in particular their hiring decisions. Individual firms are assumed to hire additional units of labour up to the point where what they add to their receipts is equal to what they add to their costs. The net return resulting from the employment of an additional unit of labour can be called the marginal product of labour. However, Marshall made it clear that a marginal productivity theory of wages should not be put forward as a general theory of wages. '. . . there is no valid ground for any such pretension. The doctrine that the earnings of a worker tend to be equal to the net product of his work, has by itself no real meaning; since in order to estimate net product, we have to take for granted all the expenses of production of the commodity on which he works, other than his own wages.'[33] To explain the wage rate, then, it is necessary to know both the technical conditions of production and the amount of employment, which together determine output per man at the margin, and then the other costs of production, which must be subtracted from the marginal product of labour.[34]

The expenses of production other than wages (assuming that we are dealing with 'no-rent' land) that arise in long-period equilibrium are interest and the earnings of management. Both of these elements are assumed to have specific supply prices in long-period equilibrium. The rate of interest is seen as the reward for *waiting*—for the postponement of the pleasure arising from consumption. 'And human nature being what it is, we are justified in speaking of the interest on capital as the reward of the sacrifice involved in the waiting for the enjoyment of material resources, because few people would save much without reward: just as we speak of wages as the reward of labour, because few people would work hard without reward.'[35]

The *normal* price of a commodity, which Marshall defines as the value

---

[31] A man in business 'would not, however, be willing to continue the business unless he expected his total net gains from it to exceed interest on his capital at the current rate. These gains are called profits.' Alfred Marshall, *Principles of Economics* (8th ed.; London: Macmillan & Co., 1920), p. 73.

[32] *Ibid.*, p. 313.

[33] *Ibid.*, p. 518.

[34] This argument was illustrated in the exercises for an agricultural economy (Sections 15.3 to 15.7) where the wage rate was equal to the net marginal product of labour but the technical conditions determined only the gross marginal product.

[35] Marshall, *Principles of Economics*, p. 232.

that economic forces will bring about if the general conditions of life are stationary for a long enough period to enable them all to work out their full effect, includes the interest required to provide the normal rate of interest on the value of the capital involved in the production of this commodity. The normal supply price of business ability in command of capital also enters into the normal price of the commodity. After those payments are subtracted, the remainder goes to wages. Therefore in long-period equilibrium, wages are a residual.

The actual distribution of income in any short period in Marshall's model depends on market conditions. He saw profits as varying more than wage rates. Profits are high or low depending on market demand and supply conditions, which are subject to disturbances. The economy need not ever be, even for Marshall, in long-period equilibrium. A great deal of his *Principles of Economics* is devoted to a careful examination of possible non-equilibrium situations.

Marshall's analysis bears some resemblance, on a formal level, to that sketched out in Section 15.8 for an industrial economy on a growth path characterized by long-period equilibrium, even though Marshall refers to a stationary economy and not to one that is growing. The wage rate is a residual in both, and it is determined after the appropriate amount to provide for the equilibrium rate of profit is subtracted from the value of output per man. However, there is a difference in the conclusions about the group that sacrifices present consumption in order to allow investment. Marshall seemed to be trying to provide a justification for rentiers' incomes by claiming that 'waiting' involved 'real' costs comparable to those of physical and mental labour. For the model in Section 15.8 a higher rate of investment, given thriftiness conditions and the level of employment, means that the real-wage rate is lower. The 'abstinence' or 'waiting' required to permit this higher rate of accumulation to take place is borne by the workers through lower real-wage rates and not by the rentiers, whose savings are increased (out of their higher incomes).[36]

15.12 Marginal productivity theories of distribution

Ricardo was a pioneer in the use of marginal principles in a theory of distribution; but as we have seen, the separation of the marginal product of

---

[36] Marshall appears to be trying to find a 'real' cost basis for the justification of rentiers' incomes in his emphasis on the sacrifice involved in 'waiting' to consume resources. Joan Robinson has pointed out the ambiguity in his use of the term 'waiting'. It is not clear whether it refers to refraining from consuming existing capital or to saving. See Joan Robinson, *Economic Heresies* (New York: Basic Books, 1971), p. xii.

labour into wages and profits was based on other grounds. With the rise of the marginalist approach from the 1870s on, attempts were made to explain all rewards on the basis of marginal conditions. In some cases, for example that of J.B. Clark, these attempts were motivated by the desire to provide a 'scientific' refutation of Marx's theory of exploitation. He reached the conclusion that 'What a social class gets is, under natural law, what it contributes to the general output of industry.'[37] This approach, which concentrates on the technical conditions of production and the demand and supply conditions for the elements of production, gives rise to various problems.

The technical conditions of production are summarized by production functions. They state the relationship, given technical knowledge, between the flows of inputs of services provided by the elements of production, measured in physical units, and the flows of output of particular types of products, also measured in physical units. In order to use these functions to provide a complete theory of distribution, all the inputs, as well as the outputs, must be capable of description in physical units. Furthermore, these inputs must be substitutable to allow for the derivation of marginal products. Various devices have been used in an attempt to meet these requirements.

There is an aggregate version of this theory in which output is shown as a function of capital and labour. Capital is treated as though it were measured in physical units, but this is not a legitimate simplification. Capital as an aggregate is measured in value terms; it is equal to the sum of the values of the individual items of capital equipment. The equilibrium prices of these items must be such as to just provide the equilibrium rate of profit. Thus capital as a value cannot be used to determine the rate of profit, since it is a function of this rate.[38] Alternatively, a disaggregated approach can be used, with each item of capital equipment and each type of labour input being shown individually in the production function. At this individual level, however, many of the elements of production are combined in fixed proportions and marginal products cannot be obtained for each of them separately. Even if this problem (which is by no means a negligible one) is waived aside, there are still difficulties with this approach because not all the contributors to production can be treated quantitatively.

The marginal productivity theory tries to provide a complete explanation

---

[37] J.B. Clark, 'Distribution as Determined by the Law of Rent', *Quarterly Journal of Economics*, Vol. 5 (April 1891), p. 313.
[38] This was one of the lessons emphasized by the recent controversy in capital theory. See G.C. Harcourt, *Some Cambridge Controversies in the Theory of Capital* (Cambridge, Eng.: Cambridge University Press, 1972).

of the distribution of total output on the basis of marginal products without reference to the social relations of production. We will examine two of the ways in which 'exhaustion' of the total product will occur under these rules. The first method is based on the assumption that the production function is homogeneous of degree one (see Section 7.18). It can be written as:

$$x = f(v_1, v_2, v_3, \ldots, v_n)$$

where all inputs and the output are measured in physical units (per period of time). Euler's mathematical theorem for homogeneous functions states that

$$x = v_1 \frac{\partial x}{\partial v_1} + v_2 \frac{\partial x}{\partial v_2} + \ldots + v_n \frac{\partial x}{\partial v_n} \qquad (1)$$

These partial derivatives are the marginal products of indicated inputs. When both sides of the equation are multiplied by the price of the product p, we obtain:

$$px = \sum_{i=1}^{n} v_i p \frac{\partial x}{\partial v_i} \qquad (2)$$

A firm with perfectly competitive markets will determine the amount of each element hired by comparing the contribution to its revenue of hiring an additional unit with the addition to its cost. The contribution to revenue is the value of the marginal product (the price of the product multiplied by the marginal product of the element), and the additional cost is the price of the element (see Section 16.2). Thus each input is hired up to the point where the value of its marginal product is equal to its price. Equation 2 states that the value of total output is exhausted if each element of production is paid according to the value of its marginal product. (But what is left of this theory if some elements of production—e.g. entrepreneurial activity—cannot be measured in any precise manner in physical units?)[39]

The definitional nature of much of the marginal productivity approach to the theory of distribution may become more apparent when it is noted that 'exhaustion' of the total product does not require a particular type of production function.[40] A perfectly competitive firm hires that quantity of

---

[39] These elements of production must be ignored by the proponents of this theory because they cannot be fitted into this approach. For example, K. Wicksell, in developing his marginal productivity theory of distribution, considered Marshall's attempt to introduce a fourth class of agents of production—namely, organization. But Wicksell did not adopt this classification because he said it 'suffers from the inconvenience that the new agency thus introduced, unlike the old, lacks *quantitative precision* . . .' K. Wicksell, *Lectures on Political Economy* (London: Routledge & Kegan Paul, 1935), Vol. I, p. 107. Wicksell then proceeded to ignore organization in order to explain distribution solely on the basis of marginal productivity.

[40] Harry G. Johnson, *The Theory of Income Distribution* (London: Gray-Mills Publishing Ltd., 1973), Chapter 3.

each element of production that equates the value of its marginal product to its price. That is,

$$w_i = p \frac{\partial x}{\partial v_i}$$

where w_i is the price of the element of production, v_i. For a perfectly competitive firm in long-period equilibrium, price must be equal to minimum average cost, by definition, when the cost curve includes rent payments to the more efficient elements of production (see Section 11.9). This condition can be written as

$$p = \sum_{i=1}^{n} (w_i v_i)/x$$

where v_i is the amount of the ith element of production hired in long-period equilibrium, and x is the rate of output at equilibrium. It follows from these two equations that

$$px = \sum_{i=1}^{n} v_i p \frac{\partial x}{\partial v_i}$$

This is the result derived in equation 2 using Euler's Theorem. This approach asserts (as an article of faith?) that all payments in equilibrium must be determined by marginal productivity, otherwise the position could not be one of equilibrium. It is no more than an assertion by definition and can never be shown to be false. The problems left unsettled, in situations where marginal products cannot be derived for all elements of production, either because of technical complementarity or the inability to obtain physical measures of these elements, are ignored.

15.13 Summary
This chapter has provided an overview of some of the more prominent approaches to the theory of distribution. The simple models of agricultural and industrial economies showed that technical relations of production provide limits within which distribution of the total product occurs, but the final distribution depends on the social arrangements in the economy and the total level of economic activity. These models also served as a background for brief sketches of the distribution theories associated with Ricardo, Marx, and Marshall. The attempt to explain the distribution of the total product solely on the basis of marginal productivity was shown to be an assertion by definition.

SUGGESTED READINGS

Dobb, Maurice. *Theories of Value and Distribution Since Adam Smith.* Cambridge, Eng.: Cambridge University Press, 1973.

Marshall, Alfred. *Principles of Economics.* 8th ed. London: Macmillan & Co., 1920. Book VI, Chapter 1.

Robinson, Joan. *Exercises in Economic Analysis.* London: Macmillan & Co., 1960. Pages 57-68.

Sraffa, Piero, ed. *The Works and Correspondence of David Ricardo.* Cambridge, Eng.: Cambridge University Press, 1951. Vol. I, pp. xiii-lxii, and Chapters II, V, and VI.

Wicksell, K. *Lectures on Political Economy.* London: Routledge & Kegan Paul, 1935. Vol. I, pp. 101-33.

EXERCISES

1. The land available for cultivation in a particular community is of three qualities designated by A, B and C. All farms are assumed to consist of the same acreage and each farm has only one type of land, so that reference can be made to A-farms, B-farms, or C-farms. The only product in this agricultural community is corn. Its production takes a year, and it requires land, seed, someone to organize production and supervise labour, and labour equipped with appropriate agricultural implements. Two joint inputs are involved in this production: 'land plus seed plus organization associated with the amount of land used' or 'land +' for short; and 'labour plus agricultural implements plus supervision of the labour employed' or 'labour +' for short. The schedules for the marginal product of 'labour +' on each type of farm are as follows:

LABOUR +	TYPE OF FARM		
	A	B	C
1	100	96	92
2	98	95	90
3	96	94	88
4	94	93	86
5	92	92	84
	etc.	etc.	etc.

(a) What would be the equilibrium allocation of labour among these three types of farms if there were 2,000 farms of each type and 14,000 labourers? What is the amount available per worker in this equilibrium situation to cover the wage rate, return for agricultural implements, interest on the wage fund, and supervision of labour? What is the equilibrium wage rate? What is the amount available per farm, for each type of farm, to cover the cost of seed and organization and to provide for rent of land? What is the equilibrium rent for each type of farm?

(b) What would be the equilibrium allocation of labour among these three types of farms if there were 2,000 farms of each type and 30,000 labourers? Answer all questions raised in (a) for this equilibrium situation.

(c) If the only difference from the conditions stipulated in (a) is that there are 1,999 farms of type A, what is the difference in total output? What is the relationship that this difference bears to the amount available for each A-type farm to cover the cost of seed, organization, and rent?

2. Prove the following statement:

In an industry that is oligopolistic, employment may vary without any variation in the wage rate in terms of the product.

16
PRICING OF THE ELEMENTS OF PRODUCTION (INPUTS)

16.1 Introduction

The marginal productivity theory of distribution emphasizes the technical relations of production. It explains the demand for specific elements of production (inputs)—for example, the demand for carpenters or the demand for copper—on the basis of the marginal productivity of these inputs and the demand for the final product. The demand for inputs is a *derived demand*. Inputs are in demand because they help produce goods that can be sold. The marginal productivity approach as applied to individual elements of production will be developed for different market structures. As we saw in Chapter 15, this does not provide a satisfactory explanation of distribution, but it is an important part of neoclassical economic theory. Some of the techniques of analysis based on marginal productivity will also be presented.

The concluding sections of this chapter examine some of the factors influencing wages and interest and define economic rent and economic profit.

16.2 The firm's demand for an element of production

The firm is assumed to have a neoclassical production function that is based on the principle of substitution (see Section 7.12). Individual elements of production have positive and calculable marginal products. It will also be assumed that the firm is trying to maximize profits in the short period. A firm will be in short-period equilibrium—that is, making the best of the situation facing it—only if it cannot improve its profitability by having a different rate of employment of any one of the variable inputs. A precise statement of the profit-maximizing position requires the definition of two

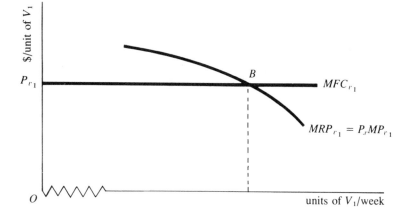

FIGURE 16.1 *Marginal revenue product and marginal factor cost for a perfectly competitive firm*

terms. The addition to a firm's total revenue if an additional (small) unit of an element of production is hired is called the *marginal revenue product* (*MRP*) of that element of production. It is equal to the marginal product of the element multiplied by the firm's marginal revenue. The corresponding addition to the firm's total cost resulting from hiring this additional unit, all other inputs unchanged, is called the *marginal factor cost* (*MFC*). A firm is in short-period equilibrium with respect to the employment of an element of production if the marginal revenue product of that element is equal to its marginal factor cost.[1]

If the firm sells in a perfectly competitive market its marginal revenue is equal to the market price for its output (see Section 9.6). Thus for an input employed by a perfectly competitive firm the *marginal revenue product is equal to the value of its marginal product.*[2] If the market for this input is also perfectly competitive, the firm can hire as many units of the input as it wants at the given market price: thus the *marginal factor cost is equal to the price of the input.* The equilibrium position for the firm's employment of a variable input under these conditions is illustrated in Figure 16.1.

The firm's demand curve for the input V_1 is derived from the marginal revenue product curve. This eventually slopes downward (only the

---

[1] This is the first-order condition for profit maximization, for which the second-order conditions must also be satisfied. For a smaller rate of employment of this element, the marginal revenue product must exceed the marginal factor cost; while for a larger rate the marginal factor cost must exceed the marginal revenue product.

[2] See Section 15.12. The value of the marginal product of an element of production is equal to the price of the output multiplied by the marginal product.

downward-sloping portion is drawn in Figure 16.1), even though the price of the product (P_x) is not affected by this firm's output because of eventually declining marginal productivity (see Section 7.13). The quantity demanded of this input in equilibrium must be such as to equate its marginal revenue product and its marginal factor cost. This quantity, given the amounts employed of other inputs,[3] is obtained from the intersection of its *MFC* curve (whose height is equal to the price of this input) and its *MRP* curve. A higher price, given the quantities employed of the other inputs, results in a lower quantity demanded of the input. However, a different price will also affect the quantities demanded of some of the other inputs, since a difference in the employment of V_1 will affect their marginal productivity curves.

The general condition for equilibrium in the employment of the variable inputs is

$$\frac{MP_{v_1}}{P_{v_1}} = \frac{MP_{v_2}}{P_{v_2}} = \cdots \frac{MP_{v_n}}{P_{v_n}}$$

as we saw in Section 8.8. The equilibrium position corresponding to a different price for V_1 is characterized by differences in the amounts employed of the other inputs of production, as well as in the amount of V_1, because these amounts must be adjusted to restore equality between the ratios of the marginal products and prices for *all* the variable inputs. Thus the quantity demanded of V_1 in this new equilibrium position will be indicated by a marginal revenue product curve that reflects the differences in the employment of other inputs. For example, in Figure 16.2 the equilibrium rate of employment of V_1 is OA when the price is $P_{v_1}^0$. The appropriate marginal revenue product curve is $MRP_{v_1}^0$ and the equilibrium position on that curve is point H. For a lower price of V_1, P_{v_1}', the appropriate marginal revenue product is MRP_{v_1}', since different quantities of other inputs are employed, and the equilibrium rate of employment, OB, is obtained from point K on that curve.

The perfectly competitive firm's demand curve for an element of production is therefore obtained by joining points such as H and K in Figure 16.2. This curve (d_{v_1}) is composed of points representing the equilibrium rates of employment of V_1 for different prices of this element of production. The prices for all the other variable elements of production and the firm's short-period production function are unchanged along this curve. Its position and slope depend on three considerations: (i) the firm's production function, which, given the values for the other inputs,

---

[3] Recall that with neoclassical production functions the marginal product of an element is defined with constant values for all the other inputs (Section 7.13).

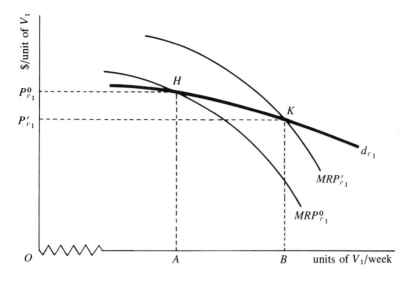

FIGURE 16.2 *Derivation of a firm's demand curve for an element of production*

determines the marginal productivity of the input being examined; (ii) the prices of the other variable inputs, which affect their employment; and (iii) the price of the firm's product. The firm's demand curve for an input displays the usual properties of demand curves. It is negatively sloped, and the elasticity of demand depends on the availability of substitutes. The effectiveness of technological substitutes for this input, other things being given, determines the extent of the 'shift' in its marginal product curve when price differs. The more readily substitutes are available, the greater the shift of the marginal revenue product curves, such as those drawn in Figure 16.2, and the greater the numerical value for the elasticity of demand for this element of production.

The derivation of a monopolistic firm's demand curve for an element of production is also derived in the manner just described. It is based on the marginal revenue product curves for the element of production whose demand curve is to be derived. Marginal revenue product ($MR \times MP_{v_1}$) is now *less* than the value of the marginal product ($P \times MP_{v_1}$), since the monopolistic firm's marginal revenue is less than the price of its product. But once this is noted, the approach illustrated in Figure 16.2 can be used for both perfectly competitive and monopolistic firms.

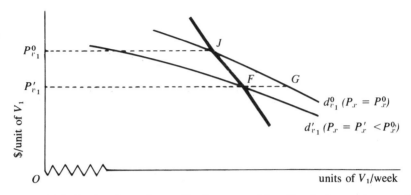

FIGURE 16.3 *Derivation of a perfectly competitive firm's demand curve for an input (product price varying with industry output)*

16.3 A perfectly competitive industry's demand curve for an element of production

The demand for an element of production is a derived demand; it depends on the demand for the final product. This will be illustrated by considering a perfectly competitive industry's demand curve for an element of production, which is based on the sum of the quantities demanded by firms in that industry. However, it is not obtained simply from a horizontal summation of the demand curves for constituent firms. These curves are derived, as in Figure 16.2, under the assumption of a given price for the firm's output. In deriving the industry demand curve it is necessary to allow for the difference in product price that would accompany a difference in the price of the element of production. Industry output, and thus the product-price facing individual firms, would differ. The way in which this difference in price can be allowed for is illustrated in Figure 16.3.

The initial equilibrium position J for the firm and industry has a price of $P_{v_1}^0$ for the input V_1, and P_x^0 for the product. The firm's demand curve for V_1, given this price for the product, is denoted by the curve $d_{v_1}^0$ in Figure 16.3. If the price of this input were P_{v_1}', then the demand for it by all firms would be higher, and their rates of output would also be higher because their costs of production would be lower. However, this higher industry output would be associated with a lower price for the product. The typical firm's equilibrium position when the price of V_1 was P_{v_1}' would thus not lie on the curve $d_{v_1}^0$, but on a *lower* curve, reflecting the lower price for its output. In Figure 16.3 this equilibrium position is at point F on d_{v_1}'. The curve joining points such as J and F is then added horizontally, over all firms, to obtain the industry's demand curve for this element of production.

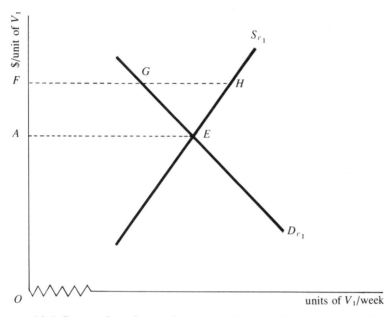

FIGURE 16.4 *Demand and supply curves for an element of production employed in a perfectly competitive industry*

The distance between $d^0_{v_1}$ and d'_{v_1} depends on the difference in the equilibrium prices for the product corresponding to the difference in the price for V_1. This points up the derived nature of the industry's demand for an element of production. The *less* elastic the demand for the product, the greater the difference in its price for a given difference in its rate of output, and the greater the horizontal distance between $d^0_{v_1}$ and d'_{v_1}—thus the *less* elastic the demand for the input V_1. Alternatively, the *more* elastic the demand for the product, the smaller the difference in its price for a given difference in its rate of output, and the smaller the distance between $d^0_{v_1}$ and d'_{v_1}—thus the *more* elastic the demand for V_1.

16.4 Competitive and collusive prices for elements of production

The determination of the price for an element of production can be illustrated with the industry's demand curve for that element. It is assumed that V_1 is employed only in the perfectly competitive industry being examined; thus the partial equilibrium approach we will use is more defensible. The equilibrium position in Figure 16.4 is at point E. The corresponding price, $\$OA$/unit of V_1, can be called the *competitive* price for this element, given the demand and supply curves in Figure 16.4.

The possibility of success from collusive efforts by sellers to obtain a price higher than the competitive price would be affected by the elasticities of the demand and supply curves. The more elastic these curves, the greater the (potential) excess supply (e.g. *GH* in Figure 16.4 when sellers attempt to establish the price $OF per unit of V_1), which sellers must keep off the market if their collusive efforts are to succeed.

A trade union can be viewed within the context of this analysis as a vehicle through which workers collude to obtain a higher price for their labour services. (It should be noted that this is only one aspect of a trade union.) The elasticity of a competitive industry's demand curve for labour is an important factor in determining a union's ability to raise wage rates, since higher wage rates may lead to an excess supply of labour that must be kept off the market. Unions may therefore try to affect the demand curve for labour. Various work rules, jurisdictional agreements about the categories of workers permitted to do specific jobs, agreements on technological change, etc., affect the degree to which other workers or inputs can be substituted for a union's members. Unions may also try to influence the elasticity of demand for the product. This activity has a long history in the garment industry, where the clothing unions have been promoting the 'union label' that is sewn onto clothes produced in union shops. The more successful these efforts, the smaller the adverse employment effects on their members of any increase in wage rates above the market equilibrium rate.

16.5 Monopsony

If the firm is a monopsonist with respect to a particular element of production, its marginal factor cost curve for that element will be upward sloping (see Section 9.12). The equilibrium position, of course, is still defined by the equality of the marginal revenue product and the marginal factor cost for the element. This position is at point *F* in Figure 16.5. The equilibrium price for the element is $OA per unit of V_1, and the equilibrium rate of employment is *OB* units of V_1 per week. Collusive efforts by sellers that alter the terms at which the monopsonist can obtain this element could now result in a higher price for the element without a decrease in the element's rate of employment.

For example, if the monopsonist is faced by the horizontal collusive supply curve S_c, he will employ a larger quantity of this element, even though the price of *OC* is higher than *OA*. His marginal factor cost is now *OC* for a large range of rates of input, and his equilibrium position is at point *K*. The potential for successful collusion thus appears to be greater here than in situations where markets for the elements of production are competitive. However, it is important to note that Figure 16.5 depicts

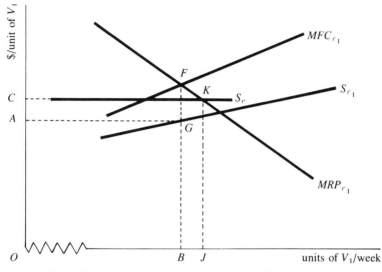

FIGURE 16.5 *Monopsony in the market for an element of production*

alternative situations for a given short period, with a given plant and a given demand curve for the firm's output. In subsequent periods of time the higher price for this element of production might foster greater substitution of other inputs for this particular input. The marginal revenue product curve for V_1 might thus lie to the left of the one depicted in Figure 16.5, and the demand for this element might be lower in future short periods. The monopsonist might also have more power than competing buyers to break up collusive efforts by sellers.

16.6 Oligopoly and oligopsony

The marginal productivity approach to the determination of the equilibrium price and rate of employment of an element of production is not generally applicable to industries characterized by oligopoly. An oligopolist firm does not have a demand curve for its product that can be defined without knowledge of the responses of rival firms to differences in its price (see Section 9.9). There is therefore no marginal revenue product curve in this case, even if the element's marginal physical product can be determined. The firm's short-period equilibrium rate of employment of a variable element of production cannot be determined by the intersection of marginal revenue product and marginal factor cost curves. It depends on the output the firm can sell at the set price for its product. The price for this element of production is reflected, along with the other constituents of standard unit costs, in the price the firm sets for its product.

The analysis of oligopolies in Chapter 14 emphasized the importance of barriers to entry and the target rates of return in the determination of prices in these industries. These barriers also protect the workers. If they are high enough to permit higher rates of return on investment over time, they may also make it possible for workers to obtain wage rates higher than those for comparable workers in competitive industries. The bargaining between firms and unions in industries with high barriers to entry can thus be viewed partly as a struggle over the higher returns permitted by the barriers to entry in these industries. The favourable position obtained by a group of workers in one of these industries may be eroded over time by technological changes and investment that affect their substitutability, or by changes that make their industry less profitable. (These changes can also occur, of course, in competitive industries.)

The supply curve for an element of production is indeterminate for an oligopsonist in the same way as the demand curve is indeterminate for an oligopolist. It depends partly on the responses of rival buyers. Therefore the cost of hiring additional units cannot be represented by a marginal factor cost curve that assumes all other things given. Even if the oligopsonist's demand curve for its output is known (e.g. if he is a monopolist), it would still not be possible to characterize his equilibrium rate of employment of this element of production by the marginal-revenue-product equals marginal-factor-cost condition. The equilibrium position would lie somewhere on the marginal revenue product curve, but there is no generally applicable analytic way of indicating the determination of this position. If the oligopsonist is an oligopolist, then the marginal revenue product curve also becomes indeterminate. Recognition of interdependence, bargaining, and collusion all have a potential role in the determination of the prices of the elements of production hired under oligopsonistic conditions.

16.7 The labour force
The supply of labour in a particular economy in a particular period of time depends on many socio-economic factors that affect (i) the size and age-composition of the population; (ii) the proportion of the population in the labour force; (iii) the time worked by individuals (i.e. the length of the working-day, working-week, and working-year), as well as the time span covered by a typical working life; and (iv) the efficiency and skill of the labour force. The size of the population and its rate of growth are not determined in any simple way by economic factors, and economists have become wary of predicting population changes. They were not always so reticent. A subsistence theory of wages, discussed in Ricardo's theory of distribution in Section 15.9, was based on the belief that population would

TABLE 16.1 *Percentage of the population 14 years of age and over in the labour force, Canada*

SURVEY WEEK	TOTAL	14-19	20-24	25-44	45-64	65+
Nov. 1946						
Male	84.9	60.2	88.5	96.8	93.2	46.3
Female	24.0	37.1	47.5	22.4	14.8	4.5
Nov. 1951						
Male	83.4	51.6	92.3	98.0	92.4	37.3
Female	23.1	32.2	45.5	22.6	17.3	4.2
Nov. 1957						
Male	81.7	44.3	89.9	97.8	92.3	34.5
Female	26.5	32.6	47.2	26.7	23.9	5.3
Nov. 1963						
Male	77.7	36.9	85.9	97.7	91.7	26.3
Female	30.5	29.4	51.2	32.1	31.4	6.3
Nov. 1967						
Male	76.5	34.7	81.9	97.1	91.3	23.9
Female	34.1	30.4	56.5	36.8	35.3	6.3
Nov. 1971						
Male	74.9	34.9	81.3	96.5	89.7	19.8
Female	36.9	29.1	60.6	42.8	36.9	4.9
Nov. 1972						
Male	74.7	35.9	81.1	96.6	88.7	18.3
Female	37.6	30.1	60.7	44.2	37.0	4.6
Nov. 1973						
Male	75.7	40.3	82.0	96.9	88.4	18.2
Female	38.9	33.1	62.5	45.9	37.5	4.3

SOURCE: For 1946, 1951 and 1957, *The Labour Force, Nov. 1945-July 1958,* D.B.S. Reference Paper No. 58 (Ottawa: Queen's Printer, 1958). For remaining years, *Historical Labour Force Statistics* (Ottawa: Statistics Canada, 71-201).

tend to grow if the wage rate was greater than the subsistence level. Malthus' *Essay on the Principle of Population* is the classic work on this approach. Its predictions about the future of mankind were pessimistic, with increasing population tending to eliminate increases in wage rates above the subsistence level.

The concept of a *labour force* is used to divide the population over a certain age (e.g. 14 years) into two groups. Those in the labour force are available for work in a particular period of time, while those in the other group are not. Unemployment can be measured as the difference between the total labour force and the level of total employment. It can therefore vary both with the size of the labour force and with total employment. In Canada, estimates of the labour force are obtained each month on the basis of a sample of 55,000 households. They are questioned about the employment, unemployment, and non-labour force activities of their members for a specific week each month. To be counted in the labour force as unemployed in a particular month, one has to be available for work and looking for work.

The proportion of males in the labour force in Canada has tended to fall over time and that of females to rise. These proportions have been affected by social attitudes, economic opportunities, and economic pressures (which also affect the overall size of the labour force). The labour-force participation rates of different age groups have also changed over time with changes in standards of living, educational opportunities, and pension arrangements, etc. The figures in Table 16.1 give some indication of how these rates have varied in Canada since 1946.

The length of the work-period has also varied over time, and it is a subject for bargaining between employers and unions. Economists have used indifference-curve analysis to try to indicate the individual's optimal choice of working time. (This approach will be outlined in the following section.)

The efficiency and skill of the workers in a particular economy depend on their health, work ethic, and training. The characteristics of the labour force can only be changed over time, since health and training can be affected only by the application of efforts and resources over a period of time (even though shortages in some areas may be alleviated by trained immigrants). The term *human capital* has been coined to emphasize the investment of time and resources in the development of individual skills.

16.8 The theory of individual choice and the supply of labour

If an individual is free to choose the length of his work period, his choice will be affected by his attitude to the type of work open to him, the wage rate for this work, his tastes for income and leisure, and his financial position if he does not work. Indifference curves, such as those drawn in Figure 16.6, can be used to illustrate the individual's optimal choice. The total number of hours in the week are represented by OG. Any point on the abscissa divides this total time into periods of leisure and work. For example, the point L_1 indicates OL_1 leisure-hours per week and L_1G working-hours. The individual is assumed to have a non-work-related income of $\$GH$ per week (e.g., interest income from bonds). His tastes for leisure and income are indicated by his indifference curves. His need for some minimum amount of leisure time is shown by the increasing steepness of the indifference curves when the amount of leisure becomes small. The indifference curves do not continue to the ordinate. Points indicating positions where there is less than the required minimum of leisure time do

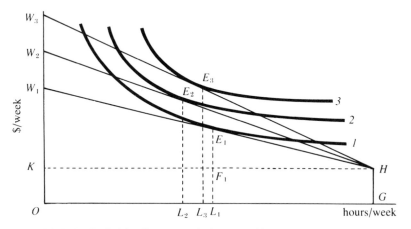

FIGURE 16.6 *An individual's optimal choices of leisure (or work) at different wage rates*

not represent viable situations and are therefore not ranked.

If the hourly wage rate for the individual's labour is equal to the numerical value for the slope of the line HW_1, his optimal position will be represented by point E_1.[4] He will choose to work L_1G hours per week for a weekly wage of $\$F_1E_1$ (his total income, taking into account his non-work income, is $\$L_1E_1$). Points E_2 and E_3 represent optimal positions for higher wage rates. With an hourly wage rate given by the numerical value of the slope of HW_2, the individual would choose to work more hours than at the lower wage rate given by the slope of HW_1. The difference in hours of work chosen when the wage rate differs can be analysed in terms of income and substitution effects (see Section 5.17).

The price of leisure in this analysis is equal to the wage rate. It is the opportunity cost of spending time at leisure rather than at work. The substitution effect of a higher wage rate thus tends to decrease the demand for leisure (that is, to increase the supply of labour). However, leisure is assumed to be a superior good; therefore the income effect of the higher wage rate will tend to increase the amount of leisure demanded. In this case the substitution effect outweighs the income effect; thus the higher wage rate leads to an increase in the supply of labour. This result will not always occur. For example, with a still higher wage rate (slope of HW_3), a smaller supply of labour would be forthcoming ($L_3G < L_2G$) because the income effect outweighs the substitution effect. For very low wage rates, when

---

[4] The distance OW_1 on the ordinate is equal to the non-labour income OK plus the product of the wage rate and the number of hours in a week (168), which is represented by OG in Figure 16.6.

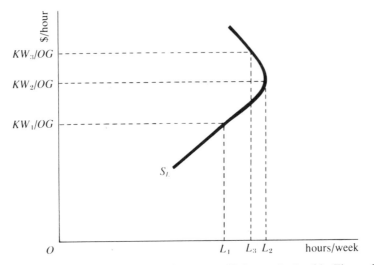

FIGURE 16.7 *An individual's supply curve of labour, derived in Figure 16.6*

hours of work are few, the income effect is very small. Thus the substitution effect is likely to be greater than the income effect. With more working hours the difference in income due to a higher wage rate is larger and the income effect *may* dominate the substitution effect.

The information contained in this indifference-curve diagram can be transcribed to a supply curve (drawn in Figure 16.7) showing the equilibrium relationships between different wage rates and the supply of labour time. This curve is *backward-bending*; the positive slope gives way to a negative slope for high wage rates because the income effect dominates the substitution effect.

This indifference-curve analysis can be extended to situations where the rate of pay for overtime differs from the rate paid during the standard work period. It can also examine the possible effects of welfare payments and negative-income-tax programs on work-leisure choices. Great care must be exercised when applying these theoretical analyses. Individual indifference curves are not known, and inferences based on observations of individual behaviour in different circumstances may be misleading because these observations may be dominated by non-economic factors.

Individuals are not generally free in modern industrial societies to choose the length of their working week, but their optimal choices may affect their actual working hours in various ways. Income-leisure preferences may affect individual responses to part-time or occasional employment or to overtime work. Absenteeism is a device that reduces the working time of those who prefer leisure even though it may result in lower income. Conversely, 'moonlighting'—the holding of a second job—permits those who prefer more income to cut down on the leisure time permitted by their primary employment.

16.9 The rate of interest

Interest is the payment for the lending of money. The borrower obtains the means to command the goods and resources that can be purchased or hired with this sum for the time-interval of the loan. Therefore interest can be seen as the payment for the transfer of command over goods and resources for an interval of time. This payment, for a particular time period (e.g. a year), is expressed as a proportion of the loan — that is, as a rate. The rate of interest is thus equal to the value of the interest payment for a time period divided by the value of the loan. This period of time is the only unit specified in the rate of interest; otherwise it is a pure number. For example, if a sum of $100 is borrowed for five years, with $12 interest to be paid each year, the rate of interest will be 0.12 per year. Alternatively, if interest payments of $1 each month are required on this loan, the rate of interest will be 0.01 per month.

There are many different rates of interest at one time in any particular economy. They differ for a single borrower according to the time periods of the loan. Short-term interest rates (the rates of interest on loans made for only short periods of time) differ from long-term interest rates. This difference is related to expectations of change in the rates of interest. If rates of interest are expected to rise in the future, lenders will prefer to purchase bonds that will mature in the near future rather than bonds with a longer term. Thus they avoid the capital losses suffered on long-term bonds when rates of interest increase (see Section 16.10). If these expectations are widespread, then short-term interest rates will be substantially lower than long-term rates. Expectations of lower interest rates in the future would decrease the spread between these rates and might even result in short-term rates being higher than long-term rates.

Interest rates may also differ for different borrowers: they are higher for loans where there is more doubt about eventual repayment. Differences in these interest rates reflect the risks as perceived by lenders. In the simple illustrations considered in the following sections it is assumed that there is only a single rate of interest and no risk in lending. Repayment on the terms specified at the time of the loan is assured.

A distinction can also be made between *money and real rates of interest*. If the price of goods has increased over the period of the loan, the command over goods represented by a given sum of money has decreased. The real rate of interest that is obtained by comparing the command over goods of the total repayment (principal plus interest) with that of the loan will be less than the money rate of interest, which is obtained by comparing the money repayment with the money loan. The real rate of interest is equal to the money rate of interest *minus* the rate of increase in prices. For example, if the money rate of interest is 10 per cent for a one-year loan and the rate of increase in prices is 6 per cent, the real rate of interest is equal to 4 per cent. Real rates of interest, which can be calculated only after the period of the loan, may turn out to be negative when prices increase sharply and unexpectedly.

A full treatment of the factors determining the rate of interest will not be attempted here. This would involve the introduction of macroeconomic analysis and a detailed consideration of markets for money and financial assets. While the rate of interest is taken as given in our examples, its effects on some types of decisions are considered.

16.10 Present values and capitalization

The rate of interest at which an individual can borrow or lend (at no risk) determines the present value of sums of money he can obtain in the future. If the annual rate of interest is r, then $1 in the present is equivalent to $(1 + r)$ next year. By lending $1 for a year, this individual will receive an interest payment of r plus repayment of the dollar loan. Alternatively it can be said that the present value of $(1 + r)$ next year is $1, since borrowing $1 now for one year will result in repayment plus interest of $(1 + r)$ next year. More generally, a sum of money, C, next year has a present value of $C/(1 + r)$.

This approach can be extended to any future time period. $1 invested for two years at an annual interest rate of r with an annual compounding of interest would provide, two years from now, a sum of

$$(1 + r) + r(1 + r) = (1 + r)^2$$

Interest is paid not only on the original dollar invested but also on the interest that has accrued on the loan after one year. Thus the present value of C in two years time is $C/(1 + r)^2$. More generally, the present value of C, n years from now, when interest is compounded annually, is equal to $C/(1 + r)^n$.

The rate of interest can also be used to *capitalize* a stream of income over time. For example, let Y_i be the income expected in year i, where $i = 1, 2, \ldots n$. Then the present value of this income stream, V, is given by

$$V = Y_1/(1 + r) + Y_2/(1 + r)^2 + \ldots \ldots + Y_n/(1 + r)^n$$

This income stream thus has a capital value of V. If it were unchanged but the rate of interest were higher, then its capital value would be lower, as can be readily deduced from this equation. The present value of an income stream that provides equal amounts (Y) annually for an indefinitely long period of time (an income in perpetuity) can be expressed very simply, using the formula for the sum of a geometrical progression:

$$V = \sum_{i=1}^{\infty} Y/(1+r)^i$$
$$= Y/(1+r)[1 + 1/(1+r) + 1/(1+r)^2 + \ldots]$$
$$= [Y/(1+r)][(1+r)/r]$$
$$\therefore \ V = Y/r$$

Bonds are loan instruments that specify the dollar amounts of interest payments during each year of the loan. An increase in the rate of interest will thus lower the market values of outstanding bonds, since it reduces the present value of these interest payments. Conversely, a decrease in the rate of interest will increase their present values. The longer the term of the bond, the proportionately greater are these effects on its value. For example, consider two bonds, each of which promises an annual payment of $10 and a repayment at termination of $100. One bond has two more years to run while the other has four years. If the rate of interest is 5 per cent, then the value of the two-year bond is approximately $109.30, while the value of the four-year bond is $117.73. With a market-rate of interest of 8 per cent, their respective values would be $103.57 and $106.65. The decrease in market value of the two-year bond is approximately 5 per cent, while the decrease in value of the four-year bond is approximately 9 per cent.

This process of capitalization can affect all assets. Expected incomes from assets are reflected in their values, and changes in these expected incomes as well as in interest rates will change these values. For example, different property tax rates in two areas with houses that are otherwise comparable would result in lower values for houses in the area with the higher tax rates, all other things given.

This process of capitalization is very pervasive in modern economies. For example, it is an important element in cost-benefit analyses (see Section 6.12). Both costs and benefits are experienced over a series of time periods, and their conversion to present values is necessary so that they can be compared. Their time patterns usually differ, with the bulk of costs generally being incurred before the bulk of benefits is available. Thus the estimates of the cost-benefit ratios depend critically on the rates of interest employed to calculate present values. The higher the interest rate, the smaller the present value of benefits relative to the present value of costs.

16.11 Saving and the rate of time preference

Individuals may choose not to exercise all their present command over goods and services. They may transfer this command for their own use (or for the use of their heirs) into the future. This transfer may be accomplished by preserving the purchasing power represented by the assets inherited from the past, and by current *saving*. For an individual, net saving in a particular period is the difference between his net income and consumption in that period. The factors determining private saving are very complex; but indifference-curve analysis can be used to indicate the effect of interest rates on individual saving. Firms also save; their savings (or retained earnings) are the differences between net incomes (after taxes) and payments of dividends to shareholders. For the average firm these savings finance a major proportion of investment expenditures. The savings of an individual or a firm can be negative in any period.

Individuals save for a variety of reasons. An important motive is concern with financial security, the provision of reserves in case of loss of a job or ill-health, and for old age and retirement. Much of this type of saving is contractual and carried out through employer pension plans and various kinds of insurance. An individual's saving may vary over his life; it is often discussed in terms of a life-cycle pattern. This displays negative saving in an individual's early working life when income is relatively low, educational expenses are high, and a household is being established. The debts are then repaid in middle life and savings begin to be accumulated to provide for old age, and possibly to build an estate. Much of this saving is therefore independent of the rate of interest, though this can still influence the total amount saved since it gives the terms at which funds can be transferred from one period to another.

The effect on an individual's saving of a difference in the rate of interest is illustrated in Figure 16.8. The indifference curves are drawn on the assumption of given tastes and given prices in the two periods. The saving is assumed to be affected only by the individual's preferences for the command over goods and his income in these two periods.[5] At the beginning of period 1 he has no assets and his income is expected to be the same in both periods (*OB* is equal to *OA*). In the absence of saving (or dissaving) he would be at point *H*. The rate of interest at which he can lend or borrow is represented in the diagram by the numerical value of the slope of the line *GK* minus one. By lending or borrowing at this rate of interest he can choose the point on the line *GK* that represents the combination of con-

---

[5] This assumption permits geometrical presentation of the analysis, but algebraic formulation makes possible its extension to more than two periods.

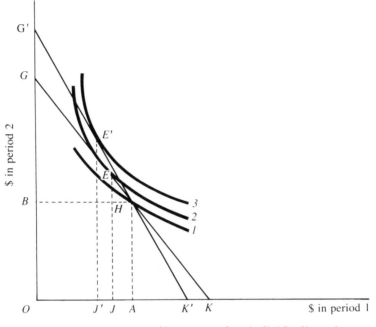

FIGURE 16.8 *The rate of interest and an individual's saving*

sumption in the two periods he prefers. His equilibrium position is at point
E; and his saving in period 1 would be *$JA*. His expenditure on con-
sumption goods is *$OJ* in period 1, and *$JE* in period 2. With a higher rate
of interest, indicated by the opportunity line *G'K'*, he would be in
equilibrium at point *E'*. In this case he would save more (*J'A>JA*). This
might not always be the case. If the substitution effect of the higher rate
were greater than the income effect, his saving would be increased when the
interest rate was higher. Saving would be decreased if the substitution effect
of the higher rate of interest (making current consumption more expensive
relative to future consumption) were outweighed by the income effect (the
individual's real income is raised by the higher rate of interest).[6]

The term *rate of time preference* is used in discussions of individuals'
saving decisions.[7] A positive rate of time preference means that an individual prefers one unit of present utility to one unit of utility tomorrow.
This method of defining time preference assumes a cardinal utility function
and is not operational unless the units of utility can be measured, and the

---

[6] Consumption in the current period is assumed to be a superior good.
[7] This term is associated with Eugen von Böhm-Bawerk, *Positive Theory of Capital* (London:
Macmillan & Co., 1891).

individual's choices observed. However, his choices can be expressed in terms of his indifference curves between purchasing power today and purchasing power tomorrow. The slopes of these indifference curves show his intertemporal rate of substitution—the purchasing power he is just prepared to relinquish tomorrow in order to obtain an extra unit of purchasing power today. The greater his rate of time preference, the larger the amount of purchasing power, other things given, he would be prepared to relinquish tomorrow in order to obtain an extra unit of purchasing power today. An individual's intertemporal rate of substitution can therefore be used to indicate his rate of time preference when his circumstances are the same in both periods.

An individual is said to have a positive rate of time preference if he values a dollar in the current period more highly than one in the succeeding period, even though he expects (with complete certainty) that his circumstances (tastes, prices of goods, and money available for spending) will be the same in each period. His time preference would be reflected in the slopes of his indifference curves. For example, if the slope of the indifference curve at point H (where his consumption is the same in both periods) has a numerical value of unity, the individual has no time preference. If its slope is numerically greater than unity, he has a positive rate of time preference. This means that at a zero rate of interest he would choose to dissave. Conversely, with a negative rate of time preference, the numerical value of the slope of his indifference curve at point H would be less than one, and at a zero rate of interest he would choose to save.

16.12 Economic rent

Rent was introduced in Section 15.5 as the payment for the ownership of land. This land would be available *to the economy* for production purposes even if nothing were paid for it. A payment can be exacted for its use, however, because land is owned and it is scarce relative to the demands for it at a zero price. Rent can thus be viewed as a surplus, in the sense that its payment is not necessary for the existence of the land or for its productive ability in its natural state. Surpluses of this type also appear in many other transactions and can be described by the general term economic rent.[8]

---

[8] 'The essence of the conception of *rent* is the conception of a surplus earned by a particular part of a factor of production over and above the minimum earnings necessary to induce it to do its work . . . in each of the broad categories of factors, particular pieces of factors may be found which earn rent.' Joan Robinson, *The Economics of Imperfect Competition* (London: Macmillan & Co., 1933), pp. 102-3.

Economic rent is the advantage an individual obtains by making a transaction. An advantage is gained when the terms of the trade are more favourable than those that would leave him indifferent about whether or not the trade was made.

If the supply curve of an element of production has some degree of inelasticity, part of the payment for it may be rent to those supplying it (for example, the wrist-twisters in Section 11.8, or the more efficient entrepreneurs in Section 11.9). Economic rent is not restricted to the supply side of the market; all participants in a transaction will usually obtain some economic rent. This was the case in the bilateral exchanges examined in Chapter 6. Consumer's surplus, which was presented in Section 6.12, is the term used to denote the economic rent obtained by a consumer from the purchase of a commodity.

Economic rent is not only very pervasive; it may also be difficult to pin down. Although it is a surplus, it may appear as a necessary payment to the individual on the other side of the transaction. This feature of economic rent can be illustrated by considering the payment for an element of production from different standpoints. From the point of view of the economy as a whole, rent is the part of any payment for an element that exceeds the amount required to keep that element in existence and available for production. From the point of view of the industry hiring a particular element, economic rent is the difference between what is paid for this element of production and the minimum amount it would be necessary to pay in order to ensure its employment in that industry. The term *transfer earnings* or *transfer price*[9] is used to describe the payment an industry must make to attract this element away from its alternative employment opportunities. These different views of economic rent are illustrated in Figure 16.9.

Figure 16.9 can provide the framework for a numerical example. Assume that the price for the element of production in this figure is $10,000 per year. This is the payment a firm must make if it is to hire a unit of that element. (In terms of Figure 16.9, A + B + C = $10,000.) If, in the industry that provides its next most profitable employment, this element could earn $8,000 a year, economic rent from the hiring industry's viewpoint would be $2,000. (Here A in Figure 16.9 would thus be equal to $2,000.) This means that if all firms in this industry acted together when hiring as though they were a monopsonist (and the owners of this element were not organized), then they could obtain this element for very little more than $8,000 per year. If $7,000 per year is the amount required to ensure

---

[9] *Ibid.*, p. 104.

The amount the hiring firm must pay to obtain this element (A + B + C)	A	Necessary payment for firm (A + B + C) rent from industry's point of view (A)
The price required to bid the element away from the next best paid employment (B + C) (transfer earnings)	B	Necessary payment for industry (B + C) rent from economy's point of view (A + B)
The amount required to make the element available for productive activity in the economy (C)	C	Necessary payment for economy (C)

FIGURE 16.9 *Necessary payments to a particular element of production and economic rent, as viewed by different segments of the economy*

that this element of production is available for production in the economy, then the rent from the economy's point of view is equal to $3,000. (In terms of Figure 16.9, we thus have A = $2,000, B = $1,000, and C = $7,000.)

The nature and degree of competition in an industry, as well as the demand for its product, will affect the magnitude of the rent from the industry's point of view. Agreements among firms to limit their rivalry in at least some aspects of the hiring of elements of production serve to keep down the prices of these elements. For example, in sports industries these agreements (reserve clauses, draft arrangements, etc.) are very important. There have been substantial increases in the payments to leading players in professional sports because of changes in both demand and the control over players by existing firms. The televising of events has increased potential revenues, while the emergence of rival leagues and the rise of players' associations have improved the bargaining positions of players.

16.13 Economic profit

Profit is a term that has been given a variety of meanings in economic theory. For classical economists, profit was the term used to describe the income of the capitalist class, and along with wages and rent it was one of the major categories of income. Neoclassical economic theorists have developed their models without reference to classes, and profit has become a less inclusive term. It has often been argued, especially by American economists, that there would be no profit in competitive long-period equilibrium because of the restrictive meaning they give to this term.[10]

A firm's profit in a particular year may be defined, according to accounting conventions, as the difference between its revenue in the year and all contractual costs *plus* depreciation in that year. These contractual costs include wages and salaries, rent, purchases of material from other firms, insurance, interest on bank loans and bonds, and costs of licenses, etc. Depreciation here includes not only the wear and tear on equipment during the year but also amortization allowances. These allowances are the funds that must be set aside to enable the firm to recover the cost of its plant and equipment over their expected economic lives. It is clear from this definition that a firm's accounting profit depends, other things being given, on the proportion of borrowed funds relative to those provided by the owners and on the way in which amortization allowances are calculated.

Economic profit is obtained by subtracting the implicit costs of the firm from accounting profit. These implicit costs can include interest, rent, and wage costs. Interest is not paid by the firm on the money capital provided by its owners; that is, the dividends paid out of accounting profits are not contractual costs. But there is an implicit cost for the use of these funds in the firms, since they could have earned interest if they were used, say, to purchase corporate bonds. Interest on these bonds, if they were considered to be the next best alternative for these funds, would be the *opportunity cost* to the owners of investing them in the firm. The firm might also own property that could be rented if not in use; thus part of its accounting profit would include an implicit rent. Implicit wages might also appear in accounting profits for firms managed by owners if they paid themselves salaries that were less than those they could earn elsewhere.

A large accounting profit can thus be turned into a much smaller economic profit. The amount remaining can be further reduced by introducing the economic rent obtained by entrepreneurs of superior ability (see Section 11.9). Instead of leading to differences in profit, differences in entrepreneurial ability can be said to result in differences in economic rent.

Monopoly profits can be earned when a firm has control over a market that is protected from entry. In such a situation a firm can have revenues

---

[10] 'In the United States . . . it is the common practise among economists to use the expression pure profit and make it refer to the income of the business after deduction of wages and rent or interest at competitive rates for all the human and property services employed in the enterprise, including both those actually paid for in the market and a wage or interest or rent for the services furnished by the owner himself. . . . followed through to its logical end . . . the owner as such would have no functions and receive no income.' Frank H. Knight, 'Profit', in *Encyclopaedia of the Social Sciences*, ed. by William Fellner and Bernard F. Haley (1934, Vol. XII), reprinted in The American Economic Association, *Readings in the Theory of Income Distribution* (Philadelphia: Blakiston, 1951), p. 537.

exceed costs even when the latter include some normal rate of return on investment. If this situation is expected to continue, however, the monopoly profits will tend to disappear from view as a result of their capitalization. For example, assume that a firm has a monopoly of a particular commodity and is sufficiently protected from potential competitors to enable it to earn a high rate of return on its original investment. Assume that its initial investment was $10,000,000 and that its annual (accounting) profit is $4,000,000. Its owners, and others who are knowledgeable about its activities, expect it to be able to earn profits of this magnitude in the future as well. Assume that potential investors regard 20% as an appropriate return on investments with the degree of risk attached to this activity. The market value of this firm will therefore be the capitalized value of a continuing stream of income of $4,000,000 per annum with a rate of discount of 20 per cent. This value is $20,000,000 (see Section 16.10). If the firm is sold for this amount, the new purchasers will earn the normal rate of return of 20 per cent and the monopoly profits will have disappeared.[11]

The capitalization of expected monopoly profits in this way has long been one of the attractions to promoters of mergers. A striking case in point is the creation of the United States Steel Corporation, which was led by J.P. Morgan. It was estimated by the United States Commissioner of Corporations that the value of the properties taken over by the Steel Corporation was in the neighbourhood of 700 million dollars, but the value of the bonds and stocks issued at the time the Company was founded was 1,400 million dollars.[12] These stocks found a market because of the expectations that the new firm, as a result of more efficient operation of the properties and the suppression of competition, could earn a reasonable return on this new capitalization. This return was subsequently expressed as a proportion of the increased value, and the monopoly profits due to the elimination of competition disappeared from view. They were transformed into the capital gains of the previous owners of the steel properties and the fees paid to the promoters of the merger.

---

[11] The original owners of the firm would have received a capital gain as a result of the revaluation of their assets. It has been argued by Harry Johnson that ' . . . the essence of the economic nature of profits [is] not an income flow but a capital gain associated with the exploitation of the possibilities of dynamic change in the economy.' Harry G. Johnson, *The Theory of Income Distribution* (London: Gray-Mills Publishing Ltd., 1973), p. 27.

[12] Reported in Frederick Lewis Allen, *The Lords of Creation* (New York: Harper Brothers, 1935), p. 301.

16.14 Summary

This chapter has touched on various topics in the theory of distribution. The use of a neoclassical production function to derive the demand curve for an element of production (input) has been illustrated. The concept of the labour force was introduced and some of the factors affecting the supply of labour were considered. Economic rent and interest were defined and the use of rates of interest to capitalize expected future incomes was explained. This capitalization can transform monopoly profits into what appear to be no more than competitive returns.

SUGGESTED READINGS

Buchanan, D.H. 'The Historical Approach to Rent and Price Theory', *Economica* (1929). Reprinted in The American Economic Association, *Readings in the Theory of Income Distribution*. Philadelphia: Blakiston, 1951. Pages 599-637.

Chamberlin, E.H. *The Theory of Monopolistic Competition*. 6th ed. Cambridge, Mass.: Harvard University Press, 1948. Chapter VIII.

Knight, Frank H. 'Profit', *Encyclopaedia of the Social Sciences*, 1934. Vol. XII. Reprinted in The American Economic Association, *Readings in the Theory of Income Distribution*. Philadelphia: Blakiston, 1951.

Robinson, Joan. *The Economics of Imperfect Competition*. London: Macmillan & Co., 1933. Chapter 8.

EXERCISES

1. Assume that an individual can choose the length of his average working day to suit himself.

(i) Derive the individual's supply curve of labour when his only source of income is the supply of his labour services. Distinguish between income and substitution effects.

(ii) Derive the individual's supply curve of labour if he also receives some unearned income (say $a per day).

2. Using indifference curves, show that an individual may save less at a higher rate of interest. What is the reason for this?

17

GENERAL EQUILIBRIUM

17.1 Introduction

The analytic methods described and developed in this book are examples of partial equilibrium analysis. The determination of price and output of a particular commodity has been examined under the assumption that the prices of all other commodities were given, and that they would not be affected by the price established for the commodity under examination. This analysis is useful for pedagogical purposes because it can be represented graphically; but it could also be viewed as the first step, the first approximation, to a more general approach. In the consideration of the effects of a tax on a particular commodity, or when determining the effects of governmental action to raise the price of some agricultural commodity, the partial and incomplete nature of the analysis was emphasized. The general interdependence of prices in the economic system has been acknowledged in this book, but it has not been investigated in any detail. The partial equilibrium analysis outlined here has concentrated on the determination of prices and quantities of *individual* commodities. A general equilibrium theory, however, is one that explains simultaneously the prices and quantities exchanged of *all* commodities.

17.2 Partial equilibrium as a special case of general equilibrium

There is no difference between partial and general equilibrium analysis where there are only two commodities in a pure exchange economy. In such a model there is only one price: the rate at which one commodity trades for another. If there is equilibrium in the market for one commodity at a

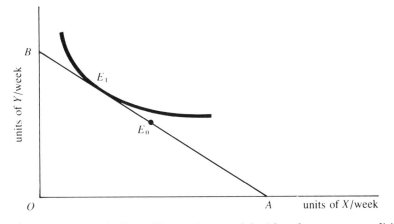

FIGURE 17.1 *Individual equilibrium in a model with only two commodities*

particular price, there must be equilibrium in the market for the other commodity. For example, if a typical individual has some initial endowment of the two commodities (*X* and *Y*),represented by point E_o in Figure 17.1, his budget line goes through this point and has a slope given by the price ratio between the two commodities. If this price ratio is an equilibrium price, as in Figure 17.1, the individual will be at E_1, where the budget line is tangent to an indifference curve. He will sell some of his endowment of *X* for some of *Y*; his net or excess demand for *X* will be negative, while his excess demand for *Y* will be positive. If the price of *X* in terms of *Y*, given by the numerical value of the slope of the line *BA*, is an equilibrium price, the sum for all individuals of their excess demands for *X* must be zero. Equilibrium for *X*, however, also implies equilibrium for *Y*, since the excess demand for *X* in a model with only *X* and *Y* is in effect the negative of the excess demand for *Y*. (This relation will be introduced more formally in Section 17.3 as Walras' Law.)

In multi-commodity models, the conclusions derived from partial and general equilibrium analyses might differ significantly. However, there is a special case of a pure exchange economy with many commodities where partial equilibrium analysis is equivalent to general equilibrium analysis. This is encountered when money is used to represent all other goods on indifference curve diagrams. The relative prices of all other commodities are assumed to be constant, and they can be lumped together as a composite commodity. The prices of these commodities are denoted by $p_2, \ldots p_m$, with $p_i = k\overline{p_i}$, $i = 2, \ldots m$, where $\overline{p_i}$ is constant for each *i*, but *k* may take different values to represent different price levels. Relative prices are then constant, since $p_i/p_j = \overline{p_i}/\overline{p_j}$. In this case, the quantity of the composite

commodity can be indicated by total expenditure on its elements divided by
k. Thus the quantity would be:

$$\sum_{i=2}^{m} \overline{p_i} q_i$$

and its price would be k.

If changes in demand and supply for a commodity do not affect the
relative prices of the remaining $m-1$ commodities, we treat this model as
one composed of only two commodities (commodity 1 and the composite
commodity) and partial equilibrium analysis gives the same result as general
equilibrium analysis. The assumption of strict constancy of relative prices
of the other commodities will not usually be appropriate. But if it holds
approximately in some cases that are of practical interest, there is scope for
the application of partial equilibrium analysis,[1] the appropriateness of
which depends on the answer to an empirical question: Do changes in the
relative prices of other commodities, induced by a change in the price of the
commodity being studied, result in a significant shift in supply or demand
conditions on the market for that commodity?

17.3 Walras and general equilibrium analysis

The full recognition of the general equilibrium concept is due to Léon
Walras, whose classic work *Eléments d'économie politique pure*, was
published in 1874.[2] The fundamental question posed by Walras was whether
the independent self-seeking actions of individuals in the economy are
consistent with the achievement of a state of equilibrium. This concerns the
notion of determinateness of the economic system, which is represented by
a set of equations that describe the desires of market participants and the
constraints on their behaviour. Are there enough equations to determine
equilibrium values for all the variables in the system? Equilibrium values
are those that economic agents consider to be the best ones attainable under
the circumstances. Walras examined this problem in various models. In one
there was no production, only exchange; goods were assumed to be given to
the individuals at the beginning of the period according to some rule of
distribution, and the individuals traded among themselves to achieve a
better allocation of these given goods. In other models production of goods
by firms was introduced. In the first edition of Walras's book he assumed

---

[1] Cf. K.J. Arrow and F.H. Hahn, *General Competitive Analysis* (San Francisco: Holden-Day,
1971), pp. 6-8.
[2] Léon Walras, *Elements of Pure Economics*, trans. by William Jaffé (Homewood, Ill.:
Richard D. Irwin, 1954).

that production was carried out under fixed coefficients, but in later editions this restriction was dropped and he allowed for alternative methods of production. All markets in these models were assumed to be perfectly competitive. We shall look at a simple exchange model.

It follows from the assumption of perfectly competitive markets that there are large numbers of individuals trading in each good. Attention is focused on equilibrium values; thus it is assumed that no trade takes place until all markets are in equilibrium. The analysis presented here does not consider the question of how an equilibrium position will be reached, or even whether it can ever be reached.[3] This analysis is concerned solely with the question of whether there are enough relations to determine a set of equilibrium values. At the beginning of our time period (say, a week), individuals have an assortment of endowments of goods and they trade to obtain a more preferred mix of these goods, which they then consume during the week. 'Time' enters into this model only in a formal sense, through this concept of a basic time period (the week). The actual process of trading, the finding of equilibrium prices, is assumed to take no time.

If there are m commodities and n individuals (with m and n being very large), the number of unknowns in the system will be equal to $mn + m-1$. There are mn equilibrium quantities to be determined, since there are m equilibrium holdings of commodities (one for each good) for each individual, and n individuals. There are also $m-1$ (relative) prices to be determined. One of the goods—say, the mth—can be taken as a *numéraire*, with the price of any other good being expressed in terms of the units of good m that can be obtained in exchange for one unit of this other good. The price of the numéraire-good is by definition equal to *one*.

To determine these unknowns there are excess demand- and market-clearing equations. Let the initial endowment for the jth individual of the ith commodity be denoted by $\overline{x}_{ij}$ and his equilibrium holding by x_{ij}; $i = 1, 2, \ldots m; j = 1, 2, \ldots n$. This individual's net or excess demand for the ith good can be written as:

$$x_{ij} - \overline{x}_{ij} = f_{ij}(p_1, p_2, \ldots, p_{m-1}; \ \overline{x}_{1j}, \overline{x}_{2j}, \ldots, \overline{x}_{mj}) \qquad (1)$$

where p_i is the (unknown) equilibrium price (in terms of the numéraire-good) of the ith good. If this excess demand is positive, the individual is a

---

[3] Walras discussed the stability of equilibrium. He argued that 'If the demand for any one commodity is greater than the offer, the price of that commodity . . . will rise; if the offer is greater than the demand, the price will fall. . . . the upward and downward movements of prices solve the system of equations of offer and demand by a process of groping ["par tâtonnement"].' *Ibid.*, p. 170.

buyer of this good; if it is negative, he is a seller. There are mn excess demand equations of this type.

A market-clearing, or equilibrium, equation for each good states that at the equilibrium prices the total for all individuals of the excess demands for that good is equal to zero. This condition for the ith good can be written in our notation as:

$$\sum_{j=1}^{n} (x_{ij} - \overline{x}_{ij}) = 0; i = 1, 2, \ldots m \qquad (2)$$

Although there are m equations of this form, only $m-1$ are independent. If these equations hold for $m-1$ of the goods, then the corresponding equation must hold for the remaining good. This feature of a set of market-clearing equations is known as *Walras' Law* and it holds because of the budget constraints on the market behaviour of each individual. They ensure that if market excess demands are equal to zero (that is, if market demands are equal to market supplies) for all but one of the goods, they must be equal for the remaining good. An individual's budget constraint can be written as:

$$\sum_{i=1}^{m} p_i (x_{ij} - \overline{x}_{ij}) = 0; j = 1, 2, \ldots n \qquad (3)$$

Summing these constraints over all individuals, we have:

$$\sum_{j=1}^{n} \sum_{i=1}^{m} p_i (x_{ij} - \overline{x}_{ij}) = 0 \qquad (4)$$

If it is assumed that the market-clearing equations of type 2 hold for $m-1$ goods—say the first $m-1$ goods—then it is convenient to re-write the equation 4 as:

$$\sum_{j=1}^{n} \sum_{i=1}^{m-1} p_i (x_{ij} - \overline{x}_{ij}) + \sum_{j=1}^{n} (x_{mj} - \overline{x}_{mj}) = 0 \qquad (5)$$

(Recall that the mth good was chosen as the numéraire for the system and thus $P_m \equiv 1$.) Reversal of the order of summation does not affect the result. Therefore this equation can also be written as:

$$\sum_{i=1}^{m-1} p_i \sum_{j=1}^{n} (x_{ij} - \overline{x}_{ij}) + \sum_{j=1}^{n} (x_{mj} - \overline{x}_{mj}) = 0 \qquad (6)$$

From our assumption of zero excess demands in the markets for the first $m-1$ goods, we know that the first term on the left-hand side of equation 6 must be equal to zero. Therefore the second term must also be equal to zero. Q.E.D.[4]

Thus in this simple economic system there is the same number of independent equations ($mn + m - 1$) as there are unknowns.

17.4 Existence and stability of equilibrium

Having a number of equations equal to the number of unknowns is a necessary, but not a sufficient, condition for the existence of equilibrium. Beginning in the 1930s, mathematicians and economists have analysed the conditions for the existence of equilibrium in perfectly competitive models.[5] They have also been concerned with both the stability of competitive equilibrium and the comparative statics of the system. The latter is concerned, as we noted in Chapter 4, with the comparison of equilibrium values that differ because of a difference in the fundamental conditions of the system—e.g. in tastes, technology, resources, etc. The former deals with the question of whether any displacement from equilibrium will set in motion forces that restore equilibrium.

Arrow and Hahn, in their review of recent work in general equilibrium analysis, have presented proofs of the existence of equilibrium for perfectly competitive systems. However, they point out that these equilibrium values may not be unique unless very restrictive assumptions are made. As there may be more than one set of values that satisfy the equations of the system, comparative statics (which compares an initial set of equilibrium values with the new equilibrium set corresponding to a new value for one of the parameters—see Section 4.2) will not provide the required single comparison. In addition, no one has yet proved that equilibrium would be stable in a multi-commodity economic system with production.[6]

---

[4] Careful readers will note that this conclusion does not depend on the mth good's being the numéraire.

[5] For a brief review of these efforts, see Arrow and Hahn, *General Competitive Analysis*, Chapter 1.

[6] The comments made by Arrow and Hahn on these questions include: 'Probably the most appealing of the possible postulates leading to uniqueness is Diagonal Dominance. This condition, if fulfilled in fact, would give a general equilibrium system a kind of Marshallian flavor, inasmuch as the properties of the demand and supply curves in the plane of the price of the good in question and the quantity supplied or demanded are in some sense the 'dominating' properties. It means that partial analysis may not make serious mistakes . . . (*Ibid.*, p. 242) . . . The most notable conclusion of our investigations in this chapter appears to us to be that for very many interesting problems of comparing equilibria, the information provided by the foundations of the models, profit and utility maximization, are insufficient in giving us definite answers to our questions . . . (*Ibid.*, p. 261). We should not be surprised if we find [in a model that includes consumption and production] that stability may become problematical.' (*Ibid.*, p. 346).

General equilibrium models can handle a very large number of variables, and even deal with them rather compactly in matrix notation: the same good in two different periods is treated as two goods. Along with spot markets, there are futures markets for goods and services that are to be delivered in future time periods. However, in trying to imagine a real-world equivalent to these general equilibrium models, we find that these futures markets pose a problem. They exist for some commodities but not for others; in particular they do not, and cannot, given the absence of slavery, exist for labour services.

Examinations of large general equilibrium models are necessarily very formal and are concerned with such things as the existence of equilibrium. Applications of general equilibrium analysis—the derivation of comparative statics results—are found in relatively simple models where the number of goods, elements of production, etc., are small. For purposes of illustration, we shall look at the pure theory of international trade, an area where some form of general equilibrium analysis has always been applied.

17.5 David Ricardo and comparative costs

Ricardo's development of the theory of international trade assumed that the ratio of the equilibrium prices of two goods depended only on the relative quantities of labour required to produce these goods. This approach offers a valid explanation of relative prices in equilibrium in the very special case where the ratio to labour of the value of the produced means of production (capital goods) is the same for all goods. Ricardo's international trade model considered two countries, England and Portugal, with each country capable of producing two goods, cloth and wine. The ratios of labour to the value of the means of production for these two goods were the same in each country, but the values for this common ratio might differ. If it is assumed that there are constant returns to scale in the production of each good, the relevant production functions can be summarized by four labour-input coefficients. The coefficients used by Ricardo[7] are shown in Table 17.1.

TABLE 17.1 *Direct labour-times (man-years) required to produce units of cloth and wine in England and Portugal*

Country	GOOD	
	Cloth	*Wine*
England	100	120
Portugal	90	80

[7] Piero Sraffa, ed., *The Works and Correspondence of David Ricardo* (Cambridge, Eng.: Cambridge University Press, 1951), Vol. I, p. 135.

In the absence of international trade, the price of cloth in terms of wine in England would equal the ratio of labour required to produce a unit of cloth and a unit of wine respectively. It would therefore be equal to 10/12. The comparable price ratio in Portugal would be 9/8. The lower price of cloth in terms of wine in England compared with Portugal is a reflection of England's *comparative advantage* in the production of cloth. (Alternatively it can be taken as a reflection of Portugal's comparative advantage in the production of wine.) If the costs of transporting cloth and wine between these two countries are not large enough to eliminate the differences in comparative production costs, it can readily be shown that an equilibrium position *with* trade is better for both countries than one without trade.

To demonstrate the potential for gain to both countries from international trade, we abstract from transportation costs. If the terms at which England could trade cloth with Portugal for wine were more favourable than the terms at which it could domestically 'transform' cloth into wine—by transferring labour (and other means of production) from the production of wine to that of cloth—then it would gain from trade. It would thus be advantageous for England to obtain wine from Portugal, instead of producing it, if the cost of wine through trade were less than 12/10ths or 6/5ths of a unit of cloth. On the other hand, trade would be advantageous for Portugal if it could obtain anything more than 8/9ths of a unit of cloth for each unit of wine. Thus there would be scope for both countries to gain from trade because their differences in comparative costs had resulted in different 'no gain' price ratios. For example, if one unit of cloth traded for one unit of wine, then both countries would gain.[8] At these terms England, with the expenditure of 100 units of labour (and a proportionate amount of other means of production), could obtain through trade a unit of wine that in the absence of trade would require 120 units of labour (plus a proportionate amount of other means of production). Similarly, Portugal would obtain a unit of cloth for the expenditure of 80 units of labour instead of the 90 it would require in the absence of trade.

This analysis has indicated the potential for gain from international trade when there is a difference in the comparative costs of producing goods in two countries, and it has shown the direction of trade, but it has not determined the terms of trade. (The terms of trade of one unit of cloth for one unit of wine were used as an example.) The equilibrium terms of trade can be determined only if demand considerations are introduced.

---

[8] This is a comparative statics exercise with two equilibrium positions being compared. No dynamic causal story is being told of the emergence of trade or of the losses to individuals in each country whose markets are taken over by imports.

17.6 Reciprocal demand and the terms of trade

The term *reciprocal demand*, introduced by John Stuart Mill to explain the determination of the equilibrium terms of trade,[9] is used to indicate a country's demand for one good in terms of the amounts of the other good it is prepared to give up in exchange. The greater a country's demand for the imported good relative to its demand for the good it exports, the less favourable will be its equilibrium terms of trade, other things being equal. To illustrate the role of reciprocal demand in the determination of the terms of trade, we shall make use of *community indifference curves*. Let us assume here that these curves are well behaved and follow all the rules for individual indifference curves described in Chapter 5. For these rules to hold, it is necessary that either all individuals in each country have identical tastes, with the pattern of demand being unaffected by redistribution of income, or the distribution of income among them is the same in all the situations compared. These are very special conditions and should not be ignored if applications of this analysis are considered.

In panel A of Figure 17.2 the two goods are X_1 and X_2 and the community indifference curves for country A are negatively sloped and convex to the origin. Also drawn in this section is A's *production-possibility curve*. This shows the maximum amount the country can produce of one good, given its resources and technical knowledge, when the amount of the other good being produced is specified. This curve, $L_A M_A$, is linear in this figure because we are making Ricardo's assumption that labour is the only primary factor of production and that the ratio of labour to the value of the means of production is the same for the two goods. The community indifference curves and the production-possibility curve for country B are shown in panel B of Figure 17.2. Country A has a comparative advantage in the production of good X_1 and B in the production of good X_2.

A country is said to be in equilibrium if, given the price ratio, it employs all its resources in producing the combination of the two goods that allows it to reach the highest indifference curve. In the absence of international trade, the price ratio in each country is equal to the slope of its production-possibility curve. The equilibrium combination of the two goods is therefore determined by the point of tangency between the production-possibility curve and an indifference curve. For country A, this combination is $O_A G_A$ units of X_1 and $O_A F_A$ units of X_2. The comparable combination for country B is $O_B G_B$ of X_1 and $O_B F_B$ of X_2.

If country A could obtain the good X_2 by trade at terms more favourable

---

[9] For a review of Mill's approach, see Jacob Viner, *Studies in the Theory of International Trade* (New York: Harper and Brothers, n.d.), pp. 535-41.

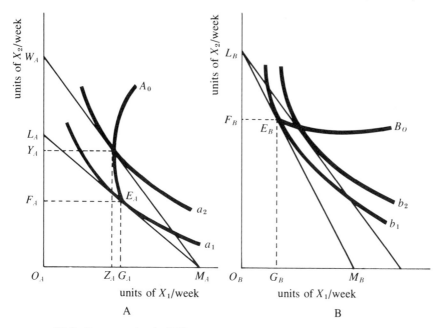

FIGURE 17.2 *Community indifference curves, production-possibility curves, and offer curves for countries* A *and* B

than those given by the slope of its production-possibility curve, it would be in its interests to devote all its resources to the production of X_1 and to obtain X_2 through trade. For example, if it could trade X_1 for X_2 at the price given by the numerical value of the slope of the line $M_A W_A$, then country A could reach a higher indifference curve, a_2, by producing only X_1 and selling $Z_A M_A$ units of X_1 for $O_A Y_A$ units of X_2. The curve joining the points of tangency between A's indifference curves and the lines whose slopes indicate possible terms of trade between the two goods is called A's reciprocal demand or offer curve. From this curve, and the maximum possible output of X_1, we can read off country A's demand for X_2 in terms of the amount of X_1 it offers in exchange. Similarly, country B's offer curve, B_o, can be derived as we consider terms of trade between X_1 and X_2 in which X_1 is less expensive to buy abroad than to produce domestically.

These two offer curves are combined in Figure 17.3 in order to illustrate the determination of the equilibrium terms of trade. The size of the rectangle, or Edgeworth-box, in Figure 17.3 is determined by the amounts of X_1 and X_2 available to both if all of country A's resources are devoted to the production of X_1 and all of country B's resources to the production of X_2. The two production-possibility curves in Figure 17.2 are brought together to

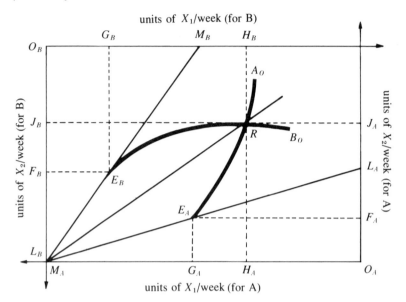

FIGURE 17.3 *Offer curves and the equilibrium terms of trade for two countries with constant comparative costs*

form the Edgeworth-box by placing point L_B on point M_A and measuring output and consumption of X_1 by country A from right to left, and measuring output and consumption of X_2 by country B from top to bottom along the ordinate.[10] The no-trade equilibrium positions for countries A and B are at E_A and E_B respectively. The offer curves $E_A A_0$ and $E_B B_0$ show the equilibrium positions for each country at alternative price ratios. The point of intersection of the offer curves is denoted by R. The slope of the line joining M_A to the point R represents the equilibrium price of X_1 in terms of X_2. At that price ratio, country A produces only X_1 and sells $H_A M_A$ units of X_1 for $O_A J_A$ units of X_2. Country B produces only X_2 and sells $J_B L_B$ units of X_2 for $O_B H_B$ units of X_1. Given the community indifference curves that determine the two offer curves, this is the only price ratio at which the reciprocal demands of the two countries are compatible. At a different price, the amount of X_2 country A would demand in exchange for a unit of X_1 would not be equal to the amount of X_2 country B would be prepared to exchange for a unit of X_1.

Both countries would be on higher indifference curves at equilibrium with trade, but the extent of a country's gain depends on where the two offer

---

[10] The Edgeworth-box diagram was introduced in Section 6.9 to illustrate bilateral exchange. The analysis of Figure 17.3 is very similar to the discussion of competitive equilibrium in Section 6.10.

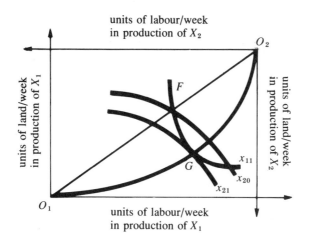

FIGURE 17.4 *Derivation of compatible outputs of X_1 and X_2 for a production-possibility curve*

curves intersect. The closer this intersection to country A's production-possibility curve, the greater country B's gain and vice-versa. A country's commodity terms of trade are equal to the ratio of the price of its export good to the price of its import good.[11] Thus country A's commodity terms of trade are equal to the slope of $M_A R$. The greater the value for the commodity terms of trade in this simple example, the greater the gain to country A.

17.7 Non-linear production-possibility curves

The development of international trade theory in this chapter has been restricted to special cases where the production-possibility curves are linear. If there is more than one primary (non-produced) factor of production, the production-possibility curves will usually be non-linear. To illustrate, let us assume that land and labour are required to produce the two final goods.[12] Labour and land can be measured in physical units and it is assumed that they are substitutable in the production of the two goods X_1 and X_2. It is assumed also that there are constant returns to scale in the production of both goods, with the production of X_1 using relatively more labour and the

---

[11] In a multi-good world the ratio of the change in an index of export-goods prices to the change in an index of import-goods prices would indicate the change in the country's commodity terms of trade.

[12] This analysis is less general in one important respect than our presentation of Ricardo's approach, since it does not include produced means of production—that is, capital goods. Output is produced only with labour and land.

production of X_2 using relatively more land. The dimensions of the box diagram in Figure 17.4 are determined by the amounts of labour and land available to the economy.

The slope of the line O_1O_2 is equal to the land-to-labour ratio in the economy. A typical isoquant for X_1 is shown by x_{11}. The output of X_1 is higher the further to the right of O_1 is the point representing the rates of input going into its production. Two of the isoquants for X_2 (i.e. x_{20} and x_{21}) are shown in the diagram. In this case output is greater the further to the left of O_2 is the final position. At point F, the land (V_2)-to-labour (V_1) ratio is the same in the production of both goods. Our assumptions about the factor intensities of the production of these goods are reflected in the slopes of the isoquants at points such as F, where the ratios of land to labour are the same for both goods.

The numerical value of the slope of the isoquant for X_1 at point F (x_{11}) is equal to the ratio of the marginal product of labour, $(MP_{v_1})_{x_1}$, to the marginal product of land, $(MP_{v_2})_{x_1}$, in the production of X_1. This ratio is greater than the comparable ratio at point F for the X_2 isoquant (x_{20}) because of our assumption that the production of X_1 is more labour-intensive than the production of X_2. If the level of output of X_1 is set equal to x_{11}, it is possible to produce a rate of output of X_2 greater than x_{20} by choosing the input combinations at point G, where the isoquants are tangent. The production-possibility curve will thus show an output rate of x_{21} for X_2 corresponding to an output rate of x_{11} of X_1. At this point we know that $(MP_{v_1})_{x_1}/(MP_{v_2})_{x_1} = (MP_{v_1})_{x_2}/(MP_{v_2})_{x_2}$. The curve O_1GO_2 is the locus of all points of tangency of the isoquants. From these points we can determine the values that are used to draw the production-possibility curve illustrated in Figure 17.5. Point H on that curve in Figure 17.5 corresponds to point G, the point of tangency of isoquants x_{11} and x_{21} in Figure 17.4.

The *numerical* value of the slope of the production-possibility curve is called the marginal rate of transformation of one product for the other. In this case the marginal rate of transformation of X_1 for X_2 $(MRT_{x_1 x_2})$ is the difference in the rate of output of X_2 that permits the rate of output of X_1 to be higher by one unit. A higher rate of output of X_1 can be obtained if more of the available labour (V_1) or land (V_2), or additional quantities of both these inputs, are transferred from the production of X_2 to the production of X_1. If a unit of V_1 is transferred to the production of X_1, the rate of output of X_2 is lower by an amount equal to $(MP_{v_1})_{x_2}$, while the rate of output of X_1 is higher by the amount $(MP_{v_1})_{x_1}$. The marginal rate of transformation of X_1 for X_2 is therefore equal to the ratio of these marginal products:

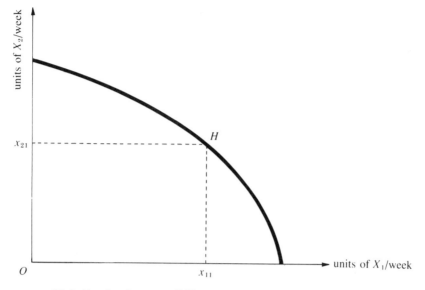

FIGURE 17.5 *Production-possibility curve obtained from information contained in Figure 17.4*

$$MRT_{x_1 x_2} = \frac{(MP_{v_1})_{x_2}}{(MP_{v_1})_{x_1}}$$

Alternatively the marginal rate of transformation can be written as the ratio of the marginal product of V_2 in the production of X_2 to the marginal product of V_2 in the production of X_1. The value for the marginal rate of transformation is the same in either of these cases. We know from the tangency of the isoquants in Figure 17.4 that

$$\frac{(MP_{v_1})_{x_2}}{(MP_{v_2})_{x_2}} = \frac{(MP_{v_1})_{x_1}}{(MP_{v_2})_{x_1}}$$

Therefore

$$\frac{(MP_{v_1})_{x_2}}{(MP_{v_1})_{x_1}} = \frac{(MP_{v_2})_{x_2}}{(MP_{v_2})_{x_1}} = MRT_{x_1 x_2}$$

The production-possibility curve in Figure 17.5 is concave to the origin. This shape follows from the two assumptions underlying this curve: (i) constant returns to scale in the production of both goods and (ii) unequal factor intensities. With constant returns and equal factor intensities, the production-possibility curve would be linear, as in Figure 17.2, which is based on the assumptions made by Ricardo in presenting his doctrine of comparative advantage.[13] Diminishing returns to scale would reinforce the concavity of the curve because the increase in the output of X_1 would be smaller for given decreases in X_2 the larger the rate of output of X_1. However, if there were increasing returns to scale, the production-possibility curve might be convex to the origin if this feature outweighed the adverse effect of unequal factor intensities.

It is important to note that each point on a production-possibility curve represents a position of stationary equilibrium. Not only are the available quantities of land and labour fully employed, but they are employed in a technically efficient manner. It is not possible to obtain a higher output of one of the goods, given technical knowledge, except by having a lower output for the other good. This analysis does not say how an economy could get on such a curve, or how it would move from one position of stationary equilibrium to another.

17.8 Non-linear production-possibility curves and international trade

When production-possibility curves are non-linear, the doctrine of comparative costs must be interpreted in terms of *comparative marginal costs*. Differences in the comparative costs of producing two goods in two countries, in the absence of trade, depend in this case on tastes, as indicated by community indifference curves, as well as on resources and technical knowledge. In Figure 17.6 the comparative costs of producing the goods X_1 and X_2 in country A, in the equilibrium position without trade, would be equal to the numerical value of the slope of the production-possibility curve at the point of tangency between this curve and a community indifference curve. This point of tangency is indicated by point E.

If a country can trade at terms that differ from its comparative costs of production in the absence of trade, the equilibrium position with trade will lie on a higher indifference curve. In Figure 17.6 the international terms of trade of X_2 for X_1 are represented by the numerical value of the slope of the line HF. Given these terms, the country at equilibrium would produce at point H (where its comparative costs are equal to the international terms of trade) and sell GN units of X_1 for RJ units of X_2.[14]

---

[13] If the production of X_1 is labour intensive and the production of X_2 is land intensive, the production-possibility curve will be concave even with constant returns to scale. As we consider lower production rates for X_2, the proportion in which the factors are available for production becomes less desirable for the production of X_1 and thus the ratio of the decrease in X_2 to the increase in X_1 (the slope of the production-possibility curve) becomes larger.

[14] This analysis can be extended to cover the determination of equilibrium terms of trade by developing reciprocal demand curves. See J.E. Meade, *A Geometry of International Trade* (London: George Allen & Unwin, 1952).

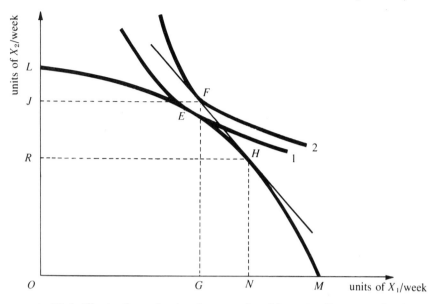

FIGURE 17.6 *Illustration of gains from trade with a non-linear production-possibility curve*

17.9 General equilibrium analysis and comparative statics

These applications of general equilibrium analysis are examples of comparative statics. Equilibrium positions have been compared, but the analysis has not shown how an economy can move from one position to the other, or considered the time required to make such a change. Each of the equilibrium positions represents a separate stationary state with unchanging technology, resources, and tastes, and producers expect that the current patterns of prices and outputs, etc. will be repeated in the future. A change in the values of the parameters will destroy the correspondence between producers' expectations and events, and the way producers respond to situations where expectations turn out to be incorrect must be built into the analysis before it can handle the out-of-equilibrium situations that follow changes.

Even though it has been shown that there are gains from trade, in the sense that the equilibrium position with trade lies on a higher indifference curve than the equilibrium position without trade, it does not necessarily follow that a non-trading country should commence trading. Before such a decision is taken, the *costs of transition* from one position to the other should be considered. Workers have to be shifted from one industry to the other, possibly from one part of the country to the other and retrained, and new combinations of capital goods have to be produced while others are discarded. *Movement does not take place along the production-possibility curve.*

17.10 Input-output analysis

Input-output analysis is an interesting application of the general equilibrium approach to the empirical analysis of production.[15] As in all applications of general equilibrium analysis, it is necessary to proceed under severely limiting assumptions. The simplifications in this case include that (i) the demands for final goods and services are taken as given and not explained; (ii) each industry is assumed to produce only one commodity (or, alternatively, a composite commodity whose constituent elements are combined in fixed proportions); (iii) each industry employs all inputs in fixed proportions and the demand for these inputs changes in proportion to the changes in the rate of output for the industry. This analysis can be illustrated by an example in which the economy is divided into three industries: agriculture and mining, manufacturing, and transportation and trade.

Input-output tables show the disposition of the output of each industry for some particular period, usually a year. Part of this output is required as an input by the industries, while the remainder goes to satisfy final demand. This category includes consumption, investment and government expenditures, and exports. Production of an industry's total output requires, in addition to industrial inputs, the services of labour, management, capital equipment, etc. In Table 17.2 the values for these latter inputs are aggregated and shown as 'primary' inputs.

TABLE 17.2 *Input-output table, three industries (fictitious annual data) (millions of dollars)*

DISPOSITION OF OUTPUT PURCHASE OF INPUTS	AGRIC. & MIN.	MANUF.	TRANS. & TRADE	FINAL DEMAND	TOTAL OUTPUT
Agriculture & Mining	800	5,000	1,000	3,500	10,000
Manufacturing	3,000	10,000	2,000	25,000	40,000
Transportation & Trade	600	4,000	1,500	8,900	15,000
Primary Inputs	5,600	21,000	10,500		
Total Inputs	10,000	40,000	15,000		

[15] It was first developed by W.W. Leontief, *Structure of the American Economy, 1919-1939* (New York: Oxford University Press, 1953).

The industries' purchases of inputs are shown in columns of the table, while the disposition of their outputs is shown in rows. With this type of double-entry bookkeeping, which includes both primary inputs and final demand, the value of total output for any industry must be equal to the value of its total inputs. Input coefficients for each industry can be calculated by dividing its purchases by its total output. Table 17.3 shows the input coefficients corresponding to the figures in Table 17.2.

TABLE 17.3 *Input coefficients for values in Table 17.2*

	AGRIC. & MIN.	MANUF.	TRANS. & TRADE
Agriculture & Mining	.08	.125	.067
Manufacturing	.30	.250	.133
Transportation & Trade	.06	.100	.100
Primary Inputs	.56	.525	.700

The first column states that in the specified year every dollar's worth of output of the agricultural and mining industry required as input 8¢ of its own output, 30¢ of manufacturing output, 6¢ of transportation and trade services, and 56¢ worth of services from primary inputs. These values are expressed in the prices of the year for which the input-output table was derived. They reflect the technology and product-mix of that year. If these input coefficients are to be used for analytical purposes—e.g. for predicting the output requirements for obtaining a specified final demand—then it must be assumed that the technology and product-mix are unchanged and that no substitution of inputs is possible. (Alternatively, independent estimates of the effects of changes in product-mix and technology can be used to adjust the input coefficients.)

To illustrate the use of the input-output table, suppose that the desired final demand (in base year prices) is \$4,000 (millions) for agriculture and mining, \$30,000 (millions) for manufacturing, and \$10,000 (millions) for transportation and trade. The input coefficients in Table 17.3 can be used to calculate the total output for each of the industries and the values for primary inputs that are consistent with this bill of final demand. The total amount of agriculture and mining output (A) required is:

$$A = .08A + .125M + .067T + 4,000$$

where M represents total manufacturing output and T total transportation and trade output. Similarly, for the other industries and for primary input (P) we obtain:

$$M = .30A + .250M + .133T + 30,000$$
$$T = .06A + .100M + .100T + 10,000$$
$$P = .56A + .525M + .70T$$

These equations can be solved to obtain the values for A, M, T, and P. They are (approximately): A = $12,000 (millions); M = $48,000 (millions); T = $17,000 (millions); and P = $44,000 (millions). It is now possible to check whether there is sufficient productive capacity (and labour) to produce the total outputs required for the desired final demand. (The matrix of inter-industry input coefficients can be inverted to handle more easily the calculation of the total outputs required by a series of alternative final demands.)

The assumptions underlying input-output analysis are very strict and the data requirements are formidable. It generally takes several years to construct a table, and technology and product-mixes might have changed considerably by the time it was available. However, input-output analysis is a very interesting example of a general equilibrium approach to the examination of real economies. Input-output tables have also proved to be very informative in showing interrelationships within an economy and have been developed for regional as well as for national economies.

17.11 Summary

Some of the techniques and simple applications of general equilibrium analysis have been presented. A full general equilibrium approach for a multi-commodity model of an economy with production is very complex. In order to ensure unique solutions for the systems of equations and to obtain comparative statics results, very restrictive assumptions have to be made about the interrelations within the model. These often make the results obtained very similar to those given by a partial equilibrium approach. However, different results for partial and general equilibrium analyses can often be obtained for simpler models where specific solutions can be derived.

Theories of international trade are examples of general equilibrium analysis. Ricardo's theory of comparative advantage and Mill's 'reciprocal demand' were presented as illustrations of general equilibrium analysis. Production-possibility curves were derived to show the interrelation between products as claimants on scarce factors of production. Input-output analysis is an empirical application of a general equilibrium approach to the analysis of production. It has been used to show the interrelations between industries and to estimate the industrial output requirements of changes in the final demand for goods.

SUGGESTED READINGS

Arrow, K.J., and F.H. Hahn. *General Competitive Analysis*. San Francisco: Holden-Day, 1971. Chapter 1.

National Bureau of Economic Research. Conference on Research in Income and Wealth. *Input-Output Analysis: An Appraisal.* Princeton. N.J.: Princeton University Press, 1955.

Morgenstern, Oskar, ed. *Economic Activity Analysis*. New York: John Wiley & Sons, 1954. Pages 3-78.

Stolper, Wolfgang F., and Paul A. Samuelson. 'Protection and Real Wages', *Review of Economic Studies*, Vol. 9 (November 1941), pp. 58-73. Reprinted in *Readings in the Theory of International Trade*. Edited by Howard S. Ellis and Lloyd A. Metzler. Philadelphia: Blakiston, 1950. Pages 333-57.

Sraffa, Piero, ed., *The Works and Correspondence of David Ricardo*. Cambridge, Eng.: Cambridge University Press, 1951. Vol. I, Chapter VII.

Viner, Jacob. *Studies in the Theory of International Trade*. New York: Harper and Brothers, n.d. Chapters VIII and IX.

18

WELFARE ECONOMICS

18.1 Introduction

In the preceding chapters, techniques of analysis have been developed for the examination of the market behaviour of both individuals and firms. These techniques, which make it possible to obtain an understanding of the factors determining such economic phenomena as the prices of products sold in different markets, were used in our study of pricing in competitive, monopolistic, and oligopolistic markets. Having analysed these markets, we will now consider the principles used by economists in deciding whether one form of market structure is better for society than another. Such evaluative considerations belong to welfare economics.

Welfare economics is concerned with those aspects of human welfare that are affected by the provision of goods and services and the expenditure of human energy and resources to produce them. It tries to establish general rules for choosing between different forms of economic organization and different economic policies. One policy is preferred to another on economic grounds because it would lead to a better allocation of goods and resources, permitting some people to be made better off without making anyone worse off, or because it would lead to a better distribution of income among persons in the economy (even though some are made better off at the expense of others). Any change in policy usually affects the distribution of income as well as the allocation of goods and resources, but economists have concentrated more on the allocative effects of changes because judgements about the distribution of income depend on the personal values of those making them. For example, cost-benefit analyses of proposals to make available new facilities or programs—such as new highways, disease-control programs, or recreational facilities—attempt to determine whether the allocation of resources could be improved; but value judgements cannot be avoided in making a decision to implement a policy with favourable allocative effects because the policy will also affect the distribution of income. Such value judgements lie outside the professional competence of economists, and we will show that the tests they have devised for deciding whether a change in policy improves economic welfare are incomplete.

18.2 Social welfare functions

In Chapter 5 utility functions were introduced to determine an individual's optimal choice of goods, given his budgetary constraints. Economists have extended the notion of a utility function to social choices, using social welfare functions to illuminate the problems involved in making a socially optimal choice, given the resources and technological constraints on the economy.[1] An individual utility function ranks alternative combinations of goods according to the individual's preferences, while a social welfare function provides a preferential ordering for society of alternative economic situations, which can be distinguished by the production and distribution of goods and services among persons in the economy. The social welfare function can be written as $W(U_1, U_2, \ldots U_n)$, where U_i is the ordinal utility function of the ith individual. The value for U_i depends on the goods and services consumed by the ith individual and on the work he performs; this value will be different in alternative economic situations when his consumption and work differ. It is customary to assume that the social welfare function responds positively to increases in individual utility, but there might be some changes in individual utility that are ignored on ethical grounds; for example, increased consumption of alcohol and drugs might increase individual utility but not social welfare.

A social welfare function that chooses between situations in which some individuals are better off while others are made worse off makes interpersonal comparisons based on judgements that are ethical in nature. The results obtained from such functions would be acceptable to any one group only if its members concurred in these judgements. Economists have therefore tried to work with social welfare functions that are based on a value judgement they believe would be widely accepted. This is known as the *Paretian value judgement*[2] and states that *a particular situation is better than an alternative one if at least one person is better off and no one is*

---

[1] They were first used by Abram Bergson in 'A Reformulation of Certain Aspects of Welfare Economics', *Quarterly Journal of Economics*, Vol. 52 (February 1938) pp. 310-34.

[2] Vilfredo Pareto, *Manuel d'Économie Politique* (2e éd.; Paris: Giard, 1927).

worse off. However, if this is the only value judgement employed, the social welfare function can provide a preferential ordering of only a small proportion of the possible alternative situations. Situations where some are better off while others are worse off cannot be ranked in order of preference without making value judgements about the distribution of income. To use only the Paretian value judgement, then, imposes severe limitations on the ability to choose between alternative situations. However, under certain assumptions this value judgement leads to the *necessary* conditions for the achievement of maximum welfare. We shall derive these conditions and examine their limitations below.

18.3 Paretian optima

An economic situation is said to be Pareto-optimal if there is no change in policy, given the values of the parameters, that would make one person better off without making someone worse off. In such a situation, production and exchange must be efficient; otherwise a reallocation of society's resources to produce a different combination of goods, or a reallocation of goods among individuals, could be found that would improve at least one person's position without lowering the utility of others.[3]

The production of a particular combination of goods is efficient if, given the availability of all the resources, it is not possible to produce more of one good without producing less of another. *Efficiency of production* implies the following three conditions[4] (the statement of which assumes neoclassical production functions, no externalities in production or consumption, and perfectly divisible inputs and outputs):

1. *The marginal rate of transformation between two goods must be the same for all firms producing both goods.* This condition can be written in terms of our notation as:

$$(MRT_{XY})_A = (MRT_{XY})_B \qquad (1)$$

where X and Y are the two products and A and B are two of the firms producing both. The common marginal rate of transformation for all firms

---

[3] Pareto optimality requires full employment of an economy's resources as well as a technically efficient combination of employed resources. If some resources were unemployed, there would be scope for making someone better off at no cost to others even if the employed resources could not be rearranged to produce more.

[4] The conditions given are first-order conditions, but it is assumed that the second-order conditions for a maximum are also satisfied. In terms of calculus, the first-order conditions for an extreme value (maximum or minimum) of a function are that its first derivatives be equal to zero. The second-order conditions for a maximum are that the second derivatives must be negative.

producing both goods is the community's marginal rate of transformation between these goods. In a two-good world of the type examined in Section 17.7, this marginal rate of transformation is equal to the numerical value of the slope of the community's production-possibility curve. (If, in Figure 17.5, the axes were relabelled with X on the abscissa and Y on the ordinate, the marginal rate of transformation of X for Y would be equal to the numerical value of the slope of the production-possibility curve with respect to the abscissa.)

If equation 1 does *not* hold, a realignment of production among the firms could increase the total output of one or both goods without requiring an increase in the rates of input of the elements of production. For example, if the marginal rate of transformation of X for Y of firm A were 3, while this rate for firm B were 2, then A should produce more of Y and B more of X. Firm A could produce, with no change in inputs, 3 more units of Y if it produced 1 less unit of X. Similarly, firm B could produce, at the same cost, 1 more unit of X if it produced 2 fewer units of Y. The net effect for the economy of these differences would be the same output of X, but an output of Y that was higher by 1 unit.

2. *The ratios of the marginal products of any two elements of production (that is, their marginal rates of technical substitution) used in producing two goods must be the same in the production of both goods.* This condition can be expressed in terms of our notation as:

$$(MRTS_{v_1 v_2})_X = (MRTS_{v_1 v_2})_Y \qquad (2)$$

The two elements of production are V_1 and V_2; the two products are X and Y. The derivation of the production-possibility curve in Figure 17.4 made use of this condition. It was shown in Section 17.7 that the failure of this condition to hold meant that a reallocation of the elements of production could increase total output.

3. *The marginal product of any element in the production of a good (that is, the marginal rate of transformation of that element into the good) must be the same for all firms producing this good and employing this element.* This condition can be written in terms of our notation as:

$$(MRT_{v_1 x})_A = (MRT_{v_1 x})_B \qquad (3)$$

The element of production is V_1, the product is X, and the two firms are A and B.

If this condition does *not* hold, then a transfer of some units of V_1 from one firm to the other could increase the total output of one or both goods. For example, if the marginal product of V_1 in the production of X were 3 for firm A and 2 for firm B, the transfer of a unit of this element from B to

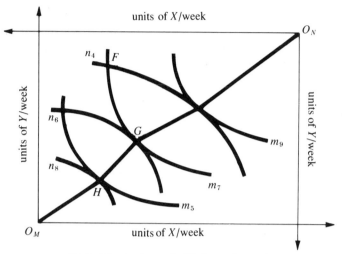

FIGURE 18.1 *Illustration of efficiency in exchange*

A would result in a net increase of one unit in their total output of *X*. Such transfers would continue to increase total output until a position was reached where the marginal products were equal (or firm *B* no longer produced *X*).

Efficiency of exchange is illustrated in Figure 18.1 with the aid of an Edgeworth-box diagram. It gives the amounts of the two goods, *X* and *Y*, to be divided between two individuals, *M* and *N*. The length of the rectangle indicates the total amount of *X* available, and the height of the rectangle shows the total amount of *Y*. *M*'s allocation is read from the origin O_M, and *N*'s allocation from the origin O_N. Each point in this rectangle, or on its sides, thus indicates an allocation of the given amounts of *X* and *Y*. Points at which the indifference curves are tangent, such as *G* and *H*, indicate allocations that are Pareto-optimal. It can be seen that, given any such point, it would be impossible to find another one where one individual is better off without making the other individual worse off. There are very many such points, and they lie on the curve $O_M O_N$. (The middle portion of this curve was called the *contract curve* in Section 6.9.) The condition for the optimal allocation of two goods between individuals who consume both is thus the equality of their marginal rates of substitution for the two goods. This can be written in terms of our notation as:

$$(MRS_{XY})_M = (MRS_{XY})_N \qquad (4)$$

For all points where this equation does not hold, it is possible to find other allocations where the position of one of the individuals can be improved without harm to the other. For example, the allocation at point F in Figure 18.1 is inefficient. A reallocation of the goods to reach point G would benefit N, while M would be no worse off.

The efficiency conditions for production and exchange must be combined in order to ensure that the appropriate combination of goods is produced. Pareto optimality requires that the marginal rate of substitution of X for Y for any individual consuming both goods must equal the community's marginal rate of transformation between these two goods. It can be written as:

$$MRS_{XY} = MRT_{XY} \qquad (5)$$

If this condition does not hold, then a difference in the combination of goods produced could improve an individual's position at no cost to others. For example, if individual M's marginal rate of substitution of X for Y is 3, while the economy's marginal rate of transformation is 2, an increase in the production of X would be advantageous. M would be no worse off if he had 1 more unit of X and 3 fewer units of Y. The economy could produce the extra unit of X at a sacrifice of only 2 units of Y. There would thus be 1 unit of Y available to make someone better off in this second position. The economy produces 1 more unit of X and 2 fewer units of Y, but individual M gives up 3 units of Y in exchange for the extra unit of X.[5]

One more condition for Pareto optimality will be presented to cover explicitly the possibility that units of an element of production can be consumed directly, as well as used to produce consumption goods. A case in point would be an individual's time, which can either be employed as labour to produce goods or consumed as leisure. Pareto optimality requires that in this case an individual's marginal rate of substitution between leisure and a good be equal to the marginal product of his time in the production of this good. If the individual's time is denoted by V, and the good by X, then this condition can be written as:

$$MRS_{VX} = MRT_{VX} \qquad (6)$$

If this condition does not hold, a difference in the time spent at work could improve the position of one person without making anyone else worse off. For example, if an individual's marginal rate of substitution of leisure time for X is 3, while the marginal rate of transformation of labour time for X is 2, an increase in his leisure would improve welfare. This individual would be prepared to relinquish 3 units of X for one unit more of time to be

---

[5] The reader can devise differences in production, given these rates of transformation and substitution, where there are additional amounts of both goods to be distributed.

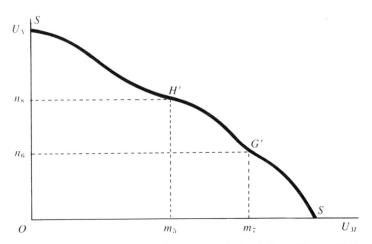

FIGURE 18.2 *Utility-possibility curve, derived from Figure 18.1*

spent in leisure, and since the subsequent decline in the output of X would be only 2 units, one unit of X would become available to make someone better off.

18.4 Utility-possibility curves and the utility-possibility frontier

For purposes of geometrical simplicity, we shall assume a community of two persons producing two goods. The information contained in Figure 18.1 can be used to draw a utility-possibility curve, SS, in Figure 18.2. It shows the combination of utilities for the two individuals that can be obtained from given quantities of the two goods X and Y and is based on the assumption that the given amounts of X and Y are allocated in a Pareto-optimal way. The utility levels (which are only of ordinal significance) shown by this curve are obtained from the points of tangency of the indifference curves along $O_M O_N$ in Figure 18.1. For example, point H' in Figure 18.2 corresponds to point H in Figure 18.1 and point G' to point G. The utility-possibility curve is downward sloping. Along the efficiency locus $O_M O_N$ an individual's position can be made better off only at the expense of someone else.

If we started with a different combination of X and Y than the one shown in Figure 18.1, we would obtain a different utility-possibility curve from the efficiency of exchange locus for the second combination. The two utility-possibility curves could intersect at one or more points or one could lie wholly inside the other.

A utility-possibility curve shows, given the quantities of X and Y available, the maximum level of utility for one individual that is compatible

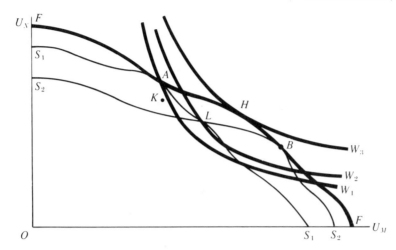

FIGURE 18.3 *A utility-possibility frontier and two of its constituent utility-possibility curves*

with a specified level of utility for the other. If these outputs are produced efficiently—that is, if the three optimal conditions for production summarized in equations 1, 2, and 3 are satisfied—the utility-possibility curve would contribute a point to the *utility-possibility frontier*. The utility-possibility frontier for the economy shows, given technical knowledge and the availability of resources, the maximum levels of utility for one individual given the levels of utility of the other. This frontier is the envelope of the utility-possibility curves corresponding to points on the community's production-possibility curve. The pair of values each utility-possibility curve contributes to this frontier is obtained from the indifference curves whose slopes, at their point of tangency, are equal to the marginal rate of transformation. *The utility-possibility frontier thus represents economic situations where both production and exchange are efficient.*

A utility-possibility frontier and two of its constituent utility-possibility curves are drawn in Figure 18.3. The frontier is labelled *FF* and the two curves are S_1S_1 and S_2S_2. The former contributes point *A* to the frontier and the latter point *B*.

All points on the utility-possibility frontier represent situations where all the conditions for Pareto optimality are satisfied. A social welfare function can order (or rank) in terms of preference combinations of utility levels such as *A* and *B* for the two individuals. However, if the only thing we know about this function is that it incorporates the Paretian value judgement, the ranking of points *A* and *B* is unknown. The information available might not even be sufficient to choose between points on the utility frontier and those off it. For example, we know that A would be preferred to K, since individual N is better off at A than at K and individual M is no worse off; but points A and L cannot be ranked on the basis of this value judgement. Even though point L represents a situation where one (or more) of the optimal conditions is not satisfied, M is better off at L than he is at A. To choose between points such as A and L, as well as between points on the frontier, interpersonal comparisons would have to be introduced. With a fully specified social welfare function we could choose the point lying on the frontier (and it *would* lie on the frontier) that maximized social welfare. For example, with the social ranking of alternatives represented by the W-curves in Figure 18.3, point L is preferred to point A and maximum social welfare is reached at point H.

18.5 Compensation tests

We have just seen that interpersonal comparisons must be added to Pareto optimality in order to find the position of maximum welfare, since Pareto optimality is satisfied at *all* points on the utility-possibility frontier. Nevertheless, economists have attempted to devise tests that would permit them to concentrate on the efficiency aspects of proposed changes, with judgements about their distributional effects being made separately. These tests make use of compensating taxes or bounties to be levied or paid by governments after a proposed change in policy is implemented.

A *compensating tax* is a levy that would keep individuals who would otherwise be better off in an alternative situation at the level of satisfaction enjoyed in the initial economic situation. A *compensating bounty* is a payment that would return individuals who would be worse off in an alternative situation to the level of satisfaction they enjoyed in the initial situation. If the sum of the compensating taxes is greater than the sum of the compensating bounties, it would be possible, by levying the taxes and paying the bounties, to make at least one person better off and no one worse off in the alternative economic situation. At first sight it would appear that this compensation test would make it possible, simply on the basis of the Paretian value judgement, to choose between situations where some individuals are better off while others are worse off. But this is not the case. This approach and the reasons for its failure can be explained with reference to utility-possibility curves.

The initial (or reference) situation in Figure 18.4 is represented by R and the alternative situation by Q. One version of the compensation test asks whether it is possible, starting from the alternative situation (Q), to make at least one person better off and no one worse off than in the reference position (R) by levying compensating taxes and paying bounties. If the

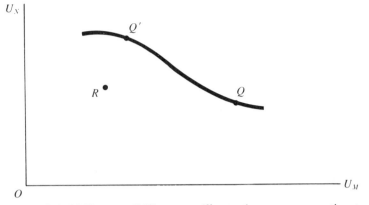

FIGURE 18.4 *Utility-possibility curve illustrating a compensation test*

utility-possibility curve through Q lies to the northeast of R (as in Figure 18.4), this compensation test is satisfied. The gainers from the move to Q can profitably bribe the losers to accept the new situation. Aggregate real income at Q is said to be higher than at R because points such as Q' lie to the northeast of R.[6]

This version of the compensation test ranks Q above R because it is possible to get to Q' by redistributing income from Q. However, the question of whether this redistribution should take place is left unanswered. If redistribution were automatically carried out, this policy would implicitly favour the *status quo*—the initial distribution of income at R rather than the distribution at Q. The automatic rejection of redistribution is also unsatisfactory, because a social choice made on the basis of the sum of the compensating taxes exceeding the sum of the compensating bounties would be based on the assumption that the marginal utility of income is the same for all individuals.[7] In both these cases, therefore, interpersonal comparisons are involved in addition to the Paretian value judgement. *At best* a compensation test can lead only to what Samuelson has called 'twere better'

---

[6] This version of the test was proposed by N. Kaldor in 'Welfare Propositions and Interpersonal Comparisons of Utility', *Economic Journal*, Vol. XLIX (1939), pp. 549-52. Another version is found in J.R. Hicks, 'The Valuation of Social Income', *Economica*, Vol. VII (1940), pp. 105-24. In order for Q to be judged better than R with this version, it is necessary for the utility-possibility curve through R to lie below Q. Kaldor's procedure is thus reversed. Q is said to have higher real social income than R if those who lose from a move to Q cannot profitably bribe the gainers to reject it.

[7] This implicit assumption about the marginal utility of income is also made when measures of consumer's surplus are used in cost-benefit studies (Section 6.12). Compensation tests and measures of consumer's surplus are related. See D.M. Winch, *Analytical Welfare Economics* (Harmondsworth: Penguin Books, 1971), Chapter 8.

statements. 'It can only assert in a negative way: "'Twere better that the Corn Laws be repealed, and compensation be paid, *if necessary.*" It gives no real guide to action.'[8]

Compensation tests can also give rise to contradictory results. In Figure 18.4 the situation at Q is judged preferable to R on the basis of the compensation test, since Q' lies to the northeast of R. However, the utility-possibility curve through point R (not drawn) may also lie to the northeast of Q. If this is the case, then individuals who would lose with a change from R to Q can profitably bribe the gainers to forego the change. The situation at Q is judged to have higher aggregate real income on the basis of the utility-possibility curve through Q, while the reverse judgement may be made on the basis of the utility-possibility curve through R. Scitovsky thus proposed a double test to determine whether welfare is higher at Q than at R. The utility-possibility curve through Q must pass outside R *and* the utility-possibility curve through R must pass below Q. In other words, the gainers by the change from R to Q can profitably bribe the losers to accept it, but the losers cannot profitably bribe the gainers to reject it.[9]

Scitovsky's double test is illustrated in Figure 18.5. In Panel A, a change from R to Q passes this test. Individual M, who gains by a move from R to Q, can profitably bribe individual N who loses, since Q' lies to the northeast of R, while N cannot profitably bribe M to reject the change to Q, since R' is to the southeast of Q. In panel B the change from R to Q fails the Scitovsky test. Individual M can profitably bribe individual N to accept a change from R to Q, but individual N can also profitably bribe M to reject this change, since R' is to the northeast of Q.[10]

Yet even the Scitovsky test is unsatisfactory. It merely rules out the possibility of the utility curves' intersecting an odd number of times between R and Q. They may intersect elsewhere, or an even number of times, between these points. For example, in Figure 18.6 the Scitovsky test is

---

[8] Paul Anthony Samuelson, *Foundations of Economic Analysis* (Cambridge, Mass.: Harvard University Press, 1948), p. 250. (Italics in the original.)

[9] T. de Scitovsky, 'A Note on Welfare Propositions in Economics', *Review of Economic Studies*, Vol. 9 (1941-2), pp. 77-88.

[10] This reversal may occur because the difference in the distribution of income at R and Q affects the community's marginal rate of substitution for the goods. For example, if there are two goods, X and Y, with N having a stronger preference for X, this good would be more valuable in terms of Y at R than at Q, since N's income is higher and his preferences are given greater weight. Let the common marginal rate of substitution at R be $X = 2Y$, and at Q be $2X = Y$, with the commodity bundle at Q having one more unit of Y and one less unit of X than the bundle at R. This bundle at Q would be more valuable if the rate of substitution at Q of $2X = Y$ were used to value both bundles, while the bundle at R would be more valuable if the rate of substitution of $X = 2Y$ were used. See E.J. Mishan, 'A Survey of Welfare Economics, 1939-1959', *Economic Journal*, Vol. 70 (June 1960), p. 224.

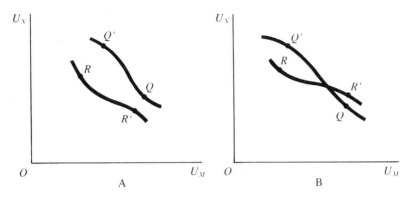

FIGURE 18.5 *Utility-possibility curves and the Scitovsky-compensation test*

satisfied for a movement from R to Q, but that does not mean that potential welfare has unequivocally increased at Q because the two curves intersect to the right of Q. Potential welfare with R may be higher for social welfare functions that attach greater weight to the utility of individual M. (For example, with the social rankings indicated by the curves W_1 and W_2, the utility-possibility curve through R is preferred to the curve through Q.) Potential welfare is higher with situation Q only if the utility-possibility curve through Q lies wholly outside the curve through R. But even here it is

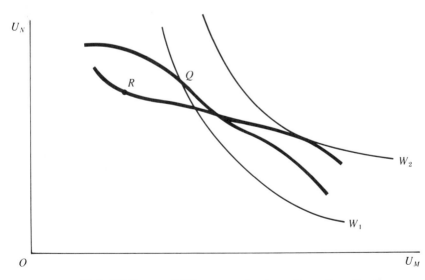

FIGURE 18.6 *Utility-possibility curves for two alternative situations*

not possible to say, in the absence of a social welfare function, that the change from R to Q is a good thing, since some individuals are worse off at Q.[11]

18.6 Cost-benefit analyses

The failure of compensation tests to provide a social ranking of alternative economic situations does not detract from their usefulness as indicators of the allocative effects of changes in economic policy. Cost-benefit analyses are an application of these tests. A *cost-benefit analysis* attempts to determine the monetary equivalent of all the benefits from a particular project and then compares them with all its costs. As benefits and costs are incurred over a series of periods, in order to obtain the appropriate sums for comparison it is necessary to reduce them to a single point of time by applying a rate of discount to a time-series of benefits and costs. If the benefits exceed the costs, the gainers from the project could profitably bribe the losers, since they could meet all its costs and still be better off.[12] Of course, some may be worse off as a result of a particular project; in this case the demonstration that benefits exceeded costs would be only the first step in deciding whether a particular project was socially desirable. The resulting distributional changes must also be judged to be acceptable.[13]

The study of the Victoria Line extension of London's underground railway system is an example of a cost-benefit analysis.[14] The social benefits attributed to the Victoria Line fell into three categories: (i) cost-savings, which included saving in fares and in operating costs; (ii) time-savings, which included the saving in time of those who switched to the Victoria Line as well as of those who benefited from the faster service on existing modes of transport because of less-congested conditions with the new line; (iii) other benefits such as increased comfort, or reduced stress, due to the provision of the new facility. These expected social benefits were projected over a period of fifty years from the planned date of completion in 1968,

---

[11] Samuelson makes this point very vividly: ' . . . a perfectly legitimate "'twere better" statement can be made as follows: "Technological change can make everybody better off in the sense that it will shift the Possibility Function outwards." We cannot deduce from this dictum: "Technological change is a good thing," since the introduction of technological change will in fact mean a vector movement from the old positions of every individual to the new positions which can hardly bode good to all.' Samuelson, *Foundations of Economic Analysis*, pp. 251-2.

[12] Cost-benefit analyses ignore the possibility of the Scitovsky-reversal discussed above.

[13] E.J. Mishan, *Cost-Benefit Analysis* (2nd ed.; London: George Allen & Unwin Ltd., 1975), Part VII.

[14] This study was carried out by C.D. Foster and M.E. Beesley in 'Estimating the Social Benefit of Constructing an Underground Railway in London', *Journal of the Royal Statistical Society*, 1963. The summary given here is based on Mishan, *Cost-Benefit Analysis*, Chapter 2.

and when discounted at 6 per cent they were estimated to be worth £86 million. The costs of construction, compounded at 6 per cent to this same date, were estimated to be £55 million. As the estimated benefits exceeded the costs, the Victoria Line was built.

18.7 Perfect competition and Pareto optimality

The conditions for Pareto optimality, set out in Section 18.3, are satisfied in a long-period equilibrium position of a perfectly competitive economy if there are no externalities in consumption and production. This situation can be verified by considering the equilibrium conditions for such an economy and showing that they satisfy the requirements for Pareto optimality.

It was deduced in Chapter 11 that in long-period equilibrium the marginal cost of a product is equal, for all firms producing that product, to its price. The ratio of the marginal costs of two goods (X and Y) produced by two firms (A and B) must thus be the same. It can be shown that this ratio is equal to the marginal rate of transformation between these goods and thus condition 1 is satisfied. A firm can alter its rate of output of X, at the expense of its output of Y, by transferring elements of production from the production of Y to the production of X. Thus we have:

$$MRT_{XY} = (MP_v)_Y / (MP_v)_X$$

where V is any one of the elements of production employed by this firm, and $(MP_v)_X$ and $(MP_v)_Y$ are the marginal products of V in the production of X and Y respectively. The marginal costs of these products are given by the equations $MC_X = P_v/(MP_v)_X$ and $MC_Y = P_v/(MP_v)_Y$, as shown in Section 8.5. Therefore,

$$MRT_{XY} = MC_X/MC_Y \qquad (7)$$

In competitive equilibrium, the ratio of the prices of two inputs used in the production of any good is equal to the ratio of the marginal products of these inputs (see Section 8.7). The prices of the inputs are the same for all firms using them, and therefore condition 2 must be satisfied. The satisfaction of condition 3 follows from the requirement that firms employ each element of production up to the point where the value of its marginal product is equal to its price. Thus, $P_v = P_X(MP_v)_X$, and since P_v and P_X are the same for all firms employing V to produce X, then $(MP_v)_X$ must also be the same. ($(MP_v)_X$ may also be written as MRT_{vX}, as in the statement of condition 3.) Efficiency of exchange (condition 4) is also satisfied, since prices are the same for all individuals, and in equilibrium their marginal rates of substitution between any two goods consumed are equal to the ratio of their prices.

The equality between the marginal rates of substitution and transformation of any two goods (condition 5) is also assured in competitive equilibrium. This follows from the equality of price and marginal cost for each good, and the identical price facing buyers and sellers for each good. The marginal rate of transformation is therefore equal not only to the ratio of marginal costs, but also to the ratio of prices, which is equal to the marginal rate of substitution.

Condition 6 combines aspects of conditions 3 and 4. In equilibrium, firms are hiring each element up to the point where its price is equal to the value of its marginal product. This can be expressed as $P_v = P_x MRT_{vx}$, since $MRT_{vx} \equiv (MP_v)_x$. If this element can also be used directly for consumption purposes, then equilibrium for any individual consuming both this element and the good X requires that $MRS_{vx} = P_v/P_x$. Condition 6 must thus be satisfied in long-period equilibrium in a perfectly competitive economy.

Equilibrium in a perfectly competitive economy (given our special assumption about the absence of externalities) is therefore *a sufficient condition* for the achievement of Pareto optimality. *However, Pareto optimality is only a necessary and not a sufficient condition for maximum welfare.* Judgements involving interpersonal comparisons must be made about the distribution of income before a choice can be made between alternative economic situations. Perfect competition is not a necessary condition for Pareto optimality; the marginal conditions could theoretically all be satisfied under socialism.[15]

18.8 Imperfections and Pareto optimality

Imperfections in markets, such as price discrimination and monopolistic and oligopolistic pricing practices in general, are not consistent with the achievement of Pareto optimality. For example, condition 4, the equality of marginal rates of substitution, would be violated by price discrimination, with different groups of customers facing different prices. Their marginal rates of substitution for pairs of goods they both consume would thus not be equal. However, this does not mean that a situation without price discrimination should necessarily be preferred to one with discrimination, since the achievement of Pareto optimality is not a sufficient condition for an improvement in welfare. Distributional considerations must also enter into making this decision. An example of price discrimination involving value judgements about the distribution of income can be found in the fare structure of the Montreal public transportation system. Persons sixty-five

---

[15] Oskar Lange and Fred M. Taylor, *On the Economic Theory of Socialism* (Minneapolis, Minn.: University of Minnesota Press, 1938).

years of age and over pay approximately one-quarter of the fare paid by other adults. A situation where adult fares are equal may be consistent with Pareto optimality, but it cannot be judged better than the current one without indulging in interpersonal comparisons.

In monopolistic and oligopolistic markets, prices of products are greater than their marginal costs. The mark-ups over marginal costs differ between firms and industries for the reasons discussed in Chapters 13 and 14. The marginal rate of transformation for the economy between two goods produced by monopolists or oligopolists (or between goods sold in different types of markets) will therefore not be equal to the ratios of their prices. And condition 5 for Pareto optimality, the equality of the marginal rates of transformation and substitution for any two goods, will thus not be satisfied. For example, consider two goods, one of which is produced by a monopolist and the other by a perfectly competitive industry. Their marginal rate of transformation is equal to the ratio of their marginal costs; but consumers equate their marginal rates of substitution to the ratio of prices, which is greater than the ratio of marginal costs (when the monopoly price, which exceeds its marginal cost, is in the numerator). This means that not enough of the monopoly good (and too much of the perfectly competitive good) is being produced. Consumers would be prepared to give up more units of the competitive good in exchange for one more unit of the monopoly good than the economy would have to sacrifice if it transferred resources to the production of one more unit of the monopoly good. It has been suggested that in such cases the appropriate public policy might be to enforce marginal-cost pricing, with prices set equal to marginal costs. If this policy were carried out for *all* products and there were no price discrimination, the marginal rate of substitution for any two goods would be equal to their marginal rate of transformation.

However, marginal-cost pricing is not a simple policy to apply, and its application gives rise to a host of other problems, such as how to finance it. Marginal costs may be substantially below average costs for firms with heavy overheads, and they would have to be subsidized if they were to be in a position to continue producing after their existing plants wore out. The methods used to raise revenues for such purposes must be designed not to violate the requirements for Pareto optimality. For example, taxation of incomes could affect incentives and the supply of labour services, thus violating condition 6: the equality between the marginal rate of substitution of a good and the consumption of a service and the marginal rate of transformation of this service and good. The taxes that would avoid this distortion are those that fall only on economic rents, but it is extremely difficult to identify and tax only rents. Of course distributional judgements are involved in any system of taxation; thus the choice of marginal-cost pricing cannot be made solely on the basis of efficiency.

Even if these problems could be satisfactorily solved, the use of marginal-cost pricing by government business enterprises or by regulated industries may not be a necessary condition for maximum welfare. It is a necessary condition only if marginal-cost pricing is observed in all other sectors of the economy. A divergence between actual and optimal conditions in one part of the economy, which is taken as given, will alter the conditions that must be fulfilled in the rest of the economy in order to achieve an optimal position. This principle is known as the *Theory of the Second Best*.[16]

Assume that the first-best solution for the economy, Pareto optimality, is unattainable because of special constraints in part of the economy. The second-best solution might then involve a departure from all the Pareto-optimal conditions. For example, if price exceeded marginal cost by some fixed proportion in one set of industries, and factor supplies (in particular, labour) were perfectly inelastic, the second-best solution would be to allow the prices to exceed marginal costs in *all* industries by the same proportion. The latter would satisfy the requirement for condition 5, the equality of the marginal rates of substitution and transformation, and the perfect inelasticity of the supply of labour would prevent changes in the supply of labour from interfering with the optimality of this solution.[17] There is no general expression for the second-best solution; its specific form would have to be determined for each case.

Economists have traditionally favoured perfectly competitive markets because of their superior performance in the allocation of scarce resources. However, in an economy with important monopolistic sectors, there is no reason to assume that establishing perfectly competitive conditions in one area would improve the allocation of resources. Economists base their preference for markets (competitive or otherwise) not only on their allocative effects but on their superiority to political or other administrative methods for co-ordinating economic activity and ensuring no surplus or shortage of goods at prevailing prices.

18.9 Externalities and Pareto optimality

The conditions of Pareto optimality were derived in Section 18.5 under the assumption of no externalities in production or consumption. They were thus expressed in terms of the individual (or private) marginal rates of

---

[16] R.G. Lipsey and K. Lancaster in 'The General Theory of the Second Best', *Review of Economic Studies*, Vol. 24 (1956-7), pp. 11-32.

[17] See R.F. Kahn, 'Some Notes on Ideal Output', *Economic Journal*, Vol. 65 (1935), pp. 1-35.

transformation and substitution. Where there are externalities, the private and social rates may diverge, and conditions 1 to 6 should be interpreted as expressing the equality between marginal social rates of transformation and substitution.[18] For example, condition 5 would require the marginal social rate of substitution between any two commodities (X and Y) to be equal to the social marginal rate of transformation between them. If there is an external diseconomy in the production of X, the social marginal rate of transformation of X for Y is greater than the private marginal rate of transformation. The amount of Y that must be sacrificed by the community in order to produce an extra unit of X is greater than would appear from the private cost of X, because of the extra inputs required to overcome the harmful externalities of producing more of X.[19] If the private, but not the social, rates of substitution and transformation are equal, then the production of a different combination of goods can result in a Pareto improvement in welfare.

An example of a divergence between private and social rates would be where the production of X causes pollution in a waterway. Producers downstream, who require clean water in their production process, would have to employ additional inputs in order to eliminate the pollution. Under these conditions, long-period equilibrium in perfect competition would no longer be a sufficient condition for Pareto optimality. The equilibrium position for the competitive industry is one where the ratio of private marginal costs is equal to the ratio of market prices. This situation is not Pareto-optimal, since the production of one less unit of X would not only permit the additional production of Y required to compensate consumers, but would also make available the elements of production absorbed by the external costs of producing that unit of X. Interference with the competitive markets through the imposition of a tax on X could thus lead to the achievement of Pareto optimality. This tax, which reflects the cost of ex-

---

[18] For A.C. Pigou the essence of externalities that create a divergence between social and private net product 'is that one person A, in the course of rendering some service, for which payment is made, to a second person B, incidentally also renders services or disservices to other persons (not producers of like services), of such a sort that payment cannot be exacted from the benefited parties or compensation enforced on behalf of the injured parties.' *The Economics of Welfare* (4th ed.; London: Macmillan & Co., 1932), p. 183.

[19] It is external technical diseconomies (Section 7.21) that create a divergence between social and private net product, and not external pecuniary diseconomies. An increase in an industry's output that raises the price of one of its inputs increases the money costs of production for all firms employing this input, but there are no increases in the real costs of production in the economy. There is a change in the distribution of real income, with the suppliers of this input benefiting at the expense of the consumers of the products in which it enters. William J. Baumol, *Welfare Economics and the Theory of the State* (2nd ed.; Cambridge, Mass.: Harvard University Press, 1965), p. 25.

ternalities, would result in a lower production of X, and private decisions made in the light of this tax would equalize the social marginal rates of substitution and transformation.[20]

This general approach also holds in the case of external economies. If an increase in the production of X lowered the cost of producing Y, the social marginal rate of transformation of X for Y would be *less* than the private marginal rate of transformation. A subsidy on the production of X would be required in order for the equilibrium position of a competitive system to satisfy the conditions of Pareto optimality. The treatment of externalities in consumption can also be handled in a similar manner.[21]

18.10 Public goods

The commodities dealt with generally in this book have been private goods. The consumption of a unit of one of these goods by an individual made this unit unavailable for others. With the recognition of externalities, the private nature of goods begins to be blurred. For example, an individual's garden might give satisfaction not only to him, but also to his neighbours and to passersby. His consumption of this good, as opposed to his consumption of a purely private good (e.g. a steak dinner), does not make it impossible for others to derive any direct enjoyment from it. In an extreme case, the consumption of a particular good by one individual does not interfere with its potential consumption by others. A good with this property is called a *pure public good*: if it is to be provided for one individual, it must be equally available for all. Examples of public goods are national defense for citizens of a country, lighthouses, and radio and television signals in a particular region.

The statement of the conditions of Pareto optimality for public goods must allow for the non-exclusive nature of such goods. Let X be a pure public good and Y a private good with no externalities in either production or consumption. Pareto optimality requires that the social marginal rates of

---

[20] In the equilibrium position with the tax, we have $P_x = MC_x + t_x$, and $P_Y = MC_Y$, where t_x is the tax per unit of output on X, which fully reflects external costs imposed by the production of a unit of X. The social (and private) marginal rate of substitution of X for Y in such a position is equal to P_x/P_Y, and the social marginal rate of transformation of X for Y is equal to $(MC_x + t_x)/MC_Y$. These two social rates are thus equal in equilibrium when a corrective tax is imposed on X.

[21] Ronald H. Coase has argued that divergences between private and social products are not sufficient to justify governmental measures to counteract them. He states: 'we have to take into account the costs involved in operating the various social arrangements (whether it be the working of a market or of a government department), as well as the costs involved in moving to a new system. In devising and choosing between social arrangements we should have regard for the total effect.' 'The Problem of Social Cost', *Journal of Law and Economics*, Vol. 3 (October 1960), p. 44.

substitution and transformation of X for Y should be equal. The former is equal to the *sum* of the individual marginal rates of substitution, since the consumption of X by one individual does not interfere with its consumption by others.[22] The conditions for Pareto optimality cannot be satisfied in a perfectly competitive market system (or in any other market system) when there are public goods. If potential consumers of a public good cannot be excluded from consuming the good, and cannot be made to pay for it, it may not be produced even though the sum of the private marginal rates of substitution substantially exceeds the marginal rate of transformation when none is produced. All payments for this good have to be purely voluntary, and many users would be tempted to become 'free riders' who make no payment. Therefore, if the good were produced, much less than the optimal quantity would be made available. There can be no Pareto-optimal solution when there are pure public goods, since all methods for financing their production might also lead to the violation of the necessary conditions for optimality (e.g. taxation of income might affect the work-leisure choice).

In the case of some public goods, exclusion of consumers can be prac-tised, or they can be made to pay in some fashion. A bridge is an example of the former, and radio and television signals of the latter. A bridge operating below capacity at all times is a public good (as soon as it suffers from congestion, it is no longer a pure public good), but its use can be restricted to those who are prepared to pay a bridge toll. For Pareto optimality, the bridge should be available (once constructed) at a zero price since there is no cost in using it (if it becomes congested, then a positive price is required to reflect the cost to users of additional traffic). The toll on a non-congested bridge restricts the services provided by the bridge and can be no more than a second-best solution. Radio and television signals sent out by commercial broadcasting stations are examples of pure public goods where exclusion cannot be practised but where consumers of the signals indirectly pay for the good. Production is financed by firms who pay for messages (ad-vertising) to be broadcast to consumers, who then purchase the goods of advertisers at prices that include advertising costs.

18.11 Social choice and individual values
This examination of theoretical welfare economics has emphasized the importance of a social welfare function. A social ranking of alternative economic situations can be made only with the assistance of interpersonal

---

[22] Individual demand curves are added *vertically* in order to arrive at the aggregate demand for a pure public good. This procedure differs from that used to derive aggregate demand curves for private goods where individual demand curves are summed horizontally.

comparisons of utility that are incorporated in such a function. The various compensation tests that have been devised in an attempt to allow a social choice between alternatives *solely* on the basis of improvements in the allocation of goods and resources have been shown to be defective. A social welfare function is therefore a necessary tool for the theoretical welfare economist. But the question arises whether it is an imposed function reflecting the tastes of a dictator or whether it can be viewed as reflecting in some democratic way the preferences of the society. K. J. Arrow has demonstrated the impossibility of arriving at a consistent social ordering with a constitution based on certain desirable ethical and democratic qualities.[23]

Arrow suggests that an ethically acceptable social ordering should satisfy four conditions. (i) It must be positively related to individual orderings. If one of the alternative social states under consideration rises or remains unchanged in the individual orderings, then it should not fall in the social ordering. (ii) Social ordering should be independent of irrelevant alternatives. In other words, the social ranking of X and Y should be the same whether or not a third alternative Z is available. (iii) Social ordering must not be imposed from outside upon the society; it must be derived from the individual orderings. (iv) The social ordering must not be dictatorial; that is, it must not coincide with the ordering of one individual within the society regardless of the orderings of others. Arrow demonstrates that it is not possible to satisfy these conditions and obtain a transitive social ordering for each set of individual orderings.

To illustrate his 'general impossibility' theorem, consider a society with two individuals, A and B, and three alternative states, X, Y, and Z. If A's ordering of the three alternatives is X, Y, Z, and B's ordering is Z, X, Y, then the society must be indifferent between Y and Z (otherwise condition iv would be violated). Both individuals prefer X to Y, and this must be the social ordering (condition iii). The social ordering, if it is to be transitive, must rank X ahead of Z, but only A prefers X to Z, while B prefers Z to X. The social ordering should show indifference between X and Z, but this results in an inconsistent ordering.

This result has very interesting implications for voting schemes, and shows that social choice cannot simply be derived from individual values in a democratic manner. However, the concept of a social welfare function can still be used by economists to examine the grounds for choosing between alternative states.[24]

---

[23] K.J. Arrow, *Social Choice and Individual Values* (New York: J. Wiley & Sons, 1951).

18.12 Summary

This brief review of welfare economics has shown that a social ordering of alternative economic situations involves value judgements about the distribution of income as well as a consideration of the efficiency of the allocation of goods and resources. The attempts by economists to obtain a ranking without interpersonal comparisons of utility have failed, but the compensation tests they have introduced for this purpose can be a useful first step in considering the desirability of a change in economic policy. Cost-benefit analyses are examples of the application of compensation tests that examine the allocative effects of specific projects.

The conditions for Pareto optimality when the economy is stationary were derived, and it was shown that they would be satisfied in a long-period equilibrium position for a perfectly competitive economy if there were no externalities in consumption and production. These are very restrictive assumptions, and if they are relaxed the desirability of a perfectly competitive price system becomes questionable. The relative desirability of perfectly competitive and monopolistic situations would be altered if dynamic conditions, such as technological changes, were introduced into the analysis.[25]

---

[24] Professor Samuelson, in his Foreword to the first paperback edition of Graaff's book, wrote: 'I wish to make clear that it is not true, as many used to believe, that Professor Kenneth Arrow of Stanford has proved "the impossibility of a social welfare function". What Arrow has proved in his pathbreaking 1951, *Social Choice and Individual Values*, is the impossibility of what I prefer to call "a political constitution function", which would be able to resolve *any* interpersonal differences brought to it while at the same time satisfying certain reasonable and desirable axioms. This Arrow result is a basic theorem of what might be called "mathematical politics" and throws new light on age-old conundrums of democracy.' J. de V. Graaff, *Theoretical Welfare Economics* (Cambridge, Eng.: Cambridge University Press, 1967), pp. vii-viii.

[25] For a spirited defence of an economic system that permits monopoly positions under dynamic conditions, see Joseph A. Schumpeter, *Capitalism, Socialism, and Democracy* (3rd ed.; New York: Harper & Brothers, 1950), Part II.

SUGGESTED READINGS

Bator, Francis M. 'The Simple Analytics of Welfare Maximization'. *American Economic Review*. Vol. 47 (March 1957), pp. 22-59.

Baumol, William J. *Welfare Economics and the Theory of the State*. 2nd ed. Cambridge, Mass.: Harvard University Press, 1965. Introduction to the Second Edition.

Coase, Ronald H. 'The Problem of Social Cost', *Journal of Law and Economics*. Vol. 3 (October 1960), pp. 1-44.

Graaff, J. de V. *Theoretical Welfare Economics*. Cambridge, Eng.: Cambridge Univeristy Press, 1967.

Mishan, E.J. 'A Survey of Welfare Economics, 1939-1959'. *Economic Journal*. Vol. 70 (June 1960), pp. 197-265.

Pigou, A.C. *The Economics of Welfare*. 4th ed. London: Macmillan & Co., 1932. Part II, Chapter IX.

Samuelson, Paul Anthony. *Foundations of Economic Analysis* (Cambridge, Mass.: Harvard University Press, 1948. Chapter VIII.

Winch, D.M. *Analytical Welfare Economics*. Harmondsworth: Penguin Books, 1971.

INDEX